The World of the Salons

The World of the Salons

Sociability and Worldliness in Eighteenth-Century Paris

Antoine Lilti

Translated by Lydia G. Cochrane

OXFORD
UNIVERSITY PRESS

OXFORD
UNIVERSITY PRESS

Oxford University Press is a department of the University of Oxford. It furthers
the University's objective of excellence in research, scholarship, and education
by publishing worldwide. Oxford is a registered trade mark of Oxford University
Press in the UK and certain other countries.

Published in the United States of America by Oxford University Press
198 Madison Avenue, New York, NY 10016, United States of America.

Abridged version of *Le Monde des salons* by Antoine Lilti © Librairie Arthème Fayard, 2005

English translation © Oxford University Press 2015

First issued as an Oxford University Press paperback, 2020

This work, published as part of a program providing publication assistance, received financial
support from the French Ministry of Foreign Affairs, the Cultural Services of the French
Embassy in the United States and FACE (French American Cultural Exchange).
French Voices Logo designed by Serge Bloch.

Library of Congress Cataloging-in-Publication Data
Lilti, Antoine.
[Monde des salons. English] The world of the salons : sociability and worldliness in
eighteenth-century Paris / Antoine Lilti ; translated by Lydia G. Cochrane.
pages cm
Includes bibliographical references and index.
ISBN 978-0-19-977234-6 (hardcover) | ISBN 978-0-19-753360-4 (paperback)
1. France—Social life and customs—18th century. 2. France—Intellectual life—18th century.
3. Salons—France—Paris—History—18th century. 4. Upper class—France—Paris—
History—18th century. 5. Elite (Social sciences)—France—Paris—History—18th century.
6. Worldliness—Social aspects—France—Paris—History—18th century. 7. Political
culture—France—Paris—History—18th century. 8. Paris (France)—History—1715–1789.
9. Paris (France)—Social life and customs—18th century. 10. Paris (France)—Intellectual
life—18th century. I. Title.
DC33.4.L5513 2015
944Ɒ.361034—dc23
2014015234

CONTENTS

ACKNOWLEDGMENTS

Working on sociability should not be a solitary endeavor. Indeed, I am deeply grateful to all the friends and colleagues who have stood by me over the years, providing comments, suggestions, and advice. First of all, this book would not have been what it is without the confidence that Daniel Roche has shown in me from the start. It is a pleasure for me to express my gratitude for his intellectual generosity and his friendship. My work was also encouraged and stimulated by many colleagues and friends, at the University of Rennes, at the École normale supérieure, and at the École des hautes etudes en sciences sociales. I am grateful to the comte de Bruce for having made available to me the notebooks of Madame Geoffrin in his possession, and to Madame Limon for having permitted me to work on the private archives of the Estampes collection in the National Archives when the items in them had not yet been inventoried.

The original version of this book, published in French in 2005, benefited from numerous discussions with colleagues, who obliged me to sharpen my arguments and who spared me from making too many errors. I would like, once again, to convey my gratitude to Pierre-Yves Beaurepaire, Gregory Brown, Caroline Callard, Roger Chartier, Jean-Luc Chappey, Christophe Charle, Michel Delon, Maria Pia Donato, Jean-François Dubost, Charlotte Guichard, Ran Halévi, Christian Jouhaud, Anne-Marie Lilti, Gilles Malandain, Dominique Margairaz, Laurent Pinon, Nicolas Schapira, and Stéphane Van Damme.

Since the book has first been published, I have been fortunate to present it in multiple places and to receive very useful comments, which have helped me to clarify my arguments and elaborate this new version. I would like to express specific gratitude to David A. Bell, Dan Brewer, Jeremy Caradonna, Barbara Carnevali, Paul Cohen, Dan Edelstein, Lisa Jane Graham, Colin Jones, Steven Kaplan, Cyril Lemieux, Jean-Clement Martin, Darrin McMahon, Jeffrey Ravel, Jacques Revel, Elena Russo, Silvia Sebastiani, Pierre Serna, Emma Spary, Jacob Soll, Michael Sonenscher, Geoffrey Turnovsky, and Charles Walton.

David Bell encouraged me to make an English version of *Le Monde des salons* and has provided very useful advice. Susan Ferber agreed to publish an English translation and has done wonderful editorial work, convincing me to tighten the argument and to make substantial cuts. I am proud to have this book published at Oxford University Press.

At the end, my warmest thanks go to Charlotte, Juliette, and Zoé, who make life so sweet.

The World of the Salons

Introduction

The most famous image of French salons of the eighteenth century is a painting by Anicet Lemonnier titled *Une lecture chez Mme Geoffrin* (A Reading at the home of Madame Geoffrin) (Fig. I.1). It shows d'Alembert reading Voltaire's tragedy *L'Orphelin de la Chine* before an audience composed of all of the eighteenth century's best-known political, worldly, literary, and artistic figures. Although it seems so true to life, this painting was done some thirty years after Madame Geoffrin's death. It was commissioned in 1814 by Joséphine de Beauharnais for her château at Malmaison as part of a triptych devoted to the glory of the arts and letters in the sixteenth, seventeenth, and eighteenth centuries, which was why Lemonnier painted all of the most famous personalities of the century, whether or not they had actually attended Madame Geoffrin's salon.[1] From the moment it was commissioned, this painting reflected a nostalgia for the salons of the eighteenth century and a desire to make them a retrospective symbol of the culture of the Enlightenment. The work, presented at the Salon of 1814, was popularized in 1822 by an engraving that included a list of the persons depicted. Even today, it is often chosen by publishing houses to illustrate works devoted to the eighteenth century. The success of this painting shows that the salons functioned as a metonym for the entire eighteenth century, if not for French culture and conversation in general. Where salons are concerned, we are often looking through nineteenth-century glasses.

The entry for "Salon" in Pierre Larousse's *Grand Dictionnaire universel du XIXe siècle* ends with these words: "The *salons* are dead. Some people miss them, deploring what they call the loss of the spirit of conversation. If that is to be understood as the art of saying nothing in an elegant style,

Fig. I.1 Anicet-Charles-Gabriel Lemonnier, "La Lecture chez Madame Geoffrin." 1804 Musée des Beaux-arts de Rouen.

the art of a boring waste of time, we will be the last to complain that the French mind has finally turned toward serious matters and thoughts."[2] By announcing the demise of the salons, the *Grand Dictionnaire universel* subscribed to a commonplace of the time, but reversed its thrust. Where the evocation of the salons usually elicited nostalgic praise of a sociability on the wane, Pierre Larousse, in an openly iconoclastic gesture, took the opposite point of view. By the early 1870s the salons had become a controversial topic, inseparable from debates about the legacy of the ancien régime and about French national identity. By reviving a critique of high society dear to French republicans, the dictionary openly contrasted this aristocratic institution of worldly frivolity with the serious matters that a republican and bourgeois France owed it to itself to confront, rather than indulging in regrets for the passing of the futile conversations of the salons.

Even today, the word "salon" remains curiously charged with contrasting connotations that evoke both the superficial amusements of a tiny elite and an ideal of intellectual communication. Far from inspiring indifference, the salons arouse immediate interest, whether their memory is celebrated or their persistence is gravely examined. A nostalgia for them is by no means exclusive to aristocratic circles; many texts have made salon life an element of French cultural patrimony and often display the very rhetoric that Pierre Larousse mocked. In contrast, salons are also perceived as temples of snobbery and insignificant chatter. The satire directed against worldliness in eighteenth-century France can still give the word *salon* a polemical charge in intellectual controversies.[3] Finally, although the present-day "salon philosopher" and the "salon writer" get bad press, philosophical and literary salons enjoy a certain prestige. Lecture cycles are called *salons littéraires* to show that they are convivial gatherings open to intellectual debate, reflecting the image of the salon as a space for free and fruitful dialogue.

This complex image of the salons, connoting refined amusements and the philosophical, even militant, engagement of an intellectual avant-garde, has an old history. With the Restoration, the salon came to be perceived as a surviving feature of the ancien régime, thus inspiring an intense nostalgia among writers of memoirs who missed the "salons of yesteryear" and among novelists who made the salon an emblem of refined prerevolutionary society. The great literary critic Charles Augustin Sainte-Beuve and the Goncourt brothers established an association between salon conversation, literature, and the role of women in high society. As a result, numerous biographies and essays recorded a repertory of dubious anecdotes and a problematic list of notable salons. Unfortunately, this abundant but undependable bibliography still remains the documentary basis for a history of French salons in the eighteenth century.[4]

Academic historians long showed little interest in salons, consigning them to a *petite histoire*, fond of anecdotes and *secrets d'alcôve*. It was only toward the end of the 1970s that they recognized the importance of salons in writing about the cultural history of the Enlightenment.[5] Today the salons have become an obligatory topic of study, divided into three principal models: the literary salon, the philosophical salon, and the aristocratic salon.

By the early twentieth century, historians of literature had forged the notion of the "literary salon," in which a woman received men of letters. It was often relegated to the margins of academic studies, alongside New Criticism's dismissal of the history of literature. Two oppositional approaches have nonetheless contributed to a renewed interest in literary studies of salons. On the one hand, the works of Marc Fumaroli present salons as an important basis to the development of French literature thanks to polite conversation.[6] Originally motivated by a desire for a rhetorical analysis of forms of conversation, these studies have narrowed to a nostalgic discourse on the lost prestige of French conversation and are often reduced to a gallery of portraits and a collection of anecdotes.[7] On the other hand, the sociology of the literary field, inspired by the works of Pierre Bourdieu, sees in salons a place for the "birth of the writer," in which the increasing autonomy of literary activity retains a dependence on the power structure and the social elites.[8] Robert Darnton's works share a similar perspective, since he sees the literary world as divided, at the end of the eighteenth century, between elite writers showered with honors who were the habitués of the salons and a group of young and bitter writers, the "low-lives of literature," who survived by publishing pamphlets.[9] The salons are not studied in and of themselves, but as settings in which writers can achieve consecration and as an instrument for the domestication of the Enlightenment, in which the heirs of the philosophes exchanged the perils of criticism for the comfort of high society.

Dena Goodman had proposed a totally different interpretation.[10] She argues that eighteenth-century salons were the central institution of the republic of letters, ruled by women and devoted to the critical project of the Enlightenment. She brings together two traditional approaches revived by the historiography of the 1980s. The first one presents salons as a female space, *le paradis des femmes*, a classical approach that has been updated in accordance with radically different perspectives in recent works in women's history, notably those that seek to evaluate the role of women in the cultural life of the ancien régime.[11] The second tradition, which emphasizes connections between the salons and public opinion, has drawn new vigor from the model of the public sphere developed by Jürgen Habermas, in which salons appear as an institution of the new bourgeois public sphere, as opposed to the traditional public space of monarchial representation.[12] For Goodman, the salons of the eighteenth century had nothing in common with their predecessors of the age of Louis XIII and Louis XIV, or with their nineteenth-century successors, which were products of aristocratic leisure. In the eighteenth century they were serious places, devoted to intellectual debate, in which the rules of politeness and a discreet governance by *salonnières* constituted the social grounding for the Enlightenment republic of letters, using an ideal of egalitarian sociability to bring together male philosophes' will to reform with female mediation.

Goodman's influential book inspired historians to reevaluate the historical importance of the salons as a cultural institution, to study seriously the women who received writers in their homes, and to take into account philosophical and moral thought on the subjects of sociability and politeness. However, using the notion of the republic of letters to think about the salons is misguided because it leads us to misinterpret both the historical significance of the salons and the social history of the Enlightenment. It induces considering salons as literary or intellectual venues, whereas they were, above all, the social spaces of elite leisure. Dena Goodman builds her argument on a restricted number of salons (those of Marie-Thérèse Geoffrin, Julie de Lespinasse, Suzanne Necker), without acknowledging that these salons were a good deal less homogeneous, socially and intellectually, than she asserts, and that they were linked to the ensemble of high society networks. Moreover, as some recent studies have stressed, the hostesses who received guests in their salons were hardly attuned to the aesthetic of the Enlightenment, and adhered to traditional representations of urbane manners (honnêteté) rather than to the intellectual project of the Enlightenment. The peculiarity of eighteenth-century sociability should not be overestimated: salons were a longstanding institution dominated by Parisian elites that outlasted the Revolution.[13]

The salons remain too often an abstract and idealized framework, almost exclusively perceived through literary praise of conversation. The expression "literary salon" presupposes that the aim of such salons was to carry on literary activity. But what was literature in the eighteenth century? What role did it play in the amusements of the social elite? Why did writers frequent the salons? Histories of "literary salons" treat these questions as self-evident and equate sociability with strictly literary interests. Similarly, identifying the salons with the republic of letters of the Enlightenment presupposes an ideological coherence and neglects the social dynamics. It does not explain the durable persistence of the salons from the reign of Louis XIII to the Belle Époque. Conversely, if the salons were merely aristocratic institutions, how are we to understand the massive presence of men of letters without turning them into unscrupulous arrivistes?

These contradictions result from the fact that salons are studied within already established fields of historiography, such as literary history, women's history, the public sphere, or even the history of the nobility. But the function of salons was to provide an interface between literary life and the amusement of the elites, between the court and the city, and between learned debates and political intrigues. Studying salons within the framework of the republic of letters or the history of the nobility leads to focus only on one facet. The situation is paradoxical: while the literature on salons is abundant we do not have a clear idea of the role they actually played in eighteenth-century society. Hence this book, based on new documentary research, proposes an overall interpretation that focuses on the forms of sociability that prevailed in eighteenth-century high society, what was referred to at the time as le monde, the world.

A focus on sociability allows for the study of the practices of conviviality among the urban elite, from the apparently most insignificant, paying a visit, to the most visible—houses that welcomed guests on a weekly basis on a fixed day of the week—without presupposing their coherence or their ideological effects. The concept of "sociability" was introduced into the vocabulary of historical scholarship in the 1960s and has been used to analyze the processes of politicization, trace the history of the phenomenon of association, study provincial academies, and describe intellectual networks.[14] It is a useful tool for understanding the social, political, or cultural stakes attached to practices that were only weakly institutionalized. Still, the term is not always free of ambiguity, as it sometimes designates a personal or collective feature of temperament. A clear distinction needs thus to be made between sociability as a tool to study social relations founded on voluntary participation, and sociability as a notion of moral and political philosophy that appeared, precisely, in the eighteenth century in the wake of theories of natural law. All too often, confusing the two leads to explaining the history of salons by reference to a supposedly innate French talent for conversation or to the existence of a powerful "ideal of sociability."[15] In contrast, beginning with an analysis of the practices of sociability allows us to understand how the salons served as a support for either imagining an ideal of sociability or denouncing it. Normative discourses need to be studied alongside a social history of practices and a cultural history of symbolic struggles.[16] Instead of explaining the one by the other, the complex connections between worldly practices and theories of sociability should be investigated.

The very word "salon" must be used with care. Although it brings with it an entire series of received ideas, in the eighteenth century it was simply an architectural term designating a large room with an arched ceiling that had appeared in the preceding century in royal châteaux and princely dwellings. In urban hôtels, this room gradually became the space in which one received invited guests, so that by the early nineteenth century the word had slowly taken on the meaning of a "house in which one habitually receives company, and, in particular, good company, and where one chats," according to the definition in Littré's dictionary.[17] This acceptance of the word was unknown before the Revolution: one spoke of "circles" or "societies." It is thus slightly anachronistic to speak of the "salons of the eighteenth century," as doing so runs the risk of overestimating the existence of an autonomous institution, associated with a specific list of hostesses, when in fact many diverse forms of hospitality prevailed within the upper levels of society.

The first occurrence of the term *salon* to designate a home in which one welcomes guests can be found in Chamfort's *Maximes et pensées*, published in 1794: "Society, its different circles, its salons, all that is called the world, is a wretched play, a bad opera, without interest; insofar as it keeps our attention at all, it does so with its machinery and its decorations."[18] Here the salons appear as "circles" and are explicitly related to a specific form of sociability, *la société*, or *le monde*. The term *société* was often used in this restricted sense to designate a social sphere that was neither private nor public, and that corresponds to the amusements of the salons. *Le monde* is an essential term for understanding Paris society of the eighteenth century, as it designates both a social group distinguished by its practices of sociability and those practices themselves. *Le monde* occupied an important place in the aesthetic and intellectual debates of the century, and many writers of the Enlightenment were fascinated by it, thus helping to give the customs and the manners of the Paris elite a lasting literary aura. The very term *mondain* underwent a change of meaning in the course of the century, moving from the religious domain to the secular, thanks to Voltaire. However, historians have shown little interest in *le monde* or in *mondanité*—that is, in the dynamics of the worldly sociability of the elites and in the representations that reinforced its effects. Worldliness was a complex social mechanism and an ensemble of signs that one had to learn to interpret, but it should not be confused with its literary representation, which gives an artificial image of it adorned with the prestige of literature. Worldliness was the specific form taken in France by the fascination that the polite elites and the people of letters (*gens de lettres*) had for each other. It was both a social arrangement that assured the preeminence of certain elites connected with the court and with cultural spheres and a group of discourses aimed at celebrating the merits of those elites.

Chamfort's statement highlights the fact that *le monde* implied interpretations that were always fraught with consequences. Satirical exposure echoed the praise of worldly sociability produced by *gens du monde* and by the writers of the Enlightenment. Historians do not have to endorse either the praise of worldly politeness or denunciations of its vain theatricality: what is needed instead is to investigate the diversity of such representations and to understand the polemical dimensions of such discourse. That is why this book avoids defining the salons ideologically. Instead, it aims to understand the logic inherent in practices of sociability, along with their effects of distinction and exclusion, and to discern the ways in which they transformed knowledge and beliefs.[19]

The subject of this book is thus not so much the "salons" themselves as worldliness. While the history of the salons all too often leads to a compilation of portraits and anecdotes, the history of worldliness concentrates on the complex mechanisms that guaranteed the social and cultural distinction of *le monde*. Comprehension of what was at stake here requires both a hermeneutics of worldly representations and a historical sociology of high society. The first of these is needed to avoid being hoodwinked by the sources; the second allows for highlighting the forms of distinction founded on the connivance of worldly circles. High society (*la bonne société*) is not a customary notion in the social history of the ancien régime, which prefers categories such as the nobility of the sword or the robe, or the bourgeoisie, even when those categories have shown their limitations, or uses the vague term "elite." Still, the constitution of *la bonne société* was one of the most efficient forms of the perpetuation of aristocratic prestige from the seventeenth century to the nineteenth century. The salons belonged to the court society, in the broad sense given to that term by the sociologist Norbert Elias—that is, a society that cannot be understood without reference to the polarity introduced by the royal court. Elias sketched out a theory of high society in which the salons corresponded to a decentralization of a worldly life that had previously been concentrated at the court.[20] But while Elias no more than hinted at such a theory, his work helps to think about the salons in the framework of an ancien régime society that, at least for Parisian elites, was still largely reliant on the chains of interdependence forged at court.

Worldly sociability was obviously a long-term phenomenon. It was a central institution in the life of Parisian elites from the beginning of the seventeenth century to the end of the nineteenth century, and its height (around 1750–1850) coincided with a period of crisis and redefinition of aristocratic prestige, during which the court nobility reinterpreted its criteria for honor and included within polite society those who conformed to its standards of behavior and acknowledged its preeminence. Long associated with military valor, and subsequently with noble birth, aristocratic prestige rested increasingly on the manners of the man of the world (*l'homme du monde*) and on the cultural practices of polite society, like theater, music, or poetry.

Sociability was an instrument of this redefinition, thanks to the writers who participated in it and celebrated it. This process took place over a long period and definitively made salons a commonplace in the French cultural imaginary. Already under Louis XIII, writers like Guez de Balzac and Jean Chapelain attended the salons of polite society and contributed to publicizing their reputation. Almost three centuries later, Marcel Proust wrote worldly chronicles in *Le Figaro*, and deployed the Parisian salons as the backdrop for *À la Recherche du temps perdu*. In the cultural history of France, *mondanité* and literature are intimately linked, and the second half of the eighteenth century is a crucial moment in this process, during which the literary elite was devoted to *mondanité* and its values.

The present book can thus be seen as a contribution to the history of worldliness. It looks at the way in which eighteenth-century social elites redefined themselves through their practices of worldly sociability and at the way some men of letters of the Enlightenment participated in that same sociability, by attending the salons. It poses questions that pertain to the material conditions of sociability, to the mechanisms of reputation, to the profits, material and symbolic, that writers gained from a frequentation of the salons, and to the political stakes of worldliness. The point is to understand the whole phenomenon, from what accounted for the success of a *bon mot* to why enlightened theories of sociability were mobilized to justify worldly practices. Moving from the salons to worldliness permits taking on some broader debates as well. What relations did worldly sociability maintain with the public sphere? How did the Parisian nobility use the idea of worldly merit and the figure of the "man of the world" (*homme du monde*) to preserve its social preeminence? Was the new political culture, characterized by an appeal to the public, compatible with the monarchical apparatus and with court intrigues? Far from being limited to a closed and picturesque world of literary salons, worldly sociability lay at the heart of the social, cultural, and political mechanisms in the eighteenth century.

Addressing such questions requires sources. Yet the salons left no archives: there are no lists of members, no regulations, no minutes, no visitors' books. This absence of documentary sources has long restricted the ways in which the methods of sociocultural history could be applied to the salons. There are, however, many sources that shed light on these supposedly elusive worldly practices. Under-exploited documentation, ranging from a vast supply of correspondence, memoirs, and diaries to the police archives, and including treatises on civility and literary sources, is abundant, nearly inexhaustible. They are usually difficult to handle. Memoirs are particularly vulnerable to a retrospective reconstruction of events, especially when they were written and published after the Revolution. But correspondence and *gazettes à la main*, which might seem more trustworthy because they were contemporary to the events they related, also pose a number of questions, given that the texts that speak of the salons are themselves caught up in the demands of sociability.[21]

The difficulty lies also in the rare and discontinuous nature of the sources, in which scraps of narrative are the only traces of worldly life. From these sources comes the anecdote, which is at once a brief narrative, an indication of social connivance, and a mode of historical writing. Historical works on the salons have often made all too much use of anecdotes, doing little more than compiling or paraphrasing them in the hope of recreating the charm of a bygone world, a practice that reproduces the very narrative forms that it claims to be studying. However, if the anecdote is removed from the realm of curiosity in which it functions, it constitutes precious raw material for a history of worldliness. Anecdotes need to be contextualized and compared. They need to be not only cited but carefully analyzed for their meaning. Most of them are the products of sociability (a salon conversation reported in a diary, for example) and, by that token, they aim at producing effects (praise, stigmatization, ridicule) within high society. To study an anecdote is thus also to raise questions about the way in which it was narrated, how it circulated, and what meaning was given to it.

Police archives, particularly the reports of the Contrôle des étrangers, offer a different point of view on the worldly sphere. Their authors did not participate in the practices of sociability but subjected them to surveillance; theirs is an outside viewpoint. The massive presence of diplomats in the salons, as well as the attention given to their surveillance by the *lieutenant de police* and the minister, indicate that the salons were not simply places of amusement. There was a political aspect to worldly life that needs to be understood.

The *World of the Salons* was published in France in 2005 in a longer version,[22] containing a chapter on the historiography of salons from Madame de Staël in the early nineteenth century to contemporary debates, an analysis of the material culture of the salons, and thoughts on the place of gambling, theater, and music in worldly amusements. The present book's argument has been tightened in the interests of efficiency. It focuses first on the social dynamics of worldliness. The salon is therefore defined on the basis of the practice of hospitality. From letters of recommendation to the constraints weighing on the mistress of the house, there arose a space of sociability that escaped the sheer alternative of "private" or "public," and that was designated by the term *société* (Chapter 1). Next, the social dynamics of the worldly sphere, considered as an interface between the court, the city of Paris, and the literary world, are studied on the basis of the mechanisms of reputation and the egalitarian fiction of politeness (Chapter 2). One characteristic specific to Parisian worldliness was the place that men of letters occupied in it. Men of letters found in the salons a way to gain access to protection networks within high society and to become identified as *hommes du monde*, a more socially acceptable figure than that of the professional writer. In exchange, they lent appeal and attractiveness to these salons while contributing to turning conversation and politeness into Enlightenment ideals that became widely shared (Chapter 3). In the second part of the book, the cultural and political mechanisms of worldly life are examined, with an emphasis on what set the salons apart from the public sphere. Studying the rituals of conversation, the uses of correspondence, and poetic games leads to an examination of the existence of a literature of society (Chapter 4). Then, I show that the dynamics of reputations in high society were founded on the oral circulation of news and opinions within worldly networks, while the public sphere was increasingly associated with print (Chapter 5). Finally, in the traditional framework of court intrigues and struggles for influence, the salons played a political and diplomatic role that constituted a veritable politics of worldliness (Chapter 6).

PART ONE

From the Salon to the World: Sociability and Distinction

There can exist a great number of little worldly societies, since they need merely be closed in order to exist; but it follows that enclosure, which is the original form of all worldliness, and which we can consequently describe on the level of infinitesimal groups (the coterie of fragment 4 of *De la ville*, or the Verdurin salon), assumes a precise historical meaning when it is applied to the world as a whole.

Roland Barthes, "La Bruyère" (1972)

CHAPTER 1

❧

Sociability and Hospitality

Le beau monde devotes four or five hours two or three times a week to paying visits. Their coaches trot through all the streets of the city and the suburbs. After a number of hesitations, one stops at twenty doorways to inscribe his name: makes an appearance for a quarter of an hour in a half dozen houses; it is the day of the maréchale, the présidente, the duchesse; one must appear in the salon, salute people, sit in one empty chair after another, and seriously believe he can cultivate an acquaintance with between a hundred sixty and a hundred eighty persons. These comings and goings in Paris distinguish the man of the world; every day he makes ten visits, five real ones and five *en blanc*; and when he has led this ambulant and leisurely life, he claims to have fulfilled the most important duties of society.

Louis Sébastien Mercier, *Tableau de Paris* (1783)

The fact that the word *salon* was unknown in eighteenth-century France does not prohibit us from using it, but it needs to be defined rigorously. When a collected correspondence or a police report affirms a certain person dined in a certain house with men of letters and "men of the world," does it mean that the group formed a salon and that the list of those present is an acceptable approximation of its habitual attendees? If we make a distinction between the salon and other dinners, suppers, and visits, do we not risk artificially distinguishing among practices that contemporaries experienced in a perfect continuity, perhaps even as identical? Should we distinguish between the court of the prince de Conti and the salon of his mistress, the comtesse de Boufflers? What are we talking about when we speak of the "salons"?

WHAT IS A SALON?

A Plural Sociability

The first thing to note is diversity. There seems to be an enormous gap between the salon of the duchesse de Choiseul, where the entire court aristocracy pressed around richly loaded tables, and that of Julie de Lespinasse, where a few guests came to talk after having supped elsewhere. We cannot get around this difficulty with a typology or a strict definition because the practices of sociability were much more diverse than historians usually assume. We imagine Madame Geoffrin's salon, for example, as a weekly meeting of a group of fashionable people and writers as they are shown in Lemonnier's painting. Things were a good deal more complicated, however. Madame Geoffrin offered not one weekly dinner, but two: the Wednesday dinner, founded in the early 1740s for Fontenelle and in theory devoted to men of letters and foreigners, and the Monday dinner, frequented by artists, art lovers, and a handful of men of letters. Started by the comte de Caylus, the Monday dinners enabled Madame Geoffrin to play the role of a protector of artists, thanks to the fortune that her husband had amassed in the Manufacture de Saint-Gobain, but also helped her to strengthen her relations with aristocrats. The guests who frequented these two dinners were not the same people, and the conversations were likely not similar.

Madame Geoffrin also gave little suppers, which were very well attended in the 1760s and 1770s. Around 1765, guests included the comtesse d'Egmont, the marquise de Duras, and the comtesse de Brionne, as well as the prince de Rohan; in later years, they included the duc and duchesse de Rohan, the maréchale de Luxembourg, and several ambassadors.[1] Madame Geoffrin was pleased to report that she made the young women of the aristocracy who frequented these suppers "faint with laughter."[2] Men of letters were few in this "more intimate society," and Marmontel insists in his *Mémoires* on the pride that he felt on being brought in to amuse this noble company by reading from his works.[3] The distinction between dinners and suppers was not necessarily rigid, and at the end of her life, Madame Geoffrin organized grand dinners on other days of the week. For example, on Friday, November 24, 1775, she gave a dinner for a large number of aristocrats, most of whom were connected with the duc de Rohan. No man of letters is mentioned in the police report.[4]

Madame Geoffrin received visits every day, in addition to her dinners and suppers. Between five in the afternoon and nine (the supper hour), she received an uninterrupted stream of visitors in her bedchamber.[5] In the

1770s, d'Alembert, who was one of her most assiduous visitors, preferred to visit with Madame Geoffrin at nine in the morning. When a newcomer was introduced for the first time, he was presented during a visit. Being received in her house did not necessarily involve dining and conversing with men of letters. When Horace Walpole, furnished with a letter of recommendation, first called on Madame Geoffrin during his first stay in Paris in 1765, he encountered no one but the duchesse de Cossé and, on a later occasion, Antoine-Léonard Thomas. Only during a second stay in Paris was he invited to a Wednesday dinner.[6] These visits played an essential role in the sociability of the salons, particularly for those who wanted to maintain their position in high society or simply demonstrate their *savoir vivre*. As Morvan de Bellegarde, a prolific theoretician of politeness, put it: "When one is of the world, one must fulfill all the duties of decorum and civility. Most people of quality, who are ordinarily fairly much at leisure and have no occupation, pass their time in making or receiving visits, and it is very important for them to learn all that must be done in order to be agreeable and to support their reputation. This is how their merit is judged, and they are blamed or praised according to whether they perform well or badly in a conversation."[7] When she came to Paris in 1786, Lady Crewe was surprised to note that "at five in the afternoon, everybody drives about to visit everybody."[8] She found it difficult to get used to the formality of French civility, which she found particularly constraining, and decided to spend an entire day responding to the visits that she had received since her arrival in Paris. She states that it was an arduous duty, but that she preferred to get such duty calls over with.[9]

Such visits were not always agreeable. The art of avoiding the unwelcome visit became a recurrent theme in treatises on civility. After a satirical portrait of the importunate guest who arrives after dinner and does not leave until time for supper, and then does so regretfully, Le Noble concludes: "It would be desirable for the Police to extend its ordinances to eliminating all the useless aspects of conversations and regulating the length of the visits of persons who have nothing to do but go from house to house boring others."[10] One remedy for this inconvenience was the invention of *visites en blanc*, which enabled people to sign a guest book at the front door of a house without actually entering. The guest book, originally created to inform visitors that the man or lady of the house was absent, was later used to say that they were not receiving that day or that they were ill. When Madame Du Deffand was ill in September 1775 and did not receive visitors, the diplomats who frequented her salon presented themselves at her doorway every day.[11] In the long run, the formula proved its utility for all visits of pure politeness, which were as bothersome to make as to receive.

The baronne d'Oberkirch discovered this practice during her stay in Paris in 1784, noting that it had become a current custom and attributing it to the "jargon and the fine air of this Parisian land."[12] As was true of court ceremonies, worldly sociability could degenerate into pure formality.

Thus the salons functioned following the dual aristocratic patterns of an open table and visits. Madame Geoffrin was perfectly integrated into this worldly sociability. She not only received guests and visitors, but also frequented the other salons of Parisian "society." A list of *visites à faire* in her notebook includes the names of such members of the highest court aristocracy as the duchesse de Bouillon, the comtesse de Noailles, the comtesse de La Marck, the marquise de Pontchartrain, and the comtesse de Narbonne.[13] On the other hand, what is known as her salon was split into different occasions: dinners, suppers, and visits. Behind the fiction of a weekly gathering, practices varied greatly. The various moments of sociability, with their different participants and their separate rituals, formed a system, the visits serving their purpose for more intimate conversations, the dinners providing men of letters an opportunity to create a reputation that would permit them to shine at the suppers. When we read that the future king of Sweden, Gustav III, attended the salon of Madame Geoffrin when he was in Paris in 1770, we immediately imagine him conversing with d'Alembert and Buffon. In reality, he went to Madame Geoffrin's house in the evening in the company of some grand aristocrats whom she had invited for the occasion.

Madame Geoffrin's case is not an exception. Madame Necker was known for her "Friday dinners," but correspondence and the police reports present a more complex picture. The Friday gatherings were not just for dinner: the Neckers received all day long, and certain guests came for supper or spent only an hour or two with them during the afternoon. Moreover, they welcomed guests to an open table on other days. When Madame Du Deffand first started attending their gatherings, she went every Saturday, then, after November 1775, every Monday.[14] In 1777, the Neckers began to receive on Mondays, at first for supper, then all day long, and diplomats were almost as numerous on Mondays as on Fridays. Moreover, up to 1783, some guests continued to arrive on Mondays, on Thursdays, and, exceptionally, on Saturdays and Sundays. The police reports state on a number of occasions that "every evening there is a large gathering" or that "a goodly company gathers in the evenings."[15] Buffon, who is often presented as a pillar of Madame Necker's salon, usually paid a visit to her on Thursday, when they could talk one on one.[16] This diversity in days for receiving callers and guests was complicated further when the Neckers were in Saint-Ouen, where Madame Necker continued to receive on her usual days, though the invited guests tended to be more aristocratic. There is an even greater variety among the houses that have been treated as emblematic of the eighteenth century. Julie de Lespinasse, for example, received every day, thus escaping the principle of the weekly "day," but she offered no food. Her "salon" was a meeting place where guests stopped by for a few hours after theaters had let out and before supper.[17]

Diverse Criteria

In the first place, the salon was a domestic space. The word "house" (*maison*), a term that the reports of the Contrôle des étrangers use frequently, recalls that the salons were based primarily on the practice of hospitality.[18] Thus the salons were clearly differentiated from other forms of sociability situated in public spaces (gardens, cafés, royal academies, for example), but also from all gatherings that implied paid membership, such as clubs or reading societies. Within the private *hôtel* or apartment, the salon was the room chosen as the place for that hospitality.

An occasional dinner was not enough to establish a salon. A salon implied a certain regularity that guaranteed continuity among those one might encounter there and the constitution of a group of dependable attendees. The dominant model, in the eighteenth century, was the weekly "day," also known as a *jour marqué* or a *repas de fondation*. That day might vary as seasons changed and years passed, but it distinguished the salon from the meals by special invitation, known in the eighteenth century as *repas priés*. The fixed reception day implied that once someone had been presented and welcomed, he could return without an invitation. Louis Sébastien Mercier, the famous author of the *Tableau de Paris*, explained: "Some people of wealth and ease usually give a dinner two or three times a week for friends and acquaintances. Once invited, you are invited forever."[19] Madame du Deffand complained of having too many people at her Wednesdays: "It is an inconvenience that is impossible to avoid when one has *jours marqués* at which a number of persons have the right to come without being invited to do so."[20] In her memoirs, Madame de La Tour du Pin recalled the essential distinction, in worldly life, between the *jours marqués* and suppers "to which one was invited, which were numerous and brilliant."[21] Unlike the *table ouverte*, a model that was both political and aristocratic, the more intimate *repas prié*, which, in the following century, became the rule in bourgeois sociability, implied a personal invitation. "The ministers," one police report states, "do not hold an open table: they invite their guests by notes."[22] These opposing modes of entertainment were not mutually exclusive, and some people who had one or more "days" also had dinners or suppers by invitation. Commenting in 1775 on Madame Necker's Fridays, a police report states: "This day is devoted to all those who have been presented; the guests are not specially invited; the house is open for all of the aforementioned who wish to go. There are other days of the social week for dinner and supper, but one is invited to them."[23]

A tenacious myth attributes to Madame Geoffrin the invention of the fixed day.[24] However, even without going back to the Saturdays of Mademoiselle de Scudéry, an identical pattern—a weekly dinner with the variation of dinner or supper—can be found with the marquise de Lambert in the first half of the century.[25] Tuesday, the day on which the marquise's friends gathered, became the metonym of her "society," which shows that the fixed day was already an important element in institutionalizing these practices of sociability.[26] Madame de Tencin was known as having two fixed days, Tuesday and Friday, although she also entertained on other days of the week. Madame Geoffrin and the hostesses of the latter half of the eighteenth century simply conformed to this model.

A third essential criterion was respect for the rules of civility and politeness, rules that governed both access to the salons and the attitudes of those who attended them. They distinguished the salons from other practices of sociability such as the *parties fines*, at which princes slummed with actresses, or bacchic societies like the *Caveau*, where writers gathered for meals at which all were expected to drink, sing songs, and deliver mocking personal attacks.

Historically, the rules of worldly politeness were associated with the presence of women. Still, this mixed male-female sociability does not imply that the salons were necessarily "governed" by a woman.[27] Many salons were in fact identified with a female figure, but some men also had special days when they received men and women for supper and conversation. Abbé Morellet, for example, received his friends for dinner on the first Sunday of each month for twelve years.[28] In his library, overlooking the Tuileries, he gathered together men of letters, but also women. After the meal, as one guest reported, "we chatted agreeably, we read prose or verse, we made music; and several artists—Grétry, Hullmandell, Capperon, Traversa, Duport, etc.—took pleasure in joining with us."[29] When Morellet traveled in England, the usual group got together at the Suards' on a Sunday and wrote him a collective letter.[30]

The fashionable salons of the duc de Biron and the maréchal de Soubise played an important role in the worldly life of the capital at the end of the ancien régime. In the final decade of his life, after an eventful career devoted to the service of the king and to *libertinage*, Louis Antoine de Gontaut, the duc de Biron, colonel of the Gardes-Françaises and maréchal de France, hosted one of the most highly reputed salons in Paris—grand dinners for foreigners on Fridays and suppers that grouped the best of high society—in which his wife seems to have played no role.[31] Similarly, Charles de Rohan, prince de Soubise, duc de Rohan-Rohan, offers an example of a salon headed by a courtier. Fermier général Le Riche de La Poupelinière received guests in his house on the rue de Richelieu with his wife.[32] After separating from her, he lived in the château de Passy, where he established a vibrant center of worldly, libertine, intellectual, and musical life. There Rameau triumphed, Grimm met Diderot and d'Alembert, and Madame de Genlis made her debut into society.[33]

Quite often a couple, such as the Helvétiuses, the Caramans, the La Reynières, and the Neckers, received visitors and guests.[34] The attribution of a salon to one member of a couple or the other can be arbitrary. Historians, for example, speak exclusively of the salon of Madame Necker, thus reducing her husband either to the role of an amiable decorative object or to a severe image of a laconic statesman vaguely irritated by the interminable conversations of the men of letters whom his wife invited to their house. The invited guests, however, were acutely aware that they were going to Necker's house and not just his wife's. When Madame Necker was not in Paris, the Tuesday and Friday gatherings, rather than being suspended, continued with her husband in charge, and the inspectors of the Contrôle des étrangers often noted that the diplomats and men of letters who frequented the salon went *chez M. Necker*. One might hypothesize that Necker cleverly focused attention on his wife in order to avoid looking like a financier who gave dinners for men of letters. He needed to ward off political adversaries, always ready to denounce the dinners and suppers as the stepping stones of his political career.

Even the salon of baron d'Holbach was much more mixed than historians have assumed. It is hard to explain the tenacious image of his "male salon" when contemporary correspondence reveals the significant presence of several women. The first of these was the baroness herself, whose coquetry, in the eyes of some visitors, provided one of the attractions of the house.[35] She was not the only woman to do the honors of the salon. The baron's mother-in-law, Madame d'Aine, was a colorful person whose escapades and petulance Diderot found highly amusing. Often present at the d'Holbachs' home on rue Royale-Saint-Roch, she lived at Grandval in a house that belonged to her husband. She received the friends of d'Holbach and she did her best to make their stay agreeable, paying particular attention, for example, to the menus of meals that were served and that were eaten "under the peril of displeasing the mistress of the house."[36] Several other women, such as Madame d'Épinay, Madame d'Houdetot and Madame de Meaux, made regular appearances, both at Grandval and in Paris, and Madame Geoffrin herself came to play faro now and then. Relating a very animated discussion with Helvetius at d'Holbach's home, Diderot commented, "We pleaded heatedly, as always will happen when one has women for judges. Mesdemoiselles Valori, Madame d'Épinay, and Madame d'Holbach were on the bench."[37]

There is no doubt that the baron appeared as the more important personage of the couple, and that the salon was primarily his. His culture, his curiosity, and his fondness for sociability imposed his tutelage—at times kindly, at times sulky—over the dinners on the rue Royale-Saint-Roch and over the gatherings at Grandval.[38] The fact remains, however, that the contrast between the d'Holbach salon and the "female" salons is a historians' invention, as is the atheist plotting that supposedly took place in the Paris home. These were two sides of the same legend, the absence of feminine censorship being thought to liberate philosophical ardor.

Not all salons were held by women. The model of a woman receiving men, and in particular, men of letters, was but one possible form of the salon. Yet, the essential criterion of the salon was a mixed membership of both men and women, the touchstone of the worldly life of the ancien régime, which set it apart from the masculine institutions of sociability.

A final criterion that defines salon sociability is the absence of an explicit objective other than sociability itself. These worldly gatherings had the sole goal of pleasurable entertainment. In this, they were distinct from forms of entertainment that were at times similar but that clearly pursued professional ends, such as the society of playwrights founded by Beaumarchais.[39] Worldly practices were leisure activities. There, "the relation established with others is more important than the activity ostensibly pursued," according to Maurice Agulhon.[40] That does not prevent participation in the salons from serving unavowed aims, or from producing effects of distinction, violence, and stigmatization. The fact that all these practices remained hidden permitted the social connection to be aestheticized.

The Frontiers of Worldliness

A home regularly open to guests who had been presented to the host or hostess and that provided a sociability in mixed company governed by the rules of civility permitted the regrouping and circumscription of a group of coherent practices based on the tradition of hospitality and conviviality of the French urban elites. It did not necessarily imply the presence of men of letters, although they were often present, nor the exclusive authority of a woman, but it did insist on the essential elements of a sociability of hospitality, on a noninstitutional system of codes, and on a mixed society, politeness, and the effects of cooptation. Finally, such a definition prevents viewing the salon as a narrowly specific form of sociability, but rather places it within the framework of ancien régime worldly society.

The mechanisms of worldly society were not limited to the salons, but were deployed in other places frequented by the social elites, the theater and the opera in particular, and also the Masonic lodges. The Masons' sociability was not as specific, egalitarian, and secret as has long been thought, but they did include other distinctive practices characteristic of the amusements of the urban elites.[41] Similarly, too sharp a contrast should not be drawn between the city and the court, Paris and Versailles, as two models of sociability, one shaped by civility and the other by etiquette. In reality, the forms of worldly social life were present at Versailles, in particular in the form of *sociétés particulières*, genuine salons within the court, such as those of the favorites, the ministers, or some courtiers. Besides, many people who figured among the "society" of Paris had court appointments that required their presence at Versailles. When the prince de Beauvau was on duty there, his wife's salon moved to Versailles, and eighty-year-old Madame Du Deffand, despite her advanced age and the inconvenience of the trip, went there for supper, as did others.[42] The court, the Paris salons, and the Versailles salons were part of the same social scene. After having attended the *coucher du roi*, the men returned to Paris or went to one of the various Versailles salons, where they rejoined "the women, the bishops, people who had not been presented [at court], and, often, an interrupted game."[43] This was the group known as "la Cour et la Ville." Without a doubt, after the Regency, Versailles never regained the cultural prestige that it had enjoyed under Louis XIV. Still, the worldly life, animated by gaming and conversation, had its place in it. The Versailles salons benefitted from the proximity of the royal couple, who exerted a clear hold on fashions and customs within Parisian high society, thus perpetuating the central role of the court in the diffusion of the social practices of the elites. The games invented in the duchesse de Polignac's salon were imitated in the Paris salons.[44]

This close connection between Parisian high society and the court was also visible in the sociability ruled by the princes of the royal family, whose practices drew on both the court and the salon, on representation, on leisure, and on etiquette and worldliness. The court of the duchesse du Maine at Sceaux is the most famous example. Theatricals, contests of wit, sumptuous *fêtes*, ballets, and fireworks: the model of this sociability was clearly the court of the young Louis XIV, and the "Divertissements de Sceaux" aimed at being the heirs of the spectacular royal amusements of Versailles as well as prolonging the memory of the Condé *fêtes* at Chantilly. The high point of such celebrations had been the "Grandes Nuits de Sceaux" in 1714.[45] Compromised in the Cellamare conspiracy, the duc and duchesse de Condé were arrested in 1718 and imprisoned for a year. After their return to Sceaux, their *fêtes*, which now had competition from those of the Regent, never regained their former luster or attendance. Still, the duchess continued to receive guests for another forty years, and Sceaux remained an influential center of worldliness. According to Charles-Jean-François Hénault, "If the court was less brilliant, it was not any less agreeable; persons of consideration and wit made up [its society]."[46] The duchess's connections with the court were reestablished; she occasionally appeared there, and in 1745 Louis XV and Marie Leszczynska paid her a visit with grand pomp. The duchesse de Condé also kept in touch with the salon of the marquise de Lambert, the most important salon of the first half of the eighteenth century, which a number of her own regular guests attended.[47] In 1747, when Voltaire took refuge there with Madame de Châtelet, Sceaux had not lost its power of attraction.[48] Performances of his plays were given there, in particular, *Zaïre, ou Rome sauvée*, which he wrote at Sceaux and had performed there in 1750, attracting a "prodigious crowd" of courtiers and prominent figures of Paris society.[49] In 1748 the comedies of Fontenelle, which Madame Geoffrin attended, were produced there.[50] In this manner, the court of Sceaux seems to have connected the century of Louis XIV to the century of the Enlightenment, as well as the court to the salons.

Other princely dwellings perpetuated this tradition during the second half of the century, in particular, those of the duc d'Orléans and the prince de Conti. The latter was the animating force of one of the principal gathering places for Paris society, in his home in the Temple district, where Madame de Boufflers, his mistress, was the central figure. The prince de Conti, a collector, a lettered aristocrat, an *esprit fort*, was fond of being called "citizen" by Rousseau even though he was the king's cousin, but was finicky about his rights and privileges. An incarnation of the paradoxes of the aristocracy of the Enlightenment, he participated in all forms of sociability, passing back and forth between the court and the salon.

From the court to the salons, as from the salons to the lodges, the history of worldly practices blurs all hasty classifications. At first glance, the court and freemasonry seem opposed in every way. The first embodied, to the point of caricature, the hierarchy and ceremony of the ancien régime operating under the guidance of an absolute monarch; the second, secret and egalitarian, developed a universalist and fraternal discourse. Both phenomena seem to have owed little to the salons, where the worldly and lettered entertainment of Parisian elites unfolded far from both the royal gaze and the secrets of the lodge. Still, from Masonic lodges to the society of the salon, and from the salon to the Palais Royal and even Versailles, the same worldly practices were often in operation. The term that described them best was *société*.

SOCIAL PRACTICES, LINGUISTIC PRACTICES
Instability and Polemics

Did the eighteenth century have a word that corresponded to what was later called the *salons*? A number of terms, with different connotations, were used concurrently. The most specific terms, those that seem to designate more precise forms of sociability—terms such as *ruelle, bureau d'esprit, cercle*—were almost always used in a polemical context, or at least with a strongly satirical intent. The term *ruelle*, which designated a space between a bed and a wall and had been closely connected with the salons of the *précieuses*, was hardly ever used in the eighteenth century. After a peak in usage in the 1650s and 1660s, the word registers a clear decline. The shift from the bedchamber to the salon as the site for sociability was in part responsible for this decline. The term might still designate conversation societies, but only in a satirical viewpoint that associated them with futility, idle chatter, and libertinage. Rousseau contrasted the person who "learned to speak only in the *ruelles*" to the male eloquence of the office-holder or the judge, and he denounced the *"ruelles* philosophers."[51]

The expression *bureau d'esprit* was always used as an ironic designation for social groups suspected of pedantry. In his famous "Satire X," Boileau applied it to a coterie of "pale authors" that is scorned by readers, subjected to ridicule as a "learned dwelling," and judged critically as having been corrupted by an all-out search for novelty: "That is where false wit [*esprit*] keeps its offices [*bureaux*] / All verse is good, provided it is new."[52] The joking association between *bureau* and *esprit* was aimed at the incompatibility between the habits of study and of the administration, on the one hand, and the manners of high society, on the other. Once that association had been fixed in the expression *bureau d'esprit*, it served to disqualify societies in which authors were too numerous and literary questions too often discussed. The phrase was popularized by a comedy that made fun of Madame Geoffrin's salon.[53] During the 1760s, Collé used the expression several times in his diary: the salon of baron d'Holbach was the *"bureau d'esprit* of the Encyclopedists"; Madame Geoffrin's house was a *"bureau d'esprit"* that he detested; and Madame Necker kept a "minor *bureau d'esprit*" that was, moreover, "ridiculously *précieuse*."[54] Madame de Genlis adds that the word is used "in derision."[55]

The term *cercle* originated at court. It was at times used to designate people gathered together for conversation. Madame d'Oberkirch, for example, writes that there was "in the evening a *cercle* at the home of Madame de La Vallière."[56] In the first edition of the *Dictionnaire de l'Académie*, the only figurative sense cited is as follows: "the company of the princesses and duchesses seated in a circle to the right and the left of the Queen. *The Queen holds the circle today. That duchess is seated at the circle.* It is also taken as the place at which that company is assembled. *Go to the circle; he is seen every day at the circle*."[57] In 1798, the fifth edition of the same dictionary extended the term to all gatherings of individuals given over to conversation and games: "It is also said, by extension, of the assemblies of men and women that are held in the houses of individuals for conversation. *That man shines in the circles. Break up the circle with a game.*" The vocabulary of the *cercle* thus reflects a spread of both vocabulary and practices from the court toward urban sociability.

Within the abundant vocabulary available, *coterie* at first referred quite vaguely to all sorts of social groups, but later it gained a negative connotation. The definition proposed by the *Encyclopédie* was pejorative: "The entire city is divided into *coteries*, enemies to one another and much scorning each other."[58] Grimm asserts that "what is admired in one of these coteries is scorned by the other; and what is even more singular about them is that usually none of these judgments is well founded."[59] Another current term, *royaume*, insists on the role of the person who receives and on the salon as a miniature court. It is generally used ironically, as it was by Madame Geoffrin's daughter, the marquise de La Ferté-Imbault, who speaks of women who, in order to be fashionable, felt obliged to "found and establish their little realms."[60]

Finally, two less specific terms were often used in eighteenth-century sources to designate what today we call salons: *maisons* and *compagnies*. The first accentuates the importance of the private residence in the sociability of the salons and sets that sociability within the field of aristocratic hospitality practices: "It is said that a man does honor to his house to say that he receives the world in his home."[61] The reports of the Contrôle des étrangers used the term frequently, for example, noting of the English ambassador that "the houses (*maisons*) of Coigny and La Vaupalière are the ones that he frequents the most assiduously."[62] The second and even more general term stressed the dynamics of aggregation. According to Furetière, *compagnie* "is said of several persons assembled in the same place or with the same purpose,"[63] but has also the narrower sense of a small number of friends assembled in a place in order to speak with one another, amuse themselves, and visit. In the eighteenth century, *la compagnie* was seldom used to designate a specific informal circle. The word was also in use with a qualifier (*bonne compagnie; mauvaise compagnie*) to speak of larger social groups that stood out for their mastery of the codes of civility. Nonetheless, at the end of the eighteenth century, the use of *compagnie* declined, whereas the lexicon of society rose.

The Society of Salons

The word *société*, much used in the eighteenth century, became omnipresent in the latter half of the century, when it designated both a specific salon and its habitués, or even the entire group of those who attended salons. In the reports of the Contrôle des étrangers its use was extremely frequent, designating, for example, "the society of Madame Geoffrin," "the society of the maréchale de Luxembourg," or "the society of Madame Necker," or specifying that the Swedish, Neapolitan, and English ambassadors were "of the society of Madame de Marchais."[64] When d'Alembert praises the salon of Madame de Lambert, he speaks of the role played by Saint-Aulaire in "that society," stating, "that woman, known for her wit, brought together in her home a most chosen society of men of letters and *gens du monde*."[65] The word was also used in the plural: Mercy d'Argenteau was happy to find his old acquaintances on his return to Paris in 1766, Madame Geoffrin in particular, but he complained to Kaunitz of the changes he noticed in the worldly life and in the quality of conversation: "It seems to me, however, that I see change in many regards: *les sociétés* have become more numerous, more mixed, and less intimate."[66]

Historians have long noted the emergence of the vocabulary connected with *société* and its many derivatives, but they almost always identify the term with the emergence of the general sense of a society as a group of individuals living in a same political community.[67] But other meanings of the term were also on the rise. The *Dictionnaire de l'Académie* specifies: "It is also taken as a company of people who usually assemble for pleasurable gatherings. Agreeable society. *He is a man of good company, he should be admitted into our society. He should be banished from our society*."[68] Here words show a semantic proximity to *compagnie*, which *société* replaces, in the nature of such gatherings, which include private *liaisons particulières* between friends and neighbors; and in the search for pleasure or amusement that is their aim.

In addition, the 1798 edition of the *Dictionnaire* states that *société* "is said about the persons with whom one lives. *That person is of my society. I would not like to make my society with that person.*"[69] The word shifts from a group that gets together to the persons whom an individual frequents. Although she appreciates the conversation of diplomats, the duchesse de Rohan is unenthusiastic about receiving them in her home: "I do not like their society as society," she writes, in a phrase that perfectly summarizes the ambiguities of the term.[70]

The polysemous term *société*, the word most often used to designate what was later called a "salon," was also used less specifically. Far from referring to a particular form of sociability, it was used to speak of any sort of voluntary association. Among the practices of sociability, its meaning was much broader than the word "salon," as it was applied to all forms of non-institutional gatherings and all forms of association, such as the "société d'hommes de lettres," cited as being responsible for the *Encyclopédie*, or, later, to the revolutionary societies. The term could also be used for scholarly institutions such as the academies: "Several of our provincial academies take on the qualities of *sociétés littéraires*."[71] These ambiguities clearly indicate the intense linguistic turmoil concerning the word *société* during the latter half of the eighteenth century.

That turmoil resulted in a new meaning of the term. *La société* designated the salons as a whole, along with those who frequented them: it was a synonym of *le monde* or *la bonne compagnie*. For example, the marquise de Pons writes to her husband about a fashionable supper given in Paris by Madame Du Barry: "All of society, men and women, was there."[72] Immediately after the Revolution, Madame de Genlis reinforced the substitution of *société* for *bonne compagnie* to designate a social elite defined by its practices of sociability. In the entry "bonne compagnie" of her *Dictionnaire des étiquettes*, she simply states, "See *Société*."[73]

By extension, "society" came to designate a specific form of sociability that corresponded to the life of the salons and gave rise to the expression *la vie de société*. It is in that sense, for example, that Rousseau utilized the word when he wrote: "I would enjoy society as much as the next man, if I were not certain to show myself there not only to my own disadvantage, but as quite different from what I am," a statement that is not a misanthropic profession of faith but the confession of an inaptitude for *la vie mondaine*.[74] Similarly, the Mniszech brothers, on paying a call on Président Hénault, judged him to be "already too infirm for society but not yet enough for belles lettres."[75] Mirabeau strikingly associates *la société* with the elites' way of life: "The rage for society in France has won over scientific men as well as the others; and if someone asked a young physician, a young lawyer, and a young preacher what is his ambition, he would answer, if he were telling the truth: It is to introduce myself into good company and to have enough to live on."[76] The use of the term in this sense, which was extensive in the latter half of the century, gave rise to numerous expressions: the words *de société* were used to describe dinner, suppers, visits, connections, amusements, theater, entertainments, verse, games, and news, as well as in such phrases as *esprit de société* and even *vertus de société*. A *maison de société* was a dwelling in which guests were received regularly, and in which those invited belonged to high society. The young Manon Phlipon, the future Madame Roland, wrote, for example, to her friend Sophie Canet that she frequented "two houses of what is called 'society.'"[77] The police inspector charged with surveillance of diplomats remarks that most of them "seem to see one another currently only in a *maison de société*."[78]

This lexical investigation highlights the absence of a specific term to designate an institution of sociability that regularly brought invited guests together in someone's home for conversation and pleasurable distraction, as the word "salon" would in the nineteenth century. It is not irrelevant that the more specific terms—*bureau d'esprit, ruelle*—were the most polemical and that the word most frequently used, *société*, was also the most polysemous. The lexical field of sociability was a polemical field, but it was also a field of experimentation where the political concept of "society," so important in Enlightenment thought, led to a number of neologisms (*socialité, sociabilité, socialisme*). Among late eighteenth-century authors and theoreticians of social art under the Revolution, the linguistic and conceptual elaboration of *la société* owed much to theoretical reflection on forms of connection and on sociability.[79]

WORLDLY HOSPITALITY

The Economy of Salons

Hospitality came at a price that was not within everyone's reach. It was not enough to be witty and have friends in order to create a salon; it also required a dwelling spacious enough for company and the means to furnish it, decorate it tastefully, and prepare food for guests. The model of aristocratic hospitality that governed the salons demanded that the host or hostess be prepared at any time to welcome a large number of dinner or supper guests. That posed no problem for most of the grand aristocratic *hôtels*, where high-level government functionaries usually gathered. The duc de Biron, who had one of the greatest fortunes in France, had no difficulty serving dinner every Friday to some forty persons in his magnificent *hôtel particulier*.[80] Not all of those who received guests were as rich as he, however, and his model was not easy to follow, even at a more reduced scale, because it required a solid fortune, which explains why the financiers were really the only bourgeois in a position to rival the aristocratic salons. The salon of Laurent Grimod de La Reynière and his wife Suzanne Françoise de Jarente was one of the most brilliant of these financiers' salons. Appointed fermier général in 1753, in 1770 La Reynière bought a *hôtel* on the rue de la Grange-Batelière, which he furnished sumptuously and where he began to receive regularly. A large polygonal dining room with fountains accompanied a salon decorated in a Pompeian style.[81] In 1780, La Reynière resigned his post as fermier général and built a magnificent *hôtel particulier* between the rue du Faubourg-Saint-Honoré and the Champs-Élysées.[82] Decorated with a large collection of paintings, it was among the "houses famous for their beauty and the richness of their furnishings" visited by foreigners.[83] Finally, La Reynière also owned the château de la Thuilerie at Auteuil, a former hunting lodge of François I surrounded by five hectares of gardens, where he received during the summer.

La Reynière's salon was famous for the gastronomic refinement of the suppers served, and the master and mistress of the house were always prepared to serve as many as was necessary: "It was ten o'clock; we were about to sit down to table, when ten or twelve carriages parading in the courtyard announced fifteen or twenty unexpected guests at a supper for three. Happily the cook (the great Mérillon) knew just what to do. He had in reserve a good number of outstanding entrées, and at ten thirty we were served an excellent supper for twenty-five."[84] The magnificence of these receptions bore witness to an intense effort on the La Reynières' part to be accepted in high society.

The salons frequented by men of letters also required material and financial ease. Helvétius did not owe the success of his salon to the quality of conversation alone or to the philosophes one might meet there. Edward Gibbon, who had a high opinion of Helvétius, wrote to his stepmother, "Besides being a sensible man and agreeable companion, & the worthiest creature in the world, He has a very pretty wife, a hundred thousand livres a year, and one of the best tables in Paris."[85] Madame Geoffrin's salon was supported by a solid fortune that she owed to the Manufacture des Glaces of Saint-Gobain, a company in which her husband had acted as a skilled administrator and in which she held a considerable number of shares.[86] The income that she drew from these holdings made her "rich enough to make her house the rendezvous of literature and the arts,"[87] according to Jean-François Marmontel, one of her regular guests. An inventory of the revenues of her daughter, who owed almost her entire fortune to her mother, provides figures for a more precise estimate. In 1788, the marquise de La Ferté-Imbault received an annual income of 133,000 livres, 90,000 livres of which came from holdings in the Saint-Gobain firm.[88] Madame Geoffrin also owned the *hôtel* on the rue Saint-Honoré, estimated to be worth 250,000 livres.[89] Thanks to that fortune, and without living ostentatiously, Madame Geoffrin enjoyed a richly furnished apartment, employed ten domestic servants and commissioned paintings from the most fashionable artists.[90]

Madame Geoffrin's relationship with the Manufacture des Glaces was twofold. On the one hand, the income that it provided to her and to her daughter permitted them to receive generously; on the other hand, her networks within high society and even her salon on the rue Saint-Honoré served as resources when the time came to intervene in the management of the manufacturing firm. Madame Geoffrin's skill in financial negotiations led her to put her salon to the service of discreet transactions. She occasionally organized afternoon gatherings, "business rendezvous, which were held in her home and in which she acted as mediator."[91]

Serving meals, week after week, to an undetermined number of guests could soon become costly. In 1786, Marie-Antoinette worried about Madame de Staël's expenses and expressed her concern to Necker.[92] The cost of hospitality posed a problem for Julie de Lespinasse, when she wanted to open a salon after her break with the marquise Du Deffand in April 1764 but had a disposable income of only 3,592 livres.[93] Only the financial support of people such as Madame de Luxembourg and Madame Geoffrin enabled her to afford acceptable housing.[94] Not offering dinner to her guests was for Julie de Lespinasse a constraint and not a choice.[95]

Madame d'Épinay's experience demonstrates that money was the central nerve of sociability. Some might find her case surprising. She was a witty woman, separated from her husband, who loved letters; she was friend with most of the *Encyclopédie* group and had a liaison with Grimm. She received a few writers and fashionable people in her home and obviously wanted to follow in the footsteps of Madame Geoffrin. Nonetheless, after a few years, her salon consisted only of a few good friends. The principal obstacle to its long-term existence lay in her chronic financial difficulties, which became pressing in 1762, when her husband lost his appointment as fermier général, thus reducing his resources and lowering their social standing.[96] Forced to abandon La Chevette, the country house where she had received her friends, Madame d'Épinay could no longer offer hospitality. From 1769 to 1782 she had no country house. Her more limited income forced her to rent a series of relatively modest apartments, and even to give up living in Paris during the winter of 1762–63. Well aware of the handicap to her activity as a hostess, she wrote to Galiani: "I hope [. . .] that you will put me down as one of your best friends, and that all that is lacking is an income of sixty thousand livres to have the reputation of chatting like anyone else, something about which I could not care less, to speak politely."[97] Madame d'Épinay not only makes clear the connection between her reputation for wit and the financial conditions of worldly hospitality, but also furnishes an indication of the income that she thought necessary in order to receive honorably.

What was the lower end of this economy of worldly hospitality, the minimum income required to receive guests on a weekly basis? The accounts of Madame Du Deffand, who rented an apartment in the convent of Saint-Joseph and had few expenses (given her age and her blindness) except for what she needed in order to attract society to her, provides a rare estimation of "the revenue it takes to have ten or twelve domestics and a supper for five or six persons."[98] She states to Walpole that "it is very difficult that it could be [done] with less than a thousand écus per month, " i.e. six thousands livres. In 1770, her total expenditures were 39,000 livres, divided as follows: 18,000 for putting dishes on the table; 2,000 for rent; 4,000 livres for her carriage and her three horses; 6,000 for the wages of her domestics and their uniforms; 4,000 livres for provisions of wood and light, and 4,000 livres "for my own upkeep." To pay these sums she had a yearly income of only 35,190 livres, made up of her marriage settlement, investment income, and a royal gratification of 6,000 livres per year that the queen had arranged for her in 1763 on the request of the duchesse de Luynes, Madame Du Deffand's aunt.[99] When her "gratification" was threatened, so was her salon.

The various estimates of the revenue needed to keep up a salon in Paris seem to align. The lower limit appears to have been 40,000 livres; the 60,000 livres that Madame d'Épinay sighs for would have raised her to the level of the baron d'Holbach.[100] Above that level, the revenues of Madame Geoffrin and, to an even greater extent, of the financiers or the upper court aristocracy permitted a hospitality beyond simple calculation. That higher level of revenues corresponds fairly well to the limit of the "plutocratic nucleus" defined by historians of nobility; it includes those with at least 50,000 livres of yearly income, a group that includes some sixty families throughout the kingdom, a hundred or so families who lived at the court, and about fifty wealthy financiers.[101]

In revealing the financial foundation of worldly hospitality, these estimates situate the Paris salons within a segment of Paris society that predictably consisted of the court aristocracy and the major financiers. It also confirms that those who kept up a salon were primarily hosts and hostesses whose talents for sociability were in part evaluated according to the material resources that permitted them to offer that worldly hospitality. These economic conditions of sociability concerned all the women who hoped to gain access to the "society" of the salons: expenditures were involved in simply attending them, even without "receiving" in their own. After his marriage, Jean-Baptiste-Antoine Suard, a journalist and academician, wanted to take his young wife, née Amélie Pancoucke, to the salons that he frequented, and to do this he was obliged to devote a sizeable portion of his mediocre revenues to ensuring that she was dressed and had accessories "just like the women she saw."[102] Since she owned few frocks, she often dressed just before she went out so as to preserve them. While an impecunious man of letters could go to the home of Madame Necker or the duchesse de Rochefort on foot, a woman had to rely on friends. A carriage, Tronchin writes, "is a need in Paris roughly equal to that of a shirt."[103] Happily for the Suards, Madame de Marchais or Madame Necker always sent their horses. Julie de Lespinasse, who also did not own a carriage, was often driven to her hostesses' houses, as is mentioned on several occasions in the reports of the Contrôle des étrangers.

How to Get Invited

The specific nature of worldly hospitality should also be seen from the point of view of those who attended the salons. How could one penetrate a salon? How were people invited? And how did one become a habitué? The rules governing access to these circles functioned according to a dialectic of openness—the regularity of the gatherings eliminated formal invitations—and closure—only a few, elect persons were admitted. Three conditions determined access to a salon: one had to be directly invited by the master or the mistress of the house, be presented by a frequent guest, or be furnished with a letter of recommendation. The new guest was already known to the host, directly or indirectly, and belonged to an interconnected circle of acquaintances.

Direct invitation was the decision of the host to invite someone who enjoyed a certain celebrity or whom he or she had encountered at other salons. A successful book or play could provide entrée, but even then, common friends guaranteed the politeness and the amiability of the author. Famous in France for his book on penal reform, Cesare Beccaria was introduced by Morellet, his translator, into intellectual circles and more worldly ones. Ten years earlier, Morellet had been presented to Madame Geoffrin by Trudaine de Montigny, then to Madame Boufflers by Turgot.[104] If his participation in the *querelle des Philosophes* and his brief sojourn in the Bastille brought him an invitation to the homes of d'Holbach and Helvétius, it was because he had already frequented the *Encyclopédie* group and had been received in Paris "society," where he benefitted from having several female protectors: Madame de Luxembourg had intervened to get him freed from prison. Occasionally, steps were taken to attract someone into a salon, but these were usually new salons that had not yet established a reputation. Thus Diderot writes to Sophie Volland: "There is here a Madame Necker, a pretty woman and a fine wit, who is wild about me. There is a persecution campaign to have me at her home."[105] This was probably a boast, since Madame Necker had just married and was only beginning to receive. When a hostess wanted to persuade a prominent person to come to her gatherings, the move was usually indirect. Thus Madame Du Deffand, in the early days of her salon, asked d'Alembert to bring along an abbé whom she wanted to meet, but she adds pessimistically, "You won't be able to do it: he will be, at the most, like Diderot, who had had enough after one visit: I have no attaching atoms."[106]

Usually the request would come from the would-be guest, and a recommendation was almost always necessary. Family networks played a large role, given the domestic dimension of this hospitality. The abbé de Voisenon was introduced into the salon of Madame Doublet by his brother, the comte de Voisenon, who had married one of Madame Doublet's grand-daughters.[107] In order to have Loménie de Brienne received in Madame Geoffrin's salon, his aunt, the duchesse de Luynes, turned to Madame Geoffrin's daughter, the marquise de La Ferté-Imbault.[108] Ambassadors played an important role where foreigners were concerned. They were scattered through the principal salons, which made them particularly well placed to introduce their compatriots into *le monde*. They took advantage of this privilege: Count Creutz presented most of the Swedish nobles passing through Paris to the host or hostess of the salons that he attended.[109]

Still, for most foreigners, the key was a letter of recommendation, either written by a French person living abroad—a diplomat, for example—or, more often, by a compatriot who had already frequented Parisian high society. The future king of Poland, Stanisław August Poniatowski, arrived in Paris in 1753 bearing five letters of recommendation that served as "so many entrées into five quite different sorts of society,"[110] including that of Madame Geoffrin, the English ambassador, and the duchesse de Brancas. Aristocratic tourism in Europe was facilitated by an international circulation of letters of recommendation, which reassured the recipients of the letters and certified that the bearer belonged to the European network of the Enlightenment. They also carried an assurance that the bearer would be well treated. The English historian William Coxe, who made several stays in France as tutor to the marquis of Blandford, had been furnished with a recommendation by Horace Bénédict de Saussure, a friend of Madame Necker's, but he failed to present it to her. She, nonetheless, received him as the author of a history of Switzerland, but when, several days later, she received the recommendation, sent on by Saussure, she was puzzled by Coxe's bizarre behavior and regretted having received him "on his reputation as an *homme de mérite*," which is to say, coolly. She added, "I reproach myself for all of the marks of attention that I failed to give him."[111] At least he was received, but when a distant relative of Madame Necker's, whom she did not know and who was sent to her by one of her friends in Geneva, presented himself to her without letters of recommendation, Madame Necker refused to see him and ordered her doorman not to let him in. She was later obliged to make her excuses to her Geneva friend, explaining that she had to be suspicious of everyone who simply arrived at her doorstep.[112]

Knowing how to manage the recommendations network was an essential skill for the hostess. In her address books, Madame Geoffrin often noted, next to a name, who had recommended that person. The baronne de Krüdener was "recommended by M. Suard and known by Mme la comtesse de Brionne."[113] Two recommendations were better than one, even for a baroness. The recommendation of a member of the Academy who was a friend of Madame Geoffrin's was reinforced by the favorable report of a high aristocrat who frequented her suppers. As for Monsieur Duchesne, a Piedmontese who was a close friend of Trudaine de Montigny, he was recommended by Monsieur Des Marches. But no one enjoyed as good a recommendation as Monsieur Buscher or Monsieur Granowski, "recommended by the king of Poland."[114]

During his stay in Paris in 1763, Edward Gibbon was received in most of the Paris salons. He recounts that initiation into Parisian social life in his *Memoirs*, but also in his journal and in letters he sent to his family and his friends. If he was astonished to find that his *Essai sur l'étude de la littérature*, published in French in 1761, turned out to be "the best recommendation" and earned him praise and invitations, he nonetheless arrived in Paris furnished with fourteen letters of recommendation.[115] It mattered to Gibbon that he was received as a man of the world rather than as a man of letters, and he took care to distinguish himself, by his appearance, from the "cohort of authors." He soon learned that these recommendations had very different effects depending on the person to whom they were addressed. If he was disappointed with his meeting with the comte de Caylus, who, to Gibbon's great surprise, shut himself up in his *cabinet* at six o'clock in the evening and did not open the door to him, he was delighted with the facility with which some recommendations brought him new acquaintances and new invitations. Thanks to this cumulative process, two weeks after his arrival he could take pride in having three dinner invitations for the following Sunday.[116] At the home of Madame Geoffrin, for example, he met Helvétius, who invited him to his own house, where he met the baron d'Holbach. Soon he was also received in the homes of the duchesse d'Aiguillon, the comtesse de Froulay, Madame Du Boccage, Madame Boyer, the marquis de Mirabeau, and Foncemagne.[117] According to Gibbon, "The seed was sometimes cast on a barren rock, and it sometimes multiplied a hundred fold in the production of new shoots, spreading branches, and exquisite fruit."[118]

The letter of recommendation was an important aid to the mobility of the elites of Europe. For those who were in a position to furnish one, it was also a power and, at times, an obligation, which means that not all letters were of equal value or efficacy. When Galiani could not refuse a friend a letter of recommendation for a Sicilian whom he did not know, he wrote to Madame d'Épinay to explain that it was a recommendation "with reservations."[119] To become a regular guest in a salon, it was not enough to be provided with a letter of recommendation: the newcomer had to win over the host or hostess and be invited back. Some aspirants never managed to be received in a certain salon that they yearned to join, either because their titles for acceptance were too flimsy or because they displeased the hostess. Madame Geoffrin refused to receive the baron de Wreech in spite of a warm recommendation from Grimm, under the pretext that she did not want to make any new acquaintances: "I am sixty. New acquaintances fatigue my head." Stressing that she was resolved, she added, "The gate is closed."[120]

Should this treatment be seen as a pretext or rather an effect of age? The following year Madame Geoffrin was delighted to receive the prince of Hesse-Darmstadt, whom Grimm had brought to her home: seemingly, the princely quality of the visitor permitted the barrier to be reopened. It is true that, over time, Madame Geoffrin's relations were increasingly numerous and letters of recommendation poured in from all over Europe.[121] Whatever the true situation, Madame Geoffrin's rather dry "The gate is closed" clearly shows that she intended to decide whom she would accept in her home. Some complained about how she selected her guests. Abbé Guasco, a member of the Académie des Inscriptions introduced by Montesquieu, was unlucky enough to displease Madame Geoffrin and was even suspected of being a police spy. According to a number of contemporary witnesses, he was sent away from her door and, when the abbé insisted, the doorman was obliged to push him toward the street.[122]

A guest's first presentation was thus a test in which he needed to please and to demonstrate his mastery of the codes of politeness. Mister Clerk, a Scot who had served in the English army and was much appreciated for his curiosity and his wit, suffered a bitter experience when he was presented to Madame Geoffrin:

> Baron d'Holbach had brought this foreigner to Madame Geoffrin's, and after the first compliments and a visit of a half hour, [d'Holbach] rose to leave. Mr. Clerk, instead of following the man who had presented him, as is the custom in a first visit, remained. Madame Geoffrin asked him if he went to the theater much. "Rarely.—On promenades?—Very little.—To the court, among the princes?—No one knows them less than I.—With what do you pass your time, then?—When I am comfortable in a house, I chat and I stay there." At these words Madame Geoffrin paled. It was six o'clock in the evening; she was thinking that at ten o'clock in the evening Mr. Clerk might still be in her house, an idea that made her shiver feverishly. Luck brought M. D'Alembert; Madame Geoffrin persuaded him, after a bit, that he was not well and that he should have Mr. Clerk drive him home. The latter, charmed to be of service, said to M. D'Alembert that he was quite welcome to use his carriage, since he would need it only later in the evening to take him home. These words struck Madame Geoffrin like a lightning bolt, and she never did get rid of our Scot, in spite of all shifting company in her apartment due to the arrival and departure of visits. Even today she cannot think coolly of that day; and she never goes to bed without taking measures against the dangers of a second visit.[123]

A victim of his lack of small talk and his failure to grasp custom, Mr. Clerk was not to return to the salon of Madame Geoffrin. Gleichen, who reports the same episode in his memoirs, confirms that she "consigned him to her doorstep forever."[124] Beyond the anecdote itself, Grimm's narrative also served to inform the subscribers to the *Correspondance littéraire* of the customs of Parisian "society" and of Madame Geoffrin's good manners, all the while playing on the connivance of aristocrats and European princes who could not help laughing at this bumpkin Scot.

Just as the host or hostess decided whom they would receive, they might also ban from the salon a person who no longer suited them. All that it took was an order to the Swiss guard not to let him in. After abbé Trublet had frequented Madame Geoffrin's salon for several years, she closed her doors to him because he had publicly attacked Helvétius in his journal.[125] Baron de Golz, minister plenipotentiary of Prussia, was "excluded from the society of Madame Necker for reasons of honor,"[126] or, more accurately, reasons of money, given that Necker, who had guaranteed the baron's rent for two years, was obliged to pay it for him when the debts of the diplomat, who "gambles, spends freely, and owes large sums," bankrupted him.

It also happened that the Swiss guard charged with prohibiting access to undesirables took an unfortunate initiative, as did the guard of the Spanish ambassador when he refused entry to three Englishmen who had come to the door. The ambassador, extremely unhappy about the incident, paid a call on the three and invited them to dinner the next day.[127] It is true that doormen got bad press. Grimod de La Reynière wrote bitterly: "I know of nothing more humiliating for a *galant homme* than the bowing and scraping (*salamalec*) that must be made to these insolent sentries when one wishes to enter into a *hôtel*. Far from simply showing the way, the only role that is proper for them, they set themselves up as privileged questioners and interrogate instead of answering."[128]

Versailles and Paris

Parisian salons were restricted and elitist spaces, access to which was not gained by a simple demonstration of one's talents, but by a slow process of social recognition and gradual penetration into worldly circles that often ended in failure. The salons were private places. Participation in them did not follow the model of voluntary membership that governed societies and associations, but corresponded to a model of courtly selection. As was true at court, the central role of the host or hostess was sanctioned by the rite of presentation. Just as the king had complete discretion to choose from among his courtiers those who would be called to sup in the Petits Appartements, so Madame Geoffrin and Madame Necker decided whom to invite to dinner or to supper from among those who paid calls on them. Unlike presentation at court, introduction into a salon did not require proof of nobility, but the necessary recommendations showed that the candidate already belonged to high society. The salons' court-like function did not escape the notice of contemporaries, and those who attended such gatherings did not hesitate to say that they were "paying court" to the mistress of the house. Hearing that Turgot was a frequent guest at the salon of Madame Du Deffand, Voltaire congratulated her, saying, "I am delighted that he is of your court,"[129] and Madame Du Deffand herself asked the comtesse de Brionne for her permission to *faire sa cour* to her. The term, she explained to the comtesse de Choiseul, "is often used."[130]

Even the physical disposition of the conversation circle around the hostess recalled the court culture. At the salon of Madame de La Vallière, the men sat to one side of the elderly duchess and the women to the other as she wove the strands of conversation together.[131] In her bedchamber Madame Du Deffand was enthroned in her *tonneau* with everyone grouped around her. Madame Geoffrin, too, gathered her guests around her armchair.[132]

The topographic centrality that made the salon a court in miniature signals, above all, that its very existence depended entirely on the person who received and devoted a part of his or her time and energy to hospitality. At times the effort could be considerable, less so for the aged and blind Madame Du Deffand ("As I never pay visits, one is sure to find me, which is convenient for the idle"),[133] but Madame Geoffrin found it a daily chore: "I get up every day at six in the morning, I go out every day at eleven, I have people for dinner or I dine *en ville*. I always return home between five and six in the evening, and then I do not go out again. As soon as I have returned, my room fills until nine in the evening. I often have those little suppers that you know well."[134] Morellet confirms that during the evening she received "many *gens du monde* and of the best company, for she never went out and one was sure of finding her [at home]."[135]

SALONNIÈRE OR MAÎTRESSE DE MAISON?

Historical debate on the role of women in the salons, which often focuses on the alternative of the public sphere versus the private sphere and on the ideological complexion of the salons, tends to be less sensitive to the practices of hospitality that defined the salons as a specific form of sociability. The term *salonnière* has increasingly been used by historians to designate women who received, but the term did not have that meaning in French at the time.[136] Contemporaries used the unambiguous term *maîtresse de maison* with no hesitation, and they stated, according to a frequently used formula, that the woman who received was "doing the honors of her house."[137] The term *salonnière* suggests instead that the salons were a well-defined cultural institution. It blurs their relation to the dwelling and turns the salon into an autonomous function, an occupation, almost a status, whereas Madame Geoffrin, Madame Necker, or the maréchale de Luxembourg were primarily perceived as women who received in their homes and who gave dinners or suppers. Both satires and laudatory descriptions converge in representing the salons a space for worldly hospitality in which women reigned thanks to their sensitivity to social decorum. As a privileged space for female action, the salon differed from the public sphere, without being reduced to the realm of domesticity and family space. To understand what was involved in such gatherings requires moving beyond the opposition of the public and the private spheres.

Gallantry and Sociability

The regular practice of hospitality often corresponded to a particular moment in the life cycle of women of high society. Having a "day" required both financial means and a high level of availability. For a woman, those requirements were linked to the norms of the Paris aristocracy, within which women enjoyed a high degree of autonomy from their husbands and couples might lead different social lives. That liberty was merely a toleration, however. A more favorable situation was widowhood: in the ancien régime, it was the only situation in which women enjoyed true legal freedom and financial autonomy. Several leading Parisian hostesses were widows.[138] Another situation that was fairly common in Paris "society" was an informal separation that allowed married women to live independently of their husbands. This was the case with Madame de Beauharnais, who, after marrying (at the age of fifteen) the younger son of a military family, a man thirteen years her elder, and going to La Rochelle to live with him, returned to live alone in Paris in 1762.[139] Unmarried women were much rarer, and Julie de Lespinasse stands out as an exception, both for her unmarried state and for her illegitimate birth. Without the intervention of Madame Du Deffand, and the support she offered her, Julie could never have come to Paris and played the important role that she did in worldly and literary life.[140]

Women who began to receive at a young age were rare. As Madame de Genlis put it: "It is impossible, in one's first youth, to do the honors of a table and circle acceptably; that is a social art that demands an observant mind and experience."[141] Hospitality on a regular basis often corresponded to a stage in the life of women of la bonne société: Madame de Tencin, Madame Du Deffand, Madame de Luxembourg, and Madame de La Vallière became respected authorities on Paris society when they were already mature, after a gay and busy youth. From the last echoes of the Regency to the sentimentalism of the age of Louis XVI, some women's careers reflected the century, moving from the Palais-Royal to the literary and aristocratic circles of Paris. The duchesse de Boufflers, before becoming the maréchale de Luxembourg, the protector of Rousseau and La Harpe, and the censor of all offenses against good taste, had been satirized in the chronicles of the age,[142] to the point that her contemporaries sometimes found it difficult to recognize in the respected woman the same one who, in her younger days, had inspired gallant verse.[143] Similarly, the duchesse de La Vallière, who was considered one of the most beautiful women of the eighteenth century and who had been famous for her loose ways, kept one of the best-reputed and most dependable salons of the end of the century. After he was received in her house, Lord Swinburne noted in his journal, "In her youth, she was an avowed libertine, and yet she now renders moral verdicts on what is good or bad [and] makes and unmakes reputations, *comme les autres*."[144] Finally, Inspector d'Hémery notes in his report on Madame Du Boccage, who was forty in 1749 and received writers on a weekly basis, that she "had been extremely *galante*."[145] This biographical journey from *galanterie* to *mondanité* became a commonplace that implied that a woman opened a salon when her charms had diminished and her flirtatious days were over.

There was a close connection between seduction and worldliness because both were based on an art of pleasing. For the theoreticians and champions of worldly sociability, "gallantry" was a key to social relations linked to politeness and the presence of women. For Hume, for example, gallantry, a paradigm of that sociability founded on hospitality and politeness, corresponded to the political model of monarchies and was rooted in court life.[146] The opposition between republics, which are based in a male civic sense and confine women to a domestic role, and monarchies, where women enjoy a space of their own, is a commonplace in writings on women and sociability in the eighteenth century. After Hume or Montesquieu, Mercier clearly formulated that contrast in the chapter on women in his *Tableau de Paris*. After first noting that "among republicans, woman are but housewives," he states that they possess enlightenment, good sense, and experience, and adds that their role blossoms "when the nation does not yet exist, or when it no longer exists. [. . .] Strangers to the bonds of patriotism, they hold marvelously firm to the sweet bonds of sociability. That is their veritable empire in Paris. They show themselves to be laughing, soft, and amiable."[147]

Mercier explicitly identifies a sphere of female action distinct from both the "domestic scene" and the public sphere of political action, which is "the world." In a republic, that social sphere disappears, leaving only the domestic sphere, given over to housewives, and the public sphere of patriots. In a monarchy, and even more so in Paris, *le monde* is defined by its "sociability" as a factor of social aggregation and by "representation," a characteristic feature of court society.

Familiarity with *le Monde*

Women were not reduced to choosing between the domestic sphere and the public sphere. They benefitted from having a legitimate space, governed by the laws of worldly hospitality, within which to act. The men of letters whom they received gave that hospitality an image that conformed to society's norms by stressing familiarity with high society and the social virtues of their hostesses. After the death of Julie de Lespinasse, La Harpe offered an explanation of her reputation:

> Soon Mademoiselle de Lespinasse brought together what was in all ways the most select and most agreeable society. From five to ten, one was sure to find there the elite of all sorts, men of the court, men of letters, ambassadors, foreign lords, women of quality: It was a title of consideration to be received in that society. Mademoiselle de Lespinasse was its principal attraction. I have seen much of her without being intimately connected with her. I can say that I have never known a woman with a more natural wit, less desire to show it, and more talent for making that of others shine. No one knew better than she how to do the honors of her house. She put everyone in a place of his own, and everyone was content with his place. She had a great familiarity with the world, and the most amiable sort of politeness, the sort that has the tone of interest.[148]

This value of this eulogy lies in the way in which it makes use of the stereotypes of the *femme du monde* in order to praise Julie de Lespinasse. La Harpe emphasizes her ability to make her home both a place for exchanges and a place of distinction. Enjoying her hospitality was a title of prestige and "consideration" for courtiers, writers, or ambassadors. How was it possible for a woman, born illegitimate, who arrived relatively late in Paris society without vast resources, to achieve a success of the sort? Julie's qualities formed a triptych: wit, a refusal of all pedantry, devotion to others. Her art was an art of hospitality, anchored inside the private space of her house, access to which she controlled and of which she "did the honors." If that hospitality was not obviously turned toward the public space, neither was it a simple domestic sphere, intimate and familial. For five hours every day, Julie de Lespinasse opened her home to all those whom she judged worthy. She created a space for amusement and of distinction, one of these "societies" that made up *le monde*, of which she had "a great familiarity." Similarly, in the *Correspondance littéraire*, Meister stressed her familiarity with the manners of high society: "To carry the art of conversation to that point, it is not enough to be born with great wit and a highly supple character; one must have to have been able to exercise one's talents early and to shape them through familiarity with the world."[149]

The qualities featured in this praise of Julie de Lespinasse are thus not intellectual, but rather social ones. She was an ideal *maîtresse de maison*—a term that she herself used in connection with Madame Geoffrin—who had mastered the codes of worldly politeness, was dedicated to the well-being of her invited guests, and strove to make them shine. D'Alembert, an intimate

friend, praised her "uncommon fineness of tact" and her "exquisite knowledge of decorum," even more admirable, he stated, because she had not
lived at court. Her great merit was thus to have "divined the language of
what is called *bonne compagnie*," to the point that such a sense of decorum
was at times expressed by an "excessive sensibility about what is called *le
bon ton* in manners and in discourse."[150]

Julie de Lespinasse took care to publish nothing and to restrict her
activity to her salon, which was not intellectually homogeneous. "With
the exception of a few friends of d'Alembert's [. . .], that circle was formed
of people who were not connected with one another. She had picked them
out here and there in *le monde*, but they were so well chosen that, when
they were there, they found themselves in harmony like strings of an
instrument tuned by a skilled hand."[151] The musical metaphor emphasizes
the social harmony that reigned in Julie de Lespinasse's home, not any
ideological harmony. The same stereotype can be found in praises given
to other hostesses, all insisting on their social talents and their ability
to keep a precarious, fragile, and temporary human collective running
smoothly.

This topical representation of the good hostess is shown in the oft-cited
phrase of the abbé de Saint-Pierre to Madame Geoffrin: "I am but an instrument which you have played well." Cited by Morellet, this saying has often
been presented as an indication of gratitude on the part of men of letters
for the role of the hostess. But from whom did Morellet, who did not know
the abbé de Saint-Pierre (who died in 1743), hear this praise? In a letter to
Martin Folkes, dated 1743, Madame Geoffrin, giving news of Saint-Pierre's
death, cites this compliment supposedly addressed to her.[152] Whether he
ever said anything of the sort is beside the question. Certainly Madame
Geoffrin appreciated the compliment and judged it to conform with the
image that she wanted to give, and indeed did her best to give, of herself.
She likely enjoyed reciting it to her guests and Morellet probably heard it
from her.

The posthumous success of this praise thus owes much to the fact that
Morellet relayed it, but its presence in a letter of Madame Geoffrin's reveals
her ongoing effort to present herself as a skilled hostess, generous, and an
enemy to all pedantry. "The dominant qualities of her wit," Morellet wrote
in his *Mémoires*, "were naturalness, precision, refinement, and at times
grace." He added that she "even drew some vanity from her ignorance."[153]
In another letter to Martin Folkes, the president of the Royal Society,
Madame Geoffrin took care to present herself as an intermediary, not a
scholar: "I repeat to you what I believe I have already told you, that I am
quite ignorant and that with all the desire in the world to stop being so,

my domestic occupations do not give me the time to educate myself. I shall thus remain all my life long in my ignorance."[154]

Even though she did her best to attract to her home men of letters, artists, and scholars capable of assuring the prestige and glitter of her salon, Madame Geoffrin proclaimed her intellectual incompetence throughout her life. In a letter to Catherine II, she boasted of the education that her grandmother had given her—a woman of "little instruction" but whose quick mind had earned her a "very great consideration." She also noted that the older woman "regarded knowledge as a thing most useless for a woman," but "spoke so agreeably of the things she knew nothing about that no one wanted her to know more about them."[155] In offering this portrait, Madame Geoffrin was praising herself. When asked about the comparative merits of the works of Richard Glover, an English "lacking politeness and manners," and Francesco Algarotti, a man "of an amiable figure and the best breeding," she responded, "I will never read the works of these two authors; but I strongly tend to believe that those of M. Algarotti are better."[156] Declarations of this sort are too numerous to be the result of chance. To her friend Burigny, who offered her one of their books, she responded, "I would be happy to receive them [as guests], but I do not want to read them,"[157] a quite believable statement, given that the library in her *cabinet de compagnie* contained no scholarly or philosophical books.[158] Next to the name of Dupont de Nemours in a personal notebook, she wrote, in an ironical tone, "He sent me several of his books, of which I understand nothing, and wrote me very learned letters."[159]

As a newcomer in "society" and a woman lacking an aristocratic network, Madame Geoffrin counted on the men of letters whom she received to attract others to her salon. However, she wanted to avoid the reputation of being herself a *bel esprit*, a quality incompatible with the social consideration and the worldly success that she sought. This left a narrow space, given the firm hold in people's awareness of the opposition between the aristocratic *ethos* that presided over the sociability of the salons and the image attached to the world of authors and, worse, to female authors. She knew just how to highlight her private and social virtues, placing herself at center stage as an exemplary mistress of the house, moderate, hospitable, and benevolent. "What am I in the universe, and how can one explain my success with foreigners—by a few mediocre dinners?"[160] she wrote, feigning humility, in her own eagerness to associate her reputation with the practice of hospitality. She took care to inscribe her action within the traditional framework of the "life of society," where the role of women suffered no contestation, and to present herself at all times as a perfect hostess. She managed to do so, though not without inspiring satire now and then.

Femme du Monde or *Femme de Lettres*?

Morellet's portrait of Madame Geoffrin, published in 1777, owed nothing to chance. Written immediately after Madame Geoffrin's death, it was a response to attacks on her, in particular in a play written by the chevalier Rutlidge, who presented her as a ridiculous *femme savante*.[161] This was not the first time that Madame Geoffrin had been attacked in a play: she was mocked in 1760 in Palissot's *Les Philosophes*, which, like Rutlidge's comedy, was fairly closely based on Molière's *Les Femmes savantes*.[162] Throughout the eighteenth century, Molière's comedy was the obligatory reference for denouncing the intellectual pretensions of a woman accused of transforming her salon into a *bureau d'esprit*. The polemical figure of the *précieuse* was used to stifle women's attempts to join sociability and literary publication.[163] The figure of the *femme du monde* was no longer compatible with that of woman author in the eyes of both high society and male writers.

Satire aimed above all at women who confused sociability and publication, making her salon an antechamber to her works. The ridicule played out in two registers: the woman who provides dinner for hypocrites and parasitical men of letters who prey on her with fine words, and the female author who has not herself written the books that she publishes, but makes use of the services of the authors whom she receives. The force of the satire was to combine these two suspect situations, as in Palissot's *Les Philosophes*, aimed at women authors who, by opening their house to flatterers and pedants, betray their sex and bring on domestic catastrophes. The ridicule of Cydalise, who receives philosophes, lies primarily in her literary and learned pretension. Cydalise is ridiculous because she does not realize that the so-called *philosophes* are hypocrites, but, above all, because she confuses sociability and knowledge, salon and academy.

Writers and parasites abuse her hospitality and turn her head, to the point that she forgets her domestic duties, notably love of her children and family interests: she is preparing to marry her daughter to a man of letters, her appointed flatterer who is the actual author of the book she pretends to publish.

Palissot's denunciation was efficient because it lay in broadly shared social norms. It stigmatized women who transgressed those norms and claimed to combine worldly prestige and intellectual reputation. The punishment awaiting women of the world who also aspired to be women of letters was ridicule, the principal danger that menaced the prestige of a salon. As Madame d'Épinay, a champion of women's education, recognized: "Let us conclude from all of this that a woman is quite wrong and acquires only ridicule when she sets herself up as a *savante* or a *bel esprit* and believes she can back up such a reputation; but still, she is absolutely right in acquiring the most knowledge possible for her."[164] For some women, such a desire was legitimate and is well attested, but within the space of worldly society it was wiser to avoid all publicity.

In the early eighteenth century, Madame de Lambert had long refused to publish her works, which circulated only in manuscript. She resolved to publish them, under pressure from her friends, only at the end of her life, when the social authority of her salon was solidly established.[165] Madame Du Châtelet, who stands as an emblematic figure of the female intellectual of the eighteenth century, was treated to all manner of satire.[166] The success of the salons as worldly spaces devoted to sociability and amusement, including the literary variety, thus implied a refusal of pedantry and seriousness and, above all, a radical rupture with the figure of the female author. In the eighteenth century, the hostesses with the best reputations bowed before that obligation. Those who received many writers were highly sensitive to the prohibition because they were the most exposed to becoming targets in literary polemics involving the authors whom they received. Proximity to the literary field gave their salons a power of attraction, but at the same time it rendered their social position more fragile. Those who managed to make their salon a durable feature of Parisian life conformed dutifully to the norms of worldly hospitality: they always took care to present themselves as perfect hostesses, refraining from all pedantry and all literary ambition.

Those women, who incessantly asserted that they were not learned and had no intention to become so, published no books and carefully avoided any intrusion into the flourishing print domain. On this point, there was nothing to distinguish the most aristocratic hostesses—the marquise Du Deffand, the duchesse de Luxembourg, or the duchesse de La Vallière—from Madame Geoffrin, Julie de Lespinasse, and Madame Necker. All these women limited themselves to writing practices that were considered legitimate in worldly society: correspondence and, on occasion, a social text or two. Madame Geoffrin published nothing, wrote few letters, and refused to write her memoirs, in spite of being urged to do so. Julie de Lespinasse owes her current reputation as a writer to an amorous correspondence that she never believed would one day be published. She wrote a few socially related texts (portraits, games involving synonyms) as a salon play, but ordered in her will that they be burned at her death.[167] Madame Necker, who wrote down her reflections and ideas, refused to publish them, following the advice of her husband, who wanted to avoid being ridiculed for having a bluestocking wife.[168] Even under the Revolution, when her friend Suard suggested that she write articles for his review, she rejected the idea, reasserting a totally classical position on the "boundaries of the mind of women."[169] The comtesse de Boufflers, to end the list, wrote a play and a short treatise on friendship, but she took care not to let them circulate outside the narrow circle of her friends. Not only did these women not publish, they fought energetically against the "impertinent reputation" of being a *bel esprit*, as Madame Du Deffand put it,[170] that some tried to attribute to them. The comtesse de Boufflers, who was not overly bothered by her reputation for loose morals, energetically defended herself against the accusation of being an author. She took care to tell her correspondents as much: "Regarding that insolence I have complained against the booksellers and book peddlers. Two booksellers have been summoned for a hearing before the [court of] Saint-Martin, and a peddler has been condemned to pay a fine. I send you this detail, monsieur, because I do not want to pass for an author, and I beg of you that if these false rumors have come to Holland to destroy them by any and all means that you judge the most appropriate."[171]

On the contrary, some women tried to combine sociability and publication and to be both a *femme du monde* and a *femme de lettres*. Madame de Genlis and Madame de Staël, who followed this route with the greatest perseverance, were permanently exposed to satire. In spite of everything that set the two women apart, they experienced the same difficulties and the same disappointments in their attempts to assert their intellectual ambitions while maintaining their desire to uphold the tradition of feminine and worldly hospitality. The innumerable mockeries aimed at Madame de Genlis are fairly well known, but Madame de Staël was also treated as a ridiculous personage in the latter years of the ancien régime.[172] After the Revolution, both women defended the role of women in literature, but also the memory of the sociability of the former regime.

Madame de Boccage, who was less famous, furnishes a perfect example of the incompatibility between worldly sociability and the status of a woman of letters. Born in 1710 in a commercial milieu in Rouen and married to a *receveur de tailles* (tax official) from Dieppe, Madame Du Boccage moved to Paris in 1733. She gave weekly dinners on Sunday and suppers on Monday that were attended by socialites and by authors such as Marivaux, Fontenelle, and Dortous de Mairan, who also attended Madame Geoffrin's salon. In 1710, Madame Du Boccage won a prize for poetry from the Académie of Rouen. Having thus launched her literary career, two years later she published a translation of Milton's *Paradise Lost* and wrote a tragedy, *Les Amazones*, and an epic, *La Colombiade, ou, La Foi portée au Nouveau Monde*.[173] Until then, she had kept her literary works secret. Now, her literary ambition earned her ridicule from some of the authors whom she received. Collé, for example, noted in his journal, "I would never have suspected her of writing verse; I had never noticed in that lady any pretense to *bel esprit*; no one suspected her inspiration; all of a sudden she became aware of her supposed talent, in an age in which it is customary to hide it."[174] Parisian high society was quick to follow his lead, and the duchesse de Boufflers, the future maréchale de Luxembourg, laughed at the ridicule that Madame Du Boccage had "brought upon herself by making a tragedy."[175] At Madame de Genlis's gatherings, her guests amused themselves by staging parodies of the "suppers of Madame Du Boccage." Writers were hardly more indulgent: Marmontel, who claimed to be bored in her salon, stopped frequenting it, and Grimm confided his low opinion of Madame Du Boccage's poetry to the readers of the *Correspondance littéraire*.[176] The contradiction between sociability and publication is flagrant in Grimm's definitive judgment: "Madame du Boccage had no need for this mania in order to make an agreeable place for herself in Paris. She was an agreeable figure: she is a good woman; she is wealthy; she could have in her home intelligent and companionable people without putting them in the awkward position of speaking with her insincerely about her *Colombiade* or her *Amazones*."[177] Voltaire, too, seems to have had a low opinion of Madame Du Boccage. Whereas Madame Du Boccage was proud of the visit that she made to him in 1758, at which Voltaire himself had placed a laurel crown on her head at the end of supper, Grimm, who was present, gives a quite different picture of the occasion:

> M. De Voltaire tormented himself all day long trying to write a quatrain for her, but never managed to do so: the god of verse, foreseeing the use that he wanted to make of his talents, had retired from him. Supper arrived: still no verse. The Poet of Henri IV, in his despair, had some laurel brought to him [and] made a crown of it that he posed on the head of the poor Colombiade, while making the sign of horns with his other hand and sticking his tongue far out in full view of the twenty people who were at table.[178]

A scene such as this, if it is authentic, would not have increased the prestige of Madame Du Boccage, and we can imagine the accounts that must have circulated in Parisian high society. Grimm relates this scene in 1764, just as the works of Madame Du Boccage were being reprinted but her salon was in the process of losing its prestige. She long continued to receive in her home, but her salon was gradually reduced to a small, friendly, and erudite group that left few traces. If fulfilling her desire to write, particularly tragedy and epic, damaged her salon, her salon discredited her literary career. Her poems were attributed to Michel Linant, one of the most faithful habitués of her cenacle, and her tragedy to abbé Jean-Bernard Le Blanc or to abbé Du Resnel. Collé, who did not think her the author of the play, nastily concluded, "She will not even have the sad honor to be whistled at in her own name, but under his name alone."[179]

The comte de Tilly recounted that one day, to his "great surprise," Rétif de La Bretonne arrived at his doorstep and claimed they had met at the home of the comtesse de Beauharnais, where Tilly had gone two or three times. For Tilly, that meeting had no importance: he judged that he was "in no relationship" with Rétif.[180] The social distance between them was too great for one or two meetings in a salon to be significant, and he could only be astonished by this inopportune visit. In Rétif's eyes, though, that meeting at Madame de Beauharnais's house authorized him to present himself at Tilly's door. The meaning of the connection established by frequenting the same salon was thus perceived quite differently, according to each man's social status, and did not engage them in the same manner. It is of course possible that Rétif was well aware of the social distance between them and that his act was an audacious attempt to force his way into Tilly's society. However, by shifting attention from hospitality toward the social connection it generated, from salon to *le monde,* the anecdote sheds light on the social dynamics of worldly society and the role that men of letters played in it. It is to that shift from the salon to the larger world that the next chapter turns.

CHAPTER 2

The Worldly Sphere

A list of supper guests was a most important and carefully considered item! There were so many interests to be fostered, so many people to bring together, so many others to be kept apart! One needed a very profound knowledge of convention and the current intrigues.

Madame de La Tour du Pin, Lucy de La Tour du Pin,
Memoirs: Laughing and Dancing Our Way to the Precipice

In eighteenth-century Paris, individual and collective dynamics were permanently interwoven, creating worldly hierarchies, literary reputations, personal rivalries, and fashionable neighborhoods. The worldly sphere was at once a geographical reality tied to the urban dynamics of Paris and a metaphor designating the social sites among which the members of high society circulated. It shouldn't be reduced to simple typologies that set literary salons against aristocratic salons or conservative ones against enlightened ones, because such contrasts do not correspond to how sociability was experienced in the eighteenth century. For example, an "aristocratic salon" such as that of the duchesse de La Vallière cannot be set against that of Madame Geoffrin, since Madame Geoffrin and Madame de La Vallière were friends and visited one another's homes, and their guests divided their time between their salons. The police reports speak no differently of Madame Geoffrin's salon than of that of the duchesse de La Vallière. Similarly, when Morellet tells of his entry into "Parisian societies," he mentions both the baron d'Holbach and the comtesse de Boufflers. Grimm dines with Madame de La Ferté-Imbault and the maréchale de Luxembourg dines with Madame Necker. Madame Geoffrin goes to the home of the duchesse de Choiseul, to the vast annoyance of Madame Du Deffand. Beaumarchais reads his *Marriage of Figaro* at the home of the marquise de La Vaupalière and Rousseau his *Confessions* at that of Madame de Coigny. That does not mean that the worldly sphere was homogeneous, pacific, or irenic. Quite to the contrary, it was a site for rivalries and distinctions, and event, sometimes, of symbolic violence.

THE TOPOGRAPHY OF THE SALONS

More so than networks, topographical terms correspond to the realities of the places—the "houses"—where, on set days, guests dined, had supper, or paid a visit. The map of this world is one of alliances and oppositions, rivalries and incompatibilities. When the newly arrived English ambassador and his wife gave their first supper, they invited the Choiseuls, Madame de Gramont, Madame de Lauraguais, and Madame de La Vallière, and "since they were not well acquainted with the lay of the land, they also had Madame la maréchale de Mirepoix."[1] Madame Du Deffand's remark shows that a good deal of familiarity with high society was required to find one's way, all the more so because the map was constantly subject to changes. Two years later it would have seemed normal for the ambassador to invite Madame de Mirepoix. For the historian, the real problem is not so much the complexity of the territory as the lack of cartographic guidelines and the danger of looking at it myopically. How can one draw a map of the salons, and not just those salons frequented by writers who penned memoirs? How can one escape the bias of posterity and impressionistic lists of fantastical conventions and filiations? Such lists underestimate the opacity of the worldly sphere, which was never transparent to the people living in it. What made a salon important: was it its prestige in the fashionable world, the posthumous reputation of the writers who attended it, or existing sources? It is true that certain houses are more frequently mentioned in the correspondence collections and available memoirs and *souvenirs*, notably those of Madame Geoffrin, Madame de Luxembourg, Madame d'Enville, Madame Du Deffand, Mademoiselle de Lespinasse, Madame de La Vallière, the maréchal de Biron, Madame Necker, and the comtesse de Boufflers. The only way to refine knowledge about the worldly sphere is to rely on new sources.

A Source: The Contrôle des étrangers

The reports of the Contrôle des étrangers, which centered on the activities of foreign diplomats in Paris, offer a privileged viewpoint on worldly life there.

It is the only source that provides observations of worldly practices over the long term (from 1774 to the Revolution) and shows their regularities and their evolution. A second advantage is that its reports were produced outside of the worldly sphere. Unlike the correspondence collections, which always present a privileged perspective on one figure, the police reports introduce an external perspective. Their importance resides in the position foreign ministers posted to Paris occupied in the latter half of the eighteenth century. The phenomenon was not limited—as has often been thought—to a few sympathetic figures, lettered and cosmopolitan diplomats like Count Creutz and Marchese Caraccioli. Rather, the copious reports of the Contrôle des étrangers show it was a massive phenomenon. A minimum of fifteen diplomats went from one salon to another to dine, sup, or simply spend a few hours. For example, the presence of Creutz in Parisian salons from 1775 to 1782 is mentioned 821 times, with peaks of 172 and 174 annual mentions for his last years at his post. Some of Creutz's days were almost wholly devoted to salons. On Tuesday July 26, 1776, he dined at Saint-Ouen at the home of the Neckers, then stopped in to see the marquise Du Deffand. From there, he left with the duchesse de Luxembourg to sup at Meudon with the maréchale de Mirepoix.[2] It became a tacit rule of Parisian sociability that the ambassadors were welcome guests ex officio on a host or hostess's established "days." With her usual airy insouciance, Madame Du Deffand tells Walpole that at her Sunday suppers "your ambassadors are masters to come when it pleases them: even Italians, Swedes, Laplanders are admitted: all seem equal to me."[3] Some ambassadors preferred more intimate societies and others crowded suppers, but all had an embarrassment of riches and attended several salons, usually somewhat irregularly, which explains why their numbers in any given salon varied from week to week. It was rare, however, for a diplomat to have nowhere to go in the evening, and the police inspector was surprised to note a break in the usual recital of daily suppers on Monday, December 23, 1772: "There was no supper anywhere."[4]

Whether they frequented the salons of Paris for enjoyment, to uphold their rank in society, or to gather political information, the foreign diplomats posted to Paris played an important role in worldly sociability and gave it a particular cast. Compared to other guests at a salon, the ambassador's presence was more changeable, thanks to the precarious nature of their posts.[5] Still, they seem habitués in comparison with the foreigners passing through Paris who gained entrance into the better social circles. Even after leaving Paris, some diplomats kept up epistolary contact with their Parisian acquaintances. Baron Gleichen, the former Danish ambassador, was recalled to Denmark in 1771, returned to Paris in 1774, and frequented "the same societies as [those] of the time of his office,"[6] spending his evenings with Madame Du Deffand, Julie de Lespinasse, or Madame Geoffrin. He returned to Paris again in 1777 and 1784. The deep-rooted, almost institutional, participation of diplomats in the life of the salons and their distribution among the various societies of the capital makes their comings and goings good indicators of the worldly landscape.

Considering only the houses mentioned several times in the police reports and excluding the dinners or suppers hosted by the ambassadors, sixty-two salons appear between 1774 and 1789, with quite different frequencies (see Appendix, p. 243–45). While the Neckers welcomed diplomats 640 times, other houses are cited on only a few occasions. Some twenty houses received diplomats more than fifty times, as a rule on a weekly basis. In this list are the principal salons mentioned in memoirs and correspondence, and canonized by historiography (Necker, Geoffrin, Du Deffand, Luxembourg, Boufflers, d'Holbach), but also less widely known and even largely unknown salons. The duchesse de Praslin's salon, held from 1737 to her death in1783, was attended by the highest number of diplomats, but it is totally unknown in historiography. Similarly, the salon of the duchesse de La Vallière gained few honors from posterity, although "foreign ministers and foreigners of distinction" supped there twice a week with an impressive regularity and found there a "good and numerous company," according to repeated comments in the police reports. In the mid-1770s her salon appears to have slipped, to the point of seeming somewhat deserted,[7] but it was reborn in 1779, and in the early 1780s she held suppers on Mondays, Thursdays, and Fridays. From 1783 to the Revolution, the duchesse de La Vallière gave two grand suppers a week, on Tuesdays and Fridays. The figures for the presence of diplomats, but also the numerous commentaries contained in the police reports and in contemporary documents attest to the fact that it was a durable center of worldly life.[8]

The police reports from the 1780s also show the somewhat lesser role played by the marquise de La Vaupalière, another personage that historiography has forgotten but in whose home "there is always great society."[9] She was closely connected with the social circle of the Brancas, of the comtesse de Rochefort, and of the duc de Nivernais.[10] Her second husband, the marquis de La Vaupalière, was an intimate friend of the duc de Chartres. As a couple, they stood at the center of a network of relations that included an ancient family of the Parisian aristocracy, a princely family, and a political coterie. The Count of Aranda, the Spanish ambassador, attended their salon from 1779 on, and during the years that followed, the police reports often mention the presence of "several foreign ministers." The English ambassador was by far the most assiduous guest, mentioned seventy times between 1784 and 1789.

Finally, the police reports mention dinners for diplomats given by the banker Louis Tourton every Wednesday. Interrupted for a time after his wife's death, the dinners were soon reinstated, and they continued up to Tourton's death in 1784. A Catholic who maintained excellent connections with the Protestant banks, Tourton may have found his dinners essential for strengthening the European networks necessary to the activity of his bank, one of the largest in Paris at the end of the ancien régime.[11]

If police surveillance of the diplomats reveals the importance of lesser-known salons, it also allows us to reassess others. The marquise de La Ferté-Imbault was known as the eccentric daughter of Madame Geoffrin, and her connections with the most conservative coteries of the royal court are often mentioned, along with comparisons to her mother's salon. For years Madame de La Ferté-Imbault kept a highly reputed salon every Thursday, at which she received both diplomats and the "better society" of Paris in the same *hôtel* on the rue Saint-Honoré in which her mother received.

Certain salons were frequented for only a short period. During the years from 1779 to 1782, the suppers of the maréchal de Soubise were much in fashion. Most of the ambassadors went every Tuesday to his home. In 1782, the suppers became biweekly, and the maréchal also received on Fridays. His gatherings were at the time the principal social venue for diplomats, but in November a police report laconically states, "the assemblies at the house of the prince de Soubise are no longer held," and there is no further word of them in the reports in following years.[12] The worldly sphere was permanently transformed and restructured. Only a few salons were consistently held from 1774 to 1789: they included those of the Neckers, the marquise Du Deffand, the duchesse de La Vallière, Madame de La Reynière, the comtesse de Boufflers, and the maréchales de Luxembourg and de Beauvau. Other salons appeared or disappeared. Madame Geoffrin, for example, is cited an average of forty times per year in 1774-1776,[13] but she died in 1777. In 1775 the salons most frequented by the diplomats were, in descending order, those of the marquise Du Deffand, Madame Geoffrin, the Neckers, Monsieur Tourton, Madame de La Ferté-Imbault, the duc de Rohan-Chabot, Julie de Lespinasse, the maréchale de Luxembourg, Madame Rondé, Madame de La Reynière, and the comtesse de La Marck. Madame Du Deffand died in 1782; Madame Geoffrin and Julie de Lespinasse were already dead by then, but others replaced them: the prince de Soubise, the duchesse de La Vallière, the duc de Biron, and the duchesse de Praslin, to cite the salons with the highest attendance figures. Meanwhile, the Neckers, Madame de La Reynière, Madame de La Ferté-Imbault, the maréchale de Luxembourg, and Monsieur Tourton continued to attract diplomats and foreigners to their weekly gatherings, as did the comtesse de Boufflers, the duchesse d'Enville, the comtesse de Rochefort, and the comte d'Albaret. In 1788, the diplomats attended the gatherings of Madame de La Reynière and the duchesse de La Vallière, but they also went to the Neckers, to the maréchale de Beauvau, the comtesse de Boufflers, the baron d'Holbach, the marquise de La Vaupalière, the comtesse Razoumovski, the marquise de Coigny, the marquise de La Ferté-Imbault, and Prince Galitzine.

Competition, Rivalry, Cooperation

The reports do not allow us to group salons, since ambassadors were present in most of them. If Creutz went almost every week to the Neckers, he was also at the receptions of the comtesse de Boufflers, the duchesse de Praslin, the marquise de La Ferté-Imbault, Madame de La Reynière, Madame Du Deffand, Monsieur Tourton, the duchesse d'Enville, the comte d'Albaret, and others. The Marchese Caraccioli attended no fewer than twenty-seven different salons during the years 1775–80, and Baron Blome, a Danish envoy, attended at least thirty-four different salons. The ubiquity of diplomats emphasizes their specific status within high society, but it also reveals the extremely supple nature of social networks that formed and reorganized according to friendships and quarrels, discoveries and lassitude. That same ubiquity leads to other ways of untangling the web of sociability, investigating solidarities between salons but also rivalries, which were not necessarily ideological or political, but could be shaped by a personal dislike or social competition.

Of leading importance in Parisian high society were the salons of the maréchale de Luxembourg, the princesse de Beauvau, the comtesse de Boufflers, and the marquise Du Deffand, as well as those of Président Hénault, Madame de Mirepoix, and the comte and comtesse de Caraman. The usual guests circulated and met in these salons, and genuine collaborations were established. In 1767, Madame Du Deffand and Président Hénault offered suppers on alternate Fridays.[14] On one occasion the maréchale de Mirepoix asked Madame Du Deffand "to cede [her] Wednesday to her,"[15] because she wanted to give a supper on that day. Three years later, when Madame de Mirepoix was ill, Madame Du Deffand spent the evening with her, and she wrote to Horace Walpole, "My Wednesday supper was transported today to Mme de Luxembourg's home."[16] Finally, Madame Du Deffand and comtesse de Boufflers held their salons together at Auteuil in the summer of 1780. In August 1785, the police reports indicate that Madame de Luxembourg "held a summer house" with Madame de Boufflers.[17]

Jealousies and rivalries among salons were frequent, and they were a common theme in the correspondence of Madame Du Deffand. When Madame de Forcalquier went to the Temple as the guest of the prince de Conti and was flattered rather too obviously, Madame Du Deffand wrote, quoting La Fontaine, "Take care! Take care for the cheese! They will take that lovely countess away from me, and the Idol [the comtesse de Boufflers] will seduce her."[18] The estrangement was only temporary, but the jealous attention that Madame Du Deffand paid to the state of her relations with Madame de Luxembourg, Madame de Mirepoix, or Madame de Boufflers clearly indicates that these were considerable preoccupations for her. There is also the famous episode of her rupture with Julie de Lespinasse, whom she had introduced into polite society and who declared her autonomy, to the point of opening her doors to all of the principal guests of her former sponsor.[19] The rivalry between Madame Geoffrin and Madame Du Deffand was equally well known. It did not prevent the diplomats—or Président Hénault—from going alternately to the functions of one then the other. The comtesse de Boufflers, who was quite close to Madame Du Deffand, also paid visits to Madame Geoffrin, and even participated in her Wednesday dinners.[20] Similarly, the hostility between Madame Du Deffand and Julie de Lespinasse did not prevent some of the friends of the marquise from frequenting the Lespinasse salon. Caraccioli, the Neapolitan ambassador, was an assiduous attendee of both salons, and he kept Julie de Lespinasse up to date on all that was said at her rival's gatherings.

The topography of worldly space is incomprehensible without an awareness of family ties. The salons of the duchesse de Praslin and the comtesse de Choiseul gravitated around the duc and duchesse de Choiseul, and the tentacular Beauvau family occupied an important place in Parisian society: the prince and princess de Beauvau received in Paris or in their residence at Le Val and were regular guests at the suppers of the prince de Conti and in Madame Geoffrin's salon. The nebulae of the Beauvau and Choiseul families overlapped and connections among them were many, tracing back to the two families' common origins in Lorraine. The duchesse de Luxembourg, who had close ties with both networks, became even closer to them through the marriage of her granddaughter, Amélie de Boufflers, with the grandson of the maréchal de Biron, who was also the nephew of the duchesse de Choiseul.[21]

At times hostess duties were transferred from one generation to the next. Madame Geoffrin did some of her apprenticeship in the society life with Madame de Tencin, from whom she was able to learn the art of receiving and observe how an aristocracy familiar with the intrigues of the court handled the self-esteem of the writers that it received.[22] In turn, Madame

Geoffrin tutored Julie de Lespinasse, whom she took in and to whom she lent support after her rupture with Madame Du Deffand. In the last years of their lives, they were "closely tied,"[23] to the point that Madame Geoffrin's own daughter, the marquise de La Ferté-Imbault, was quite jealous. Fanny de Beauharnais claimed that she inherited much from Madame Du Boccage, to whom she sent her portrait and who responded by sending some verse. After Madame Du Boccage's death, Fanny de Beauharnais published a eulogy of her entitled À la mémoire de Mme Du Boccage, in which she emphasized the many guests they had shared.[24]

It is much harder to identify the ideological differences that separated the salons open to the new ideas from those unwilling to accept them. It is true that certain societies, such as those of Madame Geoffrin, the duchesse d'Enville, the baron d'Holbach, Madame Necker, or Julie de Lespinasse, had the reputation of welcoming the Encyclopedists. On the other side, the salon of the comtesse de La Marck gathered together the most devout members of Paris "society."[25] During the 1760s, the comte and comtesse Turpin de Crissé, like the comte and comtesse de Brancas, with whom they were closely connected, received many of the poets close to Palissot, all of them hostile or indifferent to the philosophic movement. Still, it would be difficult to identify those poets as a conservative extreme, and Palissot's hopes to place them at the head of an antiphilosophical "party" fizzled out.[26] The connection between the Turpins and the Brancas was a family one, given that the countesses were both born Lowendal. The writers whom they received were by no means all enemies of the philosophes. The abbé de Voisenon, a good friend of Madame Turpin de Crissé, remained detached from ideological debates and maintained good relations with Voltaire and most of the Encyclopedists. Here, too, social connections were much more important than issues in the literary field or intellectual pursuits.

The guests circulated from one salon to the other, according to the dictates of family ties, political solidarities, the occasion, personal reasons, and worldly strategies. Caylus, who was hostile to the philosophes, was a featured guest at Madame Geoffrin's Monday dinners. Grimm and the marquis de Croismare, habitués of d'Holbach's salon, assiduously attended that of the marquise de La Ferté-Imbault, even while the marquise had connections with devout court circles and was openly hostile to philosophes. Condorcet himself frequented her "Thursdays."[27] Evidently, the salons of the capital cannot be qualified ideologically, and many other examples could be cited to show how impossible it is to force the geography of Paris society to follow divisions based on intellectual alliances. The princesse de Beauvais and the duchesse de La Vallière, for example, were close to both Madame Geoffrin and Madame Du Deffand. Even the maréchale de Luxembourg belonged to the "favorite society" of Madame Geoffrin.[28] Even if each salon had an identity of its own, the frequentation of one salon did not necessarily imply agreement with the ideas of its host and hostess or fellow guests. Violently hostile to the ideas of the philosophes, Madame de La Ferté-Imbaut nonetheless went frequently "to amuse herself" in the Helvétius's salon. She had met Madame Helvétius, who had always shown her great kindness, at her mother's gatherings, and she felt obliged to frequent the Helvétius's receptions, despite her dislike for "d'Alembert and all his sect."[29] Hers may be a borderline case, but it demonstrates the logic inherent in worldly obligations, and it suggests that ideological readings of salon sociability must be reevaluated.

PARIS, CAPITAL OF THE WORLD

Urban Space, Worldly Sphere

As an urban phenomenon, sociability is inseparable from mutations in Paris geography. As early as the eighteenth century, a social geography of Paris was set in place with the creation of what have been called *les beaux quartiers*—the neighborhoods of the western portions of the city, which not only displayed a social homogeneity and an architectural harmony, but also encouraged an elegant lifestyle *entre soi* (among one's own).[30] Oddly enough, the origin of this spatial inscription of *la vie mondaine* is poorly known, yet by the eighteenth century it played an important role in the symbolic geography of the capital. In 1775, the twenty-eight salons that are cited in the reports of the commission for the surveillance of foreigners were concentrated in six police districts. Here the faubourg Saint-Germain clearly predominates, reflecting the concentration of the aristocracy in that area. It boasted twelve salons, including those of Madame Du Deffand, the duchesse d'Aiguillon, the duchesse de La Vallière, and Julie de Lespinasse, as well as that of the marquis de Brancas, who lived in the quartier du Luxembourg, on rue de Tournon. That supremacy was threatened by the quartier of the Palais-Royal, which had eight salons. These were grouped around the Palais-Royal itself (to which the salon of the comte d'Albaret in the quartier de Saint-Eustache could be added), or in the faubourg Saint-Honoré, as were the salons of Madame Geoffrin, the comtesse de La Marck, and the fermier général La Reynière. Another neighborhood on the rise was the quartier Richelieu and the new areas of la Grange-Batelière and the Chaussée d'Antin. That was where the salons of the financiers could be found—Necker and the banker Tourton—but also of members of such court aristocrats as the maréchale de Luxembourg and the duchesse de Mirepoix. It is clear, then, that the map of aristocratic salons can be super-imposed upon that of the court nobility, who, since the late seventeenth century, had abandoned the Marais and lived, for the most part, in the fau-bourg Saint-Germain.[31]

During the following fifteen years, the decline of the Marais was confirmed, but, above all, there was a shift, in which the faubourg Saint-Gervais was outstripped by the expanding areas to the north-west. The prince and princesse de Beauvau, for example, left their hôtel on the rue de Bourbon in 1774 and moved to the one they had built on the rue du Faubourg-Saint-Honoré. Russians who kept a salon in Paris no longer lived in the faubourg Saint-Germain, as the Stroganovs had in the 1770s, but on the rue Saint-Florentin, as did the Galitzines. "Most of the people with whom I have habitual relations," the marquis de Bombelles wrote, "are in the faubourg Saint-Honoré."[32]

For several months of the year, the social whirl deserted Paris for châteaux in the surrounding areas. "Everyone is going to scatter in the countryside," Madame Du Deffand wrote in the month of May.[33] When Madame d'Épinay was obliged to rent out the château de la Chevrette, she was unhappy about spending the summer in Paris: "The need to economize has pinned me in Paris and makes me unable to live in the country. I am alone and isolated in the summer."[34] The situation was hardly any better by October: "What do you want me to tell you about Paris? There is nobody here."[35] Social and intellectual life slowed down even for the writers. Morellet urged Cesare Beccaria to come to Paris in the winter rather than in the summer, as it would be easier to help him make "agreeable and useful acquaintances."[36] "Summer" should be understood broadly: every year until November, the reports of the Contrôle des étrangers note that most of the foreign minis-ters are dispersed "in various country areas."[37] In 1771, the Helvétius fam-ily returned to Paris only in mid-December, when the d'Holbachs had not yet relaunched their Paris dinners.[38] Aristocrats and financiers owned resi-dences in areas of the outskirts of Paris that were known as *les campagnes*. Country houses that were closer to the capital were more easily reached, and friends went for the day or even just to have supper.[39] Other hosts welcomed guests for stays of several days and even several weeks. Conti's parties at L'Isle-Adam, Condé's at Chantilly, or those of the duc d'Orléans at Villers-Cotterêts set the tone for this social whirl.

If their *campagnes* allowed the aristocrats to undertake activities of feudal leisure (in particular, hunting and *fêtes*), and allowed for promenades and country leisure activities, they also, and especially, prolonged Paris socia-bility. Country houses were no rejection of the constraints of Parisian life or an affirmation of a nostalgia for the land and for feudalism. As pleasure houses, often detached from any seigneurial connections, these country places were part of a general extension of Parisian worldliness.[40] Madame de La Rochefoucauld makes no mystery about this purpose of country houses and she advises that they be chosen "near the capital."[41] A police report on Madame Necker's country house at Saint-Ouen confirms the importance of its ability to attract the habitués of the Parisian salons: "The place is of the most agreeable, both for its situation and for the choice of the persons of consideration and merit that gather there when Mme Necker is in residence during the fine season."[42] The duchesse d'Enville stated at a distance of one league from Paris, "One feels Paris as if one were there: the same adornments, the same tone, the same ceremonial, everything—even the visits—can be found here."[43] The proximity of these country places also permitted both the hosts and the guests to pay visits to one another. The duchesse de Luxembourg took advantage of being at Montmorency to go to Saint-Ouen to see Madame Necker. Suard, at Saint-Cloud with the duc d'Orléans, met Marmontel there when he was visiting the fermier général Chalut de Vérin.[44] In short, long stays in country houses were an important part of social distinction: "Only a completely forsaken man has to spend the entire summer in Paris. It is *de bon ton* to say 'I abhor the city; I live in the country.'"[45]

For men of letters, this country sociability posed challenges, as there were no set "days" and one had to be explicitly invited. As a friend of Trudaine's, Morellet was unhappy that he had not been invited to spend a few days at Montigny, knowing that Turgot was to be there. He said to Turgot, "I shall not see you at Montigny. M. Trudaine, whom I saw the day before yesterday and to whom I spoke about Montigny, did not say a single syllable in any way leading to inviting me there."[46] Did Turgot intervene with Trudaine, or did the comtesse de Boufflers serve as an intermediary? Finally, Morellet was invited to Trudaine's country house.[47]

The geography of sociability stretched beyond the country areas surrounding Paris, reaching as far as fashionable watering places. The best society of Paris hurried to the spas, as did the men of letters who were always willing to accompany some lady and were always astonished to find Parisian life replicated there. Marmontel accompanied Madame Filleul and Madame Séran to Aix-la-Chapelle; the d'Holbachs went to take the waters at Contrexéville; Morellet joined Lord Shelburne (who provided him with a pension) at Spa, where he met Madame de Sabran.[48] The vicomte de Ségur, a frequent visitor at Spa, later described his stays there as trips in which taking the baths was only a pretext: "Spa was the coffee-house of Europe; it was resorted to from every country, under the pretense of health, but in reality in search of pleasure."[49] Suard, more of a novice, was astonished to discover such a sizeable gathering of fashionable people in a mountain village, including some thirty of his Parisian acquaintances. He also discovered that the same practices of sociability pertained there as in Paris.[50]

The geography of fashionable society was also a symbolic geography. After La Bruyère, writers thought of the city as the theater of a struggle for distinction.[51] Louis Sébastien Mercier offered commentary on the reorganization of fashionable social life that was accompanied by the social decline of neighborhoods deserted by the élites of birth and of money. The most striking example is that of the Marais.

> Here you would be tempted to imagine yourself living in the age of Louis XIII, both with respect to manners and obsolete opinions. The Marais is to the polished quarter of the Palais Royal what Vienna is to London. There reigns, not misery, but a mass of old prejudices. There you find gloomy old fellows, enemies to every kind of modern improvement; imperious counsellors, overbearing, but unfit to read even the authors whose names have reached them; they think the philosophes should be burnt.
>
> If you are so unlucky as to sup among them, you only meet with stupid sottish men; in vain may one seek for that amiable character which ornaments his ideas by the charms of wit and sentiment. Such men are like empty chairs in a circle, that encumber the room. Amongst their furniture you find antique utensils that remind you only of ridiculous usages.[52]

Mercier continues his description of an overfed universe in which boredom and bigotry reign, where "terrible dowagers who have become incorporated with the cushions of an armchair and can no longer detach themselves" know no better amusements than reading the *Mercure*, and where even the pretty women receive only "old soldiers or old judges." The worst, he writes, is that "all of these stupid people gathered together dislike and bore one another."

The discredit into which the Marais had fallen continues a theme that ran throughout the century, of the Marais as a place of an old-fashioned sociability identified with the legal profession and dedicated to combating the philosophes. Although during the eighteenth century the Marais still displayed a degree of social diversity, it already seemed to the fashionable élites to be only a foil for more fashionable areas.[53] In 1742, Président Hénault, to whom Madame Du Deffand described the boring and ridiculous people whom she had met at Forges, responded to her that, when reading her letter, he thought himself "in the depths of the Marais, rue d'Anjou, rue Saint-Claude, etc.,"[54] which may have been, for that member of Parlement and courtier, a way of distinguishing himself symbolically from the sociability of *la robe* (the legal professions). In the second half of the century, social opposition was accompanied by ideological opposition. Grimm, after painting a vitriolic portrait of the lawyer Marchand, states:

> There is however a certain house in the Marais where Marchand passes for the most ingenious writer of the century, and where his pleasantries have a salt that has never been transported outside the limits of the rue Saint-Martin. Thus a pleasantry that had the greatest success in rue Portefoin and rue Transnonain remains absolutely unknown in the quartier du Palais-Royal and in the faubourg Saint-Germain. This is what happened this winter to the *Testament politique de M. De Voltaire*, fabricated by Marchand for the amusement of the suppers of the Marais.[55]

At this point, discrediting the sociability of the Marais became a polemical weapon. Palissot called Fanny de Beauharnais "curds of the Marais."[56] The force of the stereotype was so strong that Voltaire could think of no better praise for Catherine II than this bit of wit: "There is a long way from the empress of Russia to our ladies of the Marais who go on visits in the neighborhood."[57] The grandeur of Catherine, whose ambitions were at least European, if not universal, found its counterpoint in the pettiness of a neighborhood sociability. All satirical descriptions insisted on this theme of extreme localism and enclosure within a geographically limited horizon, to the point that the house described by Mercier was hermetically closed in and confined: neither the outside air nor the rays of the sun penetrated it. The outside limits of the Marais were seen as impenetrable frontiers closed to novelty and new ways that enclosed its inhabitants within an outdated and narrow mindset. Madame d'Oberkirch, Mercier's contemporary, drew her own conclusions: although she admitted that there might be some interest in visiting this neighborhood, she stated that "the Marais has gone out of fashion; only the magistrates remain, and some ancient debris of the former court. . . . The new ideas and the vaporous airs of today do not go there."[58]

Grimm contrasted the sociability of the Marais with that of the faubourgs Saint-Honoré and Saint-Germain, but Mercier, a few years later, contrasted it only with "the brilliant neighborhood of the Palais-Royal." While the faubourg Saint-Germain, in the eighteenth century, did in fact include most of the aristocratic hôtels and salons, it had not constructed a mythology for itself. That mythology was set in place only with the aristocratic stiffening of the Restoration and the return of the court to the Tuileries, at the time linked to the Rive Gauche. The contrast between

neighborhoods then became a social, and especially a political, opposition.[59] On the eve of the Revolution, the faubourg Saint-Germain was
simply a wealthy, aristocratic, and relatively enclosed neighborhood. No
text accorded it any specific virtue or drew it out of localism. The same was
not true of the faubourg Saint-Honoré, the genuinely fashionable district
stretching from the Palais-Royal to the place Louis-XV, which was identified with the court aristocracy, fashionable shops, and literature. As an
area, it structured the symbolic space of a capital deserted by the monarchy. The Rive Gauche still bore the university image of a vast Latin Quarter
that included the quartier Saint-Germain: the Rive Gauche was the terrain
of pedants in the schools and students, whereas the fashionable literary
world was reflected in the Académie Française and the Palais-Royal district.
Although nineteenth-century writers were endlessly fascinated by the faubourg Saint-Germain.[60] Mercier viewed the faubourg Saint-Honoré as the
center of attraction in Paris.

> There is sometimes nothing as dumb as witty people.... When one of them snags
> some small pensions or gets to know a few academicians, right away he moves
> out of the faubourg Saint-Germain and goes to live in the faubourg Saint-Honoré
> because it is closer to the Académie, to the literary coteries, and especially to
> the financiers who keep a good table: in just the same manner a devout Muslim
> moves as close as he can to Mecca. As soon as the littérateur is lodged near the
> Louvre, he forgets that he was once an ill-bred pedant in a school and that for
> ten years he walked the muddy streets of the University; with Roch-Nicolas
> Chamfort (so well named Champsec), he deems himself of the haute littérature
> because he is in the quarter of the Palais-Royal; he makes that silly statement
> with a serious tone of voice and, passing on to others that cost him nothing, he
> claims that there is no taste, no enlightenment, no wit outside of Paris; that the
> hearth of human knowledge is visibly close to the Tuileries; that the inhabitant
> of the faubourg Saint-Germain is already deprived of its vivifying influences; that
> this faubourg is only a province, and that, in order to possess le bon goût, one
> must go no farther than the rue Saint-Honoré.[61]

The determinant factor was not the presence of the Palais-Royal, but
rather that of the Académie, which polarized the republic of letters and
attracted the ambitious and fashionable social circles in which writers
had access to protection and gratifications. An alliance was formed in
the faubourg Saint-Honoré (denounced by Mercier) between men of
letters, monarchical institutions, and worldly sociability. That alliance
fixed attention on that district, making it seem the center of sociable
life. Indeed, the setting up of a symbolic hierarchy between the various

sections of Paris was a way to identify those foreign to both *haute littérature* and *le bon goût.*[62]

Parisian geography was thus closely connected to the ideological construction of Paris as the capital of sociability, a construction that included
the city itself, the royal court, and the surrounding country areas. To be
sure, worldly sociability was not ignored in the provinces. It remains the
case that Parisians consistently scorned social life in the provinces and
held the only true sociability to be that of Paris. In his memoirs, the comte
de Tilly deplores the fact that in certain provincial cities no social life had
existed before the Revolution. In any event, he states, the tone in those
cities was quite different from that of Paris and, in the final analysis, the
difference between the tone and language of the court and of the city was
as great as that between Paris and the provinces.[63] To his mind, an *éducation nationale* (standard of good manners) was established by "an invisible
chain" of imitation that stretched from the royal court to Paris and from
Paris to the provinces.[64] As a courtier, Tilly gave primacy to the court, but
as the century evolved, Paris came to be seen as the model of civility and
the capital of manners and behavior. For Duclos, for example, "Those who
live a hundred leagues from the capital are a century behind in their ways
of thinking and acting." Only by assiduously frequenting Parisian salons
could one gain the worldly ease that, for better or for worse, was the mark
of the capital: "Should a man return to the capital after a long absence, he
is found to be rusty, as they say: he may just be more reasonable, but he
is certainly different from what he once was."[65] During the latter half of
the eighteenth century, this theme of a provincial lag became commonplace, making Parisian sociability the quintessence of a French character
defined by civility: "It is in Paris that the Frenchman must be considered,
because he is more French there than elsewhere."[66] Only the royal court,
which remained the highest model of distinction, limited the prestige of
Paris: "All of the cities of the realm worry about Paris, as much out of jealousy as curiosity. Paris is not affected by any city on the globe, and thinks
only of what happens in its bosom or at Versailles."[67]

Europe Takes to the Salon

The prestige of the social scene in Paris reached beyond the frontiers of
France, attracting a large number of foreigners. The cosmopolitanism of
Parisian salons is one of the most firmly established historiographical commonplaces.[68] Nonetheless, it is worth questioning the actual place that foreigners occupied in the salons of Paris at a time when increased mobility

and aristocratic tourism brought to Paris more and more representatives of the European nobility, as well as men of letters who served them as preceptors and travel companions and wanted to profit from that connection to investigate Parisian social circles.[69]

Foreigners were often sought after and welcomed into the salons of the capital for the novelty they introduced into a world perpetually threatened by boredom and satiation. Some dinners were specifically planned for them, as were maréchal de Biron's Fridays. The banker Tourton received foreigners on Wednesdays, probably in the interest of making international connections beneficial to his financial activities. Foreigners were also much in evidence at the receptions of Madame Geoffrin, who made energetic efforts to attract them to her house, to the point that her address books, which she kept by country, mention several dozen foreigners. In the eighteenth century, this cosmopolitan hospitality became common and a characteristic trait of the better society of Paris: "Where women are concerned, the highest title in Paris is that of foreigner," John Moore states,[70] and Madame d'Épinay jokingly expresses her regret that she is not a foreigner: "What do you want Paris to do with a woman who has only merit? You must be a foreigner to make your way. We have a proverb here that says, 'No one is a prophet in his own land.' If I were freshly arrived from Prussia or from England, everyone would call me "Madame la baronne." Oh! That would really be different."[71]

The English were many and especially sought after. In 1765, Walpole, who was staying in Paris for the first time, was delighted with his reception and remarked that his compatriots were very fashionable and were received everywhere with a remarkable indulgence for their shaky French.[72] During that first trip, Walpole himself became a fashionable personage when his status as a foreigner was enhanced by a reputation for wit.[73] The success of the English was bolstered by a wave of Anglomania that lasted up to the end of the ancien régime, even during the American War of Independence, when the English were the object of mistrust and close police surveillance and the American *insurgents* became all the rage, as did Benjamin Franklin, who settled in Passy and was received with enthusiasm in the Parisian salons.

The English and the Americans did not necessarily frequent the same salons. Centers of attraction and affinities, reinforced by the practice of letters of recommendation, can be traced. Madame Du Deffand, for example, had strong ties with England, and even when enthusiasm for the Americans was at its peak, she defied the trends and remained unwaveringly faithful to her "dear English": "I understand nothing of your Americans," she wrote to Walpole, "I have declared myself a royalist; I don't know why! Perhaps

out of politeness toward the ambassador; perhaps for the pleasure of contradiction; but I do not make speeches about this question, I just admit
that I understand none of it."[74] Another known Anglophile, the duc de
Biron, received the English more than all others, to the point that William
Beckford complained that his suppers were "more crowded than ever with
ridiculous English people created for no other purpose, one might almost
imagine, than that of making those who have the happiness of fancying
themselves less ridiculous laugh."[75] Similarly, Russians were particularly
warmly welcomed by the duchesse de Praslin, to whose house "the Russian
ladies who are in this capital go every evening,"[76] and by the marquise de
La Ferté-Imbault. As for visitors from Geneva, they were received by the
Neckers, but also by Madame de Vermenoux and the duchesse d'Enville.

Many Poles visited Paris, as their nobility was extremely Francophile and
took Parisian civility as their model. According to Frédéric Schulz, a German
man of letters familiar with Polish society, "There are few wealthy families
whose members, sooner or later, do not stay for a certain length of time
in France."[77] After Madame Geoffrin's trip to Warsaw in 1766, her house
became an obligatory stop for Polish society figures. In the notebook in
which she jotted down the addresses of the foreigners whom she knew, the
Poles take up eighteen pages, and for twenty-two entries, there is a mention of a visit to Paris. After her death, the Poles flocked to the receptions
of the duchesse de Praslin, the duc de Biron, and the maréchal de Soubise.[78]
A few Poles left a mark on social life in Paris, such as the Sulkowski brothers,
sons of the favorite of Stanisław II August Poniatowski. One of the brothers spent time in Paris in 1765, when he attended the salon of Madame
Geoffrin. Toward the end of the 1770s the four brothers made frequent
trips to Paris, where the police kept them under close scrutiny, considering
them intriguers. The eldest, prince Auguste Casimir Sulkowski, had been a
court favorite in Vienna before being chased out of court circles. He moved
on to form a pro-French party in Poland, for which he sought official French
support. In 1779 he moved permanently to Paris with his wife, and the following year they were assiduous guests of the duchesse de Praslin and the
prince de Soubise.[79] Sulkowski was sufficiently at ease in these two salons
to introduce Countess Zewuska, the wife of the grand marshal of the crown
of Poland.[80] Toward the end of the same year, he himself gave a grand supper for his compatriots, to which the Praslins and the duc de Soubise were
invited.[81] After that, he launched a major social offensive. While continuing
to attend the Praslin and Soubise salons, he became an assiduous guest at
the dinners of the maréchal de Biron, made a number of appearances at
the receptions of the duchesse de La Vallière, and, above all, began to give
his own suppers, featuring concerts and balls, on Mondays and Thursdays.

Sulkowski was not the only foreigner to hold a salon of his own. Although many foreigners made only a rapid visit to Paris in the framework of a Grand Tour, others made it a habit to come periodically. Some even settled in for several years, becoming part of the landscape of the social scene. In this fashion, Lady Dunmore, the wife of the governor of Virginia, stayed in Paris with her two daughters throughout the American Revolution, fleeing the troubles at home. She was a great social success and was particularly close to the maréchal de Biron, for whom her eldest daughter served as hostess, an activity that won her the title of "Madame la Maréchale." When she returned to Paris in 1787, Lady Dunmore was fêted by all the best society.[82] The first Russians to hold a salon were Count and Countess Stroganov, who continued to receive guests until they left Paris in 1779. An important figure in European Freemasonry and affiliated to the most prominent lodges of the capital, Stroganov was particularly active in the Masons' social networks. He did not hesitate to spend considerable sums to "keep a great state [in his] house,"[83] and he gave suppers and concerts attended by "a prodigious number of French people and foreigners."[84] After the departure of the Stroganovs, the Shuvalovs became the center of Russian sociability, although, unlike the Stroganovs, they failed to attract the top echelon of Paris society. From 1784 to 1789, the principal Russian salon was that of Prince and Princess Galitzine. It was attended by the ambassadors of Russia and Prussia and, more irregularly, by Grimm.[85]

Despite all this activity, the notion of an open cosmopolitan sociability in Paris requires some qualifications. When the police reports mention receptions at the home of the Shuvalovs or the Galitzines, for example, they never speak of any French guests, which leaves the impression that in general those salons welcomed only members of the rather large Russian "colony" living in Paris in the latter half of the eighteenth century, whose social life revolved around the embassy. It appears that some Russian travelers who were not readily received in Parisian salons attended gatherings at the embassy. Those foreigners who were admitted to Paris salons included diplomats, those whom they introduced, or high-ranking aristocrats and ambassadors posted to other capitals, as well as authors whose European reputations were sufficiently well established to sharpen the curiosity of fashionable folk. For every Hume, a secretary in the embassy and a well-known historian, every Walpole, a distinguished aristocrat and the son of an English prime minister, every Prince de Ligne, a model cosmopolitan aristocrat, there were many less famous, less recognizably titled foreigners who remained outside the doors of the Parisian hôtels and knew little of the salons. As Mercier recalls, "a foreigner is often mistaken when he arrives in Paris. He has imagined that a few letters of recommendation will open the principal houses to him: he is wrong. Parisians dread connections that are too close and could become uncomfortable; the houses of the high nobility are difficult of access; those of the wealthy bourgeoisie open their doors scarcely more easily."[86]

In both correspondence and the reports of the Contrôle des étrangers, the same names recur; they are those of the few "foreigners of distinction" who usually settled in Paris for some time or made regular visits to the capital. Foreign visitors were many. Among the travelers who visited Paris every year—an annual average of 3,800 from 1772 to 1787—27 percent came for pleasure as "nobles on a trip, officers on leave, members of the clergy or intellectuals out to discover the capital."[87] Whether these were gentlemen or men of letters, participating in Paris salons usually seemed to them a obligatory step, like attendance at theatrical spectacles and visiting the curiosities of the city. Moreover, going to salons offered an opportunity to meet writers and scholars known throughout Europe, which was why Monsieur de Rens, an advisor to the prince of Holenzollern, visited Paris. A police report stated of him: "The desire to make connections here with men of letters is the principal motivation for his trip; he brought along several letters of recommendation and seeks to slip in [among] our scholars."[88] Some German intellectuals staying in Paris as the tutor of a young noble or during the course of a *peregrinatio academica* were delighted by the prestige that knowledge of the latest anecdotes about social life in Paris could lend them.[89]

For many of these visitors, disillusionment accompanied the discovery of Parisian sociability. During his stay in Paris, Fonvizin, a Russian, remarked on the vain efforts of his compatriots to win an invitation: "I will say unhesitatingly that nothing is more difficult than to penetrate Parisian society when one is a foreigner and, consequently, few have managed to do so."[90] This meant that foreigners gathered together in groups defined by nationality. Fonvizin, who found this surprising, assured his sister that Russian ladies sought one another's company and saw very few French women. The French ignored them, because "thanks to the brevity of their stay, it is not worth the trouble to make their acquaintance."[91] The comte de Tilly, who knew Parisian sociability well, agreed: "In Paris it was difficult for foreigners to inhabit the truly *distinguées* houses."[92]

This difficulty was often compounded by the linguistic barrier. To be sure, many of these foreigners read French, but few of them spoke it well enough to shine in conversation. Their awkward French might amuse, but it was also a handicap. While in Paris, Elizabeth Montagu, a grand figure on the London social scene, was held back by her French, as Madame Necker reported: "She makes extraordinary efforts to express herself in

French; listening to her, I remember the torments I suffered in England, where I understood no one and no one understood me."[93] Even Walpole complained constantly to his correspondents of his bad French, which prevented him from understanding everything said around him and obliged him to express himself in a ridiculous manner.[94]

What was hardest to achieve was an introduction the most prestigious salons. Franz Anton von Hartig, chamberlain to Emperor Joseph II, lived in Paris in 1775, where he observed that foreigners, attracted by the better Parisian society without being able to gain access to it, often had to be content with the society of "courtisanes" and with gambling houses. This did not prevent them from boasting about the merits of *la bonne société* when they returned home, however. He stated:

> But when foreigners seek the better societies in France, a number of obstacles repel those who would like to enjoy them immediately, and not have to endure the tiresome efforts of a novitiate, to which the visitors are often reduced, before they are able to be received and to take part in brilliant coteries; at that point the courtisanes do not fail to profit from the disappointment that [these visitors] feel toward a distinguished but difficult society, and take over all of their leisure time and their purses. Still, several Germans who have known no other society than that one, when they return to Paris, scorn their compatriots, citing as models several dukes and duchesses whom they had, at best, glimpsed on public promenades.[95]

Such statements must be taken with a grain of salt, since they spring from a well-known genre of satire of Parisian sociability and criticism of its fascination for foreigners. Still, they offer a useful counterpoint to oft-cited texts that express the contrary viewpoint. Aside from the few prestigious travelers who were received in the better houses, there were many visitors attracted by the reputation of social life in Paris who had to be content with the public spaces of urban sociability (theaters, cafés, and so on), when they did not succeed in penetrating Parisian salons. The "inflated diffusion of letters of recommendation" diminished their value.[96] Foreign travelers who did not belong to the high nobility rarely managed to be received, or were not invited again after a first visit. One traveler reported: "The high nobility rarely opens its doors, and the wealthy citizens do not easily authorize people to enter their homes. Only men bearing famous names or important titles find all doors open to them."[97] Diplomats acted as a filter in this process. Eager to preserve the reputations of the courts that they represented, they took care to present only important persons, giving others letters of recommendation for much less prestigious social gatherings.

In the final analysis, it seems that the presence of foreigners in the salons of Paris, although important for the circulation of manners throughout Europe and for the construction of the European myth of *la civilité fran-çaise*, was in reality limited to a restricted elite of travelers. The fascination that the salons held for foreigners rested in large part on the practices of social distinction that made them so difficult to penetrate.

HIGH SOCIETY

An Aristocratic World

The absence of sufficiently detailed sources makes a systematic study of the social composition of the salons difficult. Still, what can be gleaned shows the massive, and often almost exclusive, presence of the court aristocracy, even in the salons usually associated with literary history. It is hardly surprising that the salons of the maréchale de Luxembourg or the princesse de Beauvau were essentially aristocratic, despite the presence of a few writers. But, the composition of Madame Du Deffand's salon was not very different. From September 1779 to September 1780, she kept a journal in which she wrote down both her own outside engagements and the names of the people she received, in particular at her three weekly suppers.[98] Members of the aristocracy predominated among the 102 persons who attended her salon, including the duc de Praslin, the duc de Choiseul, the duc de Broglie, the duchesse de Luxembourg, the prince de Beauvau, the comte de Chabot, the marquise de Boisgelin, the comtesse de Boufflers, the comtesse de Cambis. She also lists a few foreigners; one magistrate, one minister (Necker); Tissot, a famous physician from Lausanne;[99] one member of the Académie des Sciences, Jean-Baptiste Le Roy; and three men of letters, abbé Barthélemy, secretary to the duc de Choiseul and a close acquaintance of Madame Du Deffand, La Harpe, and Marmontel, each of whom came one time to give a reading. Add to this several bishops who also belonged to the high nobility, such as Loménie de Brienne, the archbishop of Tours. This presents a picture of a homogeneous aristocratic sociability to which a handful of personalities were occasionally admitted.

Who attended Madame Geoffrin's salon, which is so often characterized as the archetype of the "literary salon"? The lists of *connaissances* that Madame Geoffrin kept in small green notebooks are difficult to interpret, as she rarely mentions how one person or another had been introduced to her. Without commentaries, it is impossible to tell whether the names in her notebooks represent habitual guests in her hôtel on the rue Saint-Honoré, occasional visitors, or even just correspondents. Still, these

lists reflect her networks; representatives of the highest Parisian aristocracy predominate, aside from an imposing quantity of foreigners noted by
country of origin.[100] Other sources confirm this impression. Among the
forty-seven persons mentioned by Walpole as paying her visits in 1765–66,
there is only a handful of men of letters (Thomas, Helvétius, d'Alembert,
Burigny) and artists (Vernet, Cochin, Soufflot). The few representatives
of the world of finance or the administration (Boutin, Cromelin, La Live)
are outnumbered by the many aristocrats (the duc de Bouillon, the comte
de Coigny, the duc de Fronsac, the comtesse d'Egmond, the duchesse de
Cossé, Monsieur de Sainte-Foix, Madame de Roncé, Madame de Béthune),
titled foreigners (Count Shuvalov, two Polish countesses), or diplomats
(Count Creutz, Baron Gleichen).[101] Perhaps Walpole entered only the
most prestigious guests in his journals—which in itself would be a highly
revealing gesture—but the fact remains that his journal attests to a massive presence of aristocrats at the house of Madame Geoffrin in 1765. This
tendency is corroborated by her ties with the marquise de Rochechouart[102]
and with the duchesse de La Vallière, about whom Madame Geoffrin writes
to her daughter from Poland: "Send [a note] to Madame la duchesse de la
Vallière to assure her of my tender and respectful homages and tell her that
I have sighed every Sunday evening, remembering that I was not at her
feet."[103] Marmontel dined at Madame Geoffrin's in 1765 with the comtesse
d'Egmont, the duc de Rohan, the marquise de Duras, and the comtesse de
Brionne, and ten years later, the reports of the Contrôle des étrangers mention the presence at Madame Geoffrin's of the maréchale de Luxembourg
and the duc and duchesse de Rohan-Chabot.[104] She also maintained relations with the Montmorencys and the prince de Carignan.[105] The supposed
"bourgeois predominance" in Madame de Geoffrin's salon does not stand
up to examination.[106]

Periodization needs to be taken into account in any analysis of the social
composition of Madame Geoffrin's salon. The evidence taken from her notebooks dates from the period 1765–77, the last years of her life, whereas she
had begun to receive in the early 1740s, after becoming acquainted with
Madame de Tencin. Sources for the early days of Madame Geoffrin's salon
are fewer, but it seems clear that her guests were at first recruited from
among writers and the scholars (Fontenelle, Mairan, and Marivaux) present in Madame Tencin's salon. In the 1740s, the sciences and *savants* were
in fashion. It was at that time that Madame Geoffrin began to correspond
with Martin Folkes, the president of the Royal Society, and with Gabriel
Cramer. Although she denied that she herself was a *savante* and spoke of
her letters as written in an explicitly social mode of flattery and social gossip, she transmitted the latest news, salutations, and recommendations,

and she advised Cramer to present his candidacy to the Royal Society. On occasion she even served as an intermediary on scientific questions. After Martin Folkes had asked her for information on polyps, Madame Geoffrin reported to him that she had gone to Réaumur, who spoke of the question in the preface to his latest book.[107] No similar correspondence can be found for the years 1760–70. Thus, these notes throw light on the chronological and social dynamics of Madame Geoffrin's salon, originally founded to receive a circle of men of letters and scholars to whom she rendered services and among whom she played the role of intermediary. In the salon's second phase, she continued to receive well-known writers, but the scholars came to be of secondary interest, while she based her Monday dinners on artists, professional and amateur, who attracted the best of the Paris aristocracy, thus allowing her to counter earlier accusations that her gatherings were founded on wit and satire. Her reputation was at its height after her trip to Poland in 1766, when her salon grew more and more aristocratic.

Magistrates are singularly absent in all these salons. Although the parliamentary milieu dominated social life in some provincial cities,[108] its role appears to have been marginal in Paris. There were salons dedicated to the *robins* (magistrates and judges), but their social prestige was too limited to have inspired written accounts. Among the few fragmentary remarks extant, Pougens says that he was received by Madame Lamoignon de Montrevault, along with authors such as Voisenon.[109] Dufort de Cheverny recounts how his father, a magistrate at the chambre des comptes, received men of letters twice a week with the aim of forming his son's taste. Another social circle that emerged from the parliamentary milieu was that of Madame de Vieuxmaison, the wife of a counselor to Parlement. Its most faithful participants were Latteignant, a parliamentary counselor; Antoine Bret, a minor dramatist; and Pierre Robbé, a satirical poet. Inspector d'Hémery considered her salon "the most dangerous in Paris."[110] Unfortunately, little is known about this salon, however, other than its execrable reputation.[111]

A Worldly Duel

The magistrates, who had other models of social distinction than the Paris social whirl, may deserve more appreciation for their reserve. The new wealthy elites had greater aspirations for playing an important role on the social stage. If their professional activity did not guarantee the social prestige of the men of the robe, it at least gave the financial means for competing with the lifestyle of the Paris aristocrats. Fermiers généraux and financiers built sumptuous *hôtels particuliers*, created art collections that attracted both the curious and art lovers, sponsored good causes, and gave elaborate suppers. La Poupelinière and Madame Dupin had shown the way, the latter in particular, who constructed a prestigious and durable aristocratic network.[112] Other financiers' salons attempted to follow that model, in particular those of Préninville, Fontaine, and Saint-Wast.[113] Some salons specialized in economists and scientists, as did Paulze, whose daughter married Lavoisier and held a salon of her own. Others preferred men of letters, as did the fermier général Bouret, a wealthy and powerful man who spent an enormous fortune on elaborate parties and suppers and was a friend of Suard and Marmontel.[114] Some of these salons were restricted to the worlds of finance or "the robe." A few others were quite prestigious, such as the salon of Jean Joseph de Laborde, who, as banker to the royal court, was connected with all the court aristocracy and was a close friend of Choiseul. He received "the grandest company of Paris," along with a few men of letters such as La Harpe.[115]

Some historians have seen in these salons evidence of a harmonious fusion of elites and a mixing of ranks in the shared pleasure of conversation and worldly refinement.[116] This analysis ignores the various forms of symbolic violence that the high society brought to bear against the financiers. The La Reynière salon gives some idea of these pressures. It was the most prestigious financier's salon, the one closest to the court and the only one attended assiduously by diplomats and the court aristocracy. There are several explanations for this success. Laurent Grimod de La Reynière was a third-generation fermier général. His father, Antoine Gaspard Grimod was a fermier for over three decades, and Laurent inherited and held his post until 1780.[117] After establishing alliances in the financial world, that generation of the Grimod family made brilliant marriages. In 1758, Laurent married Suzanne Françoise de Jarente, and one of his sisters married the marquis de Lévis and the other, Malesherbes, which connected La Reynière with the highest nobility of the robe and of the sword. After the 1770s, this strategy of aristocratic marriages was reinforced by the couple's investment in residences that lent themselves to the development of an ostentatious social life.

In the early 1780s, Laurent Grimod de La Reynière and his wife showed all the signs of successful integration into high society, and the days when Laurent's mother was chased down the streets of Paris to the cries of "daughter of a lackey!" because she was dressed above her station faded into the distant past.[118] The family's new position was not easily accepted by high society. Despite their marriage alliances and their wealth, their efforts to receive the best company left them open to ridicule, as several sources attest. According to the baronne Oberkirch, their house was reputed to be "the best inn for people of quality," and the socialites went to spend the evening in their home but mocked their host: "He is laughed at by everybody, whilst they eat the good things he sets before them."[119] Madame de La Reynière, who dreamed of the court and never accepted her status as the wife of a financier, found the situation cruel.

An anecdote reported by Bombelles speaks to the humiliations that La Reynière was obliged to withstand. This "story that amused all Paris at the expense of M. de La Reynière" deserves quotation in full:

> Every day his wife's mania for having in her home, as far as possible, no other guests than court people adds to her ridiculousness, and the same mania has infested poor little La Reynière [*le pauvre petit La Reynière*]. For some time now he has been teased about it, and in order to take his revenge he refused to receive at his fine Sunday suppers the vicomte de Narbonne, the son of the duchess of the same name, at the moment a highly popular young man, whom everyone agrees is witty, but about whose principles opinion is divided. Mesdames de Laval and de Matignon had taken it on themselves to introduce him at Monseiur de La Reynière's; the latter, not wanting the vicomte, explained: "Monsieur de Narbonne writes songs, so do I; but he makes his saucy, and I do not like mean people." This statement did not fall on deaf ears, and society took on the task of correcting Monsieur de La Reynière. What lies closest to his heart is his small existence, and it has long been known that he is a strong opponent of the sword (*l'arme blanche*). For this reason, Monsieur de Narbonne wrote him a note in the polite but dry and laconic style used when a man wants to indicate to another that he has a serious explanation to ask of him. One of the vicomte's servants was ordered to give this note to no one but Monsieur de La Reynière himself. The servant observed La Reynière's startled reaction to the message. Time was taken to prepare an answer; the council was assembled; finally the response was made in highly respectful terms and it was agreed that Monsieur de Narbonne would be received the following day between eleven o'clock and noon, as he pleased.
>
> One can well imagine that he was on time for the rendezvous. He presented himself in a green jacket with gold embroidery, worn over black breeches and a black vest, because the court was in mourning, and he had a large hat and a good long sword. Our friend La Reynière was astonished and trembling. At his sides, to encourage him and hold him up, he had Monsieur d'Aigremont, his relative, the former minister of the King at Trier. After salutations, Monsieur de Narbonne drew a paper from his pocket. Monsieur de La Reynière was sure that it contained a disagreeable proposition. He read it and was reassured, seeing that it was only a request for a tobacco outlet. At that point, breathing again and setting his fine little face in a smile [*sa belle petite mine*], he hastened to assure the vicomte de

Narbonne that, although he was no longer fermier général, he still had friends in the Company and that he could promise that what Monsieur le vicomte desired would be done.

This joke proved a stroke of good luck for a man whom no one would have thought about otherwise. A greater or lesser ridicule makes little difference for Monsieur de La Reynière and his wife: in this sort of affair, all things are equal. Thus all ended for the better, according to the system of Dr. Pangloss.[120]

In this affair La Reynière faced a strong opponent, given that the author of the joke was the vicomte Louis de Narbonne, a mighty aristocrat and an exemplary *homme à la mode*.[121] In 1783, Narbonne was one of the darlings of the better society and belonged to the group of "those great lords who dine at financiers' houses and find nothing to criticize about the meal other than the presence of the master of the house."[122]

This episode baldly shows that when tensions appeared, social conflicts between the ancient nobility and the newly rich arose at the center of elite sociability and might lead to symbolic violence and humiliation. Narbonne took it upon himself to remind La Reynière of the implications of social hierarchy by exhibiting the symbols of aristocratic status: the sword, his clothing, his connections with the court, and the culture of the duel and of physical courage.[123] Bombelles's account insists on La Reynière's fear, on his attachment to life, and on his horror of the *arme blanche*. A soldier and a courtier stood opposed to an office-holder, a man incapable of deciding for himself about a question of honor, represented here as a financier out of a comedy and a man far from comfortable within the aristocratic culture he attempted to adopt. Bombelles, reflecting the attitudes of "the better society," accentuates the social smallness of La Reynières: *le pauvre petit La Reynière; sa belle petite mine.*

That smallness was neither juridical (La Reynière was noble, his father was noble before him, and his wife was from a very old family), nor—obviously—economic. Narbonne's superiority rested on the symbols of the military aristocracy and on the representations that underlay the social identity of that group. Those representations were no more than devices whose real efficacy derived from the logic of his social group. The point was not to force La Reynière to take any action, but rather to ridicule him by reminding him of the social realities of worldliness. What Narbonne was demonstrating was that neither La Reynière's nobility, his connections, nor his wealth made him his equal in the social domain, and that politeness was only a fiction of equality; it was an honor for him, but it gave him no rights. What was at stake was the legitimacy of judging who was worthy to be received and who was not. If La Reynière was ridiculous, it was because he claimed to be bestowing an honor on the court figures whom he received, whereas the precise opposite was true. Like Molière's Georges Dandin, his judgment was faulty in considering money to be equivalent to consideration, and he discovered, at his own expense, that social standing depended on those who were in a position to impose it, a rule particularly true in the domain of worldly reputation.[124]

Why does Narbonne emerge the winner in this face-off? The success of his joke derives from the fact that it is approved by *le tout Paris*, as Bombelles puts it, which shows that Narbonne was fashionable, while La Reynière was still marginal in that society. His punishment is revealing: it was La Reynière's "ridicule" in the eyes of worldly Paris. Moreover, the La Reynières did not immediately get over this humiliation; their salon almost disappears from the police reports from 1784 to 1786, returning to its former size only in 1788. La Reynière's second error, after that of mistakenly judging social position, was not to have understood that the danger that threatened him was not from the sword but from ridicule, that "light and piercing arm of the *beau monde*," according to Mercier's definition.[125] Narbonne only suggested the possibility of violence; he was playing with social codes that La Reynière knew and feared, but in no way did Narbonne dream of using violence, unlike the young people who taunted La Reynière's mother in the Tuileries. In doing so, Narbonne acted as a perfect representative of the "civilized" aristocracy of the courtier, master of his emotions and of the effects that he produced in others, while La Reynière lost his composure and could not hide his fear. Narbonne was displaying his civility and his *politesse*. Social standing is measured here by worldly distinction and mastery of its codes.

But who was measuring that distinction? Who decided that Narbonne's action was a good joke and not unjustified violence? After all, the personage of the *grand seigneur* puffed up with his own birth can also be ridiculous, especially when he claims to force the rules of hospitality. Here Narbonne's support in high society was essential. It was Madame de Matignon who had introduced him into La Reynière's house, and it was she who spread the story in her own salon, where Bombelles heard it. Moreover, Bombelles's text and the way he noted the incident in his journal reflect the viewpoint of *le monde* and put a seal of approval on presenting La Reynière as ridiculous and the episode as a collective "joke." When he stated that "society took on the task of correcting Monsieur de La Reynière," the word *corriger* can be taken in the sense of "punish," but also as "rectify." In this sense, Bombelles's narrative reflects a collective operation by which high society qualified Narbonne's violence as reflecting ease and naturalness and as conforming with worldly codes.

Narbonne should not be seen here as using his social position to force a financier to receive him, but rather as a fashionable man using purely worldly means to render ridiculous a man whom high society had already teased for his excessive ambition. Social inequality was acting here through the prism of worldly hierarchies, creating a contrast between a man who set the tone and another man who had been proven incapable of managing his reputation. The episode also shows how worldly sociability perpetuated aristocratic domination, even while it modified its bases. Force, applied uniquely by the privilege of birth, would have been a ridiculous pretense, and the signs of aristocratic violence used by Narbonne are merely an enticement, calculated to fool the person who believes in them. It is thus as an *homme du monde* that Narbonne corrected La Reynière. His merit was no longer founded directly on his birth, as was aristocratic virtue, but rather rested on worldly ease and civility, of which *la bonne société* was the sole judge. In his *Considérations sur l'Italie*, Duclos meditated on this notion of merit and on its connections with the social dynamics of worldliness. In Paris, he wrote, "a man of merit is excluded from no society." He immediately added, however, "It is true that the first of such merits, in order to be received and accepted, is that of being amiable, that is, to carry into society wit and an agreeable mien. It is often enough to be a man of pleasure to be sought after."[126] Merit translated into the art of worldly amusement, of which the court aristocracy was a master, and it was sanctioned by those who had the power to impose their narratives.

An Unequal Equality

La Reynière's misadventure shows that the salons were far from being the peaceful enclaves that have sometimes been imagined, and relations of symbolic violence took an important place in them. It might be objected that La Reynière was a financier with little prestige, and the point of the stand-off was to exclude him from the better "society," or at least to oblige him to recall his subordinate place in it. Historians who see the salons as egalitarian enclaves generally base their opinion on the presence of men of letters, received on their merit alone. According to this argument, the equality that reigned in the salons attests to the new prestige of the writer, the new equal of the grandees. In reality, differences of rank and status were strong and were recognized by the most famous writers. One anecdote reported by Chamfort reflects this notion:

D'Alembert, who already enjoyed the highest reputation, found himself at the house of Madame Du Deffand along with M. le président Hénault and M. de Pont de Veyle. A physician named Fournier arrives, and on entering, says to Madame Du Deffand, "Madame, I have the honor of presenting to you my most humble respects"; to M. le président Hénault, "Monsieur, I have the distinct honor of saluting you"; to M. [de] Pont de Veyle, "Monsieur, I am your most humble servant"; and to d'Alembert, "Hello, Monsieur."[127]

Whether or not this anecdote is true, it is likely. It opposes the intellectual "reputation" of d'Alembert, which justifies his presence at Madame Du Deffand's salon, and his social status, which appears in the naming system and different levels of civil salutation. The anecdote can be read two ways, however. On the one hand, it highlights the inequality always present in salon life. On the other hand, the narrative aims at ridiculing the physician, who fails to acknowledge d'Alembert's genius. The anecdote indicates that even d'Alembert, at the home of Madame Du Deffand, amid people who celebrated him and were aware of his intellectual reputation, was never sheltered from to the reality of his social status. The anecdote lends itself to both readings. By mocking what is ridiculous in the physician Fournier, Chamfort reveals the ambiguity of high society. Reputation does not guarantee consideration, and social differences could be recalled at any moment in the form of a humiliation.

D'Alembert must have encountered humiliations of the sort, according to his *Essai sur la société des gens de lettres et des grands*, which gives evidence of a strong bitterness regarding the social situation of the learned man and the man of letters. Despite recognition of their talents, such men were far from being considered equals. "In order to persuade oneself of what I suggest about the low opinion commonly formed in the world of the estate of men of letters, it suffices to note the sort of welcome that they usually receive."[128] The interplay of mutual esteem, d'Alembert stated, was valid only to the point that it was accepted by the nobles: "This is what one perceives, especially in conversations in which one does not agree with them. It seems that the more the *homme d'esprit* steps back, the more the *homme de qualité* steps forward and seems to demand the deference that the man of wit had begun by doing without."[129] It would be useless to try to dismiss this, for although reputation depended upon talent, consideration was given only by the state. D'Alembert added: "A man of letters, full of probity and talents, is incomparably more admired than a minister incompetent in his position or a great lord dishonored: still, when they find themselves together in the same place, all attentions will be for rank."[130] The force of d'Alembert's text resides less in his denunciation of men of letters who frequent the great and more in his bitter unveiling of the hypocrisies of aristocratic good will. He reminded those who nurtured illusions about the esteem that literary success and reputation would gain for them of the iron-clad rule of ancien régime society that consideration accompanies rank.

The salons, far from rising above social differences, were ruled by customs that implied a strict attention to the social status of one's interlocutor. The maréchal de Richelieu firmly reminded Madame Favart that "the first [talent] of everyone in a society is to be sociable, and when that society has superior members, not to depart from its laws of subordination."[131] Diderot said much the same, asserting that "a knowledge of the regards attached to the various conditions forms an essential part of the seemliness and the customs of the world."[132] He went on to state: "My tone of voice can be as high and my expression as free as I want with my equal; provided that nothing escapes me that offends him, all is well. This would not be true with a person who occupies a rank above my own in society."

Still, salon conversations were not hierarchical rituals. The conversation, which supposed a certain familiarity and an equitable relationship concerning who did the talking, fit within the differential of social consideration that existed among the participants.[133] This equilibrium was always precarious. It would be accurate to speak of an egalitarian fiction, a reciprocity bestowed by the aristocrats so long as their own self-esteem was not challenged. D'Alembert, an astute observer of this worldly game, notes that men of letters "are lavish with their homages to people who believe they honor them with a look and who seem to express this to them by demonstrations of their politeness, even though it is an act of good will rather than a rightful expectation."[134] Far from being a mark of equality, politeness was a way of managing unequal relations in a nonhierarchical manner: it was precisely because the social distance was considerable between the aristocrats and the writers that the aristocrats could be amiable and seem no threat to the writers, without raising any doubt about the social authority of either group. Every participant was well aware of the rules, and none would risk, under the pretext that the framework of the salon dispensed him from hierarchical ceremonial, believing himself truly the equal of a *grand*, contradicting him, or permitting himself a familiarity. The penalty was receiving an instant reminder of the true state of social relations. The duc d'Olonne's friends called him "Bacha." "He replied to a person of very low estate who had hazarded to call him by his nickname, 'Monsieur, those whom I call "monsieur" do not call me "Bacha." ' "[135]

Politeness did not mean equality. To the contrary, it clarified social distances. Etiquette was mandatory at the royal court because it was the place where a struggle for classification among persons socially close to one another took place. In the salon politeness permitted an exchange of consideration among persons whose social status was immeasurably different. The custom (*usage*) of *le monde*, always praised when it involved the hostesses or the authors who assiduously attended the salons, consisted of analyzing things, in discerning the artificial nature of worldly equality. One text written after the Revolution and published by Suard in his *Mélanges de littérature* speaks of this meaning of worldly politeness. The text meditates on the decline of the salons and the customs of society life: "It was a code that had its laws, its rules, and its exceptions, by means of which one knew exactly on entering into a room what was owed to each of the persons present; at the same time, the politeness with which each person was obliged to clothe his claims softened the shocking effect that such distinctions might have held. The very order established among them served to render those distinctions less obvious."[136] The *usage du monde* was thus not an art of equality and happy conviviality, but rather a skill for adapting politeness to social distinctions. Suard thought that what had been lost was the order combining politeness and social inequality, civility and social classification. "Today," he notes, "people assemble without getting together; they divide up without classifying themselves, and we have neither distinctions nor equality in society."[137] It would be hard to find a better way to say that the formal equality of conversation and worldly rules, backed up by worldly custom—that is, by a very clear awareness of what those rules hid—was the best catalyst for "distinctions."

Despite Suard's conventional regret, the mechanism for distinction did not disappear with the Revolution. A century later, Proust would perfectly summarize what was at play in the amiable aristocratic stance:

> I began to know the exact value of the language, spoken or mute, of aristocratic amiability, an amiability happy to pour a balm on the sentiment of inferiority of those to whom it was offered, but not, however, to the point of dissipating it, for in this case it would no longer have any reason for being. "But you are our equal, if not better," the Guermantes seemed to say by all their actions, and they said it in the most genteel fashion imaginable in order to be liked and admired, but not to be believed. When one untangled the fictive nature of that amiability, it was what they called being well brought up; to believe the amiability real, that was bad upbringing.[138]

DISTINCTION AND REPUTATION

The salons were thus an aristocratic world, with which the new social elites merged only with difficulty and after the costly and lengthy process of adopting the way of life and the ethos of the courtiers. Politeness was not the sign of an egalitarian drawing together of conditions; it did not rest on forgetting social distinctions. To the contrary, it permitted nonhierarchical relations while retaining a sharp awareness of those distinctions. Still, as the misfortunes of La Reynière show, worldliness had not only its own signs and its own language, but also its own social dynamic. It did not just reproduce social distinctions; it produced worldly distinction.

Why Fashionable People Are More Amusing

Some historians contend that nobility, as the dominant principle of the creation of social hierarchy, was losing ground in the eighteenth century. According to them, the social and ideological dominance of the nobility was in jeopardy after a redistribution of wealth, the triumph of the ideology of merit, and the abandonment of an aristocratic preoccupation with ranks and lineages. In the bigger cities the Enlightenment and rising capitalism imposed a new social stratification determined by money and merit, thus giving rise to an "elite." That notion has gained broad acceptance within historiographical mores, but its use has changed. Whereas Denis Richet used the term to designate the cultural and ideological convergence of a part of the aristocracy and the bourgeoisie and to counter "class" analyses of the origins of the Revolution, current theses insist instead on a "fusion of the elites" within a society of urban (especially Parisian) consumption, in which the criterion of birth counted less than that of wealth and in which aristocratic culture, properly speaking, lost value.[139] This radical statement needs to be adjusted in light of the persistence of a strong noble identity, as witnessed by the sharpness of questions of rank, the hardening of court ceremonial, and the frantic genealogical investigations of the high nobility at the end of the ancien régime. Above all, it is important to distinguish between nobility and aristocracy and between juridical definitions and sociocultural ones. That the distinction between noble and commoner lost intensity in Parisian society of the end of the ancien régime does not imply the extinction of an aristocratic culture, largely informed by the culture of the court, which still enjoyed a powerful prestige.[140] Although Tocqueville was one of the first to insist on the equalization of conditions within the elites, he remarks, "There is nothing which equalizes so slowly as those surface mores which we call manners."[141]

The dynamic of social distinction at work in the salons transformed the Parisian aristocracy in to *le monde*, where politeness and wit were both personal talents and attributes of the nobility. That sociability also implied a mastery of the body that was an attribute of the courtier. As Julie de Lespinasse remarked to Condorcet, anyone wishing to advance in the *usage du monde* should consider his posture and stand up straight when he speaks, instead of bending forward "like a priest saying the *Confiteor* at the altar."[142] Such attitudes aside, along with the posture and the ways of moving and talking that offered immediate recognition of the *homme du monde*, concepts like *le monde*, *la bonne compagnie*, and *la bonne société* were largely self-referential. They defined the group in question by excluding those who did not belong to it. The only possible definitions were tautological, hence distinctive. *Le monde* was those who frequented worldly circles: as the *Dictionnaire de l'Académie* put it, *Le grand monde* "dans le langage familier signifie la société distinguée" ("in ordinary usage, signifies refined society").[143] If the discourse of legitimation emphasized mastery of social interactions as the basis of that *bonne société*, the importance of manners was in itself circular, because *le monde* was the sole judge of its own manners. *La politesse* consisted in doing what polite people do and, although there were rules of politeness, everyone knew that no one became an *homme du monde* by reading books about civility, but rather by a long socialization through contact with "good company"—a socialization rendered possible only by already belonging to that world of interconnected acquaintance.

From a perspective of the social history of culture, what we need to understand is how a social group founded awareness of its superiority on shared manners. The politeness of the salons, which was in theory egalitarian and informal, was different from the court etiquette that marked social hierarchies spatially and ritually, but its function was the same: to create a symbolic cohesion to a historical form of social elite founded on the circulation of honor. At court, that honor was connected with how the king regarded a person and showed him or her his favor; in the salons, it was the regard of others that bestowed honor and distinction. In both cases, those who participated in the group were distinguished from those who were excluded from it, as the aristocratic ethos, unlike economic rationality, rested upon an accumulation of prestige. As Norbert Elias put it, "In it [etiquette] court society represents itself, each individual being distinguished from every other, all together distinguishing themselves from non-members, so that each individual and the group as a whole confirm their existence as a value in itself."[144] Similarly, worldly sociability, which was founded both on open-ness and on restricted access, permitted the circulation of a prestige that was explicitly open to merit but in fact was restricted to a narrow social elite. Speaking of the suppers of the maréchal de Biron, Madame de La Tour du Pin stated, "It was a much coveted honour to be received at his house."[145] Hospitality produced distinction (as indicated by the very common expres-sion, "do the honors of one's house"), in proportion to the distinction of the host or hostess. To be received by the maréchal de Biron was to belong to le monde. Biron himself was above all a courtier, a symbol of fidelity to the king and adhesion to a hierarchical society in which even slight nuances of civility were the essential elements of social life.[146]

La bonne compagnie, la bonne société, la société, le grand monde, le beau monde, le monde: the hesitation revealed in the pertinent vocabulary shows an intense effort of qualification. The semantic field of the word *monde* is the one most often encountered (*monde, beau monde, grand monde, homme du monde, usage du monde, gens du monde*). To the world of travelers and savants (*le cosmos*) and the world of the theologians (*le siècle*), from the mid-seventeenth century, was added the world of polite society. The term spread and was used by Guez de Balzac, Grenaille, Méré, and La Bruyère, at first qualified (*grand monde, beau monde, monde poli*), then used alone.[147] Related expressions multiplied (*savoir son monde, être du monde, commerce du monde, usage du monde*) and attest to the proximity of this universe to the court, as in the Corneille verse: "Vous êtes peu du monde, et savez mal la cour" ("you are little of the world and know the court poorly").[148] In the dictionaries of the late seventeenth century, *le monde* comes to be restricted to a social elite defined both by birth and by its lifestyle. For Furetière, "the people who haunt the court are called *gens du monde, le monde poli*."[149] Among other meanings, Richelet mentions, "*Monde. Les gens du monde. Le grand monde. Les gens de qualité*," and gives as an example: "*il fréquente le grand monde*" ("he frequents high society").[150]

This definition bears traces of the moral condemnation with which the Augustinian tradition, continued by Jansenist criticism, regarded this group. In the eighteenth century, however, the term *monde* was more com-monly used, and lost the negative connotations of the theological tradition. Voltaire's *Le Mondain* was an important step in this reversal.[151] Apologetics for profane pleasures also applied to the way of life of an urban, polite, and civilized elite. This stabilization in the vocabulary of "the world" appears clearly in the *Encyclopédie*, where the term *mondain* was stripped of any theological meaning: "Man delivered over to life, to business, and to the amusements of the world, and of society, for those two terms are synony-mous." Moreover, several articles in the *Encyclopédie* present *le grand monde* as a model. The many meanings of the word *monde* became its force, associating the seductions of urban amusements with the prestige of the way of life of the aristocratic elite at court or in the salons of Paris.

Literature played an important role in this dynamic of worldly distinction. Belles-lettres were part of aristocratic amusement but they also granted social prestige to those who were received in the houses in which letters were honored. Talleyrand, a man sensitive to the effects of reputation, describes the fashion for salon readings at the end of the ancien régime as a rather irritating "burden" that must be taken on if one wanted to be fashionable:

> Readings after dinner were then the reigning fashion; they imparted special importance, and were reputed to give a select tone, to some houses. One seldom dined at the houses of M. de Vaudreuil, M. de Liancourt, Madame de Vaines, M. d'Anzely, without being obliged to hear either *Le Mariage de Figaro*, the poem known as *Les Jardins, or Le Connétable de Bourbon*, or some tales by Chamfort, or what was then called *La Révolution de Russie*. It was an obligation rather strictly enforced on all the persons invited; but then, the fact of being a guest at any of these houses, ranked one among the distinguished men of the day. I might say that many people whom I did not know spoke of me in good terms, simply because they had met me at some of these dinner-parties to which the right of making people's reputation had been granted. In this respect, I was like the man spoken of by the Chevalier de Chastellux: "He is doubtless a very witty man," remarked the Chevalier to some one; "I do not know him, but he goes to Madame Geoffrin's."[152]

"Dinner-parties to which the right of making people's reputation had been granted": this definition of the salons raises the crucial question of just who granted that right? How was the reputation of a salon established, which then permitted it to grant reputation to those who frequented it? The ambiguity of the formula hid a major sociological phenomenon, which was that of the social dynamic of high society that defined its participants as *le monde*. The most outstanding feature is not so much the aristocratic composition of the salons, but rather the distinction and the reputation that emanated from the presence of aristocrats and that changed aristocratic grandeur into worldly grandeur. When Madame de La Ferté-Imbault praised her mother's salon, she wrote that she "received the best company and all the genres of the court and the city."[153] As for Madame Du Deffand, she wrote, congratulating herself for enjoying a good period in her relations with the maréchale de Luxembourg, the duchesse de Mirepoix, and the princesse de Beauvau, three great ladies for whom she asserts she had no particular friendship, "I am only attentive to [them] because it makes my society less boring; the *gens du monde*, even if not admirable, are always more amusing than others."[154] This statement, founded on a belief in the special gifts of the aristocracy for pleasurable activities, is a good indication of how worldly distinction worked. Its dynamic relied on the values of the court aristocracy, but the effects of reputation that it elicited created breaches through which some who, by birth, would never have gained access to the court society could penetrate.

From the Salon to the Court: Madame Geoffrin

Among the meeting places that granted reputation, Talleyrand cites the salon of Madame Geoffrin. How did she manage to occupy such a prestigious position? Unlike La Reynière, who attempted a direct conversion of his capital as a financier into worldly capital and mistook the signs of high society, Madame Geoffrin thoroughly absorbed its norms. As we have seen, she ostentatiously adopted the image of the *maîtresse de maison* and vigorously rejected all aspirations to learning. Similarly, she patiently constructed the reputation of her salon thanks to a very sure sense of worldly communication. Her social ambition was linked with her fascination for the court. Her daughter (whom Madame Geoffrin had married to a young nobleman) compared her to Alexander for "her taste for conquest" and "her degree of ambition, passion for celebrity, and jealousy for anything that might diminish her éclat."[155] Lacking a noble pedigree, she proudly displayed portraits of herself and her daughter by Nattier, the court painter, in her salon.[156] She took care to keep up a correspondence with Catherine II and Stanisław II August Poniatowski, and she was so delighted to welcome the two sons of the king of Sweden that Galiani, who was fond of her but rarely missed an opportunity to tease her, claimed that if Voltaire were to rewrite *Candide*, he should situate the dinner of six kings at Madame Geoffrin's.[157] Joking aside, it is clear that Madame Geoffrin's successful reputation rested on two things: the presence of men of letters, scholars, and artists at her gatherings, and her ties with aristocrats and European royalty. The presence of both sorts of figures was an important resource, but it could become a handicap: receiving men of letters could earn her the reputation of a *bel esprit*, and her princely connections risked making her a female version of Molière's *bourgeois gentilhomme*.

The peak of Madame Geoffrin's career was her journey in 1766 to visit the king of Poland, Stanisław August Poniatowski, whom she had had as a guest in her house when he was a young man visiting Paris.[158] The traditional historiographical account of this journey is a triumphal one: Mme Geoffrin is supposed to have been received with all honors in both Warsaw and Vienna. After she had received the whole of Europe in her salons, Parisian high society sent off the bourgeoisie of the rue Saint-Honoré to repay the visits, surrounded by the glow of her intimate relations with the great names of literary and scientific life. Upon closer inspection, though, Madame Geoffrin's voyage was above all a remarkable communication campaign. Her stay in Poland was not quite as successful as Madame Geoffrin managed to make it seem. Stanisław August, whose time was taken up with heavy and complex political burdens, made little effort to receive his old friend, despite the gratitude he owed her and the affection he felt for her. Their exchange of letters reveals that the idea of the trip was hers and that she had to persuade an unenthusiastic Stanisław August. Madame Geoffrin, who usually was quite restrained, had welcomed his election with a total absence of humility, writing to him: "My son, my king! How many common citizens can say that? I alone!"[159] She fully intended to profit from that glory. Once the trip had been decided, the king seemed resolved to pour kindness on his former protectress and to show that Polish hospitality had no reason to envy Parisian hospitality. He knew that Madame Geoffrin's friendship could be turned to notable diplomatic advantage.[160] Her stay was ruined, however, by political conflicts at the court in Warsaw, which Madame Geoffrin could not or would not keep away from. Finally, they parted on chilly terms, as witnessed by their correspondence. In his *Memoirs* Stanisław August had some rather severe things to say about Madame Geoffrin, whose "vanity," he claims, made her an easy prey for his enemies, who, by manipulating her self-esteem, managed to push her into quarreling with the king. At that point, she indulged in scenes that were "highly turbulent, and were so to such a degree that at times they became even comic."[161] Other sources reveal that Madame Geoffrin's voyage was ridiculed by some of the Polish nobility.[162]

None of this filtered back to France. What did arrive was a long series of letters from Madame Geoffrin, in which she presented an idyllic picture of her trip and spelled out the most flattering details of the honors that had been bestowed on her.[163] She wrote to her daughter from Vienna that "the city and the court overwhelmed me with kindness,"[164] and the same day she wrote Boutin that "from the day after my arrival, my room was not opened without being full of valets de chambre and pages [bearing] compliments for me, requests for news of me, and [invitations] begging me to dine."[165] In all this she displayed a genuine talent for picturesque detail to bolster her reputation.[166] She stated that she had been "overwhelmed with attention" by Chancellor Kaunitz, and she described at length the most striking of her "brilliant successes," her meeting with Joseph II, whom, as she reports, said "such flattering things [to her] that [she] dared not repeat them."[167]

That effort was crowned with success. Madame Geoffrin's letters were copied, read, and duly circulated among Parisian high society. One journal announced that "Madame Geoffrin is about to agree to the insistent solicitations of the monarch, who calls on her," and, several weeks later, reported of the honors she had received.[168] It was reported on July 12 that "everyone is talking about the warm reception that Madame Geoffrin has received in the places through which she has passed."[169] Orchestrating the reverberations from her voyage, Madame Geoffrin wrote "I must tell you that my voyage has caused a thousand times more talk in Vienna than in Paris."[170] Later, after hearing about the effect of her letters, Madame Geoffrin encouraged interest in them,[171] and even congratulated herself that they were making "such a stir in Paris."[172] She ended a letter to Marmontel with "a thousand tender things to my dear baron d'Holbach and to the lovely baronne," a thinly veiled request that he read the letter to the Holbachs. The circulation of that letter is attested: Julie de Lespinasse owned a copy of it;[173] another manuscript copy ended up in the collection formed by Monmerqué; Morellet later transcribed it, with some modifications, into the new edition of his Éloges de Mme Geoffrin.[174]

By writing to multiple correspondents, Madame Geoffrin made sure that the interminable and convincing reports of her triumphs would circulate in aristocratic and financial circles, but also in philosophical and literary ones. Grimm reproduced a letter of Madame Geoffrin's to the Abbé de Breteuil, copies of which were circulating in Paris, in the Correspondance littéraire, stating that "One would not seem distinguished presenting himself in the world without having seen her."[175] Thanks to correspondence, news of her trip spread throughout Europe. Mariette, for example, wrote to Father Paciaudi, who had attended Madame Geoffrin's Mondays when he was in Paris in 1762, to inform him of her travels.[176] Even a person as perceptive as Madame Necker was fooled by this intense campaign. She shared the contents of Madame Geoffrin's triumphal weekly letters with her friend in Geneva, Madame Reverdill, informing her of Madame Geoffrin's successes in Vienna and Warsaw: "The Emperor, the king of Poland, all of the powers of Germany have lavished honors and friendship on her. I received a letter from her several days ago.. . . The ascendency of this worthy woman is prodigious in Poland."[177]

Madame Geoffrin knew how reputations work. Her intensive epistolary activity and the effective relay carried on by Parisian men of letters and sociability networks succeeded in converting a disappointing trip into a worldly success. In the Correspondance littéraire Grimm remarked that the "success" of the trip, which he relates, had stifled critics: "What had seemed ridiculous and even rash has suddenly become fine and interesting."[178] Worldly reputation worked that way: there was only one step between ridicule and glory, and the result was always fragile. This is shown in quite a different sense by Madame Du Boccage's trip to England in 1750.

In the glow of the relative success of her *Amazones* the previous year, Madame Du Boccage undertook a trip to England, where she attempted to be received by the king, with the duc de Mirepoix, the French ambassador, acting as go-between. The king refused, after inquiring of the duc de Mirepoix whether "women of the sort of Madame Du Boccage" were presented to the king of France.[179] Madame Du Boccage then tried, in vain, to be presented to the Prince of Wales. Furious, she wrote a letter to Madame de Mirepoix in which she accused the ambassador's wife of not having helped her to be presented. The letter circulated in Paris, accompanied by a letter of the duc de Mirepoix to his mother-in-law informing her of Madame du Boccage's misconduct. Collé took pleasure in transcribing these letters into his journal with an ironic remark about "the puerile vanity and improper conduct of that woman" and the "ridiculous part she is currently playing in England."[180]

Mme Geoffrin and Mme Du Boccage had been rivals around 1750, when they received the same authors. It is not impossible that Madame Geoffrin started her Mondays precisely to overshadow the Mondays of Madame Du Boccage. Both women dreamed of gaining access to the world of the royal court, which seemed inaccessible to these bourgeoises, and they both wagered on the glory of a detour through foreign courts. But, while Madame Du Boccage counted on literary celebrity, Madame Geoffrin patiently constructed her worldly reputation and her personal ties with European aristocracy. Madame Du Boccage, perhaps too hurriedly, less sensitive to the ridiculous aspects of the woman author, blinded by the successes of her works and sincerely hoping to be recognized for their literary merits, was soon forced to renounce her ambitions and resign herself to playing the marginal role of a *femme de lettres*, thus attracting ridicule in the eyes of Parisian high society whose support Madame Geoffrin was victoriously soliciting.

After her return from Poland, Madame Geoffrin was able to capitalize on the success of her trip in terms of reputation and worldly prestige. Better yet, when Marie-Antoinette, whom she had met in Vienna, became the dauphine of France, Madame Geoffrin took steps to be received at court.[181] This connection with the dauphine (later the queen) produced a series of successes, as La Harpe reported in a letter to Shuvalov:

Not long ago the Queen, wanting to see the paintings shown at the Louvre, had had the room closed to the public. But persons of some distinction could obtain permission to enter. Madame Geoffrin had herself put among that number, and as you shall see, she had her own reasons for doing so. She had known the Queen in Vienna, when she was an archduchess. Since then the Queen has never missed an opportunity to tell her that she remembers. As soon as she saw Madame Geoffrin, she advanced in her direction, and indicating Madame [her sister-in-law], who accompanied her: "Would you like," she said to her, "for me to present Madame to you?" You can imagine how Madame Geoffrin, to whom Madame was being presented, immediately became an important object for everyone who was there, and how Madame Geoffrin left satisfied.[182]

As this account shows, the court was both a horizon and a resource for worldly reputation. The exposition of paintings at the Louvre was a perfect transaction space. Situated in Paris, in a royal palace, it was "closed to the public" for the queen's visit, which was a way to restore the palace to its royal function and to recall that the exposition, organized by the Académie in the Salon Carré of the Louvre, remained subject to the will of the monarchs. On a word from the queen, the "public" was expelled and the salon given over to the queen's pleasure, amid the works. Still, access did not depend on the rules of protocol regarding presentation at the court but on "distinction." This left greater latitude to the queen, who could receive Madame Geoffrin and, above all, free herself from protocol by presenting Madame to her, in an inversion of hierarchies that would have been unthinkable at Versailles. The fact remains that the queen was the queen, even in Paris and even in an exposition emptied of its public. The fiction of equality that was inherent to society life was immediately a source of honor and prestige for Madame Geoffrin, who became "important," not in the eyes of the public, who had been chased out of the room, but in those of the other persons of distinction present. Thanks to oral accounts and to manuscript correspondence destined for European aristocrats (here, La Harpe's account of the occasion for the Shuvalovs), the little scene "immediately" enhanced Madame Geoffrin's position in high society by dramatizing her relations with the royal family.

The social dynamics of "the world" were based on the effects of hospitality and the mastery of the odes of *la bonne société*, and Madame Geoffrin's success lay in her avoidance of contagion from the image of the *bureau d'esprit* as a way to establish her position within the worldly sphere. The Parisian "world" was at once a social group defined by its practices of sociability and a system of values that considered its habits as defining *le bon ton*. It was too big a group for every member to know every other member directly, but small enough for everyone to know who was who. "The world" was both an extension of the royal court and an emanation of the city, which explains why it corresponded so well with the expression *la Cour et la Ville*. As an extension of the court, it was both close to it and different from it. Rules of politeness were in large part derived from the rationality of the court; worldly reputation was closely connected to aristocratic grandeur; and the court remained the horizon for worldly people in terms of power and prestige. On the other hand, high society was not the court. It was broader and included the fringes of the urban elites that had no access to the court. It was ruled by a different principle of distinction: at court, etiquette exposed internal hierarchies and ranks, whereas in society life politeness granted distinction by hiding hierarchies and by consecrating those who were part of those hierarchies. As an emanation of the city, *le monde* nourished representations of Paris as a model for fashion, urbanity, and civility. Representations of the Paris world were not based on an urban or a civic culture, but rather on a demand that the model of the capital be exemplary. By the same token, those representations were reliant on the local dimension of sociability only as a way to assert their universality.

Writers actively contributed to publicizing the universality of the Parisian world. They were not absent from the worldly sphere itself. Far from it. If sociability did not annul distinctions of rank and failed to shelter writers from violence and scorn, it did create spaces in which they could be included in the amusements of high society. The specificity of the Paris world, in comparison to other high societies (in particular, London), depended on the place that writers occupied in it and on the role that they played in the symbolic production of the "world" as social grandeur. But what did they have to gain?

CHAPTER 3

Men of Letters and Worldly Sociability

Look, she said to me, at those two people who are arguing so heatedly; they are two men
of letters. Their presence makes *beaux esprits* of the masters of a house.
Madame de Souza, *Adèle de Sénange* (1794)

The salons were not egalitarian gatherings animated uniquely by a search for conviviality. They were regulated by civility and distinction; the court was their horizon, and the redefinition of aristocratic merit in worldly terms was the game they played. Nevertheless, the existence of an ideal of reciprocal relations in polite conversation is undeniable. What accounts for the gap between practices and representations? How was the paradigm of politeness appropriated by Enlightenment thought? The "gradual transformation of aristocratic thought into Enlightenment philosophy"[1] cannot be explained through intellectual history alone. It demands looking at the place of men of letters in worldly society, for they were the principal theoreticians of *honnêteté* in the eighteenth century. Doing so means comparing social conditions of worldly exchange, debates about political and moral philosophy, and the differing discourses by which writers constructed their social identity. Those different registers, which belong within different historiographical traditions (social history, political philosophy, literary history), are closely connected, for their theoretical elaboration permitted the writers who frequented the salons to justify their worldly practices in the polemics that animated literary life. Such practices should be compared with the representations that men of letters or the philosophes created regarding their place in ancien régime society where social autonomy was quite impossible for writers. This chapter begins with the most material practices in order to move gradually toward more theoretical discourses, without assuming a unilateral causality, as we shall see. It focuses on the question: Why did the writers' relations of dependence on the social elites, of which salon life was one of the most important facets in the eighteenth century, borrow so massively from the language of sociability?

FROM PATRONAGE TO PROTECTION
Beneficence and Protection

With rare exceptions, the status of intellectual property and the editorial market in this period did not enable writers to make a living from the sale of their intellectual endeavors. At the end of the century, Diderot and Beaumarchais asked for economic independence, but it was a struggle. Parisian authors could be divided into two categories: those who benefitted from a social position and a fortune that allowed them to devote themselves to literature as a leisure occupation, and those who depended on pensions that they obtained from the king or from aristocrats.[2] The social condition of writers in the eighteenth century depended heavily on the practice of patronage. Carmontelle, Collé, and Laujon were "readers" of the duc d'Orléans; Thomas was for a few years the private secretary of the duc de Praslin; Chamford was secretary to the duc de Condé. The protection of the great was often a necessary condition for access to the manna of royal patronage or well-paying positions. In itself, the condition of author did not define a social status in the society of the ancien régime. A man could be noble, fermier général, abbé, lawyer, a member of Parlement, but not "author." As Madame d'Épinay wrote (and she was rather well disposed toward writers), "It is a bastard state, which brings together and unites all that is the greatest and all that is the most vile."[3] She adds that men of letters cannot make up a social category (*un état*), and that no particular quality permits one to identify them.

For writers of the eighteenth century, it was thus imperative to find means by which to live and to gain a valorized social identity. In that aim, the frequentation of salons was an appreciable resource. In the first place— and at times this was an advantage not to be scorned—the men of letters who frequented the salons ate there at the expense of the master of the house. Moreover, the latter offered many gifts to the writers whom they received, sometimes in the form of financial gratifications. Madame Geoffrin covered the writers who frequented her salon with gifts, and they all joined Abbé Georgel in praising "her wealth and her beneficence" and her "appearance [of being] always open" to men of letters.[4] A few years later, Amélie Suard remembered the "noble use that [Madame Geoffrin] made of her wealth," which means, in particular, that she "overwhelmed" her friends with presents until her last days.[5] In his portrait of Madame Geoffrin, Morellet speaks at length of that generosity, of which he was among the principal beneficiaries. He speaks of her "obliging attention" and her "giving humor,"[6] but he recognizes that Madame Geoffrin's generosity could, occasionally, be inopportune and that, in her need to be obliging, she paid little attention to whether her gifts were desired: "It is especially with her friends, with the men of letters that formed her society, that she satisfied, often despite them, what she called her *humeur donnante*.... She was as tormented by the need to offer her gift as one is to pay a debt."[7] Generosity, here, is described as a constraining obligation of honor. The other term used to describe the generosities of Madame Geoffrin is "beneficence," which corresponds perfectly with the new representations of the generosity of the elites, exemplified by the philanthropic movement in which Madame Necker was an important figure.[8] Until her last days, Madame Geoffrin remained faithful to that "giving humor" and to her "habit of beneficence," as the *Correspondance littéraire* put it when Madame Geoffrin, already unwell, sent four pots of coins to Antoine Thomas, then "forced him to receive a small box of two thousand gold écus."[9]

Generosity was expressed with a combination of sentiment, effusion, and disinterestedness. The gift was always anonymous and thanks were rejected. The discourse of beneficence and philanthropy provided a new garb for the old tradition of worldly charity and generosity formerly associated with life in society. In the seventeenth century, festive receptions given for friends, followed by gifts, were called *galanteries*, and Madame de Rambouillet enjoyed her reputation for disinterested generosity.[10] The exchange of gifts among people of the same social rank remained a foundational principle of worldly life in the eighteenth century.[11] The same language was used with gifts to men of letters, but the absence of reciprocity gave gift-giving a totally different social significance. It was not just a question of reinforcing a worldly connection by an exchange of gifts, but of inscribing a financial relation within worldly sociability. Assuming that Suard had money problems, baron d'Holbach offered him ten thousand livres.[12] Helvétius, thanks to his revenues as fermier général, gave pensions to Marivaux, Saurin, and Turpin.[13] After having read *Mélanie* in the salon of the duchesse de Gramont in the presence of the duc de Choiseul, La Harpe received 3000 livres from the minister.[14] The Neckers did not lag behind, granting Suard a pension of 800 livres, as they had done for other authors who had frequented their salon (for example, they set up a yearly income of 1,000 livres for Meister).[15] The income that the Neckers arranged for Suard gave rise to a story that swept the salons and dramatized the Neckers' desire for anonymity and Suard's attempts to express his gratitude, all in the language of beneficence. Madame d'Épinay reports the episode to Galiani in these terms: "An unknown individual has placed a sum of twenty thousand livres to be placed on the head of M. and Mme Suard as a lifetime income. He took a long time to decide to accept it, and finally they did accept it, on the condition that the benefactor make himself known. He did make himself known after the acceptance: it was M. Necker. This anecdote should please you."[16] The worldly game demanded that the donor insist on his desire to be anonymous and that the anonymity, at the end, be lifted.

Madame Geoffrin also provided pensions for at least three of the leading authors who frequented her salon. The principal beneficiary of her largesse was d'Alembert, to whom she gave an annual income of 600 livres, starting in 1760; in January 1772 she added to this an income of 1,350 livres (which he was to receive at Geoffrin's death), then a new *rente* of 600 livres in March 1773. Two years later Thomas was given an annual *rente* of 1,000 livres. In January 1771, Abbé Morellet, disappointed by not having obtained the ministerial gratifications that he had expected from his writings against the Compagnie des Indes, was consoled by a *rente* of 1,200 livres.[17] These "benefices" were received with "a gratitude as noble as was the beneficence to which friendship ceded," Morellet wrote after the death of his protectress,[18] using the vocabulary of beneficence and gratitude, amity and nobility of sentiment. It was crucially important to present such beneficence as the result, and even (paradoxically) the proof, of a disinterested relationship. The fact that Morellet's writings against the commercial monopolies were contrary to the interests of Madame Geoffrin was evidence of that disinterest which Morellet did not fail to point out.

This worldly economy of the gift must be distinguished from the traditional forms of clientelism and patronage that had prevailed in the seventeenth century and were still widespread. The client-sponsor institutionalized a domestic relationship between a great personage and an author, following a model of political fidelity. It often involved employment as a secretary in the service of a prince or a high-ranking aristocrat. Patronage allowed for rewarding authors for their works and transformed the client relation into a symbolic exchange.[19] It thus implied specific acknowledgment of the value of cultural productions. The prestige that those productions conferred on the protectors was sanctioned by the genre of the dedicatory epistle, which made the benefactor's generosity public knowledge, but also stressed the immeasurable distance between the positions of the patron and the writer, the protector and the protégé. In the salons, the situation was different. The gift was not to reward a specific work or service and did not call for public praise. It was somehow detached from the practices of writing, and it was presented as a friendly generosity inscribed within relations of sociability.

Madame Geoffrin showed her generosity to writers, but also to the artists who became part of her society.[20] Their presence indicates the new prestige attached to painters in the eighteenth century.[21] Madame Geoffrin put them to work and paid them well; she enabled them to meet potential clients among the *amateurs* brought to her Monday dinners by the comte de Caylus, and, like the writers, they benefitted from her gifts. The wife and the daughter of Carle Van Loo received 2,400 livres, Madame Vien 240, Vernet 600, Boucher 300. While some artists found Madame Geoffrin's tutelage and her intervention unbearable, others won her over with a mixture of availability and firmness. This was the case of Vien, although his first meeting with Madame Geoffrin was a fiasco.[22] Sent by Caylus to see this young painter, newly arrived in Paris, she suggested that he change his style. He responded vociferously and they parted company angrily. As Vien's reputation grew, and he was elected to the Académie, Madame Geoffrin could not resist the temptation to commission a painting from him. After another argument, she bought a head of the Virgin from him and was satisfied with it. Later she brought La Live de Jully, a great collector, to him, received him at her receptions, and bought new paintings from him: *La Douce Mélancholie*, for which she paid 400 livres in 1756, and four large canvases representing the four seasons.

She played the same role of intermediary with writers, helping them to sell their books. D'Hémery, the inspector of police, noted in 1751 that she sold "the rarest new books; that is, the authors sent her a dozen copies, which she was pleased to get her friends to buy."[23] Most artists regarded Madame Geoffrin as a generous benefactress and her salon as an opportunity to meet protectors and patrons, while also claiming their part in high society. When she died, Cochin wrote to Madame de La Ferté-Imbault to acknowledge her good deeds. He added: "The worthy artists whom she welcomed with so much goodness, whom she obliged on so many occasions and with such alacrity, should be no less affected than I am by her loss. They will not find, without the friendship with which she honored them, the invaluable advantage of seeing themselves in her house, connected with persons of the highest distinction."[24] Madame Geoffrin herself had few illusions about the nature of the "amity" that linked her to the artists: "I have become their friend," she wrote to the king of Poland, "because I see them often, I make them work a lot, caress them, praise them, and pay them very well."[25]

By frequenting the salons, writers and artists benefitted from the protection of their hosts, who could give them access to circles close to the court, recommend them, and intervene in their favor. The salons were important supports for the career of authors, not as a literary institution, but, to the contrary, because they permitted the authors who frequented them to leave the circles of the republic of letters and gain access to aristocratic patronage and royal largesse. Women played the role here that was traditionally theirs in the society of the court, where the royal favorite occupied the first rank in her power to protect, to act in favor of one person or another, and to mobilize the ministers and the courtiers. Whether it was a question of avoiding censorship, getting an intrepid author out of the Bastille, obtaining an audience or a pension, or canvassing for a place in the Académie, having the support of efficient protectors was indispensable. When he was just being launched in Parisian literary life, Marmontel was well aware of the importance of the salons. When La Poupelinière asked him what he was seeking in *le monde*, he answered frankly, "protectors and some means of wealth."[26] Similarly, when Amélie Suard speaks of the career of her husband "in the circle of his societies," she does not limit herself to listing the "gifts" that he received, but also evokes, on several occasions, the intervention of his protectors within the *monde*. One important acquaintance was Madame de Tessé, who intervened with Choiseul, with Madame de Gramont, and with Madame de Beauvau to help Suard and Abbé Arnaud obtain the editorship of the *Gazette littéraire*, thus noticeably increasing those men's revenues (from 2,500 francs to 10,000 francs each).[27] After Choiseul's fall, the duc d'Aiguillon took away the editorship of the *Gazette littéraire*, which put the Suards in a difficult financial position and mobilized their "friends" (that is, people who were sufficiently close to the royal court to have some influence there to help them): "Our friends were uniquely occupied in seeking a person who might have influence with the duc d'Aiguillon to ask for a pension, about which he said nothing." Among the great figures of the Paris world, the duc de Nivernais was a good prospect, as he was close to the comtesse de Maurepas, the only person who had any influence over d'Aiguillon. A great lord and a diplomat, an amateur man of letters, the author of fables, and an academician, the duc de Nivernais was the son-in-law of Madame de Maurepas. A scene was arranged during a session of the Académie, at which Amélie Suard wept emotionally while listening to d'Alembert's praise of Fénelon, thus attracting the sympathy and the attention of Nivernais, who had been placed across from her. He obtained a pension of 2,500 livres for Suard, which required that the Suards pay him a visit to thank him: "He received us with all the graces that distinguish that amiable lord, and since has invited us both to dine with him."[28]

This scene clearly shows how the social and political spheres coincided. Instead of an opposition between the court and the republic of letters, multiple spheres and resources were turned toward the court, the place of power and the distribution of favors. Salon attendance offered protections, but also a social and political know-how that could immediately be mobilized for action: "One discovered that Madame de Maurepas was the only person who had some influence over the duke, and that the duc de Nivernais could also promote some things with her." The public sessions of the Académie furnished a theatrical space, but also an interface between high society and men of letters (La Harpe, a friend of the Suards, sat next to Nivernais and passed on to him information about Amélie). Finally, worldly obligations implied a visit to thank the "amiable lord," followed by an invitation to dinner that enabled the Suards to penetrate the Nivernais's society. Two years later, in 1772, Suard again needed protectors. After having been elected to the Académie in the company of abbé Delille, his election was rejected by Louis XV. The princesse de Beauvau, whose salon he attended, was "mortified." At that point, she and her husband did their best to sponsor action at court to make him "receivable," thanks to the efforts of Madame d'Aiguillon, Sartine, and the duc de Nivernais, who wrote a letter to the king.[29]

Through its complex articulation of the social spaces frequented and used by men of letters, this example invites reexamination of relations between the salons and the Académie. It is commonly thought that the salons dictated the results of academic elections, though this deserves a closer look. Elections to the Académie played out on two levels, those of literary solidarities and of aristocratic protections. As it happened, worldly sociability provided a meeting place for these networks. As meeting places among men of letters, the salons served to resolve conflicts, and on occasion the host or hostess interceded between two quarreling writers.[30] Thanks to their relations with both Parisian high society and the court, the salon host and hostess had the means of mobilizing influential protectors, and thanks to the clientele of men of letters whom they received and protected, they could influence votes. Their power was an interface; hence it was to the advantage of writers to attend their salons if they aimed at being elected to the Académie. It was not so much as institutions of the republic of letters, but rather as worldly circles that the salons could play that role. They gave an opportunity for action in the literary field, but also with the king and with his counselors and ministers, who held the keys to the academic institution. Still, election was never a sure thing, as no social group controlled the Académie and every election mobilized multiple clans, thus encouraging competition among the protectors. Thus, when correspondence mentioned the chances of a candidate, it was always by weighing his merits, his strictly literary or scholarly titles, and his "protections," which included the houses that he frequented. When Bombelles, for example, brings up the candidacy of Morellet, he does not mention the many salons that he has attended, but rather his connections with the economists, his reputation as an *esprit fort*, and his protectors. His rival, the fabulist Florian, "has friends and powerful protectors," but he seemed too old and risked facing strong protections, given that "one wants to find a spot for Abbé Morellet."[31] The dominant impression is that of a complex game of influences and recommendations, in which those who are pulling the strings do not have all of those strings firmly in hand, in which assurances given are not always sustained, and in which the most powerful protectors use their credit and exchange favors, but without having a circle or any other person who possesses a determinant influence over the result.

Every election gave rise to a tangle of negotiations and strategies that have left few traces and that involved the court, aristocratic protections, literary or ideological clans, and networks of sociability. The academicians were subjected to pressure from their friends and protectors and must in turn have put pressure on their colleagues. Montesquieu wrote to Madame Du Deffand, "I will do, within the Academy, what Madame de Mirepoix, d'Alembert, and you want, but I cannot answer for Monsieur de Saint-Maur, as no one is as closed within himself as he is."[32] Two years later, on the occasion of the election of d'Alembert, Formont made use of the vocabulary of negotiation to congratulate Madame Du Deffand on her role: "You have had need of all the talents you possess for the negotiation; but it is not surprising, when one considers that you were dealing with the illustrious and scholarly duchesse de Chaulnes."[33] This statement was ironic, for what followed referred to the duchess's erotic powers by listing her lovers; still, it clearly demonstrates that the rival influences were not necessarily intellectual. Elections to the Académie des Sciences followed the same rule. The duchesse de Choiseul solicited the support of Madame Du Deffand for her protégé Monsieur Poissonnier, asking her to mobilize the scholars who attended her salon. This move made Poissonier the protégé of Madame Du Deffand, in spite of the failure of his candidacy. The duchesse de Choiseul wrote, "You have had the goodness, *ma chère petite-fille*, to procure for me the votes of Messieurs d'Alembert and Le Maunier for Monsieur Poissonnier at the recent election of the Académie des Sciences. Although success did not respond to such good urgings, I am nonetheless grateful to you and to those gentlemen, and your protégé feels no less [gratitude] for having stimulated your interest and obtained their suffrages; I will ask you for it again for one of the two places that are to be created."[34]

Each candidacy set systems of protections into motion, but they were not necessarily effective. Madame Geoffrin led a campaign in 1748 for the mathematician Gabriel Cramer, but did not succeed in assuring his election, despite the influence of Dortous de Mairan, a result that did not prevent her from reminding the unlucky candidate of the "thanks" that he owed to Dortous de Mairan for his efforts. Playing an advisory role, she urged him to take advantage of the peace to present himself to the Royal Society.[35] Two years later, Cramer was still in the ranks, and Madame Geoffrin assured him not only of the support of Dortous de Mairan and d'Alembert, but also that of comte d'Argenson, minister of the Maison du Roi, who had been persuaded by his son, who in turn had been approached by Watelet, a constant presence at Madame de Geoffrin's Mondays.[36] Cramer had to continue to wait patiently, for the place seemed promised to someone else. The duchesse d'Enville, who was in touch with both the high circles of aristocratic patronage and the academic networks, was fond of using military vocabulary: "I have lost no time, Monsieur, in setting up all my batteries in favor of Milord Stanhope when I learned by your letter that he desired a place in the Académie des Sciences,"[37] she wrote to Georges-Louis Lesage. She had already written to Malesherbes, Montigny, and Trudaine. Mably, who was staying with her at the château de La Roche-Guyon, had promised to write to Vaucanson and to "have someone speak" to d'Alembert. The duc de Belle-Isle and the duchess's son, the duc de La Rochefoucauld, had approached Mairan and, the duchesse d'Enville promised, if Buffon were in Paris, he would be solicited by Monsieur de La Bourdonnaye and by the duc de La Rochefoucauld. This demonstration of force reassured the duchess, and she did not think the election difficult. Three years earlier, however, she had done her best to assure the election of Charles Bonnet and had failed.[38] Games of influence were on occasion games for dupes. Assurances of support and proclamations of gratitude, which were part of the worldly game, also need to be taken with caution.

The role of the salons in the career of the writers who frequented them went far beyond academic elections. To be received in one of those houses offered possible material advantages, an opportunity to make connections with more important and more firmly established writers, and the hope of getting closer to the court. Success in le monde was thus a first stage in social recognition that might lead to Versailles, where the distribution of material advantages and symbolic credit really took place. If being received in a salon was a first step toward recognition and a promise of success, reading one's works in a salon did even more to enable a writer to gain a reputation as a fashionable author. In 1775, La Harpe aspired to the Académie. In March he read his latest tragedy, Menzikoff, in Madame Necker's salon before diplomats such as the English ambassador and aristocrats like the maréchale de Luxembourg and Madame Du Deffand.[39] The success of the play led to it being performed at Fontainebleau before the court, and Suard's friends hoped that it would please the queen, which would smooth the way for La Harpe's election.[40] The proximity of the worldly social sphere to the court permitted changing a success in a salon into royal favor and might lead to the Académie.

Madame de Graffigny's difficulties in the 1740s show that, by frequenting the salons, writers sought out active sources of patronage and ways to approach the world of the court much more than contact with their equals. After she arrived in Paris in 1739, Madame de Graffigny had a number of social relations that she could rely on, but she had to face the outright hostility of Madame Du Châtelet and, a year later, she lost her principal support, the duchesse de Richelieu.[41] Madame de Graffigny frequented literary circles, especially the theater world, where she hoped to shine. While waiting for success, which came in 1747 with a novel, the *Lettres péruviennes*, and in 1751 with a play, *La Cénie*, she settled on rue Saint-Hyacinthe and sought to bring together in her home the writers (Crébillon, Gresset, Duclos) whom she met at the Thursdays of Mademoiselle Quinault. Unfortunately, after a few dinners her salon faltered and she had some mortifying experiences. Gresset was the first to desert her. Then Crébillon, whom she greatly admired, kept her hopes dangling as he declined one invitation after another. Tired of struggling, she put an end to these dinners that "cost a great deal" without attracting as many writers as she had imagined.[42] Madame de Graffigny was not well known, and her quite modest fortune did not make her receptions very attractive. Above all, her failure was due to the fact that, essentially, what she offered the writers she invited to her home was the opportunity to meet other writers, whom they already saw elsewhere, as Crébillon rudely reminded her. Unlike Madame Geoffrin and others, she did not offer them the chance to make connections with influential protectors in aristocratic circles and especially at court.

Expressions of Gratitude

The relationship between the salon hosts and the writers whom they received was asymmetrical, but not unilateral. Writers were sought after, both for their talents and for the consideration they brought to those who received them. The writers' ability to produce verse, narratives, and texts of other sorts was necessary to warding off boredom. For fashionable people who aspired to a reputation as enlightened amateurs, conversation with writers furnished judgments, comments, and witty remarks that could be passed on about literary novelties or about the most recent play performed at the Comédie. For those with aspirations to write, and who were increasingly numerous, men of letters were sought out for advice, and even for help. Even Helvétius, according to his friend Morellet, made use of discussions he had with the men of letters whom he received: "He took some one of us off into a corner, put to him a question that he had undertaken to treat, and tried to draw from him either some argument in favor of his own opinions or some objection that he would have to destroy; for he was continually working on his book in society."[43]

Men of letters were also encouraged to publicize the merits of those who received them and protected them.[44] Here worldliness revealed its specificity. At court, protection was expressed in the vocabulary of favor and gratitude had to be public. Marmontel, who circulated between the court and the salons, passing from La Poupelinière's salon to Versailles and from Versailles to the salon of Madame Geoffrin, had access to the court thanks to verse that he had written in praise of the king and of the Pâris, friends of Madame de Pompadour.[45] Having obtained a post as secrétaire des Bâtiments, thanks to the royal favorite and her brother, he was appreciated for his talents in the traditional genre of the dedicatory epistle. Madame de Pompadour asked him to rewrite the dedications of less skilled authors aspiring to dedicate their works to her.[46] That talent gained him favor and advancement, and he later obtained the privilege for the *Mercure de France*. Ten years later, in 1763, he returned to the custom of dedications to the king, offering his *Poétique* to the king and to Choiseul in the purest tradition of court patronage and with the aim of assuring his candidacy to the Académie Française.[47]

Worldly gratitude, on the other hand, was not expressed in public, ostensible praise, but rather through the language of friendship and spontaneity in statements that were intended for restricted circles ruled by the shared codes of worldliness. Many traces of this economy of worldly praise subsist thanks to the role that correspondence played in it. Suard excelled in that art. During a stay in London he wrote to his wife, in a letter that might seem private, this long paragraph about Madame Geoffrin:

> I thank you for giving me accurate news of Madame Geoffrin. Go to see her, thank her for her remembrance, cultivate her goodness for us; one should esteem oneself better for meriting her friendship. I have seen many persons who know her here. The first words that they have said to me were to ask me for news of her. Here, people speak of her as in Paris: never has anyone enjoyed a wider and

more flattering consideration, yet the foreigners know about her no more than a quarter of what she is worth, for they do not know her goodness. I am terribly sorry to learn that she is still unwell. She has true courage: that of reason and necessity; she sees things as they are and takes them in the same fashion; that is good philosophy, but it is not learned, one cannot give it to oneself. May Madame Geoffrin enjoy it for a long time. I hope to find her perfectly reestablished on my return.[48]

Suard's laudatory tone suggests that this passage was addressed more to Madame Geoffrin than to Amélie. Amélie's response to it confirms this, since she reports to her husband several days later that she had gone to see Madame Geoffrin and "had read her the article of the letter that concerned her, which gave her great pleasure."[49] A passage like this was probably read before other guests and may have been copied, learned by heart, and repeated in other salons. Hence the text written by Suard was not meant for his wife, but nor was it aimed at an indeterminate public, as would be the case with a dedicatory epistle. It was intended for the "society" of Madame Geoffrin and those who were part of her world. The polite visit that Amélie Suard paid to Madame Geoffrin was an opportunity to read her these words of praise, which then gained oral circulation within worldly circles of sociability, following their usual practices.

The circulation of praise was a complex business. The comtesse de Boufflers wrote to the Duke of Portland to recommend to him her son, who was traveling to The Hague, and she took advantage of the opportunity to send him a copy of a letter from Rousseau, asking him to burn it. She states, "It is full of praise so strong and so above my merits that it would become a satire of me if it were ever published."[50] Portland responded courteously, "The letter will be burned and will not be seen by anyone outside my house."[51] Evidently he did nothing of the sort, as the copy of the letter is in his archives along with the countess's letter, and she likely did not expect him to burn it. The request permitted the comtesse de Boufflers to communicate Rousseau's praise of her while asserting her own modesty. She could count on the Duke of Portland to be perfectly capable of understanding, if only through hints, the language of worldliness. In reality, what was important was not whether he would keep or burn the letter, but that he not use it thoughtlessly. They were both highly aware of the difference between a restricted circulation, limited to people who knew each other well and accompanied by protestations of awkward modesty, and public diffusion. The first was framed by the practices of sociability and the rules of civility and produced praise and consideration. The second was uncontrollable; it escaped social codes and might lead to satire and ridicule.[52]

To receive an academician, a scholar, or a popular author brought prestige and social consideration to the host and hostess. Madame Necker tried
ceaselessly to reconcile Morellet with her husband, out of fear of losing one
of her guests, one of her "clients," as Tronchin put it: "I teased her about
the extreme fear that she had that her husband would be on bad terms
with Abbé Morellet, and that in losing him she might lose other guests.
She wants to keep all her clients in order to fulfill the project of celebrity."[53]
This statement illustrates a second element of the circle of worldly reputation. Talleyrand, as we have seen, insisted on the "reputation" of the man
à la mode that arose from frequenting certain societies. Conversely, when
men of letters enjoyed a certain fame, they lent consideration to the houses
that they frequented. In a letter to the Shuvalovs, La Harpe describes with
remarkable acuity how Madame Geoffrin and her social group achieved
their success:

> Madame Geoffrin is a very striking example of the consideration that the society
> of men of letters can give, and which they rarely achieve themselves, because the
> first basis for consideration in this country is the independence that is born of
> wealth and which men of letters very rarely have. Madame Geoffrin has neither
> birth nor title. She is the widow of an entrepreneur in the manufacturing of mir-
> rors. She enjoys around forty thousand livres of income, a modest fortune in
> Paris. But she is remarkable for a spirit of order and economy that doubles her
> revenue. For over thirty years she has given formal dinners for the most distin-
> guished men of letters and artists. Her house has thus become the rendezvous
> for talent and merit of all sorts, and the natural desire to mix with famous men
> has made people seek her society, in which one was sure to find them. Moreover,
> any open house that presents some enjoyments ends up gradually attracting
> the best company of the city and the Court, because the greatest problem for
> what is called "good company" is to occupy the evening, and because, in the end,
> everything comes down to fashion [*tout devient mode*] in this country. Foreigners
> above all have flocked to Madame Geoffrin's home; they were sure to see in her
> house what there is that is best in Paris, and they themselves at times being the
> best to be found among foreigners, they augmented even more the consideration
> that had attracted them.[54]

Three mechanisms are at work in this text. The first was personal reputation. Men of letters were sought after in the "open houses" and their company was a source of consideration because they were known and famous.
"Let us be amiable," Madame Geoffrin would say when a prestigious person
paid her a visit.[55] The second mechanism was that of consideration, honorable judgment about someone, linked as much to their social situation as

to their person. Here La Harpe insists on financial independence, which demarcates clearly between men of letters and those who give dinners for them and renders their relationship necessarily asymmetrical. Finally, the third mechanism was that of good company as a whole. Terms like *la bonne compagnie* or *la meilleure compagnie* referred not to a social status, but to a worldly status. The circularity of practices and qualifications is at the heart of this text, summarized by the assertion that *tout est mode*. Indeed, fashionable places are those to which fashionable people go. Here *la mode* designated the arbitrary nature of signs of value and imitation in social practices. This circularity gave meaning to the exchange between the wealthy host and the men of letters that he or she received because it permitted the transmutation of cultural celebrity into social consideration.

Still, Madame Geoffrin had to take care to appear as a wealthy protector who opened her house to guests and not as a pedant. This imperative may seem to contradict the affectation of discretion imposed by the tradition of worldly generosity. In fact, the hostess must keep her distance from both the *femme savante* and the financier of ostentatious liberalities. It is clear, in the case of Madame Geoffrin, that a double effort was necessary to make public both her generosity and her disinterestedness. In 1773, the *Mémoires secrets*, whose echoes were always favorable to Madame Geoffrin, reported a new charitable gesture:

> There is word of a story that would show much honor to Madame Geoffrin if it proved to be true. It is said that when two Russian gentlemen appeared to have been strongly taken with two paintings that the lady had bought at the sale of the late Van Loo, she had told them that they had cost her only 4,000 livres and that she had no intention of getting rid of them; but if they were so passionately taken with them, perhaps, for the right price, she could let herself be tempted. It is added that when these foreigners agreed to the sum of 50,000 livres, Madame Geoffrin, having taken out the 4,000 livres they had cost her, sent the surplus to the painter's widow.[56]

This extract utilizes the semantic apparatus of rumor. In order to be favorable to the reputation of Madame Geoffrin, the anecdote had to circulate, but under the guise of divulging a secret. The gesture was honorable if it was at once true, kept secret, and revealed. In the context of the salon, social inequalities were both visible and hidden. Madame de La Ferté-Imbault described the Monday dinners at the house of her mother in these terms: "At this dinner Monsieur de Caylus presided, and he brought many of his friends—painters, sculptors, and art lovers—thus making my mother, like himself, the benefactress and protector of penniless young people who had talent, which promptly gave her the greatest reputation in a genre in which she at first had no knowledge."[57] Madame Geoffrin's reputation derived from her position as protector and benefactor, from the weekly hospitality that she offered to Caylus and his "friends," from the help she provided, and from the affirmation of her taste.

Protection and Friendship

The central notion that made sense of the relations between men of letters and their hosts was protection. That term included material aid (pensions, gifts), recommendations, and support in aristocratic and court circles, and it called for grateful recognition. This relation, in which the man of letters received from his hosts protection and gratifications in exchange for the prestige and the reputation that he procured for them, directly or indirectly, was asymmetrical, but unlike the patronage relation, it did not make this asymmetry public and ostentatious. Worldly protection drew its force and its utility from the fact that it borrowed the language of friendship and sociability, beneficence and gratitude. This is why manifestations of gratitude were not aimed at the public at large, but at high society. The task of the man of letters received in the salons was not to produce public eulogies of the great man, on the model of Condé or Louis XIV, but rather to contribute, by his presence and by what he said of them, to establishing the reputation of the various houses within *le monde*. Although gratitude had to be discreet, it was nonetheless imperative and vigorously imposed by the rules of worldliness. The greatest reproach that high society could put to a man of letters was that he was ungrateful.

Regular presence in the salons in which they had been welcomed was thus an obligation for men of letters and at times a constraint, for it derived from gratitude. Why did Diderot attend weekly gatherings around de Vaines? "Monsieur de Vaines is a gallant man, who has done me service without knowing me, who has demanded, for all recognition, that I go to his house one of the two days in the week that he sets aside for his friends, and which I would not miss without depriving him of his dearest company. I am punctual with him only because I am useful to him."[58] Repeated absences were held against them. Diderot is continually called to order by d'Holbach and Madame d'Épinay, who complain about his absences, in the name of friendship, of course, but also recalling the "attentions" they have shown him.[59] The society life was both a resource and a trap, for it soon became difficult to remain master of one's time, and Diderot was continually obliged to justify his absences to Madame d'Épinay. At times it was preferable to avoid having too many engagements. Marmontel, after the success of *Bélisaire*, refused an invitation under the pretext that, "in the impossibility in which I find myself to fulfil all the duties of society that I have imposed on myself for the last twenty years, I avoid forming new connections, and especially those that it would be indecent not to cultivate after having formed them."[60] Participating in a "society" meant taking on duties; entering into a relation of protection could be constraining.

The act of protecting a man of letters was a legitimate and even praise-worthy social activity for financiers as well as for the court aristocracy. Laurence Sterne presented the baron d'Holbach as "one of the most learned noble men here, the great protector of wits, and the Scavans who are no wits" and a man who "keeps open house three times a week."[61] The prince de Beauvau, Collé wrote, "was quite willing to protect."[62] The pro-tector became a social figure. Describing the memorial funeral service for Crébillon, Favart distinguished three categories among the attend-ees: "actors and actresses, men of letters, [and] protectors and lovers [of literature]."[63] That protection by no means contradicted the fictive egali-tarian language of politesse. Evoking the "tone of superiority" that the great retained in all circumstances, even when they tried to hide it, Collé invented the formula, "protectional politesse."[64] Protection even borrowed the language of friendship that Madame Geoffrin or the prince de Beauvau used with the authors whom they protected.

This association of an asymmetrical relation of protection with the lan-guage of friendship is important for understanding what was at stake in these practices of sociability. One way to resolve this seeming contradic-tion would be to see in the language of amity, as in politeness, a pure lie, of which both protectors and the protected were cynically aware and with which they veiled the true relation of an exchange in which each partner pursued his interest. That interpretation rests on a purely strategic and rational conception of language that permits no understanding of why aristocrats and men of letters utilized such a language even when the pro-tection relation, in itself, had nothing reprehensible. Against that directly utilitarian or economic conception of social relations, Pierre Bourdieu resolves the enigma of an asymmetrical exchange that presented itself as symmetrical by supposing that the asymmetry or the interest were nec-essarily denied or misunderstood by the actors themselves. Their strate-gies were unconscious and they misunderstood the relations of power and interest in which they were enmeshed. The observer, from his objective position, is the only one who knows what is happening in the dissimula-tion of the function of exchanges.[65] But Bourdieu's solution would sup-pose, in the context of salon sociability, that men of letters, largely blind to the mechanisms of protection, were entirely subject to the illusion of friendship, which permitted them to pursue their true interests with no afterthought. Everything proves, to the contrary, that men of letters were perfectly aware of the asymmetrical dimension of the relation. They were continually confronted by an imperative to justify their practices that forbade them to ignore that dimension. Criticism of the strategy that is hidden behind a proclaimed disinterest is not an objective position; it is a position of denunciation, occupied in the literary field by those who were excluded from such exchanges.

If we do not suppose that men of letters practiced a coolly calculating cynicism or were able to fool themselves about the reasons behind their practices, we still have to understand how they thought about it. Hence we have to pay attention to the terms utilized and the values that they communicate. In fact, the contrast between amity, which is necessarily egalitarian and disinterested, and relations of dependence is not universal, given that it relies on the distinction between an interested sphere of action and a sphere of private and affective relations.[66] In the modern era, as historians of aristocratic clienteles have shown, the relation of service and protection was usually spoken of in an affective language that mobilized the vocabulary of friendship.[67]

The friendship in which protection was dressed was thus not a deception hiding an interested relation, but rather the discourse that made that protection possible by giving it a new meaning. In 1766, when Mably obtained a pension of 4,000 livres thanks to the intervention of the duchesse d'Enville, whose salon he frequented assiduously, he presented it to his correspondents as a *grâce* due to *amitié*.[68] Protection and amity were two sides of the same relation. That relation did not only involve material benefactions. The duchess felt herself responsible for Mably's reputation, which was also her own reputation as the protector of a great writer. After Mably's death, she persuaded the Académie des Inscriptions to put a eulogy of Mably on its program.[69]

The vocabulary of benefaction (*bienfaisance*) and gratitude (*reconnaissance*) was part of a symbolic economy of protection. It permitted envisioning such an economy, even in its most material aspects, as a moral connection. The philosophes ceaselessly returned to the theme of a friendly benefaction that created an obligation of gratitude all the more binding for proclaiming itself disinterested. Duclos devoted the last chapter of his *Considérations sur les mœurs* to gratitude and ingratitude, and Jaucourt took inspiration from that text to denounce the "ferocious passion" of ingratitude in the *Encyclopédie*, listing it as one of the most odious vices.[70] Delille wrote "Ode à la bienfaisance," which contrasts that quality with a condescending and proud generosity. *La bienfaisance* was the art of the wealthy and the powerful bringing help to those in need of it while dissimulating the distance that separated the benefactor from those who received his benefactions.[71]

An entire historiographical tradition has insisted on seeing in the salons an element of the growing autonomy of the literary field, not just as an instance of consecration, but also as a physical space in which the social and political emancipation of authors would be recognized. In reality, these social practices were inscribed in a relation of dependence that was one of protection. That did not prevent the salons from being places in which writers' prestige was recognized, and the social consecration of literary activity did not necessarily imply the autonomy of authors. The "paradox" studied by Christian Jouhaud, who shows that in the seventeenth century the affirmation of an authorial identity could be made through the reinforcement of connections of dependence toward the powers that be, offers insights for the eighteenth century as well.[72] Men of letters found in the relation of protection resources, both material and symbolic, for fashioning their social identity. The egalitarian discourse of politesse and friendship was a fiction, in the sense of a discourse based on practices (hospitality, conviviality, being fellow guests) that lent them meaning and permitted the creation and expression of personal identities. That fiction was not to be taken for granted, however. It corresponded to a new and fragile situation from which only a few profited. It was a permanent topic of debate and one that staked out its own polemic space in debates on the social identity of writers. Practices of sociability lay at the heart of those debates.

TOPICS OF THE WRITER

The representations of worldly sociability nourished a polemic in which intellectual considerations were inseparable from debates on the social identity of men of letters. At the height of the anti-philosophe offensive, Palissot depicted the Encyclopedists in the salon of a fashionable lady, and Voltaire responded by writing a new play showing Fréron, a friend and ally of Palissot, in a café. Diderot later wrote *Le Neveu de Rameau*, in which Palissot is presented as a parasite of the financier Bertin. Understanding the role of worldly sociability for the writers, not only as a source of material benefits, but also as a symbolic resource, requires restoring the ways in which that polemical space operated. When eighteenth-century writers described their social practices, their remarks were based on argumentative traditions, on commonplaces, and on well-tested literary resources that occasionally required the elaboration of new forms of criticism or justification.[73]

The intellectual context was the crisis of the republic of letters as a normative model. Whereas that ideal had dominated representations of scholarly activity from the Renaissance to the mid-seventeenth century, it no longer had many adherents, at least in France and especially where belles-lettres were concerned. The increasing gap between normative principles and social practices, after the establishment of the academy system and royal patronage, ruined the ideological power of the republic of letters. Even those who were most attached to the idea, like d'Alembert, found it difficult to give it coherent expression and hesitated between praise of the academy system and criticism of it.[74] The expression " republic of letters" was rarely used outside erudite circles and did not belong to the cultural universe of the Enlightenment, in particular that of the philosophes.[75] The elements that remained, notably a certain ideal of intellectual communication and autonomy, no longer offered the coherence of a legitimate representation of intellectual work as a social activity. Those ideals were reinvested and refashioned within new topics that provided a foundation for the social identity of literary operatives.

The Man of Letters as an *Homme du Monde*

The dominant topic was the topic of worldliness. A writer must be an *honnête homme* and adhere to the values of *la bonne société*. Within that framework, the model of the "man of letters" was a more legitimate reference than "writer" (*écrivain*) or "author" (*auteur*). The man of letters was distinguished by his lack of specialization, by his capacity for excelling in different literary genres, by his mastery of codes of behavior elaborated by the urban aristocracy, and by a disinterest in things financial. Adhering to the practices and values of the urban elites was expressed in the notion of *honnêteté* claimed by men of letters.[76]

Voltaire most fully elaborated on this topic in several texts, the most famous of which is the article "Gens de lettres" in the *Encyclopédie*. For Voltaire, the man of letters could "proceed from the thorns of mathematics to the flowers of poetry, and judge equally well a book of metaphysics and a work of drama." Cultivated and eclectic, both in his tastes and his areas of competence, the man of letters constructed himself as opposed to three figures: the erudite man, who is depicted as a pedant; the *bel esprit*, or wit, who possessed a certain charm and brilliance, but lacked "culture" and true "philosophy"; and the professional author, who intended to live by his writings. One of Voltaire's favorite themes, sketched out in this text, was a denunciation of the mercenary author as a famished scribbler. In his "Questions sur l'*Encyclopédie*" (1770), he developed at length a critique of "the unhappy species who write to live," comparing them to "bands of mendicant friars" and denouncing them as "the scorn and the horror even of the rabble." He opposes *gens de lettres* to simple authors, "hack writers," who, "chased out of society," must write to eat. His conclusion is definitive: "One commonly scorns an author who is only an author."[77]

Voltaire did not define the man of letters by the professional practice of writing, for "there are many men of letters who are not authors."[78] He situated the man of letters as much on the side of judgment as on that of production, and stated that the judgment of those who do not write, on the condition that it was founded on taste and study, was surer than that of authors, because it was sheltered "from the quarrels that rivalry breeds, from the animosities of partisanship, and from false judgments."[79] Still, Voltaire also asserted the importance of study and criticized sheer wit (*le bel esprit*). Because of that tension, he did not define the man of letters, but proclaimed the novelty of this cultural figure. The *Encyclopédie* article is constructed on praise of "our century," which had inaugurated a new era for men of letters typified by the philosophical spirit and access to *le monde*. He identifies the philosophical spirit as a denunciation of superstition and a rejection of scholasticism: "Today this criticism is less necessary, and the philosophic spirit has replaced it"; "their criticism is no longer wasted on Greek and Latin words." Access to "society," which had begun in the previous century (writers "were kept out of society until the time of [Jean-Louis Guez de] Balzac and [Vincent] Voiture; they have since made it a necessary allegiance"), is one of their principal titles of glory: "The spirit of the century has for the most part rendered them as fit for the world as for the study, and it is here where they are much superior to those of preceding centuries." By placing them in the same paragraph, Voltaire firmly links the philosophical spirit with access to places of worldly sociability, and he uses criticism of scholasticism, erudition, and pedantry to reinforce the connection.

For Voltaire, the entry of writers into the worldly scene was part of a conscious strategy for promoting philosophy by aiming at the social elites and winning over the spheres of aristocratic civility. In that way, it could establish its respectability, prove to the sources of power that it was innocuous, and win over the good opinion of those who led the public. "You are the good company, thus it is for you to govern the public," he wrote to Helvétius.[80] In another letter to Helvétius he expressed his thoughts more fully:

My dear philosophe, there is little that can be done about it, once a nation sets to thinking, it is impossible to prevent it from doing so. This century begins to be the triumph of reason. The Jesuits, the Jansenists, the hypocrites of the robe [the legal professions], the hypocrites of the court, shout out in vain, they will not find anything but horror and scorn among the right sort of people [*les honnêtes gens*]. It is in the interest of the king that the number of philosophes is growing, and that of the fanatics is diminishing. We are tranquil, and all of those people are disturbers. We are citizens and they are seditious. We cultivate reason in peace and they persecute it. They may burn a good book or two, but we will crush them in society, we will reduce them to being without credit in good company, and it is good company alone that governs the opinions of men. Brother Élisée [J. F. Coppel, an extremely popular Carmelite preacher] will lead a few idlers, Brother Menou a few fools from Nancy; there will still be some who promote convulsions on the fifth floor, but the good servants of reason and the king will triumph in Paris, in Voré, and even at Les Délices.[81]

Honnêtes gens, la bonne compagnie, la société—these were Voltaire's targets and the first milieus that had to be won over to the philosophical cause. His representation of the intellectual and political space was elitist, segmented, and vertical, inseparable from a scornful view of an unstable and easily influenced public. As a strategy that demanded the occupation of the worldly space, it corresponded to Voltaire's own aspirations, beginning with his debut in aristocratic circles, then in his hopes and disappointments as a courtier of Louis XV and Frederick II, including his life as the lord of Ferney. He consistently exhibited the same ideal of *honnêteté* incarnated in the man of the world of letters: "You say that most men of letters are not very likable, and you are right," he wrote to Madame Du Deffand, "one must be a man of the world before being a man of letters. This is the merit of Président Hénault. One would never guess that he worked as hard as a Benedictine."[82] Voltaire's idea was shared by the better part of the philosophical milieu in Paris. It constituted a topic in the sense that it furnished a repertory of values and arguments, and it was used as soon as the norms of the activity of men of letters were a matter of debate, whatever the context, whether in literary correspondence or in academic discourse.

Grimm made wide use of this topic. As an intermediary between the Parisian literary world and the European high nobility, he developed his own thoughts on the subject in the pages of the *Correspondance littéraire*. He lampooned *le bel esprit*,[83] but, above all, he constantly combatted the idea that writing books was in itself a prestigious social activity. An author could be a genius or a very bad writer; no glory derived from that professional definition.[84] Palissot or Fréron, he insisted, were not to be confused with Voltaire.[85] If Grimm found Voltaire worthy of respect, the other two men inspired only scorn in him. Thus, there was no unity among writers: "I do not believe in a corps of men of letters, nor in the respect that they demand, nor in the supremacy that they attempt to usurp, nor in any of their pretensions." Grimm preferred commerce among *bons esprits* and ideological complicity: "I believe in the communion of the faithful, that is, in the gathering of that elite of excellent minds, elevated souls, delicate and sensitive, dispersed here and there on the surface of the globe, nonetheless recognizing one another and understanding one another from one end of the universe to the other, and [I believe] in the unity of ideas, impressions, and sentiments."[86] Against the professional cohesion of men of letters, Grimm appealed to an elitist ideal of the unity of enlightened minds and of people of taste.

Jean-Baptiste Suard was one of the most determined defenders of the Voltairean topic.[87] He was both an enlightened writer, close to the Encyclopedists, and a classical man, fascinated by the model of Louis XIV.[88] The social ties between men of letters and socialites seemed to him adequate for prolonging that model, which was both social and literary. Called to deliver a discourse to the Académie Française, he took advantage of the opportunity to launch into a theory of worldliness. The model of sociability that governed the relationships between men of letters and men of high society in both the salons and at court, helped ensure the universal empire of the French language, since it made French "at once the language of gallantry and that of philosophy." Good taste, like politeness, resulted simultaneously from social convenience, of which high society held the secret, the "desire to distinguish oneself," and a cultural model rooted in the "exemplary sociability of the Nation."[89]

Some nuances aside, most writers shared the conviction that frequenting the "world" was necessary for a man of letters to learn urbane manners and fine language. The article "Dictionnaire de langues" in the *Encyclopédie* states that the ideal dictionary must be the work of a "man of letters who frequents the great world."[90] The worldly point of view, as expressed by Madame de Genlis, was even more abrupt: "An author should live in the great world. If he dedicates to society four hours of the day, there will still remain time enough to reflect on what he has seen."[91]

This topic draws its strength from its ability to associate some traditional ideals of the scholarly community with the redefinition of aristocratic value within the ways of high society. It returns to some elements of the republic of letters, such as the idea of courtesy in discussions and controversies and the refusal to indulge in personal and injurious attacks.[92] It thus contributed to legitimizing the figure of the writer as a man of the world and offered an intellectual caution to the symbolic operation of establishing worldliness as a social value. This topic and the idealization of high society sealed the alliance between Enlightenment writers and a cluster of social elites. *Le Journal des gens du monde* gives eloquent evidence of that convergence. Published by the marquis de Luchet, a friend and disciple of Voltaire, the *Journal* ceaselessly defended that topic, praised Voltaire as *maître de maison*, promoted wit, wrote that it is "easier to write well than to speak well," and praised the duc de Nivernais and the comtesse de Beauharnais, two prime representatives of this alliance between writers and high society.

The Test of Satire

The worldly topic of the man of letters was highly successful because it promoted an ideal of achievement for writers that was not based on the professional act of writing. It justified attending salons and seeking protection. Still, that topic was not hegemonic. A writer such as Charles Collé, for example, adhered to a different, and more traditional representation of the writer, which rested on a very clear distinction between the social status of the writer and that of aristocrats. The true model that regulated a writer's relationship with the aristocracy was based on patronage, and if the writer contributed to aristocratic forms of entertainment, it was because he was paid to furnish poems or plays as the secretary of a prince or an aristocrat. At the same time, the writer's practices of sociability took him beyond the spaces of high society, preferring places like the cabaret or the theatre, because the writer must "live with his equals, step back from the aristocracy, and shun the people of quality."

> This is what I have put into practice since 1737; and although I have been admitted into the courts of M. de Clermont and M. le duc d'Orléans, to whom I have been and am currently attached, nevertheless I have not ceded to the advances that the lords who surround those princes have made to me; I have prohibited myself from [attending] their suppers and living with them; I have pushed them away with politeness and respect; I have lived uniquely with my equals and have found myself quite content. I did, it is true, learn in my youth that the earthen pot must not travel with the iron pot.[93]

For Collé, the hauteur of the aristocrats and their "tone of superiority" were not condemnable but inevitable. Rather than denouncing an injustice, he stated a fact, recommended a posture of modesty, and drew the consequences. He contrasted the politeness and the protections that were the organizing principles of the life of salons to patronage and the sociability of writers among their fellows in the tavern or the café. Such an image of the writer had inspired a crowd of authors throughout the eighteenth century and guided their careers, their friendships, and their discourse just as surely as worldly success had guided Suard and Morellet and seemed to them an enviable fate. These writers had their own model of sociability, of which the society of the *caveau* was symbolic: they met there together and each paid his share of the meal. The rules of civility were sacrificed to gaiety and drunkenness.[94] Collé contrasted the friendship of writers and their frankness in the tavern to the customs of high society. In his eyes, the equilibrium that Voltaire preached, where the man of letters, turned man of the world, holds himself at an equal distance from the pedant and from the wit, was a chimera, because the men of letters who frequented *le monde* lost their way in it and became *beaux esprits*. Collé concluded: "It is a great misfortune for men of letters that they no longer live among themselves, as they used to do; the tavern was a free place where they spoke truth. Now, each of them lives in a world of which he is the sun and to which he thinks he gives light; each social whirl these days has its *bel esprit* sun, whom it spoils by airs, by pretension, by self-love, by vanity, or otherwise."[95]

Similarly, it was on the terrain of sociability that the partisans of *honnêteté* responded to him. Grimm attacked the dinners of the fermier général Le Pelletier, at which Collé had been a guest, and where frankness and gaiety were the rule: "If gaiety could not be found in a circle without admitting debauchery, biting and bitter pleasantries, tough ways and manners, I would renounce gaiety."[96] Frankness, which Collé praised, was disqualified in the name of politeness, measure, and *honnêteté*. Given the European crowned heads who were among his readers, Grimm placed himself on the level of connivance: "you can easily judge how agreeable, polite, and *honnête* that commerce was bound to be." Immediate reprobation should be aroused by such sociability. Finally, by denouncing the opposition that such writers established between "gaiety" and "cold reason," Grimm explicitly placed himself on the terrain of ideological confrontations, given that reason was associated, within the literary field, with the figure of the "philosophe." Like Voltaire, Grimm refuted the opposition of reason and gaiety by proposing politeness and gentle manners as vectors of a fruitful association of those two qualities. To the "hardness" of customs and manners, the philosopher opposed the symbiosis of reason and gaiety under the auspices of polite entertainment.[97]

Palissot's play *Les Philosophes* represents an essential episode in the polemics aimed at the Encyclopedists, whom he places in a salon that is recognizably that of Madame Geoffrin. Ideological criticism (the morality of individual interest, irreligion) is doubled by a satire of the worldly practices of the intellectuals, a satire that lies at the heart of both the play and the scandal. Palissot's attack used the weapons of satire and comedy borrowed from the seventeenth-century repertoire; it was directly inspired by Molière's *Les femmes savantes*. *Les Philosophes* also borrowed themes from a play by Gresset, *Le Méchant*, which had met with great success in 1747 and which featured Cléon, a libertine hypocrite, who lived in the house of Orgonte and manipulated the credulity of his host, but also that of his wife, Florisse, whom he courted.[98] This quite obviously resembled the plot of *Tartuffe*, with the important difference that false religious devotion has been replaced by worldliness, politeness, and wit.

Palissot imported this hypocrisy into the literary field, focusing on the relations between authors and a hostess. The salon became a privileged setting for a confusion of ranks. While classic patronage devised a hierarchy and fixed each person in his place, worldly sociability hid that asymmetry, and hypocrisy shuffled the cards by trying to convert the high social status of the protectors into literary greatness. The violence exerted on a manipulated host sets off another sort of violence, one that occurs within the literary space and claims to impose on it a heterogeneous grandeur founded on participation in high society. The "tyranny" for which their adversaries so often reproached the philosophes consisted of an illegitimate transfer of grandeur from the worldly sphere to the literary sphere.[99]

Comedy and satire lent themselves to unveiling hypocrisy. They were genres often utilized by authors who are hard to situate in any ideological category, who had little in common with Catholic apologetics and stood violently opposed to the Encyclopedists. Palissot himself used them repeatedly, from *La Dunciade* to *L'Homme dangereux*.[100] His friend Poinsinet wrote a comedy in 1764 entitled *Le Cercle*, in which it was easy to recognize the salon of Madame de Beauharnais. Spurred on by Palissot's difficulties, Poinsinet did not attack the hypocrisy of writers, but rather the vanity of fashionable society and the scorn with which aristocrats viewed authors.[101]

The genre continued to thrive after the polemics of the 1760s. In *Le Bureau d'esprit*, published in 1776, Rutlidge returned to Palissot's plot lines and produced a transparent satire of the salon of Madame Geoffrin, who was dying at the time.[102] The fictional hostess says of one young poet, "I protect him, he will be in my Academy; thus his reputation is assured; but the point is to sell his work, and that is not so easy." Her sole piece of advice to her daughter is, "Always protect."[103] The aim of this play was to denounce the protection relationships and the coterie reflexes of the Encyclopedists' boosters, but a second edition published the following year was prefaced by a violent critique of the "philosophical sect" and its "persecutions" of literature. Dorat, in turn, preceded his comedy *Merlin bel esprit* with an "Epistle to the great men of the coteries," which sharply attacked the philosophes, their arrogance, and the salons they frequented: "Your Sévignés are silly chatterboxes."[104]

Satire and comedy were the favorite weapons of those intent upon unveiling the hypocrisy of the philosophes, who in turn reproached their adversaries for their lack of civility and politeness. In Diderot's *Le Neveu de Rameau*, all those who had attacked the sociability of the philosophes are presented as the "fools" of the financier Bertin. Guided by interest alone, frequenting "bad company," in which none of the standards of the *grand monde* were respected, they are dehumanized, branded as animals, and compared to "wolves," "tigers," or "a menagerie."[105] Nothing could be further from worldly customs and the ideal of the man of letters than this noisy, sweating, and gesticulating Nephew whose conversations Diderot takes care to situate in a café.[106] Diderot attacks the ridiculous flatteries that the Nephew and his friends lavish on their patron and his wife, condemning them as archaic relics.

The Patriotic Writer

Rousseau's criticism of worldly society was much more radical than mere satire of wit and conversation. He not only attacked the presence of men of letters in the salons, but also the foundations of *politesse*. *Julie, ou, la Nouvelle Héloïse* eloquently reworks the main themes of criticism of *le monde* as a space of hypocrisy, falsity, and vacuousness. The letters that Saint-Preux writes from Paris mock conversation in Parisian salons, where "one learns to plead with art the cause of the lie, to shake off, thanks to philosophy, all the principles of virtue, to color one's passions and one's prejudices with subtle sophisms, and to give error a certain fashionable twist, according to the maxims of the day."[107] As in the first of his *Discours*, where Rousseau begins with conventional praise of the culture that he then attacks, Saint-Preux's first letter contains praise of worldly conversation that is close to parody and that Rousseau takes care, in the printed edition, to qualify as "well-worn commonplaces."[108] After a few pages, however, Saint-Preux becomes more critical of the salon's hypocrisy: "No one ever says what he thinks, but what it is convenient for him to make others think; and the apparent zeal for truth is never in them anything but the mark of interest." It is impossible to trust anything; the words that are spoken refer only to a perfectly codified social game in which one's words, one's convictions, and one's acts are in no way related. The essence of Saint-Preux's criticism is that he sees actors, totally deprived of inner thoughts, and uniquely focused on the effect produced: "Up to now I have seen many masks; when shall I see the faces of men?"[109] Rousseau views this permanent theatricality as a dehumanization, and at this point, the metaphor of the theater is rivaled by those of automats, mechanical contraptions, and marionettes. The "spectacle" offered by high society has a terrifying monotony: "You will say that these are so many marionettes nailed to the same board or pulled by the same string."[110]

Had Rousseau limited himself to this criticism, he might have been simply a censor of fashionable society, of self-centeredness, and of futile conversations. The force of his denunciation, however, broke with the previous century's tradition. Julie reproaches Saint-Preux for adopting the tone of high society he stigmatizes even in letters unveiling its lies.[111] His style, she tells him, betrays worldly contamination; the *gentillesse* of his carefully shaped expressions replaces the lively and natural flow that denotes the force of sentiment. She reproaches him with judging too rapidly, on appearances, and with "moralizing at the expense of his hosts." In the long run, she warns him: "I hold as suspect any observer who takes pride in his wit; I always fear that, without thinking it so, he sacrifices the truth of things to the brilliance of thoughts, and plays with his phrases at the expense of fairness."[112] In short, the danger that lurked for the satirist was to fall prey to the very failings that he denounced, to sacrifice authenticity.

Forced to agree, Saint-Preux then reaches a higher level of generality and discourse, passing from "national satire" to "philosophical observation."[113] He no longer mocks the national conversation; the things that had to be understood and denounced were the effects of economic and social modernity, life in the big cities, and the sociological laws that impose the authority of a small group of wealthy people, "a handful of impertinents who count only themselves in the universe and are hardly worth the trouble of counting, if not for the evil that they do there."[114] Satire becomes social criticism, blended with Rousseau's political theses against the corruption of the wealthy.[115]

The salons, however, also corrupt the philosopher. Rousseau argued against those who asserted that the man of letters must live in high society order to know it: after a few weeks, Saint-Preux is "completely in the flow," moving from theatrical spectacles to "suppers in the city."[116] When he plunges into high society, Saint-Preux loses himself, floats "from caprice to caprice." He ends up doubting his own sentiments, and painfully acknowledges his own degradation. He experiences the conflict between the external honors of opinion and the sentiment of "inner grandeur" that he feels when he is with Julie.[117]

Saint-Preux thus discovers, following the example of Rousseau himself, the paradox of the philosopher in *le monde*, who cannot escape the failings that he denounces, even when he claims to raise himself to the level of critic.[118] Even while denouncing the abusive role of a small minority of the aristocracy and the worldly taste of writers who choose their characters and their subjects exclusively from within that restricted elite, Saint-Preux does the same thing in his letters, as Julie rather sharply points out.[119] Rousseau had experienced much the same thing at the start of his career, when he frequented Parisian high society and benefitted from the success of his first *Discours*.[120]

On the philosophical level, Rousseau's criticism of salon life was aimed at the reign of individual interests, which prohibited all communication, all true exchange, and, in a word, all sociability.[121] True sociability, which implies a strong inner presence and a convergence of sentiments, was possible either in the harmony of a small circle of close friends or in the political fusion of the city. Rousseau himself never claimed to be a "man of letters". Quite the contrary. His rupture with the world and his egalitarian ideal implied a radical refusal both of the traditional conception of patronage, as illustrated by Palissot, and of the worldly conception of protection, granted under the cover of a fictive friendship, that was the foundation of the social identity of the man of letters. Rousseau's refusal of protections and protectors reinforced his rupture with the aristocratic milieus that had been favorable to him: Madame d'Épinay, Conti, Madame de Luxembourg.[122] He mistrusted "donors, eager for the glory of overcoming my resistence and of forcing me to be obliged to them in spite of myself."[123] And he denounced protection as an attack on his autonomy: "I would soon have been reduced to exhibiting myself, like Punchinello, at a charge of so much per person."[124] Every donation, every gift seemed to him an intolerable charge on his independence; once, he sent back in a fury a basket of game from the prince de Conti.[125] Both aristocrats and Encyclopedists reproached him for his ingratitude; on the other hand, his attitude attests to the asymmetry that underlay worldly exchange. Rousseau unveiled the nature of the amity between men of letters and aristocrats: he denounced the terms of the exchange and declared the writer's independence.[126]

Declaring himself a citizen author; with neither a place nor a political sphere to call his own, he claimed his only "place" as the works he had written and the personage had created for himself and whose acts and statements were reported in gazettes throughout Europe. While fairly systematically breaking his ties with his friends and protectors, he wove others with his innumerable readers—through reading[127] Roussseau, who had genuine success in the bookshops, paid careful attention to his publications.[128] He represented a totally new conception of the public, one quite different from that of the principal stars of the Paris Enlightenment, for whom only the enlightened opinion of a small number mattered. That Rousseau's readers were many within Paris "society" changed nothing: Rousseau's relation with his public rested on an ideal of sentimental identification.

The political dimension, the striving for autonomy, the appeal to the public, and the pursuit of social criticism all clearly distinguished the topic of Rousseau from the criticisms to which Collé or Palissot subjected the sphere of worldly sociability. A similar distance separated Rousseau and Molière, Palissot's avowed model. Where Molière mocked excess, Rousseau attacked the very foundation of that classical morality by opposing to it a radically different morality of disinterest and the heart's transparency. At base, Palissot and Voltaire spoke the same language, that of a morality in which friendship and interest were not incompatible. Rousseau overturned the edifice, as he made it clear in his *Lettre à d'Alembert sur les spectacles*, the basic text of his rupture with the philosophes, in which he denounced Parisian high society and attacked Molière, accusing him of having rendered virtue ridiculous by allowing *la bonne société* to laugh at Alceste in *Le Misanthrope*.[129]

Rousseau's denunciation of worldliness offered writers new resources for thinking about their activity, for conducting their careers, and for justifying their social practices. In the early 1770s, it echoed the new "patriotic" language. Such statements borrow even their form from the literary repertory of drama, but also from a Rousseauist discourse of persecuted innocence and transparency of sentiment and from an appeal to the public.[130] This new political language spoke of *la patrie* and *la nation* as legitimate communities, as opposed to the voice of the sovereign or to high society.[131] It denounced both absolutism and the corruption of morals, and it aspired to regenerating the homeland by transforming the national character, judged to be overly futile, and returning to a policy of virtue of republican inspiration.[132] Contrary to the politeness of *le monde*, the patriots proposed a quite different conception of virtue founded on simplicity of customs, the language of sentiment, and a stricter separation between the private and the public spheres. Against the effects of distinction and reputation typical of high society, they set up their own judgment, identifying with the public of their readers.

For writers at the end of the ancien régime, the combination of the figure and the work of Rousseau and patriotic political discourse provided a

full range of topics for criticism of academic institutions and worldly sociability, alongside a framework for reading works (virtue, and a rupture with
worldly topics and with wit) and a strategy (appeal to the public, which was
no longer identified with *le monde* but with the "nation"). Rousseau's posture as a writer, his stylistic choices, and the representation of high society
in his writings helped to create the attitudes of the patriot writers at the
end of the ancien régime in their sweeping denunciation of worldliness,
wit, and despotism. For newcomers, experience of the literary field was
hard to obtain: the easy posts seemed to have been distributed already, and
access to the academies, the Comédie-Française, and the salons was difficult. There were, however, new representations of the possible relations
between the writer and society.

The appearance of a new language and new strategies for self-presentation
allowed authors of the two last decades of the ancien régime to break with
the model of the *honnête homme*. They experimented with new ways of
expressing their identity as writers, presenting themselves as "patriots"
guided by the interest of the public.[133] Worldliness was a prime target,
given that it permitted denouncing both aristocratic luxury and writers'
submission to socialites.

The autonomy of men of letters became a political and patriotic imperative. Alliance with *le monde* must be followed by alliance with the people. In
this new framework, *politesse* was no longer denounced as hypocrisy, but
as social violence. "There is a politeness more humiliating than haughti-
ness; it is that of the Great," as Grimod de La Reynière wrote, to pick only
one example.[134] Moral criticism of appearances was succeeded by a political
criticism of social domination.

Models and Identity

These topics permit us to gain a better understanding of literary life at the
end of the ancien régime. Writers made use of coherent groups of values
and arguments when they denounced the practices of their adversaries or
when they were called on to justify themselves.[135] Of course, these topics
are rarely found in a "pure" form except in some manifestos, as most writers
occupied and defended complex positions, shifting according to biographical events and conscious or unconscious strategies for adapting to changing political or literary circumstances. In the 1770s, for example, Mercier
served as the archetype of the patriot author. In his combative *Du théâtre*,
he takes on Rousseauist accents to denounce satirical comedy and its com-
promise with fashionable society: "Irony becomes the favorite figure of the

poet because it is that of the *beau monde*, and that *beau monde* is composed of three to four hundred conceited fops who do not know how to exist."[136] Other texts show, however, that Mercier could not totally renounce a certain fascination for the prestige of worldliness, wit, and polite conversation: "The man who lives in society and in a society in which ranks are unequal, in which functions cross one another, soon feels that laws need a supplement, which is politeness; it recalls a sort of equality; it announces an underlying beneficence."[137]

Among the philosophes, Diderot presents a particularly interesting case. If many philosophes seem to have had little doubt about the wisdom of Voltaire's strategy and the worldly topic of the man of letters, Diderot remained haunted by a Rousseauist remorse. In 1757–58 he had chosen his camp, broken with Rousseau, and, under the guidance of his friend Grimm, embraced a career as a man of letters and was received as a guest by Madame d'Épinay, the baron d'Holbach, and Madame Necker. Rousseau thought that the rupture was not a question of incompatibility of humors, but a choice of a lifestyle. "Diderot," he wrote to Madame d'Épinay, "is now an *homme du monde*."[138] Unlike Grimm, however, Diderot was no more at ease in the salons than his old friend was. Madame Geoffrin preferred not to receive him, and he seems not to have gone to the receptions of Julie de Lespinasse or Madame d'Enville. He long remained persuaded that the protections assured by his acquaintances in high society would enable him to bring the *Encyclopédie* to publication. What was important was to conserve his independence of mind. Still, he finally had doubts, especially when he was obliged to suffer the uneven humor of the baron d'Holbach and the reproaches of Madame d'Épinay. Diderot complained often of the solicitations of his "friends," who wanted to impose worldly constraints on him. "Those people do not want me to be me," he wrote to Sophie Volland about Grimm and d'Holbach. "I shall plant them all there, and live in a hole. That project has been rolling about my head for a long time."[139] What if Rousseau had been right? What if, despite his folly, about which Diderot had no doubts, he had seen clearly when he stressed the impossibility of being virtuous and independent while surrounded by Parisian dissipation?

To exorcize that doubt, on which the entire question of the relations between writing and the power structure depended, Diderot wrote *Le Neveu de Rameau*, a work in which the dialogue form in no way reflects worldly conversation, but rather expresses inner turmoil. This work included a virulent attack on Palissot and his friends, but the "Bertin menagerie" was a convenient adversary. The challenge of *Le Neveu* was greater: it threatened the basic position of the philosophe in his confrontation with the histrionic figure of the bad conscience. Diderot had to keep conjuring up the figure of the Nephew to assure himself that he was not, like his character, a flattering valet, an illusionist, and a parasite of the great.

In a long letter to an anonymous addressee published in 1776 in the *Correspondance littéraire*, Diderot remarked: "I will never joke with a *grand*; pleasantry is a beginning of familiarity that I do not wish to grant nor take with men who overuse it so easily and whom it is so easy to offend." The man of letters should "prefer the society of his equals, with whom he can augment his enlightenment and whose praise is almost the only [kind] that can flatter him, to [the society of] the great, from whom he has only vices to gain to repay him for the loss of his time. He is with them like a tightrope dancer: between lowness and arrogance. Lowness bends its knee; arrogance raises up its head; the worthy man holds his straight."[140] The road that Diderot had chosen was a narrow one, at some distance from both the submission of the protégé and rupture à la Rousseau. The comedy of domination, relations with protectors, and the will to continue, even at the cost of compromising one's sensibility, are justified only if the enterprise is worth it, and if one is not one's own dupe. Diderot's last years were thus years of remorse and justification.

His *Essai sur les règnes de Claude et de Néron* was an explicit reflection on the role of the philosopher. In the second edition Diderot introduced a long critique of Rousseau's folly and ingratitude. Those vibrant lines were less a satire than his own "apology."[141] The entire text is infused with self-justification, and it ends with a series of self-directed questions ("Am I an *homme de bien*?") and questions about Seneca ("Are Seneca and Burrhus *honnêtes gens*, or are they only two cowardly courtiers?") that express the nub of the problem. Can one be an *honnête homme* and live in the world without being a courtier? For a man of letters, is solitude not the better choice? "Whatever the advantages attached to commerce with *gens du monde* for a scholar, a philosopher, and even a man of letters, and although I am aware of those advantages, I dare believe that his talent and his customs will find themselves better from the society of his friends, solitude, and reading the great authors, from an examination of his own heart, and from frequent consultation with himself, and that very rarely will he have occasion to hear, in the best constituted circles, anything as good as what he says to himself in his withdrawal."[142] Torn between justification and implication, Diderot finally seems to tip toward doubt and skepticism. His litany of questions ends on a skeptical note: "Agree, reader, that you know nothing about it."

Rousseau chose the radical path. Diderot represented the other face of the modern writer, defined both by his responsibility and his uneasy conscience, ceaselessly choosing between concessions to his times and the mirage of the beautiful soul, and permanently subject to the imperative of justification.

THE INVENTION OF SOCIABILITY

From Civility to *Politesse*

While debates over civility are often closely associated with the seven-teenth century, civility and politeness remained the subject of many publications in the following century. Collections of maxims and precepts about how to succeed at court and in high society were still popular. *La Nouvelle école du monde, nécessaire à tous les états et principalement à ceux qui veulent s'avancer dans le monde*, by the prolific writer Alexis-Jean Le Bret, was a fairly conventional accumulation of worldly precepts (do not speak at too great length; do not interrupt others; do not speak of yourself or be rude or affected) that made no attempt to provide any moral or philosophical justification of those precepts.[143] The archetype of the genre in the eighteenth century was Moncrif's *Essai sur la nécessité et sur les moyens de plaire*, published in 1738, a work that went through several editions and that Voltaire admired. Equally at ease at the court as in the Parisian world, knowing how to please both the queen, for whom he wrote religious poems, and actresses, for whom he wrote libertine verse, Moncrif was a prime example of a man of letters and courtier, whose social ubiquity was based on his ability to please.[144] Far from any moralistic ambition, the work proposed an enchanted vision of society in which the desire to please provided politeness with the sentiment lacking in ceremonial.[145] The genre became increasingly pragmatic during the second half of the eighteenth century. Abandoning all psychological reflection, it was reduced to just practical advice. Pons-Augustin Alletz, for example, published a *Manuel de l'homme du monde* that cited Moncrif and was mostly a dictionary of general culture.[146] Written for provincials who had come to Paris, for foreigners, and for young people making their entrance into the world, the work is a minor *vade mecum* that completely adheres to the worldly norms it publicizes.

Another current in the writings on civility was the Christian redefinition of *honnêteté*. In the late seventeenth century, the tension between the idea of universal civility and the worldly norms of *honnêteté* deeply involved the religious question. What place should religious precepts, which were supposed to regulate the behavior and direct the upbringing of children, have in civility? Erasmian humanism had not been impermeable to the religious dimension of social norms, but it held that dimension at a distance and founded its ethics on the identity of appearances and being, a stance that Jansenists and moralists challenged during the second half of the seventeenth century.[147] Before this attack, Antoine de Courtin was the first to attempt a Christian redefinition of civility. He was not rethinking

Erasmus's civility for children, but rather worldly *honnêteté* and the rules for life at court that were based on the hierarchy of estates. Jean-Baptiste de La Salle, on the other hand, returned to Erasmus's project, but inspired by Courtin's work.[148] The notion of *bienséance*, as central to La Salle's work as it is to Courtin's, connects moral teaching and a respect for social distinctions. On the one hand, civility for children, which overlaps the worldly rules, becomes autonomous and offers a specific corpus destined to the education of the young and to incorporation into social norms.[149] On the other hand, the works of Courtin and De La Salle inspired many publications that attempted to reconcile Christian morality and the rules of a worldly *honnêteté* identified with the court and, in particular, with Parisian high society. *L'Honnête homme chrétien*, published in 1715, used the *honnête homme* as a slogan, simply equating the formula with the virtuous man.[150] Other authors attempted a real synthesis. The most famous of those was Jean-Baptiste Morvan de Bellegarde, who published a number of impressive works on civility in the late seventeenth century, but also treatises on Christian morality.[151] Bellegarde's criticism of the abuses of the court society was an important step in the Christian redefinition of worldly civility, and it had many imitators in the eighteenth century, like François Marin, who published in 1751 *L'homme aimable*, a treaty of the "fine gentleman." This was a socially conservative work, which proposed smooth behavior and defended a nonegalitarian world.[152] One cannot be an *homme aimable*, Marin stated, "without submitting oneself entirely to the yoke of religion."[153]

A third attempt to reformulate the idea of *honnêteté* was the insistence on the secular and moral dimension of politeness, founded on natural law and sociability rather than on theories of Christian politeness. The first episode was the now forgotten, but then highly important book by François-Vincent Toussaint, a friend of Diderot and Grimm: *Les Mœurs*. In this book, Toussaint broke the connection between politeness and religion and defended both a deist position and a natural ethics. For Toussaint, politeness was a social virtue: it required "constant attention, which inspires humanity, on pleasing everyone and offending no one."[154] It was not based on religious morality but on the natural sociability of man.

The Sociability of the Enlightenment

The word *sociabilité* appeared as a concept in France in the late seventeenth century and enjoyed widespread success during the Enlightenment. At the time, "sociability" was an abstract concept of political philosophy used to account for what urges human beings to live in society. Whereas the

modern use of the term is both sociological and psychological, in the eighteenth century it was philosophical and anthropological.

Its importance in the social thought of the Enlightenment cannot be
doubted. "From the principle of sociability flow all the laws of society," the
Encyclopédie states. At first the notion of sociability owed much to the theorists of natural law. Pufendorf had made it a central concept of natural law.
Even while picking up the anthropology of human weakness developed by
Hobbes, Pufendorf stated that natural sociability, founded on the rational
and enlightened interest of individuals, pushed them to associate with one
another and live peacefully together.[155] The theory of natural sociability had
a great influence in France, in particular thanks to Barbeyrac and his trans-
lations and commentaries. It was transferred from juridical discourse to
philosophical discourse thanks to the Encyclopedists and provided the foundation of their social thought.[156] Unlike the theorists of natural law, some
authors described sociability, not as the consequence of human weakness
and a calculated utility, but as a natural feeling that brings man to seek his
like. Shaftesbury, notably, stated the importance of good will and sympathy.
A third definition of sociability came from Mandeville, who developed a theory of the social in his famous *Fable des abeilles* that owed nothing to either an
initial natural sentiment of sociability or to a contract founded on a utilitarian calculation, but rather was based on a mechanism of interests and their
involuntary convergence. That mechanics of interest became a fundamental
paradigm of the intellectual culture that, from the Jansenism of Nicole to the
invisible hand of Adam Smith, led to the emergence of economic thought.[157]

Of course, those three founding definitions did not demarcate intan-
gible positions. Each author elaborated a position of his own between the
contract theories and the theories of the self-institution of the social and
between a pessimistic and an optimistic anthropology. Hume and Smith
articulated a thought of social self-institution that left a large place for the
mechanics of interests and a theory of sympathy as a natural moral sentiment.[158] Diderot merged the philosophy of natural law with the thought of
Shaftesbury, whose *Inquiry Concerning Virtue* he translated and who exerted
a genuine influence on him in his formative years.[159] The article "Sociabilité"
in the *Encyclopédie* attempted to take a middle position, inspired by both
natural law and the theories of benevolence.[160] At that point, the debates
on sociability seem to have been situated at a level of generality far from
worldly norms and rules of conversation. Still, they offered those norms a
theoretical underpinning by posing questions as important, in the eighteenth century, as commerce, manners, and civilization.

Following Montesquieu and Vicent de Gournay, Physiocrats and liberals
founded *le doux commerce* on the theory of natural sociability and on the

notion of reciprocal relations between individuals.[161] But if this "commerce" can be thought of as reciprocal and sociable, it is also because the word includes all forms of exchange, in particular, conversation. Enlightenment thinkers ceaselessly explained the harmony of commerce by the harmony of conversation, and vice versa.[162] Society rested on an exchange of goods, but especially on an exchange of words and knowledge that always referred to sociability, the "connection among men by a commerce of ideas and by the exercise of a mutual beneficence," as Diderot and d'Alembert put it.[163] The vocabulary of commerce and the conversational ideal created a common field of reference and an attention to the social forms engendered by conversation, as attested by the recurrent use of the commercial metaphor in treatises on civility.

The second point of convergence concerns manners. The intellectual confrontation between the neorepublican thinkers and those who thought of society in terms of commerce led, in England in the eighteenth century, to a redefinition of virtue, no longer thought of in the austere terms of civic humanism, but through a refinement of manners aided by the development of commerce and the progress of the arts.[164] In *The Spectator*, Addison and Steele attempted to promote politeness and conviviality; Addison states, "I shall be ambitious to have it said of me that I have brought philosophy out of the closets and libraries, schools and colleges, to dwell in clubs and assemblies, at tea-tables and in coffee-houses"[165] From a stylistic point of view, that attempt resulted in the genre of the essay in dialogue form. The choice of the essay refers back to the Socratic model of the exercise of philosophy and to a form of writing that the seventeenth century had honored, but it also explicitly referred to the refinement of worldly conversation. In France, the development of the philosophical dialogue responded to the same logic. From its beginnings in the seventeenth century, it became an important tool for publicizing philosophy by emphasizing the possibilities of the new (Cartesian) philosophy in its opposition to the dogmatism of the Scholastics, and in the rise of a new (and less learned) public for philosophy.[166] During the century of the Enlightenment, philosophical dialogue underwent both a quantitative and qualitative change, and the model of the friendly chat ceded to an exhibition of worldly forms of intellectual commerce.

This change in the status of dialogue is attested by a tendency among authors to anchor dialogue within the fictive situation of a spoken exchange proper to worldly society.[167] One of the distinctive traits of the philosophical dialogues of the eighteenth century is the presence of a female figure. From Fontenelle's marquise to Diderot's maréchale, that female figure is worldly and serves to indicate both the pedagogical destination of the dialogue and the ways in which the Enlightenment dealt with social difference.[168]

That does not mean that philosophical dialogue resembled worldly conversation. The inscription of that sort of dialogue within a worldly situation and décor was a fiction, a writerly technique. However, its existence
indicates a vast zone of interference between the representations of
worldly conversation and the ideal of an enlightened intellectual communication. When Shaftesbury insisted on the importance of both politeness
as a permanent effort to refine and develop moral sense and sociability, on
the one hand, and philosophical communication, on the other, he returned
to the theme of politeness as something that "polishes" minds by rubbing
them together, and privileged wit, humor, and raillery as dialogue forms of
a search for truth.[169]

Reflection on manners was not limited to questions connected with writing; it also inspired a social anthropology. In describing French monarchical society, Montesquieu elaborated a genuine "paradigm of manners," as
Céline Spector has put it.[170] France was a nation of an *humeur sociable*[171]—
that is, a society in which cohesion rested on the dynamic of self-esteem,
an apprenticeship in politeness, the logic of honor, and the cultivation of
taste. A search for honor and distinction was the principle that permitted social harmony. Montesquieu described a social mechanism within the
monarchical system in which "virtue," a republican principle, was absent.[172]
If politeness, denounced by the moralists as false, could once again be
viewed positively, it was precisely because it produced social ties.

Unlike Montesquieu, most of the philosophes tried to find foundations for the moral value of politeness. A search for the *fondements de la
morale* outside of revealed religion was one of the principal tasks of the
Enlightenment. Some authors sought them in natural religion, others in
interest, but all insisted on "social virtues."[173] Voltaire defended a concept
of virtue judged by the standard of society and the notion that benefits
attract other benefits, and he rejected religious definitions, saintliness in
particular: "Can I call virtue anything but that which does good?. . . But
how? Wilt thou admit of no other virtues than those which are useful to
thy neighbor? How can I admit any others? We live in society; there is
therefore nothing truly good for us but that which does good to society. . . .
Virtue between men is a commerce of good actions: he who has no part
in this commerce, must not be reckoned."[174] Even materialist philosophes
like d'Holbach and Diderot were obsessed by the question of morality and
wanted to found an *ordre des mœurs* that would refute the immoralist mate-
rialism of La Mettrie.[175] D'Holbach systematically attempted to base this
morality on the notion of a natural and rational sociability, because he
deemed the social status of man to be a fact of nature that pushes him to
experience the utility of society and seek his fellow men, who are necessary

to both his security and his happiness.[176] "Virtue," he wrote, "is really only sociability."[177] In *La Morale universelle*, d'Holbach presented an apologetics of the "social virtues" that contributed to the happiness of others and were dictated by the enlightened interest that urges men to live in society. As he described them, those virtues corresponded perfectly to the qualities traditionally praised by treatises on worldly conversation and manuals of civility.[178] In particular, d'Holbach praised *la complaisance* (complaisance, obligingness), which he declared to be "the soul of life,"[179] and politeness, acquired by familiarity with *le monde*, whose practice is "an act of justice and humanity."[180]

In his synthesis of traditional discourse on politeness and the new discourse of natural law, d'Holbach substituted reason for birth as a condition of sociability. He thus potentially enlarged to all of humanity the qualities of a worldly sociability founded on reciprocity. Above all, he offered the philosopher a privileged position: because the philosopher, by definition, had deeply investigated the political and philosophical bases of social life, he owed it to himself to be particularly sociable and polite: "The most enlightened men should know their true interests best and, consequently, stand out for their sociability."[181] The philosopher, a man who makes enlightened use of his reason, was thus particularly apt as a man of the world.[182] This argument enabled d'Holbach to devote many pages to a question that might seem prosaic: Should a philosopher participate in the *grand monde*? Returning to the moderate position of Voltaire, he asserted that a writer should attend high society venues in order to become more polite and to speak about it more pertinently, although without losing his taste for working in the "whirlwind of the world." Criticism of worldly excesses assigned to the philosopher a position of equilibrium within the literary sphere, given that he was both a socialite and a scholar, frequenting *la bonne société* while still saving time for his work.[183]

The theory of sociability developed by d'Holbach, far from defending the autonomy of a particular and egalitarian social space, attempted to base the whole of social order, with its distinctions of rank and estate, on the principles of sociability and social utility.[184] Worldly *politesse*, already theorized according to this model, offered d'Holbach a springboard for thinking about social virtues and a basis on which to build an order of practice based on a natural sociability within the inegalitarian society of the ancien régime. In return, *politesse* supported the philosopher's position as an intermediary between learning and worldliness.

The last place where the political philosophy of sociability and theories of politeness coincided is in the area of customs and manners, operating through the notion of civilization, a term that designates an endogenous process for the transformation of law and manners, but also a project for cultural mutations.[185] In this, the Scottish philosophers and historians who traced the evolution of civil society were influential in connecting the economic, the political, and customs.[186] Adam Smith, for example, introduced the natural sociability of Pufendorf into an evolutionist theory of civilization founded on the progress of commerce.[187] By removing manners from the naturalist tradition, the philosophes inscribed them within history and questioned their relationship to political change. Voltaire's history of *mœurs* is, mostly, that of the various stages of civility.[188]

Thus the writers of the Enlightenment reworked the classical notions of the theories of civility on the basis of the new language of sociability, an essentially eighteenth-century notion of moral and political philosophy. The rules of politeness were no longer tied to religious precepts or to the glory of the prince, but rather to an enlightened interest, to the social utility of human virtues, and to the progress of custom. In this reformulation, the many meanings of *société* permitted frequent exchanges, in both directions, between general moral questions and the sphere of worldliness. The adjective *sociable* allowed an easy transfer from one register to another. Whereas *sociabilité* was always used on the abstract level of political philosophy, *sociable* designated, at the same time, an anthropological fact (man is a sociable animal), an element of the national character (the French are sociable), and a trait of individual psychology (certain individuals are more sociable than others). Constant comparisons are made between *l'homme sociable* and *l'homme aimable*, as in Duclos and in the *Encyclopédie*.[189] When d'Holbach states that "the true *savant* should be the most sociable of men,"[190] he cleverly plays with the ambiguity between the theory of natural sociability and mastery of the aristocratic codes of behavior in society. His *Morale universelle* reaches "a kind of lexical apotheosis" of the vocabulary of society.[191]

Abbé Morellet furnishes an excellent example of the convergence of philosophy of sociability and the arts of worldly conversation. Morellet was a perfect representative of the second generation of the Enlightenment, and particularly of the intellectual eclecticism of the philosophes. A man engaged in all the literary and economic quarrels of the century, he drew from several theoretical currents. A disciple of Gournay and a close friend of Turgot, he spent his entire life preparing a dictionary of commerce, only the prospectus for which was published. He translated Beccaria and Smith's theory of moral sentiments, and he helped Suard translate Robertson. He spent his last years in a revolutionary world that was no longer his own, then under the Empire managed to reconstruct an institutional position for himself and to defend the heritage of both the philosophy of the

Enlightenment and the salons of the ancien régime. In 1812, when he, Thomas, and d'Alembert republished their praises of Madame Geoffrin, he contributed a text entitled "De la conversation" that returned to and developed in his own way Jonathan Swift's *Hints toward an Essay on Conversation*, which Morellet had translated in 1778.[192] Morellet's interest in the arts of conversation was longstanding, but it took on new importance.

Morellet sang the praises of a worldly conversation directed by the rules of politeness and civility, and argued for its superiority over the written word as a means of intellectual formation: "Conversation is the great school of the mind, not only in that it enriches it with knowledge that one could only with difficulty have drawn from other sources, but in rendering [that knowledge] more vigorous, more just, more penetrating, more profound.. . . The majority of men, and even those who have given the most cultivation to their minds, hold a large part of their learning from conversation."[193] The pedagogical qualities of conversation come from the "strong attention" that it requires and that are absent from reading. Its superiority led Morellet to praise men of the world formed in that "great school of the mind," a classical theme found throughout the century, for example in Madame Necker's writings: "One profits more in speaking with an *homme d'esprit* than in reading his works; for [reading] recalls only the major ideas that occupy him and necessarily neglects the developments and the ideas less apt to make an impression."[194] In an equally classical way, Morellet develops a list of faults to be avoided "to be agreeable in society."[195] At first glance that list hardly seems original. It includes inattention, the habit of interrupting, the will to dominate, the spirit of contradiction, dispute, private conversation substituted for general conversation, and pedantry. Morellet defined the last, with Swift, as "an overly frequent and misplaced use of what we know in ordinary conversation," but he remarked that pedantry is even more often found in the tone and the manner of what is said than in its substance.[196] For a conversation to succeed, it must respect the external forms of *honnêteté* and *la galanterie* or, in Morellet's terms, have an appropriate "tone" and display "manners."

Although Morellet's essay can be read as a simple variation on the classic motifs of the arts of conversation, it is much more than that, for it is infused with Enlightenment ideals of sociability. Morellet defends the place of learning and, unlike the classical theorists of conversation, he rehabilitates learning and study: "One knows well only what one has studied and studied well."[197] He even justifies a flagrant breach of the rules of politeness in the case of a particularly knowledgeable man who takes the time to explain his theory at length.[198] Morellet thus sets himself apart from all earlier authors of treatises on conversation, for whom knowledge in no case justified talking too long, and made doing so even more open to condemnation as pedantic and boring. Behind an apparent continuity in themes, differences appear between Morellet and a classical theorist of the *honnête homme* like Méré, who stated that "among the persons of the world, what is linked to study is almost always poorly received."[199] Similarly, where a more traditional champion of conversation such as abbé Trublet stated that an "assemblage of well-pursued and well-connected reasoning" had no place in conversation because, above all, people seek amusement in it, Morellet insisted that "conversation lives on the connection of ideas."[200]

Adopting the commonplace of conversation as a "school," while safeguarding the specificity of knowledge and argumentation, led Morellet to defend the moderate position adopted by men of letters since Guez de Balzac and constructed by force of oxymorons, in which conversation is described only by the stumbling blocks that threatened it and restricted it without defining it, forcing it to be neither too playful nor too serious, to please while instructing, and to instruct while pleasing.

This median position asserting the necessary connection between worldliness and knowledge posed the question of the aim of philosophical knowledge. The superiority of conversation found its true reason for being in a broader diffusion of philosophy. "Few people read, or read with enough attention, to take their opinions from books, and it is that small number of readers who transmit their ideas by way of conversation to all the rest of society."[201] Books reached only a small number of enlightened spirits who were accustomed to reading and reflecting on what they read and who were, for the most part, scholars and men of letters. The conversation they had with elites in high society permitted the enlargement of the audience for new ideas.

Morellet placed his praise of conversation within a theory of civilization. Whereas Swift had been content to justify his essay by a few rapid phrases about the innocent pleasure of conversation, Morellet began his essay with a long digression on the "utility" of conversation and on its moral and social justifications. Conversation, he wrote, permits "perfecting the morality and the sociability of man."[202] Bringing conversation back down to linguistic exchange, he made it a criterion for the disciplined mores of civilization, and he devoted several pages to demonstrating that the march of a barbarian people toward civilization is necessarily tied to the discovery and mastery of conversation. "It is to the habit of conversing that the principal differences that distinguish the civilized man from the savage man must be attributed," he stated in a passage that owes much to the preliminary discourse of the *Encyclopédie* and can be read as a refutation of Rousseau. Morellet distinguished two sorts of commerce, corresponding to "two degrees of sociability." The second of these, which satisfies the "needs of the mind," is more important in the constitution of society, as it permits the containment of the passions and the purification of taste.[203]

This analysis leads Morellet to reinterpret the qualities of conversation as "social virtues." Because *le monde* represented the social connection par excellence, conversation, which anyone could engage in, became a metaphor for society as a whole. The tension between the norms corresponding to the conversation of an elite and the demand for universality in verbal exchange was resolved, once again, by the equivocal vocabulary of society. For example, if lack of attention is a fault in conversation, it is because "listening is a social law."[204] Taking this to its logical end and inventing a neologism: in conversation, Morellet writes, "inattention is always a crime of *lèse-société*."[205]

Ranging from the liberalities of Madame Geoffrin to moral philosophy, the topics treated in this chapter might seem disparate. Nonetheless, they form a sociocultural configuration that allows us to comprehend both the reality of worldly exchange and the reasons for the adherence of some men of letters to that model of sociability. Worldly sociability gave men of letters access to the protection and the gratifications of the social elites, but it also enabled them to elaborate new representations of the writer and its place in ancien régime society. Writers themselves played an important role in the configuration of that sociability by their ability to produce texts, eulogies, and letters, but also, and more generally, by their participation in worldly amusements and by their acceptance of the codes of aristocratic behavior. Parisian worldliness was a literary and intellectual one.

"Society" was thus both an order of practices—that of life in society—and a social group—*le monde*. It designated a space of sociability, which produced distinction and domination, in which the struggle for social classification was expressed in the language of sociability that contrasted those who belonged to it and those who did not. Worldly sociability permitted the production of social domination, but also its denial. Where court ceremonial, founded on etiquette and distance, concentrated on making hierarchy visible and on producing domination by exhibiting that hierarchy, worldly sociability encouraged domination by covering it with the language of amity and sociability. That sociability was the place of an alliance between Parisian elites and certain writers around a model of the man of the world with which nobles, courtiers, and men of letters could identify.

PART TWO

News and Opinion: The Politics of High Society

It is very odd that a lady who has a Wednesday has no news.

Montesquieu, Letter to Mme Du Deffand

CHAPTER 4

Word Games: Literature and Sociability

Most men say only conventional things in conversation. Men of letters would not even dare to say frankly what they think of Homer, even though he lived three thousand years ago.

Suzanne Necker, *Mélanges*, 1798

The expression "literary salon" is a nearly perfect example of a historiographical notion that seems obvious but contains ambiguities that can lead to error. It seems natural as the definition of a social space (the salon), an activity (literature), and individuals (men of letters). But the combination is far from evident and overestimates the role of literature in worldly sociability. What did people do in the salons of the eighteenth century? They ate; they played theatrical games and other games, even for large sums of money and at times until dawn; they listened to the young Mozart giving a concert or admired a follower of Mesmer as he hypnotized volunteers. Amorous intrigues might be launched or ended in a salon, and certain guests might drink more than was reasonable. The pleasures of the salon were more varied than has been imagined, and they corresponded to the different forms of amusement of the urban elites, which were marked by a permanent theatricality.[1] Literature itself was a worldly practice. What literature are we talking about, after all? Before becoming a playful and somewhat old-fashioned literary genre, in the seventeenth and eighteenth centuries, *poésie de société* for example was a social activity governed by the rules of polite commerce. Its first quality was as a social performance in which a system of representation cannot be dissociated from a speech situated in the very space of worldly relations.[2]

Without seeking to be exhaustive, this chapter attempts to answer to these questions: Outside of the normative treatises, what was salon conversation like? What were the rules and the effects of the circulation of texts within high society? Was the salon a place of literary production? What place did literature occupy within it?

SALON CONVERSATION

Conversation as Gaiety: The Art of Pleasantry

The *mot d'esprit* or witticism was a verbal performance that depended on the vivacity of a rejoinder. It brought together a sense for language and a feeling for what is appropriate, and it revealed both intellectual and worldly qualities. The *mot d'esprit* was always saluted as a performance, something based in individual mastery (or at times collective mastery, when *bons mots* arrive in series and in response to one another). It prompted a group cohesion that could be recognized in the collective laughter that greeted the *bon mot*. Its success depended upon its being understood, and on listeners who possessed an equal vivacity. That success provided evidence of the wit of the author of the *bon mot* and that of the circle surrounding him. Finally, success was generally based on the effect of connivance that binds a group together against the outside world.

"*Bons mots*," Madame de Staël wrote to Gustav III, "are the events of Paris. They are the subject of conversations for several days."[3] Transmitted by conversation, by multiple visits, and by correspondence, the witticism circulated within worldly society and assured the reputation of its author as an *homme d'esprit* and an amusing person. "A pleasantry of M. de Voisenon is running through the world" the *Mémoires secrets* noted in August 1762. The *bon mot* also enhanced the reputation of the host and hostess by spreading the image of a house in which guests amused themselves and were witty.

By occupying high society for a few days before being forgotten, the most successful witticisms extended the temporal range of sociability. As an oral and fugitive bit of repartee, a *bon mot* was picked up and commented on. Some even escaped the oblivion that was the fate of salon chitchat. Repeated, they were then set down in correspondence, published in news sheets and gazettes, and then in the *ana* (collections of witticisms and pleasantries) that supported collective memory. The tradition of worldly society was based on the memory of old *bons mots* pronounced by a few great figures, such as Fontenelle or Madame de Sévigné. Fontenelle's long life permitted him to make the connection between the salons of the mid-century (such as that of Madame Geoffrin), back to those of the first half of the century, where he had been an assiduous guest (of Madame de Lambert and Madame de Tencin), and even to those of the reign of Louis XIV, which he had attended in his youth. To Amélie Suard, Fontenelle seemed a ghost when she heard him preface an anecdote with: "I remember that one day I heard Madame de La Fayette say in the house of Madame de Sévigné. . ."[4] The eighteenth century regarded Madame de Sévigné as a great model of the worldly tradition of an earlier age. Madame Geoffrin kept in her library the *Sevignana*, along with the *Maintenoniana*,[5] and Madame Du Deffand was fond of citing certain witticisms of the marquise that had become a part of a shared repertory.[6]

As time went by, how was this worldly repertory transmitted? The fate of Talleyrand's first *bon mot* illustrates the fragility of worldly memory. Invited for the first time to the home of the comtesse de Boufflers, Talleyrand was approached by the duchesse de Gramont, who sought to embarrass him. She asked him what had struck him as he entered that made him say, "Ah! Ah!" Without letting himself be intimidated, Talleyrand responded calmly that she had not heard him correctly and that he had said "Oh! Oh!" That response won him a reputation for wit and a good number of invitations. Thanks to his quick reaction, Talleyrand made a great success of his entry into *le monde*, for the anecdote was repeated and contributed lastingly to his legend. However, this response does not seem to us irresistible, and the reasons for its success are now unclear. Talleyrand himself, in his *Mémoires*, called it a "wretched reply" and expressed amusement at its unexpected and disproportionate success: "That wretched reply caused general hilarity; I continued to sup, and did not say another word. On leaving the table, a few persons came up to me, and I received for the following days several invitations which enabled me to make the acquaintance of the persons whom I was most anxious to meet."[7]

When Sainte-Beuve related the anecdote eighty years later, in 1862, but before the publication of Talleyrand's *Mémoires* in 1891, he attempted to retain or restore its exemplary status, quoting it according to "the tradition," and thus suggesting that it had been repeated by generations of socialites. His version differs from that of Talleyrand himself, given that for Sainte-Beuve the scene took place at the home of the maréchale de Luxembourg. The most striking thing about his version is that Sainte-Beuve tried to justify the success of the "Oh! Oh!" when he quite obviously did not understand it, since he attempted to inject a bit of wit into it: "It was in fact quite different; there was a nuance of surprise or admiration that escapes us but that indicated the accent, the refinement of which was immediately sensed."[8] Much like us, Sainte-Beuve did not appreciate the wit of Talleyrand's retort: its humor "escaped" him and he was reduced to suppositions. Still, Sainte-Beuve himself was still following the same tradition: he did not read the anecdote in someone's memoirs or in a history book, but picked it up in a salon. He did not doubt its *finesse*, which had been appreciated and recognized. The long-term success of the exclamation gave proof of a wit that was now perceived to lie in its effects alone but that was not open to doubt. In Sainte-Beuve's text the anecdote is not so much aimed at proving Talleyrand's wit as it is that of Madame de Luxembourg. It is inserted in a long passage in which Sainte-Beuve tries to show her refinement in her readiness to recognize talent at the least sign. Thus it was not Talleyrand's repartee that was exemplary, but rather its success, because it proved the elegance of Madame de Luxembourg's salon. Talleyrand's response was droll because it had been appreciated. That its fine wit "escapes us," as Sainte-Beuve says, attests even better to the discernment of Madame de Luxembourg, whom it did not escape.

The long life of this anecdote shows that a *bon mot* was a collective creation, and that its success depended on the arbitration of worldly society. What made a response a *bon mot* or a *mot d'esprit*? Its success. The intrinsic quality of most of these sallies is hard to determine, even for contemporaries, who often pronounced contradictory judgments about them.[9] It was its immediate validation by the other guests, in the form of laughter, then the circulation of the statement, that transformed a response into a *bon mot*, whereas an icy silence would have sealed its failure.[10] The witticism produced a good reputation in three ways: first, it made its author into a man of the world, sought after as a man of wit. Second, it assured the reputation of the salon in which it had been pronounced, of the house in which witty things were repeated, and of the mistress of the house who knew how to recognize men of wit and attract them to her. As the witticism circulated, it reflected well on *la bonne société*: everyone worked to make sure that the statement that had enjoyed such success merited it. The third level was the most durable one: that connivance continued to be effective a century or two later. It did not really matter that the worldly tradition that Sainte-Beuve reflects had modified the conditions of Talleyrand's repartee. The message was the same: society was extremely witty.

The validation of a *bon mot* by collective reaction was more important than theoretical distinctions that might attempt to define the quality of the witticism. In principle, the *mot d'esprit* was set apart from the much humbler *calembour*, a pun or play on words, which was based essentially on similar sounds.[11] Even the marquis de Bièvre, although a great promoter of puns, recognized this hierarchy: "When the subtlety of a retort does not consist in an ambiguity but in an ingenious idea express with precision, it is no longer a play on words; it is a genuine *bon mot*. Only people of wit emit them, whereas the play on words is the wit of those who have none."[12] He himself, however, had great success in the 1770s thanks to works that were little more than a series of parodies of *calembours*, but also thanks to his plays on words, which were repeated in all the salons. Similarly the marchese di Caraccioli, who was much appreciated for his Mediterranean gift of the gab and for his reforming and enlightened mind, never hesitated before a play on words or a pun, either in high society or at court.[13] The function of the play on words in worldly conversation was to encourage gaiety and amusement rather than serious conversation. It functioned like a short circuit in that it cut off serious discussion, which was always suspected of introducing boredom or dissent. When the duchesse de Maine, a cultivated woman who did not disdain talking about philosophy, started to compare the merits of Descartes and Newton, the marquis de Sainte-Aulaire, whose opinion she had asked, improvised a response in verse that had the company nodding in agreement:

Bergère, détachons-nous
De Newton, de Descartes:
Ces deux espèces de fous
N'ont jamais vu le dessous
Des cartes, des cartes, des cartes![14]

Aside from the intrinsic quality of this conceit, its worldly value seemed sufficiently high for Hénault to remember this riposte and write it down in his *Mémoires*. It had done its job of assuring the triumph of gaiety and the pleasure of the moment over intellectual discussion. It had reestablished the harmony that might have been threatened by philosophical debate. It had recalled the rights of worldliness, hence was taken to be in high praise of frivolity.

Still, the play on words is an extreme example of worldly conversation. It may lead to equivocal statements that threaten the very possibility of conversation. Gaiety, which lay behind worldly commerce, implied a distance from satire or folly, the rival figures of laughter. Worldly pleasantry took care to distinguish itself from foolish gaiety in its farcical or intoxicated version by its insistence on the rules of civility and its rejection of corporal humor.[15] The problem with satire was that a pleasantry was apt to be aimed at someone. How to reconcile, within the framework of worldly life, the demand for gaiety and a concern for civility, which implied not upsetting anyone? The ambiguities of the pleasantry, which hung suspended between group cohesion and possible aggression, were concentrated in one word: *raillerie*.

In the seventeenth century, raillery lay at the heart of reflection on civility. The term designated all sorts of agreeable pleasantry with a punchline, but it was also used in the more restricted sense of a pleasantry directed at someone. In this it was related to sarcasm and mockery. In its broader sense, raillery was a shared pleasure and an adornment to conversation. It prompted agreeable laughter at ridicule. A defining trait of the *honnête homme* was to "hear raillery" and not take offense, even when he was its target. In its second sense, the term focused on its aggressive dimension. Satire was denounced as an insult or an offense.[16] From Faret to Mademoiselle de Scudéry, every author tried to distinguish the joking repartee, which connected society, from misplaced sarcasm, which troubled its harmony.[17] In the eighteenth century, the second of these tended to predominate, while the aesthetic and moral sense of honest raillery became an archaism. Theorists of civility and sociability flatly condemned it because it harmed society by introducing aggression and suspicion. D'Holbach exclaimed, "What strange gaiety it is that consists in pointed railleries, offensive sarcasms, and desolating satires!"[18] Raillery came to be judged by its result. By his reactions, the target of raillery became the sole judge of its legitimacy, and the art of the man of the world was no longer to understand raillery, but to know how to convey its meaning. In Chamfort's words, "It is an excellent rule to adopt on the art of raillery and pleasantry that the author of the one or the other must take responsibility for the success of the joke with the person in question, and should that person become angry, the other is wrong."[19]

The only conversational practice that permitted laughter at the expense of someone without openly breaking the rules of civility was the sort of teasing known as *persiflage*.[20] It consisted in praise that everyone except the targeted person knew to be ironical. It was an allurement, a disguised violence that ridiculed the victim without his being aware of it. As Louis-Sébastien Mercier describes it, "*Persiflage* is a continuous raillery under the misleading veil of approbation: one makes use of it to lead the victim into all sorts of ambushes set for him."[21] The use of the vocabulary of trapping is eloquent here: *persiflage* juggles the worldly rules of civility and of approval and praise at the expense of someone who is less skilled at mastering codes and subtleties. In principle, the target of *persiflage* is someone who does not understand worldly language and who, lacking experience in high society, takes counterfeit coin for genuine and makes himself all the more ridiculous by being enchanted with such praise. Raillery created dissension within the worldly collective, *persiflage* soldered the circle together by the symbolic exclusion of an outsider or a newcomer. It was thus a worldly practice par excellence in which the man of the world or the philosophe who indulged in it veered away from the ideals of *honnêteté* and approached the figure of the libertine.

Conversation as Spectacle: The Art of Story-Telling

It would be wrong to imagine salon conversation as consisting of one lively and striking repartee after another. Such conversations resembling theatrical dialogue would have been exhausting. Most of the reports of conversation that we have from correspondence, journals, or memoirs insist above all on the art of telling a story. To be a good conversationalist was to have mastered the art of cleverly relating an anecdote, a curious fact, or an event. The *conte* was a small theatrical spectacle presented before the entire circle that amused, informed, and gave each guest a chance to contribute a commentary or a word. Abbé Galiani, according to his contemporaries, was the archetype of the salon man and a master of the art of conversation. His verbal exploits are often mentioned, but only rarely do we learn the exact nature of this talent. Galiani did not lack humor, and some of his *bons mots* were famous,[22] but his brilliant conversation was less dependent on the art of repartee than on his ability to recount a fable or improvise an apologue to justify a paradox that had just been suggested. "There was nothing," Marmontel tells us, "either in politics or in morals, about which he had not some diverting story to tell."[23] At the home of d'Holbach or Madame Geoffrin, Galiani combined a cynical fondness for paradoxes with an actor's talent that made him the "prettiest little harlequin," but on his shoulders there was "the head of a machiavel."[24] Diderot also expressed enthusiasm for the storytelling talents of the Neapolitan abbé and thought them the ideal remedy for boredom: "It is a treasure on rainy days. I was saying to Madame d'Épinay that if cabinetmakers produced his like, everyone would want to have one in his country place."[25] Although Diderot was not always persuaded by the pedagogical bent of Galiani's tales or by their contents, he could not resist their "gaiety": "The basic matter is miserable in itself, but in his hands it takes on the strongest and gayest color and becomes an inexhaustible source of good pleasantries, and at times even of morality."[26]

What made Galiani's conversation attractive was thus his gaiety and, above all, his talents as an actor that permitted him to make the most of tales that would have seemed flat if related by others. His was a true performance, oral and gestural. One day at d'Holbach's home, when Diderot, d'Holbach, Galiani, and others were engaged in a conversation about genius and method, Galiani improvised a fable about a nightingale, a cuckoo, and an ass. Diderot commented:

> The abbé's tales are good, but he performs them in superior fashion. One cannot resist. You would have laughed to see him stretch his neck out and do the nightingale in a little voice; bring it back down and take on a raucous tone for the cuckoo; prick up his ears and imitate the stupid and heavy gravity of the ass: and all of that naturally and without even trying. That's because he is pantomime from his head to his toes.[27]

Marmontel, too, insisted on Galiani's command of gesture that combined "an unaffected elegance" in his gestures with "the ludicrous air of the person who told" the story.[28] He added that Galiani took little part in the conversation aside from telling his tales. "But when he had acted his part he no longer formed any part of the company" and he patiently "awaited the watchword to return on the stage." That description, which is far removed from what the models of conversation dictated, suggested that what was most important in conversation was gaiety and theatricality, each participant intervening in turn, aware of taking center stage and of shining by amusing the others. A last example gives the measure of the scenic qualities that abbé Galiani's conversation played into. It comes from a text by Morellet that relates a conversation of atheists at the home of the baron d'Holbach. This well-known text has been used to show the particular flavor of d'Holbach's salon and the freedom of thought that reigned there, but it can also be seen from a different point of view to observe in it the practices of worldly theatricals in the conversational setting. After having listened to Diderot and Roux speak of their atheism, Galiani returned several days later and defended the existence of God.[29] Far from insisting on Galiani's arguments, Morellet stressed his performance as an actor. After dinner and coffee, Galiani plumped himself down in an armchair, crossed his legs like a tailor, took his wig in his hands, and gesticulated while he spoke. The quality of the spectacle given by the voluble little Neapolitan abbé struck Morellet as memorable: "I no longer recall the rest of the abbé's development, but it was the most piquant thing in the world, and it was the equal of the best spectacles and the most lively amusements."[30]

Aside from highlighting Galiani's personal talents, these descriptions of his oral performances throw light on the nature of worldly conversation. For Marmontel, Madame Geoffrin's chief attribute lay in the stories she would tell: "Her real talent was that of telling a story well; in this she excelled, and readily employed it, without art or pretension, however, but just to set the rest an example."[31] What is essential here is the association between the story, gaiety, and amusement. The other lesson we can draw from Galiani is the worldly efficacy of the "paradoxes" that the tale-teller developed and that enabled them to show off their wit and capacity for merrily backing an unexpected opinion. During a dinner at Madame Geoffrin's, the comtesse de Boufflers "was charming; she did not say a word that was not a paradox. She was attacked, and she defended herself with so much wit that her errors were almost as good as the truth."[32] Whether or not her opinions or arguments were well founded mattered little when they were presented as paradoxes admired for the oral jousting they permitted.

Because it lent itself to spectacle, the *conte* transformed the circle of listeners into spectators and each listener in turn into an actor. Better still, professional actors were perfect tale-tellers in society. At a reception of the baron de Bensenval, Dugazon achieved a genuine tour de force, making the entire assembly laugh at his account of the burial of the mother of the Vestris family, famous dancers, in what his listeners agreed was a remarkable performance: "Dugazon recounted a story as no one has ever done before." In doing so, he used imitation to *contrefaire* the various protagonists of the scene, in particular, the inappropriate fit of laughter that stuck one of the Vestrises. "The details of this story are of a truth that carried the day over the sadness of the subject, and the imitation of the bursts of laughter was so true that the most serious of men were forced to smile."[33] Imitations were much appreciated. D'Alembert, who possessed this social talent, used it liberally in the salons that he frequented.[34] The comte d'Albaret was the best known of the imitators admired in worldly circles. He was particularly appreciated for imitations of Voltaire that made all of high society laugh: "But to see M. Albaret's imitation of M. de Voltaire?—it was a living portrait, it was a mirror in which he seemed to be reflected. I have seen persons sit motionless in astonishment, so perfect was the imitation."[35] With d'Alembert's imitations and the little comic scenes of the comte d'Albaret, conversation could easily turn to parody and came close to being social theater, all the while remaining within the framework of improvisation. Several young aristocrats, the chevalier de Boufflers or Donnezan among them, were popular among high society for their talents as imitators and their skill at amusing people: Madame Du Deffand nicknamed them *les facétieux* and even *la troupe facétieuse*.[36] It is true that presence of amusing guests was not absolute insurance against boredom. "We had three jokesters and we had no jokes," Madame Du Deffand noted bitterly on one occasion.[37]

This sort of fashionable humor was not the only amusement that worldly society indulged in. Some took advantage of it to gain acceptance into the salons of the capital thanks to a particular talent. One man named Touzet brought delight to the salons by hiding behind a screen and imitating an entire choir of nuns.[38] "This way of contributing to the amusement of society is not exactly a road that leads to consideration," the *Correspondance littéraire* noted, "but it gives a sort of existence to Paris and access to good company, where that class of persons would never have figured without the amusement that they procure." Among these *facétieux* Grimm cites the comte d'Albaret, but also a Mademoiselle Delon from Geneva who, after marrying a gentleman and taking on the name of the marquise de Luchet, received all of high society. She was connected with a forage dealer who could imitate an English accent to perfection and went by the name of "milord Gor." One of his imitations bordered on hoax when he took advantage of a "lady of quality" who had taken him for a real English physician and permitted him to perform a medical examination. Madame de Luchet made the mistake of recounting the event, the story did the rounds, and the lady in question called the police, who intervened, arrested the false physician, and reprimanded Madame de Luchet. "A woman taken by the police is no longer received anywhere, and the poor devil de Luchet fell into utter misery." Such adventurers were well received as long as they amused and maintained the appearance of respectability, but their position collapsed as soon as scandal broke out.

From Galiani's pantomimes to the imitations of the comte d'Albaret, the echoes of worldly conversation can at times seem rather far from the models presented in treatises and summaries of the arts of conversation. Conversation was primarily a spectacle valued for its ability to distract, amuse, and surprise, but also to give fine talkers a chance to shine. As Madame Necker put it: "Conversation is quite different from thought: thought is reality, and conversation is spectacle."[39] Conversation was not a simple exchange of thoughts, nor was it by any means transparent communication. To the contrary, it implied a strong self-awareness. Comparison with the actor's art sprang up quite naturally:

> If Ariane, when she is in her accesses of sadness, forgot that she was playing a role, her attitudes would be uncouth; she would repeat herself twenty times; she would grimace. Similarly, when one speaks, one must never forget that conversation is the garb of thought. How, then, can one be distracted in that moment, when one must think at one and the same time about what others are saying and what they are—men, women, great lords, stupid people, witty people, men of business or of letters—about what we are, about what we say to them, and about the manner in which we say it; about gesture, tone of voice, facial expression, and correct language; about the propriety and the politeness of a word and about the refinement and the correctness of an idea? We must keep in mind, what is more, that it is by way of conversation, by a word, by a phrase, that we give a good or bad impression of ourselves.[40]

The theory of dramatic art on which Madame Necker based her comparison is Diderot's, and it relied upon the lucid distance thanks to which the actor is in perfect control of his or her emotions and effects. That self-awareness obliges the speaker to keep permanent vigilance and always remain attentive to what the others say and do and, above all, to what they are. The enumeration of grades of social status confirmed that, if politeness implied respecting a fiction of equality, salon conversation demanded exacting attention to the social status of one's interlocutors. Finally, conversation was an art of appearances in which each participant judged and knew that he was being judged and in which reputation was constructed by the gaze of the other.

To be sure, this insistence on the theatrical dimension of conversation, in which each person strives to give a good image of himself, does not contradict being natural, which was, for Madame Necker and everyone else, a sacrosanct rule of conversation. The worldly *naturel* referred to an art that demanded considerable work to assure mastery over the effects one wanted to produce in others. There was nothing spontaneous about it. *Le naturel* in conversation was acquired by frequenting *le monde*, just as in the theater it was acquired by rehearsal. It was quite acceptable to prepare conversations by learning by heart a few phrases to be used at the right moment, as Madame Necker recommended, and by thinking ahead of time about topics to help the conversation flow. What was important was that all of that preparation not show and that the illusion of naturalness be given. Otherwise, one exposed oneself to mockery, like a certain lady who announced, in a salon, "To speak much and well is the talent of the *bel esprit*; to speak little and well is the character of the wise man; to speak much and badly is the idiosyncracy of the fatuous man; to speak little and badly is the misfortune of the stupid man," only to hear the response, "And to speak as you do, madame, is to speak like a book."[41]

Conversation as Politics: The Art of Praise

Was that stinging retort, the sharpness of which was hidden under its ambiguity, ever actually delivered, and if so, under what conditions? The art of the quip, the amusing retort, and the killing witticism that annihilates the victim are what stand out from salon conversation, customarily viewed as a sort of verbal fencing match or a duel of wit. In reality, the art of conversation was above all an art of skillful praise, of saying agreeable things to others. Worldly conversation always looked back to its origin in the royal court and to its political nature. Laudatory statements were common coin and perfectly normal in conversation. Praise that seems to us exaggerated, if not ridiculous, and in which we tend to suspect a note of irony, was perfectly well received. Praise in Parisian social circles, like praise in the court setting, did not shrink from hyperbole, but it avoided paradox. It seems that no one was bothered by hearing his praises sung in a salon. Quite to the contrary, laudatory speech was an essential part of worldly life, and it is important to understand its function.

Such praise needs to be distinguished from flattery, however. In classical French literature flattery, whether it is that of the parasite who seeks to obtain material goods (La Fontaine's crow and his cheese is the paradigm here) or that of the courtier who hopes for favors, is a false discourse that aims at fooling and manipulating the other person. It differs from the worldly system of praise, which corresponded to "the *conventional* repudiation of the potential for aggression intrinsic to all human relationships."[42] Flattery is, at base, an aggression, given that it functions as bait that leads to a clear loss for the flattered (the crow swears in vain that he will not be taken in again, and there is no more cheese), whereas praise can be inscribed within a reciprocal system of compliments in which the demands of civility come to the aid of both parties' amour propre. Praise had a function of aggregation; it nourished sociability and reinforced the collective nature of the group. The salons were like mutual admiration societies in which each participant was paid by the praise with which he covered others and by the praise he received. Not only did the cohesion and the durability of a circle come at that price, but it was mutual admiration that permitted the circulation of such praise, for every compliment reflected back on all the habitués of the group by means of a genuine "group narcissism."[43] Every salon was pleased to imagine itself as particularly distinguished and supported that opinion by exchanging compliments that, at court, would be reserved to the king: "There is no company so bad that it does not imagine itself being good company,"[44] the prince de Ligne wrote with a smile.

The demand for praises reached an extreme in the sociability of Le Riche de La Poupelinière, where it bordered on flattery. La Poupelinière adored music, but he liked compliments even better. He recognized, however, that his freedom to say what he wanted was not the rule in his salon: "I have put my friends in a situation in which none of them would dare tell me a truth that I would not be happy to hear."[45] When an author's amour propre became involved in worldly praise, the exchange of compliments could become comical. The prince de Ligne drew amusement from the terms of exchange: "I get along with men of letters with praise for praise and as much verse as they wrote for me."[46]

Worldly expressions of praise were often addressed to women. Such compliments were part of *galanterie*, an essential part of the society life.[47] As a strategy of seduction, praise addressed to a woman was a variation on flattery, deceitful discourse dictated by the specific objective of obtaining the favors of the woman being flattered. As a civility, on the other hand, it was part of the worldly economy of praise in which someone sought to be "amiable" by reinforcing the amour propre of the person or persons addressed, but without pushing the artifice outside the bounds of convention and manifestations of worldly savoir faire.[48] Madame Du Deffand was amused by the circulation of such laudatory talk. After having supped at the home of Madame de La Reynière, she wrote Walpole to say, "I told her that you find her the most beautiful woman in France; as a result, she believes you to be a man of the greatest merit."[49] The most effective praise was, in fact, indirect, one person taking on the task of repeating the praise pronounced by another.

Within worldly society, not everyone was to be praised in the same manner. A large part of knowledge of the high society lay in distinguishing what was due each person and how to say what one's interlocutor wanted to hear. An apprenticeship in worldly politeness, whether this was in the society of the prince de Conti or that of Madame Geoffrin, was a political training, and the courtly dimension of salon conversation was an open secret. Only newcomers—foreigners, for example—needed any explanation. That is the meaning of the lesson in worldly politics that Madame Geoffrin gave the young Stanisław August Poniatowski during his stay in Paris. He frequented the house of the maréchal de Noailles and one day, in the presence of the comtesse de La Marck and Madame de Brancas, the maréchal asked him what people abroad said about French ministers. Poniatowski answered with a long compliment, to the effect that throughout Europe everyone was hoping for policies directed by the maréchal de Noailles. But unfortunately he added, "I have heard the same people say the like about the marquis de Puisieux."[50] Vexed, the marshal left the room without responding, leaving Poniatowski with the comtesse de La Marck and Madame de Brancas. They scolded him and explained that he had committed a blunder that had "shocked them to the highest degree." They continued: "Are you unaware that monsieur de Puisieux owes everything that he is to monsieur le maréchal de Noailles, but that he is not of a sort ever to be compared with him?" The young Polish lord was thus reminded of the importance of respecting hierarchy in nobility and client networks. Madame Geoffrin, her protector in Paris, was angry when she learned of the blunder, an account of which seems to have circulated among the salons. When Poniatowski next presented himself at her home she gave him a chilly welcome, interrogated him "with an angry air," and explained, "Learn, *grosse bête*, that when a man asks you what people are saying of him, he wants you to praise him and no one but him."[51]

The young Poniatowski had been naïve: he thought he was being asked a question when he was being solicited for praise. He thought that conversation served to inform, where it was here a social and political sham whose customs and codes he had not yet learned. Thus he needed a translation of the language of worldly society, where the real meaning of words is not always their explicit meaning. Madame Geoffrin even reserved more subtle lessons for more experienced students, for example pointing out to Gleichen that, in spite of the fact that he was a diplomat, the resources of silence can at times be more flattering than spoken praise. He stated, "She taught me to be silent in order to listen in such a way as to make people think that they had said the finest things in the world."[52] As this shows, the sociable function of conversation did not imply forgetting rank and social position, and the art of praise was also an art of showing one's own worth. For one and all, the reputation drawn from conversation was socialized, in the sense that it was valid only for the judgment that the circle produced when it qualified a swift response as a *bon mot*.

THE SOCIAL USES OF LETTERS
Correspondence and Worldly Networks

Despite being a tenacious commonplace, correspondence is not a faithful image of salon conversation. The letters exchanged by socialites are sources for the historian, but they are also emanations of worldly sociability, hence they should be read as both acts of writing and worldly practices. Correspondence served to remedy distance and maintain interpersonal connections within high society. When the marquis de Paulmy visited Poland from 1760 to 1762, he kept up a correspondence with Hénault, and in every letter asked him to salute Madame de Mirepoix, Madame de Séchelle, and Madame Du Deffand, with whom he also corresponded directly.[53] Guibert, who was both the epitome of the *homme de salon* and an indefatigable traveler, alternated between stays in Paris, where he ran from one visit and one supper to another, and journeys to Germany, Switzerland, and throughout France. When away from Paris, he wrote regularly to his Parisian friends, and his letters were minor events, not only for Julie de Lespinasse, who awaited them with impatience, but for all the circles he frequented, where the members of the circle read them and lent or sent them to one another. As soon as a letter arrived in Paris, whether it was addressed to the comtesse de

Boufflers or the chancelier d'Aguesseau, news of it went out and Julie de Lespinasse was told of it. On returning home one evening, for example, she found a note from one of her friends telling her that he had received a letter from Guibert. The next day she waited in vain for a visit from the friend, but ran into him at the house of Madame Geoffrin. The letter was read there, and Julie de Lespinasse noted with satisfaction that Guibert mentioned her three times.[54]

Correspondence structured networks that were looser than the worldly ones and extended connections of sociability, with foreigners in particular. Walpole asked Madame Du Deffand to send him very detailed news of Parisian life. He pressed her for the names of her guests, the people in whose house she went to supper, and the persons she met there. Thanks to this information, he maintained close contact with worldly Paris and fit easily into its society on his return. Similarly, Galiani demanded from Madame d'Épinay fairly detailed chronicles and news of the hostesses whose gatherings he had attended in Paris. When Madame d'Épinay's letters became overly political under the Maupeou government, Galiani objected: "Is that a reason for my not knowing what the Helvétiuses are doing? What are Madame Geoffrin, Madame Necker, Mademoiselle Clairon, Mademoiselle de Lespinasse, Grimm, Suard, the abbé Raynal, Marmontel, and all the honorable company doing?"[55] It was not only a matter of having news, but also of transmitting one's own news and of not being forgotten by Parisian high society.[56]

Interaction between epistolary exchange and worldly sociability went far beyond the desire of individuals who were away from Paris to maintain an affective and worldly connection with Paris circles. The essential question is how that correspondence circulated. Who read these letters? To whom? Were the letters copied? Under what conditions? At what risk?[57] Aside from intimate letters though, within high society most correspondence had an extremely complex circulation that was governed by subtle codes.

At times, letters were written by more than one hand. D'Alembert served Julie de Lespinasse as a secretary by writing down letters that she dictated from her bath. The duchesse de Choiseul and abbé Barthélemy often wrote letters together to Madame Du Deffand in which they chronicled life at Chanteloup. Several people are often mentioned as receiving a letter. Galiani encouraged Madame d'Épinay to read his letters to the habitués of her salon, and even to make copies for them. He stated, "You know that I would like it if my letters were read and seen by all my friends. This is not out of vanity. It is to keep me in their memory. It is because I would like to speak with them and cannot do so. It is because I eat in Naples, but I still live in Paris."[58] The justification for this sort of request was of course friendship and distance. But Galiani's insistent denial of epistolary vanity is scarcely persuasive. During the first years of this correspondence (1770–72), Galiani was concerned about the publication of his *Dialogues*, and his preoccupation for the book's success is an almost obsessive topic. In this context, it was crucial for him to remain in his friends' minds. He felt obliged to write amusing, even droll, letters to maintain his reputation as an original and brilliant conversationalist—a reputation that would contribute to the success of his book.

Galiani worked hard on his letters, which only seem spontaneous and informal. He probably intended to have them collected and printed, should the opportunity arise. In any event, on several occasions he encouraged Madame d'Épinay to keep them safe and to gather together all the letters that he had sent to friends in Paris. Now and then he mentions to her a missive that he had recently sent to another of his correspondents and that he thought particularly amusing, suggesting that she procure a copy to read in her salon, but he also suggested that she add it to the collection, seeming to see no problem in such a move.[59] Galiani's letters functioned on the model of the stories and pleasantries that had guaranteed his success in Parisian salons. He expressed irritation when some of his correspondents refused to show his letters and kept them for themselves. What seems today like a normal practice appeared to him as an unacceptable abuse of power and a deliberate refusal to play the game: "I have received a letter from Madame Necker, but since she does not show you my responses, I will answer her quite tardily and through my office."[60] Tiring of running after the letters that Galiani indicated to her, Madame d'Épinay eventually found a way around the difficulty and suggested to Galiani that when he wrote a fine letter he send it to her first, so that she could make a copy of it, promising to then convey it to the addressee.[61]

How could people keep up a private correspondence in letters that were intended to circulate and be read by many? After penning a virulent passage about Suard and Morellet, whom she suspected of having written an anonymous article criticizing Galiani's book, Madame d'Épinay specifies, "Do not answer me on this topic, as I want to be able to read your letters to society."[62] Galiani's response was destined to a worldly and collective use; it would be integrated into the practices of sociability, hence its author had to weigh his words and avoid speaking of things that did not concern "society." The other solution was to write letters in segments, separating what was of a worldly nature and what was more appropriate for private correspondence. When she speaks of the difficult situation of her son, Madame d'Épinay specifies to Galiani that he should answer in a separate note.[63]

The two principles coexisted. Correspondence was a relationship between two people set within a network of worldly practices. This is why, although it is essential not to mistake correspondence for private or intimate texts, it would be wrong to see them as quasi-public texts. As we have seen, Madame d'Épinay did not always manage to see Galiani's letters, since the circulation of correspondence followed unwritten laws based on tact and civility. When Galiani complains that Madame d'Épinay had not read the letter he wrote to Madame Necker, Madame d'Épinay answered him that it was not astonishing, given that she saw Madame Necker only rarely and, above all, was not that close to her: "We are not at all on terms of communicating our letters to one another."[64]

Epistolary Exchanges

To whom could one show letters received? Was it obligatory to allow them to be copied? How broad a distribution was deemed legitimate? There is no clear answer to these questions because they involve both the worldly meaning of letters and their political meaning. The correspondence between Madame Du Deffand and Voltaire provides a good example of these ambiguities. There was nothing private about their exchange of letters, in which social, worldly, and political themes dominate.[65] Their relationship was of long standing: they had met at Sceaux and had friends in common, notably Formont, whose death in 1758 offered an occasion to launch an abundant correspondence that continued until Voltaire's death. They esteemed one another, feared one another, and dealt carefully with one another. To flatter Madame Du Deffand's classical tastes, Voltaire repeated tirelessly, "We must return, Madame, to the century of Louis XIV."[66] The marquise knew Voltaire well enough to praise him incessantly, stating that he was the only great writer of the eighteenth century.[67]

Until 1764, Madame Du Deffand, without being favorable to the philosophes, received several of them in her home—d'Alembert in particular—and could thus pass for their ally. However, her decision to favor Palissot in 1760, her repeated attacks against the philosophes, and her rupture with Julie de Lespinasse and d'Alembert in 1764 distanced her from the philosophical current. Her correspondence with Voltaire did not suffer from that shift, however. For Voltaire, what mattered was the position of the marquise in high society and her links with the duchesse de Luxembourg, the prince de Conti, and the Choiseuls. In the 1760s he constantly urged Madame Du Deffand to transmit his admiration to the duchess: "I put myself at the feet of Madame la duchesse de

Luxembourg,"[68] he wrote on several occasions. Madame Du Deffand was quite willing to take on this role of intermediary and at times made the first move: three years later, at the death of the duc de Luxembourg, she signaled Voltaire that he should send a word to the duchess. He did so, but the note was received with ambivalence, as Madame de Luxembourg reproached Voltaire for his attacks on Rousseau.[69] Voltaire responded to Madame Du Deffand with a plea destined for the duchess: "I hope that Madame la Duchesse de Luxembourg will render me the justice to believe that I do not at all hate a man whom she protects, and that I am far from persecuting a man so to be pitied."[70] In several of the letters that followed he proclaimed his respect for Rousseau in a courtier's language: "I begin, madame, by begging you to put me at the feet of Madame la maréchale de Luxembourg. Her protégé, Jean Jacques, will always have rights over me because she honors him with her kindnesses, and I shall always love the author of the *Vicaire savoyard*, whatever he may have done and whatever he may do."[71] Later, Madame Du Deffand acted as an intermediary with the Choiseuls, to the point that they ended up as a third party in the correspondence.

Madame Du Deffand herself gained a good deal from this correspondence with Voltaire. In the first place, there were the letters themselves. They proved that the marquise was a regular correspondent of Voltaire's, which contributed to her prestige. Walpole described her as a woman who "corresponds with Voltaire" and "dictates charming letters to him."[72] Ten years later, the *Mémoires secrets* presented the correspondence as one of her last claims to glory: "She was once renowned for her graces, her wit and her mischievousness: she always kept up some connection with the philosopher of Ferney, and he has just addressed an epistle to her."[73] Voltaire's letters were read in her salon, where they were appreciated and commented on. She wrote him to say, "Your letter is charming; everyone asked me for copies of it." On another occasion she said about a missive that he had sent to her, "You make us spend very agreeable moments."[74] She often recommended that he add a word for one of her visitors, as she did for William Robertson, who wanted to dedicate a copy of his *History of the Reign of Emperor Charles V* to Voltaire: "I would like him to be able to see your response; thus I beg you that it be of a mind to satisfy him."[75] In this particular case, Voltaire provided only minimal service, a few amiable lines that Madame Du Deffand would have to extract from the rest of the letter, for the subsequent paragraph was a good deal less amiable. Certain of Voltaire's letters give the impression of a mosaic of paragraphs destined for different interlocutors. Madame Du Deffand took it upon herself to make extracts and to read them to the persons concerned.

This mix of sociability and flattery was even clearer when the Choiseuls entered the scene. Voltaire never moderated his praises when speaking of the powerful minister and his wife. Since Choiseul was the superintendent of the postal service, Voltaire addressed to the duchesse de Choiseul unsealed letters and packages destined for the marquise Du Deffand. This means that the Choiseuls were the first to read letters in which Voltaire took care to praise them. In a letter of March 1769 explicitly destined to be read by the duchesse de Choiseul he praises the merits of the duchess and adds a "confidence" that Choiseul shared with him, writing to him that his wife made his happiness.[76] The duchess, the first reader of the letter, sent it on to Madame Du Deffand, adding that the passage had given her particular pleasure.[77] These laudatory statements did not remain among Voltaire, Madame Du Deffand, and the Choiseuls, since the letters were read in Madame Du Deffand's salon and by the duchesse de Choiseul herself. Madame Du Deffand related to Voltaire the success of his letters when read to her guests by the duchess in person: "*La grand-maman* does not want to leave it to anyone else to read you; she did it in a superior manner, with a tone of voice that went to the heart, an intelligence that made everything felt and remarked; to tell the truth, she wanted to mumble the passages that regarded her, but I would not suffer it, and I forced her to articulate them more distinctly than all the rest. These [passages] are the ones that are the most applauded, because they are the most just and the most true."[78]

Voltaire's letters also permitted Mme Du Deffand to be aware of Voltaire's doings and sayings, always a highly appreciated topic of conversation. When, for example, the rumor circulated that Voltaire had confessed and taken communion, Madame Du Deffand, who found that hard to believe, rushed to take up her pen and ask Voltaire for confirmation.[79] In addition to the letters themselves, Madame Du Deffand constantly reminded Voltaire to send her his new works, which was, for him, a way of putting them in circulation. Faithful to his customary strategies, he often pretended not to be the author of these works, but the marquise was rarely fooled. That perspicacity enabled her to keep the duchesse de Choiseul from making a serious gaffe: the duchess was about to write to Voltaire all her negative thoughts about *Guèbres* when Madame Du Deffand told her that he was quite certainly its author.[80] While maintaining the pretense of protecting a young playwright, Voltaire sent several letters to Madame Du Deffand urging her to campaign for the play: "Shout out loud for these good Guèbres, Madame, shout and make others shout."[81]

Within the framework of worldly practices, epistolary exchanges tended to escape from private correspondence and become fodder for salon conversations. Still, the tacit rules governing this circulation were complex, in part based on nuance, a sense of decorum, tact, and an interpretation of the other person's intentions. At times Voltaire insisted on the need for discretion, and he even instructed Madame Du Deffand to burn one of his letters after she had read it.[82] He was disturbed when he thought that she had circulated a letter that might cause a falling out with friends: "Ah! Madame, Madame, what have you done? You have let a letter circulate that has raised a quarrel with people whom I love and who love me."[83] This time Madame Du Deffand succeeded in justifying herself, but on other occasions she made mistakes. In March 1764, she discovered, to her fury, that someone had "printed, without her knowledge" a letter in which Voltaire spoke of Moncrif in terms that could be misunderstood, expressing regret that no one still read him.[84] One of her guests (whom she later identified as Turgot) was reported to have learned the letter by heart. Moncrif does not seem to have been offended, but Voltaire regretted "that unfortunate letter, which pirates published,"[85] and he recalled the incident in future letters. His expression was a strong one, and the incident shows that between reading a letter aloud in a salon and printing it a boundary had been crossed that qualified this use as piracy. Published, the letter left the legitimate domain of worldly circulation and became open to unexpected interpretations and uncontrolled uses.

Writing enjoyed the special status of serving as proof. One might argue endlessly about a witticism or an anecdote, for everyone knew that it might have been distorted or even invented. A written text, however, whether in the author's hand or copied before a trustworthy witness, was irrefutable proof that put an end to discussion and engaged the author, who could no longer deny his statements. In fact, as long as circulation remained oral, it was always possible to protest that the content of the letter or the conversation had been distorted; as collective productions of high society, rumors did not involve those who originated the particular statement in the same way that a written text or a certifiable copy did. Voltaire, for example, was quick to make the claim of denial when one of his judgments was passed around. What was essential was there not be a written copy to confound that denial.

The circulation of quotations was thus governed by fairly complex rules that required perpetual negotiation among the expectations of the correspondent, worldly imperatives, and cultural codes. Morellet, who kept up a thick correspondence with Lord Shelburne, learned this when the Leyden *Gazette* published a letter on free trade that Shelburne had sent to him. Scandalized, Shelburne complained to Morellet immediately about this public use of his letter. For an Englishman involved in politics and used to public political debate and to the role of the gazettes, the difference between private and public was quite clear, while it was much less so for Morellet. Worldly rules were unstable and left room for uncertainty. But Shelburne was not naïve, and he was well aware that letters circulated within salons in Paris. He surely knew that Morellet was reading his letters and copying them. On the other hand, it was imperative that they not appear in the newspapers. Morellet's reputation as a correspondent rested on his mastery of the worldly networks within which he circulated the letters that he received. For Shelburne, Morellet's trustworthiness, but also his political interest, was based on his position in the Parisian world and his experience, which should have permitted him to make Shelburne's letters known in certain social spheres without their becoming public.

A SALON LITERATURE

Collective Writing?

Contrary to common knowledge, the salons were only rarely places for collective literary production. The tales that Voltaire wrote for the society of the duchesse du Maine were not the fruit of collective composition.[86] Similarly, although at times Diderot used baron d'Holbach's salon to recruit authors, it is impossible to establish a genuine connection between the baron's hospitality and the editing of the *Encyclopédie*.[87]

The salon of Mademoiselle Quinault, where the members of the "Société du Bout-du-Banc" gathered, was an exception to that rule. From 1741 on, Jeanne Quinault, a famous actress, gave weekly dinners attended by Caylus, Madame de Graffigny, Duclos, Sallé, Berthier, Périgny, the duc de Nivernais, and Crébillon. That first circle of writers and men of the world was occasionally augmented by other guests. These dinners were better known for their amusements than for any philosophical ambitions.[88] Thanks to a parlor game in which losers had to promise to write a tale, a group of frequent guests published a volume called *Recueil de ces messieurs*[89] that contained some of the tales that had been read at Mademoiselle Quinault's receptions.[90] Although the book was published anonymously, it publicized—even by its title—the existence of a collective, friendly, and literary sociability that featured literary amusements. It also demonstrated the strong cohesion among the habitués. Relations of hospitality were paralleled by a fiction of institutionalization, as signaled by the collective name, "Société du Bout-du-Banc," given in the *Recueil*. When Mademoiselle Quinault no longer gave her dinners, that half-worldly, half-bantering tradition, which was based on a parody of institutionalization, was taken up by the comtesse Turpin de Crissé and her guests, who called themselves the "Order of the Round Table" and also published a collective effort, *La Journée de l'Amour, ou, Heures de Cythère.*[91]

Nonetheless, the *Recueil de ces messieurs* was not really the product of salon sociability. Each author wrote his contribution independently, being assigned a title with no further information and unaware of what the others were doing. The contributions were brought together, outside the dinners, by Quinault and Caylus during the autumn of 1744, and Madame de Graffigny herself does not seem to have known who had written what.[92] The *Recueil de ces messieurs* was, in fact, a quite different sort of enterprise from the *Chroniques des samedis*, composed by the friends of Mademoiselle de Scudéry a century earlier, which remained in manuscript form and helped to commemorate the chosen sociability of Scudéry's friends within a restricted and privileged readership.[93] In contrast, the *Recueil* was published immediately and contained no allusion, except in the title, to the gatherings that had taken place at the homes of Quinault or Caylus. The front matter includes a notice of a page and a half "from the printer to the reader" to state that the collection was made at the request of a lady, who found it boring, which had pushed the printer to present it to the public. The aim of the work was not to publish or celebrate the sociability of Mademoiselle Quinault's friends, but rather to deliver a set of more or less parodic texts. The result was judged to be disappointing, even by Madame de Graffigny. It seems that she was the only person who took the exercise seriously, while the others saw it as a joke and an opportunity to parody genres that were fashionable, such as that of *Les Étrennes de la Saint-Jean*, a work published a few years earlier.[94]

The habitués of a salon might collaborate in writing a play or a poem, but the salon as a place of sociability lent itself poorly to writing. Readings, on the other hand, suited it perfectly. During a stay in Saint-Ouen with the Neckers, Suard decided to return to Paris because, he wrote to his wife, "there will be a reading at Madame Geoffrin's and I am invited."[95] The session was planned in advance and invitations to attend it had already been sent out. The salon was thus a reputable space where judgments were produced, but also a first audience that authors had to take into account. Readings also provided a way to spread word of works that could not be published. Sedaine, for example, read his play, *Paris sauvée*, whose production had been forbidden, at the home of the Trudaines.[96] Certain works were known for a number of years thanks to salon readings. In 1751, Madame de Graffigny expressed her delight at persuading Helvétius to come to her home to read his poem *Du Bonheur*, which she had heard in 1744 at the home of Mademoiselle Quinault.[97] Grimm and Marivaux praised the poem in subsequent years, but it was not published until 1772.

At a time when the elite model of solitary reading was dominant, collective reading remained an activity prized by high society[98] In Paris salons, reading aloud was both an amusement that at times could resemble a theatrical performance and a social event to which guests were invited and promised novelty and pleasure. The marquise de La Vaupalière did not hesitate to invite sixty guests to listen to Beaumarchais read from *Le Mariage de Figaro*.[99] Such readings of new works by their authors were not the special privilege of certain salons: Chastellux, for example, made six readings while staying in the home of the duc d'Orléans.[100] The duchesse de Luxembourg invited Madame Du Deffand to listen to La Harpe read his *Barmécides*. The piece was so long it took two Monday evenings, two weeks apart, to finish, but Madame Du Deffand was satisfied with the result, and La Harpe's performance as reader had something to do with its success.[101]

Social Verse and Worldly Games

The eighteenth century was long held to be a century without poetry. However, poetry was omnipresent in urban society of the age, and notably so within high society. One of the greatest stage successes of the century was Piron's *La Métromanie*, a play about the mania for writing verse.[102] Periodicals, correspondence collections, and memoirs all testify to the vogue for verse in all its forms: slight occasional works, songs, petitions, epigrams, and more all bear traces of being destined for circles of sociability. From the *Mercure de France* to Grimm and Meister's *Correspondance littéraire*, social verse was the daily fare.

Occasional verse did not confine its circulation to worldly circles, news sheets, or even printed periodicals. It was also published in the form of specific collections, where it was often qualified as *poésie fugitive*, thus contributing to the formation of a literary subgenre.[103] The connection between occasional verse and the practices of sociability is undeniable and in nearly all cases explicit, as when it is labeled as *vers de sociétés*.[104]

In Parisian salons, the ability to produce verse for all occasions drew on a repertory that was no longer that of the canon of classical poetry, but included *la poésie galante*, songs, and comic-opera airs. Performances of such verse might be oral and improvised, but improvisation was often mimed. The minor events of life in society were opportunities for versification, both for men of letters and men of the world.

When the comte de Genlis discovered among the papers of the maréchale d'Estrées after her death an unpaid bill for 4,000 livres for white wine that had been sold to the marquis de Conflans, he requested payment of the sum due by sending the bill, along with a bit of verse to be sung to "Grégoire's air in Richard the Lion-Hearted," to which the marquis de Conflans responded in kind.

A minor and apparently quite prosaic occurrence thus inspired a contest of wits between these two aristocrats, prominent figures in the worldly life of the final years of the ancien régime. It is noteworthy that the two *couplets* were sung to a tune that was currently popular, drawn from *Richard Cœur de Lion*. The two poems were found sufficiently well conceived to circulate in the salons and to inspire Meister to put them into the *Correspondance littéraire*, thus giving a still broader circulation to the image of two witty men of the world creating light verse as easily as Voltaire. The poems may even have been intended for wide circulation and to be repeated, sung, and read in high society. The dual poetic performance of these two aristocrats gave public exposure to their wit, and it denotes the importance of a poetic competence as a social skill. A man of the world was expected to be able to turn out an agreeable bit of verse just as he had to know how to use a sword. If arms made the military virtue of the gentleman, verse made the reputation of the socialite.

Some men of the world made a specialty of society amusements. For those who remained faithful to the aristocratic ethos, which was incompatible with publication, worldly distractions furnished a legitimate framework for literary activity. The chevalier de Boufflers was certainly the most famous and the most representative of these amateur poets.[105] Brought up at the court of Lunéville, he abandoned the seminary for a military career. In 1761, he wrote a successful tale, *La Reine de Golconde*, and spent his time traveling and frequenting the salons between adventures.[106]

The many gifts that were exchanged among the habitués of the salons on festive occasions or holidays were accompanied by brief poems, which were at times considered more important than the gift. In 1772, the latest rage in the salons was *parfilage*, an amusement that consisted of unwinding bobbins of gold thread to make braided decorations.[107] That year everyone in Paris society gave gifts of objects and animals made of gold thread. "It is the current folly; which makes display and magnificence shine because what is extremely expensive is reduced to nothing," Madame Du Deffand explained to Walpole when she sent him a collection of songs written at Chanteloup to celebrate a pigeon in gold thread that the princesse de Beauvau had just given as a Pentecost gift to the duchesse de Gramont.[108] The verse songs celebrated the worldly relationship and the generosity and wit of the princesse de Beauvau. The gold thread pigeon did not last long, since it was to be unraveled, but this gift typical of Parisian high society was commemorated in poems that circulated as far as London and of which Madame Du Deffand kept copies.

Salon poems were a social diversion. Like *bons mots*, they were intended to amuse and entertain, to be repeated and to do honor to their author and to the society for which they had been conceived. Madame de La Ferté-Imbault kept the pieces produced in her society and created a dossier of the poems that had been written for her "various societies" over a span of thirty years.[109] Julie de Lespinasse also carefully kept society pieces and copies of letters.[110] Prominent salon hostesses were not the only ones who kept such pieces, which circulated from one circle to another. Collecting poems and songs was a widespread practice, and the value accorded to verse was no longer directly connected to the memory of live performance, since the immediate connection with sociability was broken, or at least stretched.[111] To bring together a large number of them, nonetheless, was proof of active social networks, and a collection allowed its owner to feel at the center of worldly life. To Mathieu Marais, who had sent him two fairly mediocre songs, Président Bouhier responded, "I thank you for the one and the other. One is always happy to know what is current."[112] Moreover, when his correspondent spoke to him of some satirical verse, Bouhier hastened to ask him to send a copy: "What you say to me makes my mouth water. There is an infinity of occasional pieces of this sort, which it would be good not to lose."[113]

In salon life, a writer's ability to produce verse easily was a valuable skill. Such a person was asked for poems to flatter one figure or another, to celebrate a worldly occasion, or to accompany a gift.[114] Some writers even specialized in occasional verse. Abbé de Voisenon was a tireless author of society verse and songs. His *Œuvres mêlées* overflow with poems written to accompany a gift, such as an "*Étrenne* from M. Le duc de G*** to madame la duchesse de Choiseul, giving her a little lamp to burn incense," or "Verses of madame de B*** to Madame de Laborde on sending her an eggcup." Some verses celebrated even lesser events, such as a poem entitled "To Madame de *** on a butterfly that she caught."[115] Voisenon, who was of fragile health but tirelessly delivered mocking banter, was the incarnation of those eighteenth-century "butterflies" whose entire works consisted of amiable nothings and fleeting but graceful images of the "futility" of the age.[116]

Some authors did not hesitate to display their capacity for versified praise as a way to advance in the world. Ponce Denis Lebrun, for example, the author of many odes and of a poem on nature, whose publication he announced as imminent for some twenty years, enjoyed a good reputation as a lyric poet.[117] He was also clever at composing satirical epigrams and circumstantial pieces. He enjoyed close relations with the comte and comtesse de Brancas, to whom he addressed verse for all occasions. Because she had him woken at six in the morning, he composed a poem in which he compared her to the dawn. The final conceit was obvious: "These two divinities wake me too early in the morning."[118] Lebrun also knew how to use his poetic talents to penetrate the most fashionable salons. In 1760 he composed an ode to Buffon that met with great success and allowed him to be received at Mme Necker's home: "Suffer that I implore of you, in the name of the sublime old man whom you love, the grace that is the most flattering for me, that of being allowed to pay you court."[119]

Once received in a salon, authors continued to furnish poems in praise of the mistress of the house and of the guests, poems to accompany gifts, and poems that contributed more generally to the common entertainment, which was their principal function. A letter of Madame de Staal de Launay to Madame Du Deffand reveals this expectation and the inappropriate nature, in a worldly setting, of serious and solitary work. When Voltaire and Madame Du Châtelet were staying with the duchesse du Maine, Madame de Staal de Launay complained of their absence from all participation in the entertainments: "They do not show themselves at all during the day. They appeared yesterday at ten in the evening. I do not think that anyone will see them earlier today; one is describing important events, the other is commenting on Newton. They do not want to join in on gaming or a promenade: they are indeed non-values [*non-valeurs*] in a society within which their learned writings have no relation."[120] Judging by the standards of "society" and by those of collective amusement, the intellectual work of Voltaire and his companion had no value. Happily, Voltaire soon caught up with his tasks and, several days later, Madame de Staal announced to her correspondent that he had produced some "gallant verse" that "repaired somewhat the bad effect of their unusual conduct."[121]

Society poetry had a gallant and playful function. Literary parlor games such as *bouts-rimés* (composing verse from set rhymes), charades, and synonyms were not exclusive to seventeenth-century salons, as some historians have believed, persuaded that such mental games had been supplanted by critical and philosophical conversation in Enlightenment salons. To the contrary, Madame Necker, for example, had no qualms about entering into a *bouts-rimés* contest with Thomas: they had to write a poem in praise of Madame de Vermenoux using a set list of rhyming words.[122]

Aside from *bouts-rimés*, Parisian high society continued to delight in other traditional forms of literary games, such as the portrait, at which Madame Du Deffand was the acknowledged master; charades and synonyms, whose popularity was increased, in the latter years of the ancien régime, by the publication of the abbé Roubaud's book on the topic.[123] Madame de Créquy who counted Roubaud among her most assiduous guests, was extremely fond of this exercise.[124] The linguistic exercise of defining two synonyms, insisting on the nuances of difference between them, had become a worldly game particularly appreciated. It permitted the players to display a certain virtuosity and, above all, a sense of linguistic nuances.[125]

Madame de Staël also tried her hand at synonyms. Her short texts on "Véracité et franchise" [truth and frankness] and "Trait et saillie" [quip and sally] proved a great success. Meister reproduced them in the *Correspondance littéraire* with praise.[126] Like everything fashionable, the synonyms game lent itself to parody, and the success of those of Madame de Staël attracted satirists. The comte de Thiard was the first to enter the fray with a synonym parody "most appropriate for making the fashion pass away" on the words *ânesse* and *bourrique* (both she-ass, with overtones of stupidity and stubbornness).[127] He took the occasion to ridicule both the role of women in society and purist tendencies.[128] Two months later Meister related a "much bitterer" parody. This time, the author had written a close pastiche of Madame de Staël's synonym on *franchise* and *véracité*, but compared the terms *naturelle* and *précieuse*. The joke worked two ways. By striving for a fine distinction between two opposites, it exposed the very principle of the synonym game to ridicule, and the choice of terms obviously led to applying the term *précieuse* to the author of the original synonym piece.

The salons of the eighteenth century still closely resembled those of the seventeenth century. *Bons mots*, contests of wit, *bouts-rimés*, and occasional verse met with the same success. Literature was still profoundly tied to aristocratic entertainment, and only gradually detached itself from the "oral, collective, and ephemeral forms of language-related creation."[129] To be a man of letters meant being able to amuse a gathering or affect worldly hierarchies through ridicule, praise, and acceptance. That persistence of worldly literature was even more evident in poetry than in prose. Whereas prose invented new forms of writing, poetry remained largely dependent on worldly theories of taste.[130] Even when poetry sought to express the new ideals of the Enlightenment, it was not incompatible with the maintenance of a traditional taste, as shown by the success in the salons of didactic and descriptive poems of the years 1760 to 1770 (Saint-Lambert, Delille, Lemierre, Roucher). Moreover, the authors of that poetry did not refuse to try their hand at society poetry. Saint-Lambert, a gentleman philosopher, man of the world, and disciple of Helvétius, wrote occasional verse in which he saw "refinement of the mind," "playfulness," and "the talent to seize, in certain circumstances and in the moment, what is most piquant and most agreeable."[131]

The rupture that led to modern literature, while asserting itself as an aesthetic form independent of social and political authorities, also brought about a new conception of the destination and the circulation of texts, which freed themselves from *sociabilité* and demanded a universal audience. Unlimited publication was the goal of texts that assumed an identical and unknown reader. On the contrary, the texts that circulated within the salons were not necessarily aimed at a broader public. They were produced for specific social circles, and they drew their efficacy from their ability to circulate within that world. From society-based jokes to society verse, their value was a social value, which depended on the unmediated success of performance.

CHAPTER 5

Society's Judgment and
Worldly Opinion

There is ridicule in communicating to the public in a book all the society praises that one has received.

Madame de Genlis[1]

Conversation, which was an art of exchanging pleasantries, telling stories, and offering flattery, was also an art of delivering opinions. Salons are thus often seen by historians as an arena for critical discussions and a powerful vector of public opinion. But worldly conversation was very different from rational communication and the salons were not public places. Instead of applying a theoretical model of conversation, it is worth studying precisely the formation and circulation of opinions within the salons, while being attentive to the dynamics of imitation and reputation and to the culture of connivance that were so important in high society.

THE FORMATION OF WORLDLY OPINION
News of a Little World

The connection between conversation and opinion is usually erroneously posed in terms of topics that were taken up or prohibited. In any attempt to survey conversation from extant sources, what is immediately striking is the variety and diversity of topics discussed, which range from literary quarrels to questions of foreign policy, from the latest spicy anecdote to

Chinese civilization, and from court intrigues to Paris theater. It was not the importance of the item that gave news its value, but rather its novelty. Whether it reported a fact or something someone had said, the news item had to be original, amusing, and easy to repeat. By its very nature, a news item was ephemeral, and it was abandoned with the same haste with which it had been reported, for it was part of an economy of worldly entertainment, valuable only for its ability to grab momentary attention.

The form that conversation took and the attraction of novelty equally valued items concerning major political or diplomatic events and those reporting the loves of an actress, the latest witticism, or a judgment of a play performed the night before. During the War of Austrian Succession, the duchesse d'Aiguillon, self-appointed gazetteer to high society, told Maupertuis a number of anecdotes about Voltaire's relations with a dancer, commenting, "That's the news of the Opéra. Given the situation Europe is in, this is not the most interesting news, but it is what everyone is talking about."[2] This emphasis on the equality of all news is also evident in Fonvizin's words: "Here people are completely indifferent to everything except news, whatever it is, which people are delighted to spread throughout the city and which makes up the spiritual nourishment of Parisians."[3] The flow of news items, which knew no other hierarchy than that of novelty, supported the image of Parisian frivolity. Mercier described the "facility" with which "one passes from one object to another." Skillful Parisian conversation depended on a rejection of the principle of discussion and on perfecting a quick overview of interchangeable topics. Its aim was not to deepen understanding of a question or to exchange ideas, but rather to reinforce the feeling of belonging among those who had mastered the virtuosity of that conversational form. Topics were arranged in no other order than that of novelty and curiosity: "It is impossible to know by what rapid transition one passes from an examination of a play to a discussion of the affairs of the Insurgents; or how one can speak at once of a fashion and of Boston, of Desrues and of Franklin."[4] The quick succession of news items was valued for the witticisms it enabled and for the way in which it nourished a conversation that was reluctant to return to yesterday's news. Conversely, an absence of news made conversation languish. A few months after his arrival in Paris in September 1765, Walpole complained about the paucity of events. During the first month of his stay, one subject of conversation occupied everyone: had the duchesse de Boufflers caught smallpox for a second time? After that, he reported to his friend Mary Coke, the salons lived for ten weeks on the illness of the dauphin, and after his death Madame Geoffrin herself admitted that there was nothing left to talk about.[5]

The most interesting news items—those that most attracted the attention of the salons—concerned members of Paris "good society," their successes and failures, their advancement at court and their love affairs. When
Madame Du Deffand, who constantly complained of the unspeakable boredom of worldly life, finally began a letter with the enthusiastic statement,
"We have had great news yesterday," the reason for her excitement was the
prince de Hénin's appointment as a colonel of grenadiers and Monsieur de
Castries's command of a gendarmerie.[6]

It did not much matter whether or not such news was true, as long as it
nourished conversation. Most of the anecdotes that circulated were unveri-
fiable "in this Paris where the next day it would have been ridiculous to
recall what it would have been ridiculous to doubt the day before."[7] Belief in
the veracity of a news item was grounded in an ephemeral consensus that
suspended the question of its truth. It would have been just as inappropriate to contest a news item under discussion in a given circle as it was boring
to relate a bit of stale news. In both cases, veracity was unimportant.

The example of baron d'Holbach shows clearly that one could be a philosopher in one's study and a gossip in the salon. An appetite for news was
a veritable passion for him, as Meister recalls in the eulogy he published at
d'Holbach's death:

> Perhaps one of the most violent passions that occupied him throughout his life,
> but especially in his latter years, was curiosity: he loved news as a child loves toys,
> and by that sort of blindness that is so natural to all passionate customs, he put
> very little choice into it: good or bad, false or true, there was nothing that had no
> attraction for him, and there was even nothing that he was not ready to believe.
> It truly seemed as if all the credulity that he had refused to news of the other
> world he reserved, in toto, for that of the gazettes and the cafés. He even took
> pleasure in having people recount in the smallest detail an event all of whose
> circumstances demonstrated its falsity.[8]

Even in d'Holbach's salon, worldly conversation did not provide an
opportunity for philosophical discussion, and incredulity was seemingly
suspended by the effects of a playful curiosity. D'Holbach lost his temper
at Grimm when the latter expressed doubts about a story that the baron
had learned of that very day at the Palais-Royal and which he had enjoyed.
Irritated by an incredulity that spoiled his own pleasure, he snapped,
"That is how you are," but then said, with a friendly smile, "You never say
anything, and you never want to believe anything."[9] Grimm had broken
the unspoken rule that the pleasure of all required an indifference to the
veracity of information. Similarly, each member of the circle was expected

to contribute to this passion for news by adding surprising bits to the conversation.[10]

News circulated among urban public circles, the gazettes, and the salons by complex circuits. The salons seem to have been hubs where information flowing in from the court, the literary world, the journalists, and the cafés intersected. Conversation, even in d'Holbach's salon, was less focused on the diffusion of enlightened theories or the exercise of critical reason than on a mastery of news items and their circulation. That mastery was an essential social goal as the prestige or the attraction of a salon could be measured by the freshness of the news that circulated in it. The hierarchy of the salons corresponded to a geography of information.

Still, the salons were only one link in the circulation of news, given that conversation was fed by rumors from the court, news from cafés and other public places, and anecdotes from the Académie. News was one of the reasons men of letters were sought in the salons. If the aristocrats were more apt to be aware of political news and goings on at court, writers had the merit of bringing literary news and judgments on works and authors, but also of having connections with the gazette writers and the universe of the cafés and public places. The salons played the role of distribution center, where information circulated in the form of the *nouvelle à la main*, a handwritten news sheet, was validated by the collective sanction of high society, then found its way into news sheets, gazettes, and police reports, into the more daring works of fiction, and into conversation at court. This image of frivolity does not imply that the worldly circulation of news was an inconsequential game. Mastery of news had important social effects.

Rumors and Reputations

Norbert Elias has shown that gossip plays an important role in the cohesion of the best-established groups and in their domination over lesser groups.[11] For Elias, the density of circuits of communication and the rapidity with which news is transmitted is proportional to the social cohesion of the group. Tittle-tattle and ill-natured gossip have a function of social control over the members of the dominant group and form a barrier against would-be new members of the group; they are inseparable from the positive bits of gossip that report an adventure that has happened to a mutual acquaintance and that spreads a flattering image of the entire group. Similarly, the worldly gossip that circulated in Paris salons fed the ideal representations of high society by relating a *bon mot*, a fine action, or a successful reading, but also reported on the faults of those who had transgressed certain codes. The misadventures of La Reynière or Madame Du Boccage showed the impact of such talk. In both cases, they were outsiders whose integration into the social world was interrupted, temporarily or definitively, by such rumors. The social stakes of conversation were great: conversation guaranteed the cohesion of high society and its symbolic domination by shutting the door of the salons to those about whom too many tales were in circulation.

The punishment inflicted upon an individual stigmatized by the verdict of high society was ridicule. This quickly spread through worldly networks by conversation and by correspondence, both of which lent themselves perfectly to the communication of a lethal witticism or short, amusing anecdote. One evening in 1766, Madame de Forcalquier and Madame Du Deffand were victims of a carriage accident in front of the hôtel of the duc de Praslin. They asked for the hospitality of the house, which was refused to them by a surly Swiss guard. Since they knew the master of the house well, they swept by the guard, entered, and awaited the duke's return. However, after the duke had returned, none of the servants wanted to bother him by telling him of the women's presence, so that they were obliged to leave. Praslin's reputation was tainted by his unmannerly servants. Madame Du Deffand hastened to recount the anecdote in a letter to Président Hénault; the letter was read at his suppers and word of it spread from there. "That letter was read by everyone who had been at his house, and all of those who were present repeated it to everyone they saw: thus nothing made as much fuss as this adventure or gave more ridicule to Monseigneur de Praslin."[12] By relating the anecdote to Walpole, but also by telling him of its success and of the ridicule to which it had exposed Praslin, the marquise reinforced the effect of the incident and established the interpretation of it that she wanted. In other circumstances, such a story could have been recounted to the detriment of the two ladies and their impromptu and disdained visit, but Du Deffand ensured that the anecdote would continue to circulate among Walpole's friends and correspondents and bring further negative commentary against Praslin.

The mechanisms of ridicule were abundantly described in the eighteenth century. Many authors insisted on the efficacy of that "light and piercing arm of the *beau monde*."[13] The paradigm of fencing was an obvious though symbolic choice for describing this mixture of civility and violence, elegance and combat, a light touch and a death blow. Foreigners were often struck by the importance of ridicule, fear of which conditioned behavior and imposed extreme conformity. For Fonvizin, France was the "nation in which *ridicule* is what is most terrible. It matters little if one says about someone that he has a wicked heart or an impossible character, but if one says that he is *ridiculous* he is lost, for everyone flees his society." In the highly codified worldly society, ignoring the customs, arbitrary though they may be, was enough to render someone ridiculous. The way to avoid ridicule lay in imitation, which was the principal resource of foreigners, who always took care not to betray insufficient mastery of the codes. Fonvizin notes with amusement: "There is no surer way to create for oneself, for life, a reputation as an imbecile, to damage one's reputation, and to lose oneself irremediably than to ask in public, for example, for something to drink between dinner and supper. Who would not rather accept to die of thirst than drag himself through scorn for the rest of his days because he quenched his thirst?"[14] The satirical intent is undeniable here, but Fonvizin accurately portrays ridicule as a symbolic death even more terrible than physical death in the eyes of those who lived in high society and had taken on its values.

This raises the question of authority in worldly society. Who was ridiculous, and in the eyes of whom? Worldly customs varied, they were subject to fashion. "Ridicule consists in shocking fashion or opinion," Duclos remarked, adding: "Given that fashion is among us reason par excellence, we judge actions, ideas, and sentiments by their relationship with fashion. All that is not in conformity with it is found to be ridiculous."[15] By integrating ridicule into the paradigm of fashion and arbitrary customs imposed by imitation, Duclos posed the question of conformity and its opposite, the originality affected by *petits-maîtres*, fops who hovered between fashion and ridicule. The *petit-maître*, a literary and polemical figure, was a caricature of the man of the world. Actually, success distinguished a fashionable man from the ridiculous *petit-maître*.

Success in worldly society was measured by the ability to render verdicts that would be repeated, thus putting the seal of approval on a reputation. During the latter half of the century, the maréchale de Luxembourg served as both a moral and a social authority to whom people referred when they wanted to know who was worthy of being received. "On a sentence of Madame de Luxembourg, one was banished from all fashionable tables." Her verdicts were enforceable thanks to her prestige and her mastery of customs and codes, and they drew further strength by being circulated. Madame de Luxembourg thus personified the arbitrary quality of worldly judgments. By recognizing her authority, high society delegated responsibility to her for legitimating its own cohesion. She herself conformed to these standards by adopting a radical position in which everything was judged by the standard of *le bon ton*, for which she herself was the guarantor.[16] Her knowledge of manners enabled the maréchale de Luxembourg to shore up her authority and gave her opinions broad influence. Her ability to invite the most eagerly sought-after personalities or to ruin the consideration enjoyed by a man of the world encouraged those whose positions were unsure to follow her advice and attempt to please her, making her "the instructor of all of the youth of the court."[17]

At that point, conversation took on an important social value that had little to do with parlor games. The salon of Madame de Luxembourg was an obligatory experience for young aristocrats that even ranked above presentation at court: "One had to be in her good graces to find a proper husband. Not one young bride would have risked her presentation without first going to show herself at the maréchale's: she was a veritable authority."[18]

From Ridicule to Fashion

The social effects of ridicule were always associated by eighteenth-century authors with fashion. Under their seeming commonplaces, discourses on fashion and ridicule were important elements in political and social debate.[19] Debate was not limited to economic questions, controversy about luxury, or the consequences of the new urban consumerism for codes relating to clothing. It raised the question of social and symbolic hierarchies. Fashion drew support from a social imitation that led to establishing a hierarchy of social groups according to their proximity to the court, but also to an urban model of innovation.

The worldly sociability of the eighteenth century corresponded to a shift from custom-imitation to fashion-imitation.[20] The models that were imitated were no longer the aristocracy and the court as social bodies capable of commanding obedience, but individuals who dictated fashion. Nonetheless, unlike the later phenomena of celebrity and fashion, worldly sociability still owed much to custom-imitation. It legitimized practices by appealing to tradition, and it did not hide the social hierarchies that underlay its distinctions. The court nobility displayed the same ambiguities concerning worldliness, by declaring openness but regulating society based on conversations, gossip, and stigmatization by means of ridicule.

In her *Dictionnaire des étiquettes*, Madame de Genlis defended the virtues of ridicule in the name of a worldly and aristocratic ideal in which control by high society was the best guarantee of virtuous conduct: "Whoever entirely mocks ridicule, living in *le grand monde* will soon get to the point of mocking decorum and then virtue."[21] The connection between virtue and worldly conformism was justified using the aristocratic theme of honor. "A great sentiment of honor makes one sensitive to ridicule," Madame de Genlis asserts, before depicting ridicule as a punishment meted out by opinion. "It is by the sort of influence that opinion exercises within a nation that one can better judge the mores of that land."

Parisian salons thus produced a worldly opinion, founded on individual judgment and maintained by the circulation of tales, rumors, and verdicts.[22] High society possessed hierarchy, authorities, and mechanisms of imitation, intimidation, distinction, and stigmatization that designated the concept of fashion: "One obtains nothing in this land if one is not *à la mode*," the marquis de Bombelles remarked.[23] For some, fashion was justified by the very way in which "good society" functioned, where ridicule was necessarily the mark of a moral vice, and where the fashionable man pleased by means of social virtues. For its critics, fashion was, to the contrary, a perversion of values. They associated it with the big city and with luxury and held it to be the principal instrument of alienation.[24]

THE LITERARY WORLDLY SPHERE

Politeness and Imitation

The judgments formed in the salons were not directed only at people, but also at literary works. These were read in society and gave rise to commentaries that were repeated from one salon to another. The author who read a play or a poem in a salon had no intention of subjecting it to criticism; rather, he expected compliments, applause, and support. It would be a fault to deprive him of these, as the point, for the listeners, was to conform to worldly norms, which were politeness and compliance. As Madame de Genlis emphasizes, no one had ever seen "an author whistled at in a salon."[25] In 1775 Guibert had read his play, *Le Connétable de Bourbon*, "to everyone," but he refused to have it performed or have it printed, La Harpe stated, "apparently to reserve to himself the pleasure of reading it without being exposed to the danger of being judged."[26]

The reaction of the listeners in a society reading was thus dictated primarily by the rules of politeness that demanded that the author be congratulated and applauded. What was expected at a society entertainment was mutual pleasure and an avoidance of all tension. As with society praise, moderation was not proper: salon readings were met with frenetic applause, as a very demonstrative reaction was required in order not to "seem an imbecile."[27] The same held true for theatrical or musical performances. As she often did, Madame Du Deffand observed these social rules with consummate art. After a supper at the home of the comtesse de Boufflers in Auteuil in the company of Gibbon, the comte de Creutz,

Caraccioli, and Madame de Vierville, during which Amélie de Bouffflers sang and played the harp, she wrote ironically to Walpole: "The diplomatic folk were in ecstasies, Gibbon feigned ecstasy, and as for me, I limited myself to exaggeration."[28]

The personal relationship between the author and his audience, worldly connivance, and the rules of sociability were a good deal more important in this context than a critical relationship with the work. The same was true of society theater, which blurred the distinction between actors and spectators. The spectators of society theater had little in common with the audiences for public theater, which asserted its criticism, rowdy reactions, and incivility.[29] The listeners at a reading or the spectators watching a society play had not paid to attend a performance and were expected to express satisfaction. Unlike public theatergoers, they could never interrupt the actors and contest the interpretation or the program.[30]

Contemporaries gave much thought to the distinction between public judgment and society judgment. One instance of this appears in a passage of La Harpe's *Cours de littérature* in which he speaks about Roucher's *Mois*. La Harpe attempts to understand how that poem, which he considers completely lacking good qualities and which was a failure when it was published in 1779, could have enjoyed such a great success in salon readings. "How has everyone been so long and so generally infatuated when the author recited what after then no one was able to read without boredom and disgust?"[31] To answer that question, La Harpe threw himself into analyzing the social conditions of judgment.

La Harpe distinguishes three forms of the reception of texts: public presentation, private judgment, and society reading. The first corresponded to the public theater, the strongest and most coherent representation of the literary public in the modern age. From the dispute over *Le Cid* to the debate over seating patrons in the *parterre* (stalls), the theater was a privileged topic for reflection on the public as a collective. In ancien régime France, the theater was one of the few public spaces in which individuals brought together in one place could express themselves collectively.[32] It was an emblematic form of aesthetic judgment, one in which "the assembled public that senses a fault immediately manifests its discontent, as it does its satisfaction when it senses a beauty." La Harpe's description signals the specific forms of sociability of a noisy and active *parterre* in which the public's reactions are immediate, with whistles or interruptions indicating discontent, and heavy applause expressing the spectators' pleasure.[33] The judgment of the theater public was on the level of pleasure and emotion. The spontaneous and unanimous reaction of persons whose only connection was their presence in the same public space in order to attend the same spectacle was the guarantee of an authentic evaluation: "At that point, there is judgment," La Harpe states.

The other site that permitted an evaluation of the worth of a literary work was *la lecture de suite*, uninterrupted reading carried on in one's study or *cabinet*, "book in hand," as La Harpe put it. A retreat into reading a text permitted the formation of a judgment thanks to "reflection," without which there could be no criticism. The result was "rare and difficult," because it required a technical competence that served as a base for critical authority.

Salon reading fell into a third form of reception, which La Harpe contrasted with the two other forms. He opposed continuous reading "in the *cabinet*" to recitation "in society," which was often a fragmentary reading that made all critical evaluation problematic. He compared the "assembled public" capable of judgment to the salon "audience" led astray by the author's enthusiasm and by the illusion created by reading "in society." That sort of reading did not produce a public judgment or permit even connoisseurs to judge a work, because it relied on the effects of seduction, politeness, and imitation. "The enthusiasm of the author is communicated to the audience all the more easily because nothing troubles the illusion." This argument is both circumstantial, because Roucher's fine voice contributed much to the success of his readings, and more general, given that it refers to the entertainment that salon reading was expected to provide. The illusion, which pertained to the merits of the work, was due to the enthusiasm of the author and the personal ties that he maintained with the spectators. Their reaction was thus not connected with the immediacy of pleasure or displeasure, nor with critical reflection, but rather with the constraints of worldly sociability.

Politeness in fact governed the way in which opinions had to be expressed within the salon. It automatically produced applause and regulated the very rhythm of a reading: "In society, politeness, and even the very appropriate deference for an author who gives you a mark of complaisance and confidence, hardly permits you to stop him in his reading, if it is not in places where it gives you particular pleasure." Unlike the silent reader, the listener cannot control the way in which the text is read. The very notion that a critical hearing might resemble a critical reading becomes impossible.

For La Harpe, politeness was not a simple relationship between two individuals, but a group relationship that had profound consequences for the conditions in which judgments are forged in society. Central to La Harpe's analysis was a "spirit of society" that generated imitation and emulation. "Among us, the spirit of society consisted in large part of rivaling one another in exaggeration when [approval] was set into motion." Influential members of the circle might impose their own judgment (or the judgment that they wanted to prevail), leaving it to social dynamics to amplify praise and declarations of enthusiasm. Social distinction took the form of imitation and conformity: "When things had arrived at that point, it was no longer a question of judging, but only of seeming better informed and more sensitive than the other by giving more hyperbolic forms to one's praise." La Harpe also insisted on the constraints that the circle put on its members through loud applause, suspending individual judgment and reducing the autonomy of individual appreciation: "Faults, even if they have been felt internally, soon disappear before the noisy and lively impression of applause, especially when there are genuinely good parts, and there are some in *Les Mois*. At that point each person is struck only by what has pleased everyone; and what displeased each one is nearly forgotten or is unconfirmed." The very possibility of individual judgment was threatened by the mechanisms of worldly society. Inner feeling and the individual capacity to react to a text were "effaced" by the expression of polite praise.

The mechanism of mutual imitation combined a voluntary decision (each person wanting to imitate the others and above all to imitate those whose prestige he or she admired and who set the tone for gatherings) and the constraints of collective norms (that of politeness, which was also a power of the group over the individual, imposing on him the need for unanimous praise). Imitation was thus both active and passive; it was motivated by desire and by obedience.[34]

The judgments produced on the occasion of society readings or performances were not "motivated judgments," to use La Harpe's term—that is, reasoned judgments supported by arguments. They were society judgments, which did not rely on a public and critical use of reason, but on the exercise of the social and cultural competence of worldly politeness. Their function was neither to exercise an expertise nor to produce an aesthetic evaluation, but rather to reinforce the cohesion of the worldly collective.[35]

It is the same sort of distinction that Kant had in mind when he published in 1784 his famous text "What is Enlightenment?" in which he defined the public use of one's reason as "the use which a person makes of it as a scholar before the reading public."[36] He explicitly connects the historical construction of a public in the Enlightenment to printing, to reading as a competence, and to publication as a universal ability to speak up. For Kant, only that universal use tied to the written word could be qualified as a "public" use. Conversely, the judgments produced or exhibited within particular familial, social, or professional communities cannot be considered "public." Circles of sociability founded on orality and profoundly inscribed in the practices of elites of the ancien régime had no part in that rational debate.[37] Consequently, if the public sphere is defined, as Habermas does, by the public use of criticism by private individuals, then the salons had no part in it. They were instead spaces for the consecration of *le monde*.

The Dynamics of Success

How did the shift from society judgment to worldly opinion take place? How did successes that guaranteed the author the applause of a few dozen persons become genuine collective enthusiasms shared by a large portion of high society? Salon conversation was helpful in the circulation of prefabricated judgments, whether they featured praise or criticism. The *Manuel de l'homme du monde* insisted on the need to accept opinions that had a broad consensus so as to avoid the risk of expressing a different judgment. The taste was for conformity, and it was more important to know what should be said of a work or a book than to know its contents.[38] The principal merit of these judgments was to be witty, compact, and easily memorized. Madame Necker recommended that they be prepared in advance:

> People often ask us our opinion on the subject that most occupies society, and it is then a well-known little ruse to have a judgment all prepared in two lines that puts together a fine idea, an antithesis, and a delicate sentiment. For example, someone asked Saint-Lambert, "What do you think of the poetics of La Harpe and Marmontel?" "One says too simply what must be said, and the other too ingeniously what should not be said." This cleverness emphasizes the wit: one does not repeat an eloquent tirade; one cites the witticism and the person. The value of a judgment such as this is not so much in its pertinence as in its form.[39]

When a work had been read with success in several salons, praise of it was rapidly passed on. Those who had attended a reading told of the pleasure it had given them, and the work, known to only a few, was for the moment the latest news in all the salons.

The worldly success of a work depended on the authority of the salons that organized word of it. "Each house is a temple, and has its idol, and in spite of all, needs to have the incense burner on hand," Madame Du Deffand noted.[40] Thus Saint-Lambert's *Les Saisons* owed its worldly success to the salon of the prince and princesse de Beauvau, good friends of the author.[41] That success was not limited to Parisian high society, as correspondence spread word throughout European networks. Madame Necker wrote to Lesage: "We are awaiting with impatience *Les Incas* of M. Marmontel and *Les Saisons* of M. Saint-Lambert. The first of these works seems to me a masterpiece of imagination. The second is full of sensibility, poetry, and a sweet sadness, and it penetrates one and disposes one to attention."[42] Even before these works had been published, Madame Necker had already formed an opinion of them, cast in a stereotypical formula in which we can hear an echo of the conversations that followed the reading of these works in Parisian salons. Madame Necker did not even take the trouble to say that she had heard them read, and her statement constructs an expectation at the same time that it exhibits an already formed judgment. Rather than an incentive to discussion, she offers a commentary that her correspondent was invited to repeat.

Singing the praise of *Les Incas* and *Les Saisons* was not the sole point of this letter. Only a few years after her arrival in Paris, Madame Necker had made her way into high society and proven her talent for relaying information and her knowledge, not only of current happenings in the literary sphere, but also of works for which expectation ran high that she had already read. Making reputations was also a way to construct her own prestige. The author who was praised and the hostess who praised him linked their reputations in a complex game that operated somewhere between social consideration and literary reputation. A hostess was credited with making an author fashionable, circulating praise of him and giving credit to others' praise, and his success reflected back on her. Julie de Lespinasse, hoping to persuade Madame Geoffrin to send a letter to the king of Poland praising Guibert, wrote to the latter, "Do you know that one could take vanity in praising you and liking you?"[43] She counted on Madame Geoffrin seeing the advantage in attaching her name to the reputation of this young officer who was also revealing himself to be a successful author.

The circulation of praise structured the whole of the worldly networks. Opinion took the form of hyperbolic judgments, repeated all the more willingly because they reflected on those who had expressed them. In a letter to Gibbon, Madame Necker gave a detailed description of how worldly opinion functioned in Paris, where it was supported by a genuine habitus of exaggeration and by the role of the worldly women who were uniquely capable of cultivating an author's fame. In it, she contrasts sociability in London, where politics occupied minds and leveled reputations, and Paris sociability, where conversation was uppermost. Because London did not encourage women to enliven conversations, it was not favorable to great literary reputations, even for an author such as Gibbon. The English were too busy over their "business" to permit high society to build reputations: "It is in Paris that it is agreeable to be a great man. For it is there alone that one seeks to please by the vivacity of conversation and that one makes his sentiments pass into the souls of others by the perfected art of exaggeration."[44]

"The perfected art of exaggeration": this definition of salon conversation stresses its social effects by associating the role of women with theatricality, the aesthetic dimension of speech, and a certain playful distance. Paradoxically, Parisian frivolity offered genius an opportunity: it ensured durable enthusiasm and infatuation by focusing attention on literary reputations, while the English reserved their enthusiasm for topics that touched on interests and were less reliant on the imagination and on exaggeration. Voltaire himself, Madame Necker stated, owed part of his prestige to that art of exaggeration. Soon after Gibbon published his *History of the Decline and Fall of the Roman Empire*, Madame Necker warned him, "I know that your work has made a prodigious amount of noise and yet three more years of war in America will make your noise fade into the distance. Your politics, that mountain that crushes everything, stifles even giants and permits only the appearance, from time to time, of those who, like you, raise that immense weight by torrents of flame."[45] That curious metaphor allowed Madame Necker to skim over an essential question: is that fame confined within the realm of worldly society or is it possible to transform it into public successes? If it was agreeable for an author to see his success amplified by the echo chamber of worldly conversation, it was not always easy to convert worldly praise into public success.

Worldly Success, Public Failure?

The career of many eighteenth-century literary works was launched in the salons. Certain ones, like *Le Mariage de Figaro*, later triumphed at the Comédie-Française or when they appeared in print. This was not the most frequent case, however. Many of the works that aroused the greatest enthusiasm when they were read or played in high society met with resounding failure once they were printed or performed in a public theater. If La Harpe was surprised by the destiny of Roucher's *Les Mois*, a work praised to the skies by the salons and neglected by the public, he himself could measure the distance that separated society from the public at large. His play *Mélanie* had met with considerable success in the salons of Paris, with daily readings that aroused the "enthusiasm" of the best "society."[46] When the play was finally printed, criticism was severe and general disappointment all the greater. "It is worthy of remark that people had an infatuation and enthusiasm for *Mélanie* when the author went from house to house reading it [in contrast to] the sort of outburst that it suffered when it became public," the *Correspondance littéraire* noted.[47]

All the narrations that relate disappointment when a text moved from the salon to print or to the theater insist on the opposition, at once spatial and social, between the opinion of "society" and that of the public. This example is taken from the *Anecdotes dramatiques* of Joseph de La Porte:

> Never had a play been announced with more éclat within *le monde*; people spoke of it as of a prodigy. The ancients and the moderns were going to be eclipsed. People lavished the most pompous praise on the author; he was promenaded about Paris as if in triumph; people competed to see who would have the merit of producing him. He could hardly keep up with recitals of his work; everyone [*tout le monde*] wanted to hear it, and everyone, after having heard it, cited it as a masterpiece. This phenomenon, which shone in only a few private houses, finally burst before the eyes of the Public, and it disappeared in an instant, like those slight flames exhaled by the earth that fall back precipitously.[48]

This text repeats familiar distinctions. *Le monde* is defined by a restricted social space that lent itself to distinctive practices of imitation. Despite their social narrowness, such practices of sociability enjoyed high visibility, as the equivocal *tout le monde* ironically suggests. The judgments that were produced reflected the order of obligatory and hyperbolic praise, thoughtless collective infatuation, and the influence of fashion. La Porte explicitly contrasted this flash in the pan with another source of judgment invested with a legitimacy that seemed to him indisputable: the public. That opposition between the practices of sociability, which maintained the illusion of value, and the tribunal of the public, which rendered justice, was not an isolated occurrence. Rather, it was an essential element of representations of literary judgment. The most systematic formulation of this question is given by Helvétius in "Of the Difference between the Judgments of the Public and those of Private Societies."[49] Here *le public* refers to all citizens, the nation in its collective and political dimension, and the *sociétés particulières* correspond to *la bonne compagnie, le monde,* and the salons. The judgments of those social groups could not claim any general application; they were dictated by the particular interests of each group and by the worldly conventions that were considered good breeding and were customary in that group. Helvétius theorized that the opinions of *le monde* can never be the same as those of the public at large. A person or a work could not please both the private societies and the general public because their interests were not the same. Whereas the historiography of public opinion postulates a continuity between sociability and public, the authors of the time insisted on all that separated them.

The forcefulness of these representations, along with the effective difficulty of controlling the public reception of a work, or even predicting it, made any attempt to translate worldly success into literary success hazardous. Authors were thus led to develop complex strategies, as shown in the case of Collé, whose *La Veuve* had first been performed, with great success, in the theater of the duc d'Orléans and then at that of Monsieur de Magnanville. In 1763, when Collé agreed to have the play performed on a public stage, he presented the Comédie-Française with a watered-down version of it, which was accepted. In order to compensate for the loss of meaning in the text, he accompanied the public performance with a print version of the original text so that "the public will know the back side of the cards."[50] Collé clearly describes three different ways in which a play could be read or performed. Society performance, away from the public space of police control and cultural institutions, left a good deal of liberty to the author, but it was addressed to "society," which provided a cooperative audience seeking entertainment. The print edition reached a public of solitary readers who rendered a collective judgment that escaped the localisms of society successes. Public performance proposed a text carefully controlled (by the actors and by the censor) and subjected to certain norms of decorum, offered to spectators who felt themselves to be a public by the fact that they were grouped together. Among these three modes, readers and spectators grasped the play in different ways. The complex strategy that Collé thought necessary in order to avoid failure reveals an acute awareness of the gap between a society success and public recognition. As things turned out, it was not enough: *La Veuve* was a flop at its first performance at the Comédie-Française.

THE HUME-ROUSSEAU AFFAIR
Worldly Reputations and Public Opinion

In the summer of 1766, a violent quarrel broke out between David Hume and Jean-Jacques Rousseau. What began as a personal dispute mobilized all of high society and even became a public affair that involved personal reputations and relations between larger forces. It constitutes an ideal case for studying the formation and the circulation of worldly opinion and its dynamics, but also its porous borders with the public sphere.

In 1765, Jean-Jacques Rousseau was seen as a persecuted philosopher. He was forbidden to stay in France after the *prise de corps* decree of June 9, 1762 following the scandal sparked off by *Émile*. At Geneva, his *Lettres de la montagne* resulted in his being persecuted. The comtesse de Boufflers managed to persuade David Hume to take Rousseau across the Channel. Relations between the two philosophers rapidly went from bad to worse. Rousseau suspected Hume of plotting against him. When Hume proposed that Rousseau get a secret pension from the king of England, Rousseau accepted the idea, but soon expressed embarrassment, which Hume interpreted as a refusal. Rousseau responded to Hume's requests for an explanation with silence, then, on June 23, by an accusing letter in which he announced that he had unmasked Hume. On July 10, Rousseau sent Hume another very long and virulent letter outlining all of his suspicions. By then the dispute was already much talked about in Paris, for Hume had written two rather sharp letters to d'Holbach, dated June 17 and July 1, in which he called Rousseau a scoundrel. The news spread rapidly in Paris, then in England. The dispute had turned into an "infernal affair," according to Du Peyrou, Rousseau's friend and publisher. This episode marked a turning moment in the life of Rousseau, who lost his last support, found himself more isolated than ever, and entered into a world of paranoia.[51]

Historians have focused on two moments: the rupture between the two men, a fertile terrain for psychological interpretation, and the written polemic that was addressed to public opinion. In this passage from a private conflict to a public polemic, however, it is the intermediate phase that best offers an understanding of how worldly society grasped the quarrel and how the quarrel escaped out of that society's hands, to the point of becoming a fully-fledged public affair. Rarely was the opposition between the mechanisms of worldly opinion and the effects of print publication so visible or so commented upon. In order to understand the speed with which news circulated, making and unmaking reputations, the polarization of the worldly sphere must be considered. Hume himself was surprised: "I little imagined that a private story, told to a private gentleman, could run over a whole kingdom in a moment; if the King of England had declared war against the King of France, it could not have been more suddenly the subject of conversation."[52]

Why did a private argument between two writers elicit so much talk? To read the numerous letters exchanged during the summer of 1766, it seems that one of the essential points of contention was to what extent the details of the quarrel itself were to be divulged. In the letters that Hume exchanged with his friends in Paris the principal question was whether or not to publish the documents. All of his letters speak of the choice between a restricted circulation of information, reserved to high society, or publication, which consisted of "putting before the eyes of Paris" details of the affair.[53] At first, the Paris networks with which Hume was in touch—that is, the groups centered on the baron d'Holbach, d'Alembert, and Julie de Lespinasse, or the comtesse de Boufflers—all advised him not to publish a summary of the dispute, but rather to show the letters within *le monde*, as the worldly code of reputation dictated. Adam Smith, who was in Paris at the time, judged Rousseau as being wholly in the wrong, but believed Hume should not "publish" anything.[54] He should be content with insisting on Rousseau's "ridicule" by "exposing" his letter, showing it at court and to the minister involved in Rousseau's pension, but without letting it out of his hands, so that it could never be printed.[55]

D'Holbach and d'Alembert were even more explicit about avoiding publication. Rousseau must be discredited in the eyes of high society without making public a dispute that risked harming the prestige of Hume himself. The judgment of the social elite was preferable to the dubious judgment of the public. D'Holbach wrote to Hume that "the public commonly judges very badly the disputes of which it is made the arbiter." What mattered, he added, was to maintain "the esteem of enlightened and unbiased persons, the only judges whose opinion a gallant man desires."[56] D'Alembert sent him a similar warning: "I advise you to think twice before putting your complaints before the eyes of the public because these sorts of quarrels often only inflame obstinate fanatics, and because the indifferent take advantage of the occasion to say bad things about men of letters."[57] The philosophes had many reasons for wanting to avoid a public dispute. That it would emphasize the disunion of men of letters and philosophes was one. The judgment of high society was to be privileged over that of the public. In particular, they feared the polemical process that could lead to publication. "If you once opened warfare, one brochure would lead to another, and you would never be rid of it," d'Holbach warned, urging Hume to mistrust "polemical writings."[58] D'Alembert shared his distrust of the public, for which he professed no great esteem. He engaged Hume to "look at [the situation] twice before making this story public, that is, do nothing hastily or before having reflected on it well, because it is always disagreeable and often harmful to have a trial in writing before that stupid beast called the 'public,' which likes nothing better than to have something bad to say about those whose merit makes it feel uncomfortable."[59] D'Alembert's arguments combined an extremely negative view of the public, a distrust of the forms of public polemics, and a judicial metaphor that evoked the mechanisms of famous law cases.

The philosophes' spontaneous reaction pointed to alternate options. On the one hand, print publication opened a polemical field that nothing could control. On the other hand, the worldly circulation of information had its own rules and operated by means of salon conversations and letters that were shown around but not printed. That circulation permitted men of letters and socialites close to Hume to control rumors and to impose the interpretation given to the episode. In the middle lay the notion of "reputation," which returns like a *leitmotif* in the exchange of letters. In the eyes of high society, Hume had little to fear: he was *le bon David*.[60] For two years he had been a fashionable man for whom the salons competed, to the point that Walpole nicknamed him "The Mode." He made up for being less famous than Rousseau by having a great reputation in worldly society, which upheld his innocence: "There is no one here who does not know M. Hume," the duchesse d'Enville wrote to Moultou, as if that were irrefutable proof of Rousseau's guilt.[61] Even Rousseau's friends warned him that high society was prejudiced in favor of Hume: "He enjoys a very well established reputation," Coindet remarked.[62]

Hume quite well understood that worldly networks were important for his reputation. During the months of May and June, while he was attempting to put pressure on Rousseau to accept a pension from George III, Hume turned to the comtesse de Boufflers and the maréchale de Luxembourg, thinking they might exert an influence on Rousseau. However, after he had received Rousseau's letter of June 23 and understood that the rupture had taken place and it was up to him to make the first move if he wanted to impose his version of the facts and destroy Rousseau's reputation, he wrote to the baron d'Holbach. Far from seeking to calm these troubled waters, as the comtesse de Boufflers would have done, d'Holbach was eager to learn about Hume's complaints in his own words. Although he did not lend out Hume's letters, he had them read to all who paid him visits, who then rushed to pass on his statements condemning Rousseau.[63] A friend of Rousseau, who had learned that the rumors were coming from d'Holbach "and from his friends" and sought to learn more, wrote: "I have not seen these letters, I have done everything I could, in vain, to get copies or extracts of them, [but] the Baron is content to read them to anyone who wants to hear them, and, as you can easily judge, reflections are not spared."[64] Although the comtesse de Boufflers was on Hume's side, she bitterly reproached him for having contacted d'Holbach first, who only "spread" Hume's accusations.[65]

D'Holbach's spreading the word of Hume's complaints, formulated in virulent terms, was the nucleus of the affair. The difference between circulation within worldly society and publication was thwarted by the uncontrollable diffusion of rumors. Despite d'Holbach's precautions, the information leaked out of the worldly networks that controlled the Paris salons. Although few had seen Hume's original letter to d'Holbach, it was reported that "extracts are running through all of Paris."[66] Everyone sought information, wanted to know the exact terms of the letter, the conditions

of the dispute and Rousseau's reproaches. The flood of words and letters—
what letters speak of as *bruit* or *bruit general* went so far as to become
bruit public as the comtesse de Boufflers put it. This uncontrollable proliferation of rumor challenged the possibility of maintaining the distinction
on which the philosophes' strategy was based.[67] They had experienced the
porous nature of the worldly networks, along with their inability to keep
information under perfect control, especially when the newspapers took
affairs into their own hands.[68]

At that point, Hume had to change strategy. Because it was impossible
to prevent "publicity,"[69] he was advised to accept this new situation and act
accordingly by publishing the documents of the dispute as quickly as possible. On July 21, d'Alembert announced to Hume that his friends had met
and now advised him to "give this story to the public with all its circumstances." This change of tack was motivated by a realization, an anticipation, and a challenge. The realization was that of the *bruit* that the dispute
had caused and in which the "public" was showing an interest. Because
the rumor had escaped from the control of the salons to reach the public,
that public must be addressed directly, which necessarily involved print.[70]
Anticipation focused on another publication, the memoirs that Rousseau
had begun to write, to which Hume was urged to respond in advance.
Finally, the decision to publish was reinforced by a veritable challenge
launched by Rousseau in early August. He stated to bookseller Pierre Guy
that Hume would never dare to publish their correspondence because he
would unmask himself.[71] This letter, which was circulated widely, backed
Hume into a corner.

The dynamics of the dispute and the decision to change strategies highlight the ambiguity of the term "public." The public was the undifferenti-
ated mass of those whom one did not know, who could be reached by print
but also by far-reaching rumors. It designated both the result of an uncontrollable divulgation and an institution of judgment. Once an affair was
"public," there was no more evading the issue, and publication had to be
total.

The unwelcome public nature of the dispute had changed the situation: holding back information would be an admission of weakness rather
than a sign of civility. Everyone experienced the public quality of the affair
as a deplorable constraint that modified their capacity for action. Certain
correspondents faulted the awkward haste with which Hume had communicated his complaints to d'Holbach, others blamed d'Holbach himself,
and still others the role of the press. The decisive element, however, was
Rousseau's celebrity and the failure of Parisian high society to measure its
consequences. Rousseau was not only a man of letters; he had become a

public personage whose every move and word were reported in gazettes throughout Europe. During the several weeks that he spent in Paris before going to London, his presence at the Temple was the principal event of the capital.[72] No sooner had he arrived in London than the newspapers published satires against him.[73] The worldly sphere in Paris, which was governed by connivance and reputation, stood opposed to the regime of celebrity, which was based on the mechanisms of collective identification made possible by the press and the printed word.[74] In the press and in the texts published in response to the *Exposé succinct*, anonymous reactions were often favorable to Rousseau and used the language of sentiment to express their certitude that "the author of *Héloïse* could only be innocent."[75]

Silence and Justification

The newly public nature of the dispute modified both its form and its content by imposing a judicial vocabulary with such terms as "the accused," "trial," and "proof." Rousseau, of course, was called on to explain his conduct and offer proof of his accusations.[76] After having been in the position of the accuser, Hume soon found himself obliged to justify the very violent terms of his letter to d'Holbach, especially after the letter had become nearly "public." Turgot told him clearly: "In the eyes of all the partisans of Rousseau, who are many, you [have] become his accuser and as such are obliged to justify the imputations and the qualifications with which you have blackened him."[77]

In order to justify himself and save his reputation, Hume had to establish Rousseau's guilt. But exactly what was Rousseau guilty of? In order for Hume's accusations not to seem disproportionate, he had to show that Rousseau's fault concerned not only the relations between the two men, but also Rousseau's attitudes in his social relations. Hume and his friends based their claims on the norm that governed relations between the social world and writers, which was the recognition of beneficence. Hume was painted as a "protector" and "benefactor" of Rousseau, whose "ingratitude" was denounced.[78] That ingratitude seemed almost unnatural, because, not content with failing to express gratitude, Rousseau had gone so far as to accuse his protector. Julie de Lespinasse declared her astonishment: "It is inconceivable that a man who owes you so much should have resolved to fail you."[79] The duchesse de Choiseul was even more explicit: she doubted whether Rousseau, who "has always refused himself the sweet pleasure of gratitude so as to spare himself the slightest obligation" was an *honnête homme*.[80] As for Madame Geoffrin, who followed the affair from Poland, she confirmed her conviction that, although Rousseau had a fine mind, he had "a very black soul."[81] Garat commented, "It was impossible that Madame Geoffrin, for whom beneficence was a need of the highest necessity, should pardon Rousseau, who had no liking for benefices or benefactors."[82]

The dispute had a history, which was that of Rousseau's relations with the Paris salons, and the protagonists in the dispute did not hesitate to draw upon it. Their confrontation dramatizes, through the various discourses of justification, two elements of the relations between the writer and high society. Rousseau dips into the rhetorical and fictional repertory of his works while Hume used the arguments of worldly *honnêteté*, given that he clung to that representation of the social world.[83]

Rousseau and Hume did not place their dispute on the same level. Rousseau reproached Hume for a group of acts that he judged to be suspect and unfriendly; Hume thought that the central point was Rousseau's refusal of the pension. By insisting on this point, Hume was certain of attracting to his side all those who could not understand why anyone could refuse a pension, and who therefore judged Rousseau's behavior to be inexplicable and unacceptable. As Turgot put it, "No one in the world will imagine that you asked for a pension for Rousseau in order to dishonor him. Because except for him, no one will think that a pension would have dishonored him."[84] By working to obtain a pension for him, Hume could not escape being Rousseau's benefactor, which put the question of protection and beneficence at the center of the affair. Following a similar logic, the comtesse de Boufflers demanded explanations from Rousseau in the name of the protection relation that, in her estimation, linked them: "You have in France friends and protectors. You have consulted none of them. . . . Madame the maréchale de Luxembourg and I impatiently await your explanations."[85] Rousseau was in fact remaining silent, refusing to justify himself. He stated explicitly to Du Peyrou that he did not want to play the game of worldly correspondence that circulated and fed rumors. As for his friends' accusations, Rousseau reduced them, in the face of all the evidence, to "little female gossip" that inspired him to comment, "Women are made to chatter and men to laugh at them." While worldly logic identified honor with reputation, Rousseau operated in the opposite way, asserting his independence and his refusal to justify his actions: "They believe that my reputation is dependent upon an injurious letter; that may well be; but if they believe that my honor depends on it, they are mistaken."[86] Hume was concerned for his "reputation," but Rousseau affected disinterest, launching a rhetoric of the persecuted man who rejects an unequal fight and of the solitary man who owes explanations to his conscience alone.

That attitude, which peaked in the writings of his final years, drove his partisans to desperation. François Coindet begged him, in vain, to provide clarifications: "I beg of you the grace of not letting this letter go without response: instruct me as to how I can parry the poisonous blows launched against you."[87] It was wasted effort, however: Rousseau did not respond. The comtesse de Boufflers, furious over having no news, also attempted to draw him out of his muteness: "The silence to which we are forced harms you more than any other thing."[88] When he finally did respond to her, after a month of silence, it was to send her an ironic and almost insolent letter.[89] When Hume finally passed on to printed publication, Rousseau, to the great surprise of his adversaries, maintained his silence and refused to respond, even disdaining the articles in his favor that appeared in the English newspapers and the pamphlets in response to Hume. How can we explain Rousseau's silence?

Rousseau and Hume did not conceive of their justifications in the same manner. Hume spoke the language of "facts and proofs" as d'Holbach had recommended to him.[90] Rousseau, on the other hand, refused to enter into that logic, which he had tossed aside from the beginning in his letter to Hume of July 10: "The first care of those who weave atrocities is to put themselves under the cover of juridical proofs; it would not be good to charge them with atrocities."[91] This was a position that determined all of Rousseau's line of argumentation, beginning with this letter and continuing into the following months. To demands for proof, he opposed an intimate conviction: "Inner conviction admits another type of proofs that govern the sentiments of an *honnête homme*." His own suffering seemed to him incontestable proof of the plot that was being formed against him: "One tells me nothing; I know only what I feel; but as people have made me feel it well, I know it well." Faced with demands for clarification, he thought that the expression of his suspicions would be enough to do him justice.[92] When the comtesse de Boufflers reminded him of the rules of worldly prudence, he retorted, "You want me to refuse to accept the evidence; that is what I have done as much as I could. That I contradict the evidence of my senses is a piece of advice easier to give than to follow; that I believe nothing of what I felt, and that I consult on that matter the friends I have in France. But if I must believe nothing of what I feel, they will believe it even less, those who do not see it and feel it even less. What, Madame! When a man comes eye to eye with me and strikes me again and again with dagger blows to my breast, before daring to say to him that he is striking me, must I go far off to ask others whether he has struck me?"[93]

Unlike Hume, who ceaselessly asked his Paris acquaintances for advice (which was also a way to interest them in his cause), Rousseau remained silent, then wrote that he was ceasing to write, and finally responded to his friends that there was no reason for producing a rebuttal because his accusations were founded on what he felt deep within himself. Being the only one to "feel" the blows that had been inflicted upon him, he had no need of advice. That attitude, which left the field free to his adversaries, both in the salons and in the print sphere, reflected the coherence of a paranoid sensibility in which an exacerbated mistrust led to isolation. That isolation was paradoxical, however, for Rousseau inaugurated an attempt that led, in the great autobiographical texts of the last years of his life, to his turning that weakness into force. All the while refusing to justify his acts, he reacted to the "plots" against him by publishing his silence and his isolation as if they were proof of his innocence. "I do not live at all in the world, I am unaware of what happens there, I have no party, no association, no intrigue."[94] Solitude and the unhappy awareness of self became his best justification, which he charged literature and posterity with confirming: "If I knew that M. Hume would not be unmasked before his death, I would have difficulty believing in providence."[95]

Worldly Networks

When he deserted the worldly sphere, Rousseau left the field free to Hume and his partisans. In fact, the history of this affair, which had begun as a private break in relations between two individuals and which soon became an event for high society throughout Europe, then a public polemic, illustrates the role of worldly networks. Letters circulated and crossed one another. When the marquise de Verdelin, a friend of Rousseau, was obliged to spend the month of August at Bourbonne, she asserted that she constantly received letters in which her Parisian friends informed her of the latest developments. "I have received twenty letters in which people tell me a thousand things, one more striking than another. . . "; "One sends me word from Paris. . . "; "One says in *le monde*. . . "; "One wagers that. . . "[96] This epistolary activity reveals the state of a worldly geography polarized by the dispute.

Three groups can be discerned. First there were Hume's friends, who gathered in the salons of the baron d'Holbach and Julie de Lespinasse. They were the overseers of the assassination of Rousseau in worldly society. Although the uncontrolled publicity of the affair made them fear being caught up in polemical complications, they managed to seize the advantage. They functioned on a collective model: d'Holbach spoke in the name of his entire "society";[97] d'Alembert and Julie de Lespinasse, who wrote joint letters, asserted that all their friends were "unanimous" and that d'Alembert "speaks in the name of all."[98] At first this group functioned as an echo chamber for rumors of the rupture. Then it was transformed into center of collective elaboration for Hume's strategy. A genuine war council was held at the home of Julie de Lespinasse, where "all, unanimously" decided that Hume must publish. They drew up a battle plan and a list of words of advice to be followed that Julie and d'Alembert were then charged with transmitting to Hume. Finally, when Hume had made up his mind to publish the documents, these salons played an active role in their preparation for publication. Hume sent the manuscript to Trudaine de Montigny, who was to pass it on to Turgot and d'Alembert, to whom Hume delegated full editorial responsibility.[99] Suard, commissioned by d'Holbach's salon, translated Hume's text into French, while d'Holbach and d'Alembert took over the tasks of correction, adding a few pieces (in particular, a declaration by d'Alembert), and seeing the text through the printing process. This means that those salons were not only spaces for exchanging opinions, but also for taking action and moving toward a publication that mobilized their combined energies.[100] The salons of the baron d'Holbach, Julie de Lespinasse, and d'Alembert played the most important role; but they were joined by Trudaine, whose gatherings served as a relay station and council; Helvétius, who was at Voré for the summer (where d'Holbach joined him); and even the duc de Nivernais, to whom d'Alembert showed the manuscript before publication.[101] Within this group, a logic of solidarity produced unanimity and a radicalization. Morellet and Duclos, for example, rallied to Hume's cause, definitively breaking with Rousseau. Under these circumstances, Turgot stands out as an exception. Present at the meeting at Julie de Lespinasse's home, his position rapidly evolved, and he wrote two long letters to Hume that shine for their moderation and their detailed analysis of responsibilities. He reproaches Hume for having misinterpreted Rousseau's first letter and for having made too much of a fuss about the affair, thus making the rupture irreparable. Although he placed himself on Hume's side, he attempted to read nuances into Rousseau's fault, the reasons for which he tried to understand. Moreover, he made himself the spokesman for Malesherbes, who was quite familiar with Rousseau's *modus operandi* and preached appeasement.

In contrast, Rousseau's friends were less well organized and, above all, had little support in high society. They hastened to inform Rousseau of what was being plotted and expressed their frustration at not being able to come to his aid. They were quite ready to fire off counter-charges, however, or, more simply, to find out the latest news. Coindet proposed going to see d'Holbach, whom he did not know. Others drifted away, bewildered by Rousseau's conduct and overwhelmed by the publication of his letters. Even George Keith ("Milord Maréchal"), for whom Rousseau professed an intense friendship close to filial love, refused to get mixed up in the dispute and preferred to put an end to his correspondence with Rousseau so he could "end his days in peace."[102] The marquise de Verdelin, who had contributed much to persuading him to follow Hume to England, found herself caught up in the storm. At first she sought above all to glean information about a rupture that had affected her deeply. She strove to reason with Rousseau,[103] corresponded with Coindet, and tried to urge the comtesse de Boufflers to go to England to serve as a "mediatrix."[104] Incapable of explaining the misunderstanding between two men whom she admired, she blamed Thérèse Levasseur, "that imbecile female that he has near him."[105] She later reasserted her friendship with Rousseau, with whom she continued to correspond, but refused to take up his defense, seeking above all to protect her own reputation from the consequences of the dispute. She managed to borrow a copy of the correspondence before it was published by d'Alembert, and she intervened with him to omit her name from the print version.[106]

Finally, there was a third group that gravitated around Conti and the salons of the duchesse de Luxembourg and the comtesse de Boufflers, women who were known as protectors of Rousseau but were also close to Hume. At first the comtesse regretted not having been informed soon enough, a negligence that threatened her position and her role as an intermediary between the two men.[107] Unlike the preceding group, these ladies had no interest in the dispute and did their best to calm it, but faced with the publicity given to the affair and Rousseau's obvious desire not to accept their protection, they took on the defense of Hume. Like Turgot, they reproached Hume for his haste and they tried to understand the reaction of Rousseau, but without justifying it, and they worked to paint him as an unhappy fool rather than a scoundrel. All the same, their defection sounded the defeat of Rousseau's position among Parisian elites, and Tronchin, who detested him, could declare triumphantly: "Mesdames de Luxembourg, de Beauvau, and de Boufflers, my good friends, have abandoned him. Now people speak of him only as a wicked rogue, there is only one voice on the matter. Never has a man sunk more rapidly to the bottom."[108] Relations still persisted between the two groups. D'Alembert sent the comtesse de Boufflers a copy of the letters that he had received from Hume,[109] and she corresponded with Julie de Lespinasse and invited Adam Smith to visit her so that she could read him the letter she was about to send to Hume.[110]

Madame Du Deffand occupied a somewhat special place within this social configuration. She was close to the comtesse de Boufflers and the duchesse de Luxembourg, and her connections with Voltaire and Walpole situated her decisively among the adversaries of Rousseau. With a bantering tone, she observed the ways in which her friends attempted to extract themselves from the difficult situation in which Rousseau had put them. "I do not know what side his lady protectors will take," she wrote to Walpole. She supposed that the comtesse de Boufflers would abandon Rousseau, but was not sure about the maréchale de Luxembourg, who was proud of her reputation as a "protector" of Rousseau: "Not being able to dominate, she wants to protect. She is fond of Jean-Jacques and is not fond of M. Hume, but the Temple and l'Isle-Adam are necessary to her amusement; she faces a conflict."[111] How to decide between her protection obligations and her society connections, which had to do with worldly entertainment? All summer long Madame Du Deffand, who discussed this affair with all her correspondents, was eager for news. She had access to the letters that were exchanged, thanks to her relations with Rousseau's two female protectors.[112] Even when those two women seemed to have definitively sided with Hume, Madame Du Deffand claimed not to be duped. Refusing to take the affair seriously, she designated the protagonists by nicknames, as if the whole affair were a fable or a parody, and claimed to unveil the mechanisms of their positions: "That Maréchale and the Idol (Boufflers) are still fanatics of the Dromedary (Rousseau), and although the Idol spoke in different terms to M. De Guerchy, she attempted to fool him, because she does not want to lose her fame in England, nor does the Peasant (Hume) diminish anything of the cult that she has received there."[113] For Madame Du Deffand, discourses and justifications, great words and great sentiments, were always brought down to the dimension of a society amusement, a shadow theater in which everyone pursued his vainglory and where freedom consisted in not being duped and in laughing on the sly.[114]

For three months the dispute was played out in *le monde*, inspiring correspondence and conversations. For some, as for Madame Du Deffand, the interest in the vicissitudes of the dispute was a matter of curiosity and entertainment. For others, it was an extremely serious affair in which the reputations of both Hume and Rousseau were at stake, but also those of all who had joined their causes. With the publication of the *Exposé succinct*, the heart of the polemic left the sphere of worldly society, even though it continued to contribute to conversations, to move to the sphere of public print, where articles and pamphlets were coming out, one after the other and responding to one another, most of them favorable to Rousseau. A few weeks later, Grimm returned to the polemic to draw his own conclusions.[115] Grimm, who was close to d'Holbach and had broken with Rousseau some time earlier, was by no means favorable to the latter, but he intervened very little in the dispute. In his *Correspondance littéraire* he addressed, in manuscript form, a very selective readership that by and large shared the interests and the values of Parisian high society. His intervention was not on the same level of publication as the *Exposé succinct*, a fact that permitted him, for example, to give his readers names (Boufflers, Verdelin) that the *Exposé* omitted. Taking a detached stance, Grimm was critical of Rousseau's attitude, which was to be expected, and he insisted on the echoes of the dispute, returning to a phrase of Hume's: "A declaration of war between two great powers of Europe would not have made more noise than this quarrel." It was precisely that *bruit*, that transformation of a dispute into a public trial, that lay at the heart of his analysis. Since he had not been involved in the publication of the documents, Grimm could stick to principles. He spoke in favor of separating worldly reputation from public debate and reproached Hume for having published. In his eyes, Hume had acted wrongly when he "consented to put the public into the confidence of a trial that was in no way important to it." Recalling his own brushes with Rousseau, Grimm depicted himself as a detached man of the world refusing to enter into the arena of public polemics. This strong reaffirmation of the worldly model of the man of letters who is suspicious of the public and prefers to rely on the judgments of an enlightened social elite concluded with a manifesto on style in which Grimm denounced the rhetorical emphasis of Rousseau's letters, which he judged to be very inappropriate. He preferred wit to that eloquence of sentiment.

Despite the success of the metaphor, the confrontation between Hume and Rousseau was not a trial. Unlike the major judicial affairs of the latter half of the century, their dispute could not be brought to a conclusion by an explicit verdict. The support of a worldly network allowed Hume to protect his social and intellectual reputation within the sphere of the Paris salons and to find support when at last he decided it was necessary to take recourse in print publication, but publication was insufficient to bring the dispute to a close to his advantage. On the other hand, Rousseau's celebrity and the support that he received in many articles and pamphlets published in response to the *Exposé succinct* were not enough to keep him from being "sunk to the bottom" and to lose his protectors in high society, along with the support of many friends. For several months, Parisian high society and the leading men of letters in the capital threw themselves into a private dispute between two writers, and the volume of the dispute produced its own stakes: for some philosophes, the question might have been to defeat Rousseau; for others, it was to defend their friend; for aristocrats, it was surely to assert their authority over the writers whom they protected and not to let themselves be swept away by public polemics. But everyone spoke the language of reputation.

The dynamic of this dispute confirms that the social sphere defined by the salons did not function in the same way as the public sphere of print publication. That dynamic was founded on mechanisms of imitation and intimidation, on the existence of worldly authorities capable of imposing a judgment. The distinction between the worldly sphere and the public sphere that structured the social world of the Parisian elites in the latter half of the eighteenth century makes it easier to understand the sharpness of debates over fashion or over the effects of ridicule, but also the persistent mistrust of the effects of publication. Conversely, worldly society could not remain enclosed within itself. Successes in the social world were not enough for the writers, who sought to transform them into public successes on the stage or by means of the book. News was subjected to the porousness of the worldly networks, which opened onto other information networks. The dynamics of divulgation perturbed the strategies for worldly control over reputations. In the second half of the eighteenth century, it became increasingly difficult to ignore the undefined public of readers, which was gradually acquiring a legitimacy constructed by means of literary, religious, and political controversies. One could attempt to avoid having an affair become public and, in society, mock the judgment of the "stupid beast" that was the public, but it was no longer possible to ignore its authority.

CHAPTER 6

Politics in the Salon

We would never advise anyone to speak of politics at the table: the moment in the day when one is the least capable of governing oneself is a poor moment to be concerned with governing the State; there are so many other subjects of conversation that are more appetizing and gayer that there is no less stupidity than imprudence in choosing that one. Literature, theatrical spectacles, gallantry, love, and art are unquenchable sources of joyous topics.

Laurent Grimod de La Reynière, *Almanach des gourmands* (1805)

In 1805, in his new role as a gastronome, Grimod de La Reynière attempted to distinguish between the world of pleasures and that of politics. When this former *enfant terrible* of Paris society became nostalgic for an idealized sociability, he found that politics and worldly entertainment did not mix well. Did this precept based on prudence and decorum, which later became a commonplace of bourgeois politeness, make any sense to the habitués of Parisian salons in the eighteenth century? Contrary to the cliché, the salons did not exist in isolation from politics. Connections joined the salons and the traditional politics of the ancien régime, a politics that thrived at the royal court, in the various coteries, in governmental intrigues, and in diplomatic policies, and that had a privileged role in the formation of a public opinion. Some see the salons as places dedicated to a literary and abstract politics, where men of letters, according to Tocqueville's famous phrase, became the principal political men. Others, following Habermas, see the salons as an institution of a public literary sphere whose critical spirit shifted to focus on political institutions. However the sources almost never hint at theoretical discussions about the constitution of the kingdom or the foundations of authority. Instead, they reveal the importance of conversations linked to the traditional politics of the monarchy, whether these were diplomatic and military news items, relations of force between ministerial coteries, or conflicts between the royal power and the parlements. All such events and questions fed worldly conversations and made the salons strategic places that the actors in the political game did their best to control. The connections between worldly reputations and political action were complex: they shed light on the political use of society news and the way in which worldly networks were penetrated by political fidelity. It is that worldly politics, which the Revolution did not immediately destroy, to which this chapter turns.

THE POLITICS OF WORLDLINESS
Political News

If echoes of salon conversation bearing on that "literary politics" for which Tocqueville blamed the philosophes were rare, worldly discussions, in contrast, were full of news of the court: this is what Madame de Sévigné called "politicking."[1] Salon participants commented on nominations, told anecdotes about political figures, repeated the latest rumors of someone's disgrace, and discussed confrontations between the royal power and the parlements. This is hardly surprising, given that the habitués of Paris salons, from Necker to the prince de Beauvau, from the maréchal de Soubise to the duchesse d'Aiguillon, from Choiseul to the maréchale de Mirepoix, included many people who were active in the traditional political operations of the monarchy.

Salon conversations on politics are particularly conspicuous over the short time-span of a political event. To cite one example, Chancellor Maupeou's move to establish authority over the parlements inspired a great many commentaries. Madame d'Épinay and her friends were speaking of Maupeou "in their *soirées*," and in a letter to abbé Bathélemy, Madame Du Deffand stated that politics occupied the heart of Parisian conversation, where it competed with theatrical spectacles, new books, and the chronicle of the latest scandal.[2] Political events also gave rise to songs that circulated in the salons. In 1773, for example, when conflict arose between Louis XV and the princes, Madame Du Deffand sent abbé Barthélemy "the song in which our princes are celebrated; our songwriters do not have a light touch, but it suits those about whom it sings."[3] Political information was a serious affair, but it was submitted, as were all other subjects of conversation, to the entertainment principle around which worldly society was organized. High society much appreciated such songs, and even ministers (especially when they were not in power) copied and collected them.[4] Politics provided an occasion for *bons mots* and songs, which Chamford mocked by citing (or by imagining) the witticism of a young noble: "I am sorry about the loss of that battle: the song is worthless."[5]

In the political struggles that shook the monarchy, these songs were not necessarily meaningless trifles, however, and their purpose was not exclusively entertainment. Their circulation could reveal political positions and opinions. Madame de La Ferté-Imbault, for example, who was violently hostile to Maupeou, took the trouble to transcribe and carefully conserve songs written against him.[6] Although it would be a mistake to overestimate the ideological effects of these songs, they do reflect a certain relation to politics, that of both adhesion and detachment, in which a joking tone and derision corresponded to a refusal of over-enthusiastic engagement. Such songs fitted in seamlessly with other forms of worldly amusement, but they also circulated in other milieus where their effect may well have been different.[7]

An interest in politics in the salons, where political information was primarily news and was expected to take the worldly forms of narration, the anecdote, or the pleasantry, also appeared in the way in which news about the royal family circulated. In 1765, the long illness of the dauphin was the subject of all commentaries. Walpole, who was in Paris for the first time, was astonished by the wealth of details that accompanied conversation about the dauphin's health. On one occasion, the daily health bulletin on his condition issued by the royal physicians the night before and mentioning a bowel movement was read during supper at the home of Madame Du Deffand. Already astonished that information of this sort would have been given at the table, Walpole was surprised again when Madame Du Deffand added that the dauphin had upset his chamber pot and his bed linens had had to be changed.[8] Decorum was set aside because the body of the dauphin was a political body—that of the heir to the throne—and a worldly body that excited curiosity. Within the political equilibrium of the court, the life of the dauphin was a fact to which Madame Du Deffand's guests were sensitive; in Parisian suppers his illness was the latest fashionable subject, and everyone sought to share information about him, even when it was less than appetizing.

Whether news was about the royal family or military or political affairs, the center of rumors and information was the court. It was still true, in the latter half of the eighteenth century, that all political life was organized around anticipations of events at court. This was the case in 1769, when the rumor circulated that Madame Du Barry was going to be presented at Versailles. The news, first presented as sure, then denied, then again given as certain, had all the elements to focus the attention of Paris high society. Not only was the place of a new favorite no small matter at Versailles, but the official presentation at court of a former *courtisane* was fodder for scandal. Finally, the presentation was a personal defeat for Choiseul, whose hostility toward the favorite was manifest, and a victory for his adversaries. In the salons of Paris and at Chantilly, everyone waited impatiently for news from Versailles.[9] For some, it was a bit of court news with a whiff of scandal; for others, the political dimension was of essential importance.

The proximity of the court, which enabled people to obtain political news rapidly, granted additional distinction to some. Julie de Lespinasse wrote to Guibert: "It was said yesterday that the archbishopric of Cambrai would be given to Cardinal de Bernis and that the duc de La Rochefoucauld would go as ambassador to Rome. Perhaps the Abbé de Véry will be named first, but only to get him made a cardinal and prepare the way for M. de La Rochefoucauld; that was the talk of yesterday at my fireside, and if I were to name to you the persons present you would see that if this news does not become true, it was at least not absurd."[10] This bit of news was of particular interest to Julie de Lespinasse, since Véri and the duc de La Rochefoucauld were regular members of her circle. Their personal futures were dependent on political decisions taken at the court, and provided fodder for society talk. Who were the persons present whose opinion made the news credible? Perhaps Turgot himself, the new minister, who was close to both the duc de La Rochefoucauld and abbé Véri. In this instance, it was Julie de Lespinasse's connections with certain ministerial circles that permitted her to obtain credible news, thus enabling her to provide a conversation topic and burnish the reputation of her salon.

The comtesse de Boufflers benefitted from her proximity to the prince de Conti. The long letters that she sent to Gustav III of Sweden show that she was perfectly informed about happenings at Versailles, where she went regularly and followed with interest and intelligence the relations among political forces and between the government and the parlements, and, in particular, relations among the ministers. Her letters were genuine diplomatic dispatches in which she commented on nominations, rumors, and the influence that various people had at court. Her judgments reflected how closely each event contributed to Conti's political action. At the death of Louis XV, for example, she analyzed the new situation and described the new ministers according to their relations with Conti.[11] To a certain extent she served as an intermediary between Gustav III and Conti, who had ambitions to play a high-level political role. When he died, she spoke of his death as a "national loss" and painted him as a "hero," a "great Prince," and a zealous defender of "rights" and "liberties."[12]

Madame Du Deffand's salon offers an enlightening example of the connection between certain societies and the political coteries. Beginning in the mid-1760s, Madame Du Deffand was a close friend of the duchesse de Choiseul. The friendship between the two women soon shifted to the political terrain. Until then a distant observer, Madame Du Deffand made common cause with the Choiseuls, organized supper parties for them, and kept up an intense correspondence with the duchess. Abbé Barthélemy, the duke's secretary and the duchess's confidant, became a pillar of the salon on the rue Saint-Joseph, which was made up, for the most part, of people close to the minister. Madame Du Deffand felt herself accountable, even in her worldly activities, for Choiseul's interests and political reputation. This was why, in March 1770, she quarreled with her friend the comtesse de Forcalquier, who defended Choiseul's adversaries in the government.[13] Their dispute took place in the home of Hénault, and the account she gave of it to Walpole shows how the polite manners gradually retreated before a political confrontation, albeit one that took place within the practices of sociability: "The period before supper went by marvelously. Mutual excuses for not having seen the other, promises to see one another more often. We sit down at the table. Until the fruit all goes well; unfortunately someone got around to speaking about the edicts; at first everything was quite sweet; little by little people became heated."[14] The political discussion, concerning the edicts of the contrôleur général, shifted to rumors and each guest gave a different version of what had gone on in the Conseil du Roi. Differences of opinion led to personal accusations: Madame Du Deffand reproached the comtesse de Forcalquier for having been motivated by familial rancor, given that her cousin had not received the military promotion that he had hoped for, while she herself was accused of a servile attachment to Choiseul. Conversation soon degenerated into a dispute, and the two women left the salon to settle their quarrel in the bedchamber. Thus political discussion broke down all possible exchange and forced the two protagonists to take refuge in partisan solidarities, expressed in the traditional language of friendship. "Never have I spoken of your friends in a way that could displease you, you owe me the same courtesy," an angry Madame Du Deffand proclaimed, firmly defending Choiseul's interests. At that point Madame de Forcalquier accused her of "gathering" and "distributing everywhere" writings against her own friends. This changed Madame Du Deffand's stance as an outraged friend into one of an interested propagandist; the comtesse de Forcalquier even escalated tensions by suggesting that Madame Du Deffand was senile.

Beyond the anecdote itself, which shows how a convivial supper begun with an exchange of polite questions could degenerate into a political dispute, this episode sheds light on the political solidarities that permeated high society. Political attachments could conflict with worldly geography: in a period of strong political tension, when the Choiseuls' social group was becoming increasingly fragile, the peaceable practices of society life could no longer prevent the expression of conflict. For all that, the dynamics of worldly society did not break down, however. At first, accounts of the dispute circulated in several salons. According to Madame Du Deffand, it was Madame de Forcalquier who had taken it on herself to "recount it to everyone."[15] The anecdote then circulated in a variety of circles, ending up by reaching the Choiseuls, through the Beauvaus, two weeks later. Finally, Madame d'Aiguillon, a friend to both women, took up the task of reconciliation by inviting Madame Du Deffand. The conflict was thus resolved by an act of hospitality and mediation, and the elasticity of sociable connections made it possible to restore harmony. Reconciliation was only possible, however, because the political situation permitted it. When simmering tensions resulted in Choiseul's dismissal, his exile to Chanteloup, and his replacement in the ministry of Affaires Étrangères by the duc d'Aiguillon, Madame Du Deffand could no longer pay calls on the duchesse d'Aiguillon. In the salons, however, she continued to play the role of a silent but attentive agent for Choiseul: "Do not fear either tepidity or indiscreet zeal on my part. Not being able to be useful to you, I listen with close attention and great interest to all that is said, but I do not speak."[16]

Salons were propitious places for political action. Intrigues could be carried out in them in an attempt to wield an indirect influence on decisions made at court, and that use of worldly space in no way contradicted other amusements. During the first half of the century, the salon of Madame de Tencin was at once a site of political intrigue and a society open to men of letters. Madame de Tencin, a friend of Montesquieu, Marivaux, and Piron and a model for Madame Geoffrin, was deeply involved in political affairs, which even led to her being exiled by the minister Fleury in 1730. It was said of her that she "perfectly possessed all that was called at court intrigue, politics, and stratagem,"[17] which did not prevent her from making her Tuesdays an important cultural setting and from writing novels that she published anonymously.[18]

In many ways, Madame Cassini's salon could be seen as playing a similar role during the second half of the century, combining literary sociability, worldly *libertinage*, and political intrigue. For one thing, Madame Cassini received writers in a hôtel on the rue de Babylone.[19] La Harpe put on *Mélanie* in her salon in 1772, before "the most brilliant company in Paris,"[20] and Madame Cassini herself played the leading role when the play was performed at Sannoy in the home of Madame d'Houdetot after being banned in Paris.[21] She also participated in a number of intrigues during the reign of Louis XV. In 1773, for example, "the intriguing Madame de Cassini" dazzled the prince de Condé with the idea of an appointment as *grand maître de l'artillerie*, while negotiating behind his back with the duc d'Aiguillon. "Madame de Cassini disguised herself as a man and went at night to negotiate and pursue intrigues with the duc d'Aiguillon and the prince de Condé, whom she deceived," according to Madame de La Ferté-Imbault, who was close to the prince.[22] Madame Cassini's stepbrother, who was known as the marquis de Pezay, is a good illustration of such an alliance of letters and political intrigue. Of fairly modest birth, he first attempted to make a career for himself in the army and through poetry, establishing connections with Dorat's circle, frequenting Fanny de Beauharnais's salon, and publishing society works and comic operas. His thinking was that of an enlightened reformer: he studied the administration, he wrote a eulogy of Fénelon, and he became connected with Diderot, who introduced him into d'Holbach's salon and charged him with writing the article on "valeur" for the *Encyclopédie*.[23] During the same period, he took on the title of marquis de Pezay,[24] and thanks to his stepsister he succeeded, by dint of intrigues, in becoming closer to the power structure. His hour of glory came with the accession of Louis XVI, with whom he kept up a secret correspondence and whose confidence he managed to obtain, which won him a place in the Sartine administration, perhaps even playing the role of an unacknowledged counselor. In 1777, after a failed mission to Brittany, he lost the favor of the king and he died a few months later. This surprising career shows that between the salon of an intriguing woman, a space open to political action and permeated by ambitions aimed at the heart of monarchic power, and the circle of baron d'Holbach, where Diderot recruited some of his collaborators, the distance was not so great. Some guests circulated from one to the other; political news and literature were discussed in both; and it was at the home of Madame Cassini that guests braved the authority of the archbishop of Paris by performing a forbidden play that featured the suicide of a young nun.

For those who participated in them, the salons permitted access to the world of power and the possibility of attracting the protection of powerful people. Men of letters were not the only ones concerned here. The marquis de Mirabeau, who did not have his own Paris networks, used the salon of the comtesse de Rochefort to defend the interests of his brother, a knight of Malta. She also served him as a privileged informer, hastening, for example, to tell him that Choiseul was going to be named minister of war, an event with immediate consequences, as the vicomte de Castellane, a relative of Mirabeau's, had "full credit" with Choiseul. He was thus "available to do you all the services that you need."[25] A few years later, Mirabeau was anxious to find a place for his younger son and, with this aim in mind, assiduously frequented the Noailles's society. Announcing to the comtesse de Rochefort that he was getting ready to spend two days in Saint-Germain with the duc de Noailles, he justified himself in these terms: " You will ask me what I have to do there, but I have a younger son, and until his wretched older brother breaks his neck, I have every reason to treat the Noailles with circumspection when, on occasion, they treat me with the greatest distinction, and that child would be well settled, for a younger son, with a brigade in the Gardes du Corps."[26] Frequenting salons and country houses was a political necessity for those who wanted to advance their careers or their fortunes. The royal court existed not only at court: it had flowed into the privileged places of worldly sociability, as a number of sources confirm. Bombelles, for example, complains of having to do the rounds of the country houses in the summer: "Running around the outskirts of Paris, the duties that I have to go there to do are really tiring things, but obligatory as soon as one has a fortune to be made."[27] The language of pleasure and entertainment gave way here to that of "duties."

Attending salons might also serve as a step toward a political career. The meteoric career of Cardinal de Bernis offers an example of a reinvestment in the political domain of a success in worldly society. His qualities as a man of the world, which were based on his literary talents, allowed him to frequent the houses of prominent persons. Made fashionable by his good looks, his poems, his social talents, and his "very sociable and very amiable character,"[28] he made the most of those qualities to go from one salon to another to find protectors. The baron de Montmorency took him under his protection, advising him "to spread himself about in *le grand monde*"[29] and presenting him at Madame Geoffrin's salon. At the age of twenty-nine, he was elected to the Académie Française, thanks to the backing of "all the best company of Paris and Versailles," who interested themselves in him,[30] but he took care not to limit his reputation to belles-lettres. To that end, he stopped assiduously attending gatherings at the Académie: "[he] avoided therefore the sort of ridicule that people in society would certainly have put upon [him]" if he had too exclusively frequented men of letters.[31] However, he made use of that position to continue to attend salon gatherings and find protections there. He was received by the duc de Nivernais and the comtesse de Pontchartrain, and became a currently fashionable personality. "The ladies the most in fashion at court and in the city disputed with one another for the pleasure of giving him supper,"[32] wrote his friend the marquise de La Ferté-Imbault. The acquaintance that made his fortune was that of Madame Le Normant d'Étiolles, the future marquise de Pompadour, with whom he struck up a friendship at the home of the comtesse d'Estrade. When the future marquise became the mistress of Louis XV, Bernis served her as a confidant, a move that soon won him a pension, then an ambassadorship to Venice and the launching of his diplomatic career.[33]

Bernis's career, which was accelerated by his relations with the royal mistress, again highlights the connections between the salons and the court. Even beyond the case of the marquise de Pompadour, who was received as a young woman at the home of Madame Geoffrin, the worldly sphere was both a social space and a political space. Madame de La Ferté-Imbault, for example, attempted on several occasions to put her worldly networks to the service of her friends. She had connections in quite different milieus, given that her salon brought together aristocrats and diplomats as well as men of letters. In 1770, she acted as an intermediary between the prince de Condé and the parliamentarians.[34] A few years later, when her friend Maurepas returned to power, she attempted to mobilize the habitués of her salon in favor of the minister. Since Choiseul still appeared to be the most obvious potential rival to Maurepas, Madame de la Ferté-Imbault obliged the comte d'Albaret, who was one of her attendees, to stop frequenting the former minister's salon.[35]

Oriented toward the court, the salons tried to learn its news but also to influence appointments to positions at court and in the governmental sphere. Political interests and worldly interests constantly mingled and were usually expressed in the same language of friendship, protection, and gratitude. That common language also borrowed from forms of sociability typical of the salons such as the news item, the *bon mot*, the song, and praise. The politics of worldliness lay both in the political efficacy of society talents and in the salons' ability to reformulate political interests in worldly language. When ministers themselves held a salon, the political dimension of the worldly connection was even more flagrant.[36]

The Salon in Exile: Choiseul at Chanteloup

Chanteloup was a country house turned permanent residence and worldly and political center of sociability, a sort of court in exile or an opposition salon. The château, which had once belonged to the princesse des Ursins and had already sheltered one disgraced minister, Bolingbroke, was bought in 1761 by the duc de Choiseul, who had it enlarged and reconstructed. Beginning in 1766, the duchess spent several months a year there. Although the hospitality of the all-powerful minister could not have been totally without political meaning for those who paid visits, Chanteloup was primarily the domain of the duchess and her friends. Choiseul stayed there only for brief periods.

After Choiseul fell from grace in December 1770 and took refuge at Chanteloup, the château became an important site in the political geography of the kingdom. Historians have often insisted that Chanteloup shifted to being a center of political opposition toward which the eyes of all those unhappy with the politics of chancellor Maupeou and the duc d'Aiguillon turned, but have rarely examined how that opposition functioned.[37] In 1770, the situation was no longer that of the sixteenth century or the early seventeenth century, when malcontent princes published manifestos, called on their friends and clients for support, and levied troops. Not for a minute did Choiseul give any sign of troubling public order: he withdrew when royal confidence and favor were no longer his. At Chanteloup he led the luxurious life of a prince in exile, received visitors, played games and gambled, conversed, and sponsored theatrical performances. Somehow, from there, Choiseul acted upon, or maintained the fiction of acting upon, being the center of the political scene.

Numerous aristocrats came to spend a few days at Chanteloup. That success can be explained by the irreverent atmosphere of the end of the reign, accentuated by the insurrection of the princes and the unpopularity of Maupeou's power grab, but also by their confidence in Choiseul's rapid return to power. Above all, that endless stream of visitors made Chanteloup something of a center of worldly society that maintained unbroken ties with the court and with Paris. Since every visit there required authorization from the king (which was generally accorded), a trip to visit Choiseul necessarily took on a political dimension.

What went on at Chanteloup during those four years? The sources present the image of a daily life dominated by games (billiards and trictrac), meals, and long conversations. Dufort de Cheverny, who owed much to Choiseul and went to Chanteloup immediately after the minister's fall, found there a good number of "society" pursuing amusements. It was important that life at Chanteloup appear to be in a sociable and friendly key. At the same time, the continuous presence of large numbers of guests contradicts any image of an intimate society. In the evening, Chanteloup seemed like a court, and women were expected to be dressed and coiffed as they would be at Versailles. Madame Du Deffand wrote to Barthélemy that "to go to Chanteloup is to go to court; it is to seek out the *grand monde*

[and] amusements, to put oneself to *le bon ton*, acquire the *le bon air*."[38] Politics and worldliness were inseparable in this salon of exiles, where the dismissed minister held a substitute court. To show support for Choiseul was at once an assertion of a worldly loyalty, a political *fronde*, and a matter of fashion. If the maréchale de Luxembourg went to Chanteloup, Madame Du Deffand explained to Walpole, it was because it was "*du bel air* right now to be in what we call the opposition."[39]

The letters of the duchesse de Choiseul and abbé Bartélemy often contain a list of departures and arrivals. The latter wrote to Madame Du Deffand: "There is a flux and reflux. I think I am at the mouth of a port, where I see a ceaseless stream of ships of all nations coming and going."[40] Those lists of visitors (which Madame Du Deffand passed on) had an obvious political function: they stated that Choiseul's party continued to exist, and that the minister, despite his disgrace, remained an actor in the political game. He himself later gave physical form to the political dimension of the visits he received in his exile when, in 1777–78, he had a pagoda built at Chanteloup that he dedicated to all who had come to pay him a visit.

These incessant comings and goings also permitted Choiseul to keep up a strong connection with the capital. Newly arrived guests brought the latest news, while those who left hastened to tell of their stay in Touraine on their return to Paris. Similarly, the abundant correspondence that Madame Du Deffand exchanged with the duchesse de Choiseul and abbé Barthélemy was both worldly and political. In her own salon and in various circles, Madame Du Deffand spread news that she had received at Chanteloup. Abbé Barthélemy called his own letters "the Chanteloup gazette" and jokingly compared them to political gazettes. Madame Du Deffand transmitted the political and worldly news of Paris to Choiseul. She was well placed to collect information, decode the slightest deeds or words, and report on the positions of those who were rallying to the cause or betraying it. For that reason Choiseul engaged her to keep up his connection with the maréchale de Mirepoix, whereas the latter, who had supported Madame Du Barry, had a falling out with the Choiseuls.[41]

Continuing to frequent the duchesse d'Aiguillon, whose son had succeeded Choiseul as the minister, was not an easy matter for Madame Du Deffand. The duchess, who lived with her son, could not invite Madame Du Deffand, a friend of the Choiseuls, to her house.[42] On the other hand, they could meet on the neutral terrain of other *sociétés*. The contacts that she maintained with the duchess allowed Madame Du Deffand to play the delicate role of intermediary. Every move required tact, and even a woman so practiced in the politics of worldliness could at times commit an error. When Madame Du Deffand praised Madame d'Aiguillon in a letter to the duchesse de Choiseul, the latter responded that she was not surprised, something that Madame Du Deffand hastened to repeat to Madame D'Aiguillon. When she learned of this, the duchesse de Choiseul wrote her friend a furious letter: "How could you have imagined to say *coquetteries* about me to Madame d'Aiguillon?"[43] She declared herself shocked and insulted that anyone could think she might have wanted to "pay her court." She felt "compromised" by Madame Du Deffand's lack of delicacy and demanded that she repair her mistake, even if it vexed the duchesse d'Aiguillon. Madame Du Deffand had considered the letter as part of the usual commerce of the exchange of politeness, which it was up to her to provide in her role as intermediary. The duchesse de Choiseul insisted instead on the political context that had rendered positions asymmetrical and suspected worldly praise of concealing political flattery:

> When her son was in a situation more troublesome than [political] disgrace, and my husband in a position more promising than favor, it was up to me to convey to Madame d'Aiguillon all my esteem for her, in order to soften the bitterness and bring closer the distance that the difference in our situations necessarily put between us. Today everything has changed. Her son has power; my husband is left with nothing but honor, and it would be a low move unworthy of me to seek to please Madame d'Aiguillon. I would seem to be asking for her benevolence, her protection.[44]

This is a fine lesson. Worldly politeness was not beyond the reach of political evolutions, differences in power, or shifts in fortune. A compliment, even one as discreet as Madame Du Choiseul's, takes on meaning in function of the political situation, and its consequences must be evaluated in terms of moral reputation, given that the duchess felt herself to be "compromised." By repeating the compliment to Madame d'Aiguillon, a worldly practice that was familiar to her, Madame Du Deffand was thus accused of lacking political sense. "It is to you that I say this, and not to her, nor in order for that to be repeated to her." Worldly politics was an affair of nuance, interpretation, and tact, and it is possible that the duchess's protestation was above all a political act and a dramatization intended to ward off criticism.[45]

At the death of Louis XV, the *lettres de cachet* against Choiseul and Praslin were annulled. The prince de Beauvau wrote to Choiseul that he could return to Paris. He arrived in the capital on June 12, and the following day presented himself at the king's levée at La Muette. Proper society in Paris gave him a triumphal welcome, but Choiseul's hopes of a rapid return to power were soon disappointed. On June 17 he returned to Chanteloup, which would remain an important center of political sociability for years. The following winter, the Choiseuls returned to their Paris residence, which was once more a worldly center open five days a week with at least forty invited guests. Madame Du Deffand even had the unpleasant surprise of meeting Madame Geoffrin there.[46]

Despite this open-handed sociability and the support of Marie-Antoinette, Choiseul did not succeed in returning to his former power. His worldly networks remained extensive, but the organization of factions at court had changed with the new reign and some of his friends now supported Turgot.[47] Above all, a newcomer began to crystallize the hopes of the reform-minded aristocracy: Necker gained the support of many who had been close to the former minister, such as the Beauvaus and the Boufflers.

Salon and Power: Necker

Was the Neckers' salon the place in which the minister's political strategy was constructed? While historians only barely raise the question, contemporaries were less circumspect.[48] Condorcet, who was one of the most virulent critics of Necker and of the support he obtained from men of letters, never missed a chance to make the connection at his Friday dinners. In 1775, when Turgot was in power and had to deal with Necker's criticisms, Condorcet congratulated himself because he had received the support of Voltaire, who "has not hesitated between a banker who provides dinners for men of letters and a statesman who is already their defender."[49] When Necker came to power, Condorcet continued to attack him, at the risk of quarreling with his friend Amélie Suard, a protégée of the Neckers, to whom he sent letters denouncing men of letters who had rallied to his cause: "It is said in our cantons that M. Necker is converting. The ceremony will be held at Saint-Sulpice. Abbé Maury will preach, the priest will say mass; Abbé Raynal will be the deacon and Abbé Morellet the subdeacon. The chevalier de Chastellux will be the choirboy, and everyone will eat Friday dinner at the house of the daughter of the Infant Jesus. I think men of letters are going mad."[50] While these accusations were polemical, Madame de La Ferté-Imbault, although more favorable to Necker, insisted on several occasions on the connection between Necker's political career and his wife's salon. Even Marmontel, who was close to the Neckers, states in his *Mémoires* that Necker's career was Madame Necker's principal concern when she began to receive men of letters.[51] That unanimity attests that the connection between Madame Necker's "society" and the political success of her husband was obvious to contemporaries.

The salon was broadly seen as that of both of the Neckers, even at times of Necker alone, whether the observer was Madame Du Deffand or the inspectors of the Contrôle des étrangers. Madame Necker also identified fully with the political work of her husband, whom she ceaselessly praised and defended. In 1781, when he was dismissed, she wrote a letter to Gibbon in which she used the first person plural to speak of her husband's work and his departure: "We cannot yet understand that we have been constrained to abandon an administration in which success has always followed purity of intentions."[52] Finally, this salon was not a simple "literary society," because the Neckers received the duchesse de Luxembourg, the comtesse de Boufflers, the Beauvaus, Madame Du Deffand, and a number of diplomats.[53] The diplomats frequented the salon more because of Necker's political role than for the men of letters they met there, as indicated by their attendance, which rose and fell according to the political fortunes of his ministerial career. Their numbers peaked in the years 1779–81, those of his highest political attainments. Afterwards, they declined quite visibly, and the salon almost disappears from the reports of the Contrôle des étrangers before reappearing again during the last years of the ancien régime, when Necker became the hope of the liberal opposition, and returned to power.

The political dimension of the Neckers' salon concerned not only diplomats but also men of letters. Morellet furnishes a good example of conflict between practices of sociability, intellectual controversies, and political struggles. A habitué of Madame Necker's salon, he found himself in disagreement with Necker over the interests of the Compagnie des Indes, which led the two men into public polemics.[54] Despite Madame Necker's concerns, he continued to frequent her salon. Grimm, Galiani, and Diderot reproached him for selling his pen to the government and professed their astonishment at seeing him profit from the Neckers' hospitality while he was exchanging polemical barbs with his host.[55] When the conflict became truly political and Necker attacked Turgot's political positions, Morellet's situation seemed untenable. To spend his Fridays at the home of a man whose works he refuted publicly was already a delicate matter; dining every week with the political adversary of one's friend and protector would be incomprehensible. At that point, Morellet published a fairly violent refutation of Necker, then gave up attending his salon.[56] Although he had to give up the Neckers' hospitality, he maintained cordial relations with them. This enabled him to persuade Necker to assign the post of treasurer of the Administration des Domaines to his brother Jean-François.[57] The Neckers were witnesses at the marriage of Morellet's niece to Marmontel, and the latter, who lived with the Morellets, continued to go to the Neckers' recep-tions.[58] Morellet had occasion to encounter the Neckers, but he could no longer "cultivate them in their own home."[59] In 1781, when Necker was dismissed, Morellet felt he could legitimately return to his home.

The political dimension of the Neckers' salon, at least during his ten-ure as minister, is thus beyond doubt. It was perceived in that sense by contemporaries, who knew well that the hospitality offered by a minis-ter, even though it was delivered through his wife, was not an indifferent matter. How the salon served Necker's career needs examination. First, it permitted the Geneva Protestant banker to join Parisian high society at a time when he was doubly foreign to it.[60] In this sense, his patronage was a very clever way of playing with the codes of le monde by presenting himself as an enlightened protector of men of letters. Rather than displaying his wealth, his ambition, and his desire for glory, Necker left center-stage to his wife, while he stood by as an indulgent husband and discreet protector. This strategy paid off, and it permitted him to build important support among men of letters, but also within the high aristocracy of Paris who fre-quented his house and who, in turn, invited him to their houses. Madame Du Deffand created a weekly supper at which he was the principal figure. Madame Necker's ability to ally herself with all the various leaders of high society, to frequent equally Madame Du Deffand, Julie de Lespinasse, and Madame Geoffrin, helped Necker to rally the support of disparate groups. Thus, even as he stood opposed to Turgot's economic policies, Necker man-aged not to alienate some of the contrôleur général's supporters. Julie de Lespinasse, for example, frequented the Neckers' salon, and it seems that the duchesse d'Enville played a role in Necker's nomination by intervening with Maurepas.[61]

For her part, Madame Du Deffand played a role as intermediary between the Choiseuls and the Neckers.[62] In October 1776, when Necker was named director general of the Treasury, she asked the Choiseuls to make it known that they approved this choice and took it upon herself to inform Necker of their response.[63] She went to supper at the Neckers in order to try to obtain details about his nomination, and she hastened to inform the Choiseuls, who were at Chanteloup, about what she had learned.[64] For Necker, sup-port from the Choiseul party was valuable reinforcement. The prince and princesse de Beauvau, for example, who were very influential and close to Choiseul, were taken to Saint-Ouen by the marquise Du Deffand, and they supported the career of the director general of finance.

Choiseul's friends remained influential but in the new political configu-ration it was primarily the Maurepas clan that had to be swayed. Here, the Neckers' principal advantage was the marquise de La Ferté-Imbault, with whom they had established friendly relations, even though she detested the philosophes whom they received. Even before Necker became minister, she enabled him to gain the good will of Louis XVI's principal minister.[65] In 1781, at a moment of great tension before Necker's resignation, she tried to dissuade Necker from withdrawing.[66] Necker's resignation caused a cooling off with Madame de La Ferté-Imbault, who supported the party of Maurepas.[67] Their relations were reestablished during the 1780s.

The Neckers' salon thus permitted them to join high society and to create solid political support. At the same time, Necker used the support of the men of letters who frequented his house to forge an image of himself as a cultivated man interested in both administration and letters. In 1773, he spoke before the Académie in a speech praising Colbert that permitted him to downplay his status as a Calvinist banker and to pose as an enlightened and eloquent reformer. The salons orchestrated the success of this speech, and the men of letters whom he received diffused his image as a protector of letters and philosophy.[68] When Necker gained power, Meister, whose pension the minister paid, presented the "elevation of M. Necker" to the subscribers of the *Correspondance littéraire* in a highly favorable light and assured them that his fame was connected with letters: "The confidence that His Majesty has deigned to accord to this illustrious foreigner honors letters, which have contributed to making him known; and the triumph that merit has won on this occasion over vain prejudices must perhaps be regarded as a proof of the progress that reason and Enlightenment have made in France."[69] Subsequently, Necker maintained that reputation by choosing topics that enabled him to display his interest in public questions. In 1775, he published his *Réflexions sur les blés*. In 1788, his return to power was preceded by the publication of a book on religious opinions. Hardly surprised to see the Académie salute Necker's book, Madame de Créqui wrote: "He is rich, a man of wit, and pays back the academicians with good dinners."[70]

The famous episode of the statue of Voltaire paid for by subscription can be seen in a similar perspective. The idea arose at the house of Madame Necker and has often been presented as a writers' initiative, an homage of the republic of letters to its great man.[71] It can also be read as an episode in Necker's promotion as a protector of men of letters. The subscription was in fact open, beyond professional writers, to all those who loved letters, be they men of the world or even sovereigns. Voltaire himself was not fooled, and he seized the occasion to become closer to Necker. At first, when he was informed of the project, he wrote a series of stanzas to Madame Necker in which he thanked her, as if the initiative had come from her.[72] In 1776, when the statue was finished, Voltaire sent her an epistle in which he associated the statue with Necker's nomination. He also recalled the past connection between Necker and men of letters at the time of the prize that the Académie accorded to Necker's eulogy. Finally, he proclaimed his allegiance to him.[73]

Thanks to the complementary nature of their marriage, Madame Necker served as an intermediary between authors and her husband. Necker managed to avoid the ridicule of the financier who receives writers by appearing an educated a man of the world without exclusive connections with any one sector of worldly society. He was also extremely sensitive to the evolutions of political culture and to the role played by the notion of public opinion.

Necker appears to have introduced this new element of public opinion into the traditional political game, the influence of which he addressed in his works or the preambles to his edicts. He was one of the first to build his career on his popularity, and he had few qualms about publishing his famous *Compte rendu au roi* of 1781, a work that for the first time made the monarchy's budget public knowledge. It might be argued that Necker based his actions on public opinion, and that the men of letters who frequented his salon relayed his publications to that public opinion. But who read *Sur la législation du commerce des grains*? If the *Compte rendu au roi* was a success in the bookshops, how can its impact on "public opinion" be measured? If the theater "public" was a participant in the literary game whose verdicts could be disputed but not ignored, the political "public," for its part, existed only virtually and had no way to express itself. Certainly there were *bruits*: people talked in the cafés and in the gardens, rumors circulated in the streets and in the houses and came to the attention of the police, but they were subjected to divergent evaluations. The distance was immense between the ideal of public opinion put forward by the lawyers, the Jansenists, and the men of letters, and the reality of politics. The abbé de Véri, an incisive observer of political life in the reign of Louis XVI, insisted on the gap between public opinion, which everyone claimed was on his side, and the personal opinions of the courtiers with whom the king had to deal. It left the interplay of reputations, both in the salons and in the court, to take its course: "One can thus be wrong in advising princes to listen to everyone and to believe in the opinion of the public. A good or bad reputation is perhaps the seal of truth; but the difficulty for sovereigns is to discern it well. It often arrives to their ears only by way of passionate and interested persons; everyone credits his own personal opinion to the public."[74] Necker built his rise to power on this give and take between the traditional ways in which political life functioned and through which the networks of influence and the coteries attempted to control the opinions of the king, on the one hand, and, on the other, the new arrangement introduced by the notion of public opinion, which, for the moment, remained a great but silent unknown quantity.

It may be helpful to look more closely at how Necker himself defined the "public opinion" that he claimed was with him. According to Keith Baker, Necker was representative of the new theoreticians of public opinion as a rational and stable political tribunal to which those who governed owed an account.[75] This analysis underestimates the originality of Necker's thought, however: his theory of public opinion is quite different from the one expressed by authors such as Malesherbes.[76] For Necker, public opinion was not the result of the diffusion of printing and the formation of a rational collective opinion. To the contrary, Necker defined public opinion in terms associated with worldly opinion and with society life. It did not appear in connection with public debate, the effects of print products, or individual reason, but rather was linked to practices of sociability and the fluctuations of reputations: "The spirit of society, and the desire of consideration and praise, have established a tribunal in France, before which everyone who attracts public notice is obliged to appear; there public opinion, as from a throne, distributes praises and laurels, and establishes, or ruins, reputations."[77] Public opinion had still here its traditional connotations of collective judgment on moral reputations.

Even though Necker attempted to distinguish public opinion from the fluctuating opinions of the various coteries, the importance that he granted to the vocabulary of praise, imitation, and reputation, as well as to *l'esprit de société* (which Necker connected to public opinion on several occasions), make this text an original enterprise. Although *esprit de société* and *opinion publique* belonged to two different languages in the 1780s, Necker brought them together on several occasions and attempted to bridge the gap separating worldly sociability from the public. He embellished worldly opinion, which made and unmade reputations by imitation and distinction, with the positive attributes of public opinion. Since public opinion had begun to figure rhetorically in political struggles, Necker chose to become its herald, while identifying it with the mechanisms of worldly sociability he had actually mastered.

Necker thus saw public opinion as specifically French, hence unfathomable to foreigners. According to him, it corresponded neither to the English political model nor to a European phenomenon connected with the Enlightenment, but rather to the political and social model of the French monarchy. In France, he wrote, the preambles to edicts must be addressed to public opinion, a gesture that was useless in despotic governments, where public opinion plays no role, but also in "free countries, such as England."[78] According to this statement, which implicitly referred to Montesquieu, public opinion corresponded to the specific nature of French society, ruled by honor, politeness, and gallantry, where opinions converged thanks to the spirit of society. That spirit, Necker wrote, "has an unbounded sway over a sensitive people, who love not only to judge, but to cut a figure in the world, who are not divided by political interests, weakened by despotism, nor overcome by turbulent passions. . . a nation, in which, perhaps, a general propensity to imitation prevents a multiplicity of opinions and weakens the force of those that are too singular."[79] Public opinion, as Necker conceived it, was not a force for contestation, but the result of the convergence of opinions in the worldly sphere.

The ways in which Necker attempted to fuse the language of sociability, the effects of imitation, and the fluctuations of reputation with the language of public opinion and the public nature of political debates led him to consider what made politics function in the eighteenth century. In his correspondence with Maurepas before being called to the ministry of finance, he played with the ambiguity between public opinion and high society on several occasions. He wrote, for example: "I flatter myself that public opinion will tell you that your benevolence toward me is not wrong and that, at the earliest opportunity, a number of persons who count for much at the Court and in the City will let you know that they share your sentiments."[80] Men of letters also helped him ensure the success of his publications, which were less aimed at the broad public as at the salons. Almost a year before the publication of *De l'administration des finances de la France* (1784), an early version of the work circulated in manuscript and inspired the guests in his salon to send letters full of praise, to which Madame Necker took care to respond at length.[81]After the publication of *De l'importance des opinions religieuses* in 1786, Madame de La Ferté-Imbault called Necker a "great Caesar" and stated that she "prostrates herself before him." Madame Necker responded with protestations of friendship and assured Madame de La Ferté-Imbault that she had "always hoped for her support for M. Necker, in which [she had] placed all her amour propre."[82]

That worldly strategy, which relied on her sociability networks to guarantee the promotion of Necker's works and policies, was noted by his adversaries and became a recurrent argument in criticism against him.[83] His critics missed no opportunity to draw attention to the "suppers" that Necker gave for *beaux esprits* and aimed directly at the minister's alleged political strength, "the fanaticism that he has inspired within *la bonne compagnie*." Necker's enemies presented the courtiers and political coteries that rallied to him as "*grandes dames*, beautiful women, pretty ones, witty ones, and above all intriguers." They did not produce public opinion, but rather a simulacrum of it destined for the court. Necker's master stroke would thus consist of using his writings to promote the importance of public opinion, which he feigned to address, just as the political game focused on knowing who could pass for its interpreter. His adversaries were acutely aware of his political strategy and of the role of worldly practices in that strategy.

SALON DIPLOMACY
Sociability and Representation

The participation of diplomats in the high society of Paris was due in part to their massive presence in the city, but it also responded to a political necessity. After the Peace of Utrecht at the end of the War of Spanish Succession, there was little doubt that sociability was an integral part of an ambassador's job description or that worldly entertainment had become a "diplomatic duty."[84] Hence one of an ambassador's principal functions was to "represent" his sovereign, and court ceremonial was traditionally the place par excellence for that diplomacy of prestige and glory.[85] During the latter half of the eighteenth century ambassadors were seldom present at Versailles. They went to Versailles on Tuesdays for the audience, lunched with the minister of foreign affairs, then hastened back to spend the evening in Paris. This may have been a result of a shift of worldly life from Versailles to Paris. Maintaining one's ambassadorial rank with respect to the court nobility implied representing one's sovereign in the salons of high society as much as appearing at court. This was also true of receiving visitors and guests: foreign diplomats regularly gave grand suppers or balls, following the lessons of Callières, who had taught that an ambassador must be "liberal and magnificent" and must "often give fêtes and entertainments for the principal persons of the court in which he finds himself."[86]

Some ambassadors held an open table for their compatriots; others more or less regularly gave dinners or suppers for other diplomats posted to Paris. These suppers were not necessarily reserved for foreigners, however, and they often provided the ambassadors with an opportunity to receive the court aristocracy. Still others adopted the practices of sociability of Parisian high society to the point of having their special "days" in certain seasons. Spinola, the Genoese ambassador, gave a dinner every Monday for several of his colleagues, followed by "the usual gaming."[87] Aranda, the Spanish ambassador, arrived in Paris in 1773; two years later he was maintaining "a great state [in his] house,"[88] giving dinners and suppers several days of the week. Not only was he defending the prestige of Spain, but he was also affirming his own status as a grandee of Spain and former prime minister to the Spanish crown. By 1778 he had become perfectly integrated into Paris high society and "kept a good and well-regulated table, and without begging anyone, he often had a large attendance because everyone was welcome there."[89]

Receiving visitors, guests, and colleagues, and offering meals and entertainments was not only a question of prestige and rank. The ambassadors who frequented *le monde* and spent their evenings in Paris salons were eager to "know what was going on," to gather information, and to keep their ears open for news and rumors. The art of the diplomat, which involved a combination of perspicacity, dissimulation, and penetration, found in the Paris social world a field of action equal to its measure.

Worldly News, Diplomatic News: The Battle of the Salons

For the ambassadors, the salons were strategic strongholds that they needed to occupy in order to be the first to hear the rumors that they fed into their dispatches, but also in order to influence the circulation of information. Their first task was to be informed, to know the political news that often circulated in the salons before being taken up by the gazettes. The inspector charged with surveillance of the foreign ministers noted that they "continue to move through the city and the houses of their acquaintances to gather the news, and seem extremely occupied by the latest news";[90] a week later: "the foreign ministers have continued to move through the city and the houses of their society in the evening to gather the news."[91] Such news, which was the reason for the diplomats' political interest in the salons, came from the court and consisted of rumors of someone's disgrace, someone else's nomination, or some gesture or word from the king. Stormont, the English ambassador, was "accustomed," on Wednesdays, to "go out in the evening before finishing his mail in order to learn some news at the home of Madame Du Deffand."[92]

In moments of political uncertainty, a race for information between ambassadors took place in the salons. In 1775, for example, the death of the maréchal de Muy, the minister of war, perplexed the diplomatic corps. The foreign ministers, the police inspector reported, "went from one to another of the houses of their society to gather opinions concerning the successor to this minister in the War Department."[93] When the comte de Saint-Germain was named to the post, diplomats and distinguished foreigners were so astonished that they "did not fail to go to the houses of Madame la marquise Du Deffand, Madame Geoffrin, and Madame d'Espinasse [*sic*]"[94] to obtain more specific information. For the diplomats posted to Paris, those three salons, which historians have often considered "literary salons," were primarily places for gathering political information from people close to government sources.

The vocabulary of news was common to worldly sociability and diplomatic information. The diplomatic news item, however, was theoretically subject to an imperative of veracity, or at least verisimilitude, as the basis of its political value. Still, the way in which news functioned in society, where it was valued primarily for the story it enabled and for its ability to inflate the reputation of the person who reported it, at times ended up contaminating the diplomatic information network. News heard in the salons and reported in diplomatic dispatches, which might be a simple society rumor, was then corrected in subsequent dispatches. Certain diplomats went farther: the minister of Prussia, Baron Golz, counteracted the paucity of news by stuffing his dispatches with false information and invented conversations.[95]

Conversely, the diplomats soon understood that they could make full use of the salons as a springboard for spreading news or rumors favorable to their country. In a context in which worldly opinion played an important role in political and diplomatic decision making, a skilled control of the news that circulated within proper society was mandatory for the ambassadors. At times the police reports reflect these strategies. For example, when Baron Golz dined on April 27, 1786, at the house of Prince Galitzine, he attempted to put an end to rumors about the illness of Frederick II.[96] Similarly, a report dated April 1778 indicated that the Russian lords in Paris were using the salons they frequented to spread word of a possible commercial treaty between Russia and France about which they supposedly learned from letters received from St. Petersburg.[97]

America in the Salon

The American War of Independence presents a good vantage point on salon diplomacy. Paris high society took a passionate interest in the war. Highly contradictory diplomatic and military news circulated in the salons, often signaled in the police reports with the formula, "on dit que." In April 1778, for example, the rumor spread that the court of Spain was hesitating to support the American "insurgents."[98] Discussions that followed military news led to judgments that were repeated and took on political value. At one of Madame Necker's receptions, when conversation turned to losses the Americans had sustained in warehouses that contained stocks of shoes, among other things, the duke of Richmond, a pillar of the opposition to the English government, declared, "That is no great affair; they will fight without shoes," a statement that was immediately repeated and that the police inspector carefully noted.[99] The distance of the theater of operations made salons fertile grounds for rumors and the presence of a few noble Frenchmen in America made the events there even more interesting. Stormont, the English ambassador, profited from a situation in which news was rare, unsure, and avidly awaited, to conduct a systematic campaign of worldly disinformation. He tirelessly repeated false news, always favorable to England, going from salon to salon to announce a naval victory of the royal forces or a rout of the "insurgents." Although fashionable people seemed never to tire of such dubious and partial information, the police inspector grew increasingly skeptical about "news" spread by the ambassador that always turned out to be false. In April 1777, for example, Stormont "reported in the houses of his society" that the royal army under the command of General Howe had routed the Americans, killing three thousand men. Although official news later corrected this information, he continued, in the days that followed, to spread rumors about the defeats of the "insurgents."[100]

Obviously, Stormont's persistent false announcements of English victories led to a decline in his credibility and eventually raised only a faint and amused interest.[101] Stormont even went to the extreme of spreading a rumor about a secret, a rumor that could not be countered and that inspired all sorts of questions: "A rumor is spreading among the foreign ministers that the ambassador of England says that for some time now he has a secret that he does not care to communicate to anyone."[102]

The Americans were not lacking resources in this information war, as they could count on Benjamin Franklin, who had proven himself capable of perfect integration into Parisian high society and had mastered the art of spreading such rumors as he found convenient. All he needed to do, for example, was to insinuate during a supper, with a knowing air, that he was confident about the military situation to have suppositions flow through the salons and be relayed to Vergennes, the minister of foreign affairs, by the police reports.[103] At times an ostentatious presence, a symbolic gesture, or a clever word became news and provided fodder for salon conversation. During a dinner at the home of the duchesse de Deux-Ponts, a toast was offered to the health of the American Congress in the presence of Franklin, who added, "and to the happy alliance with the king of France." Those who had been present at dinner hastened to report the event in the other societies they frequented. From the salons, the rumor of a treaty between France and America spread through the cafés, in particular those frequented by the English living in Paris, who then judged war with France to be inevitable.[104]

The political rivalry between Stormont and Franklin also played out on the terrain of worldly sociability, a situation that posed serious questions of decorum for the hostess. Franklin was a close friend of the duchesse d'Enville and her son, the duc de La Rochefoucauld, who was translating the Constitution of the United States with Franklin's aid. In February 1778, however, a diplomatic incident was narrowly avoided. The duchesse d'Enville had invited Franklin to a concert at her home, forgetting or being unaware that Stormont and his wife would attend the concert. The duc de La Rochefoucauld was obliged to write to Franklin to persuade him to stay away so as to avoid an unfortunate encounter with the English ambassador.[105] Sociability again played a role a few months later. In the days before Stormont departed Paris in March 1778, the police scrupulously noted all the visits that he received.[106] On the day of his departure, Monsieur Le Play de Chaumont gave a dinner honoring Franklin and other Americans.[107] The duc de La Rochefoucauld was delighted: "Finally, Sir, we see your Nation and our own declared friends, and the liberator of America made public plenipotentiary in France; one can now safely invite you to a concert, and Milord Stormont has made way for you."[108]

The Spy in the Salon

As a general rule, the Paris police spared no effort in their surveillance of foreigners, whom they suspected of being active spies. Vergennes's attention to the words and deeds of the diplomats shows that in the eyes of the power structure the presence of diplomats in the salons was directly connected with their political role. It was thus important to know what "people have said that day in a good house."[109] Inquiries were directed at the many foreigners who lived in Paris and who frequented the diplomats. An Irishman, O'Byrne, who made several sojourns in Paris, where he was introduced into high society and played high-stakes games, was suspected of being employed in secret negotiations in London.[110]

In the case of Baron Boden, the police expressed certainty, developed over a number of successive reports, rather than suspicions. From 1769–71, Boden, who enjoyed the confidence of the Prince Royal of Prussia, stayed in Paris on the prince's business, sending him the information that he managed to collect. "He had slipped, for that purpose, into the houses of the foreign ministers and into several good houses."[111] After a trip to Dresden late in 1771, he soon returned to Paris, where he established connections with all the diplomats posted to the capital. According to a new report in August 1774, certain ambassadors began to mistrust him, which led him to concentrate on the "good French houses."[112] It seems that Boden had done a good job as a political informer: several years later, he became a minister of the Landgrave of Hesse-Cassel, a post that permitted him to continue his activities in a more legitimate manner. He frequented most of the salons, but particularly that of Madame Dupin, whose house he visited almost every day during the 1780s.

The minister of foreign affairs and the lieutenant of police were particularly suspicious of salons hosted by foreigners, which served as a natural base of operations for ambassadors within worldly society. Countess Shuvalov was closely watched because the Russian minister, Prince Bariatinski, "goes every day to that house, both to confer with the count and to learn the news that M. Seiffer, a German physician, gathers throughout Paris and brings there."[113] Among the foreign women who received and whose activities were kept under surveillance, Baroness Rieben was well known to Inspector Buhot, who had arrested her in 1757, at the beginning of the Seven Years' War.[114] Madame Rieben, a twenty-six-year-old Swedish woman, had settled in Paris three years earlier, following her lover, Monsieur Knyphausen, who had served as an adviser to the Swedish legation in Paris and later as minister plenipotentiary of the king of Prussia.[115] Knyphausen dined every day at her house in the company of other foreigners of distinction, such as the duke of Mecklenburg and the Danish ambassador. In July 1756, after the first offensives of Frederick II in Saxony, d'Argenson made some inquiries about Baroness Rieben, whom he believed to be Prussian, and six months later, after the departure of the minister of Prussia, inspector Buhot and commissioner Rochebrune ordered a search of her house and had her imprisoned in the Bastille. They found several letters from a certain Manem, "mad but dangerous," who was offering his services to the king of Prussia. The baroness had been swifter than the police, however; the ambassador's papers, which she had been keeping, had disappeared by the time of Buhot's search. Obliged to let her go, the lieutenant of police suggested to her that she leave the country, which she refused to do under the pretext of health problems. A year later, she was still in Paris and Buhot had to order her to leave France within the month.[116] Thanks to dilatory maneuvers, however, she ended up remaining in Paris.

She was still there twenty years later. Police reports show her comfortably installed at Chaillot in 1778–79, giving receptions several times a week for the ambassadors of the United Provinces, Prussia, Saxony, and Denmark. The police continued to be suspicious of her worldly activities and had surveillance put on her, thanks to her servant who was a police spy.[117]

The police and the government may not have been the only ones who worried about the presence of spies in the salons. As they frequented the salons in search of news, the ambassadors were faithful to their role. "One of the principal functions of the ambassador is to spy," Abraham de Wicquefort declared.[118] It was when roles were less clearly defined that suspicions arose. Grimm, for example, who was officially the minister of Saxe-Gotha, was also considered to be an agent of Catherine II. After a dinner with him, Bombelles commented: "He much amused us by anecdotes about the little courts of Germany. If you have to live with suspect people, it is a good thing if they are likable."[119]

Princely Voyages

During the final thirty years of the ancien régime several foreign sovereigns visited Paris. They generally did so under assumed names, though the fictitious anonymity fooled no one, given that the voyages had been announced, awaited, celebrated, and at times accompanied by publications.[120] Among other advantages, anonymity permitted the royal visitors to escape ceremonial activities and visit the capital as if they were ordinary citizens. It allowed them to spend their evenings in the salons, which was a way of enjoying the aristocratic amusements of the capital, but it also had a political dimension. Joseph II, for example, wanted to meet prominent politicians: he visited Madame Necker in order to speak with her husband, and Madame d'Enville in order to see Turgot.[121] It was at the Neckers' home that Madame Du Deffand crossed paths with Joseph II following his two-hour conversation with the directeur général des finances.[122]

During his Parisian sojourn in 1784, Prince Henry, the brother of Frederick II, paid visits to "all the most significant personages."[123] That intensive occupation of the worldly sphere can be explained by the secret diplomatic mission with which Prince Henry had been charged by his brother. The duc de Nivernais and Grimm served him as intermediaries, the latter guiding the prince to the principal salons of the capital.[124]

In 1770, Gustav III, then the crown prince of Sweden, also frequented most of the Paris salons. Gustav, a twenty-six-year-old prince, had been educated in the French manner and spoke French perfectly. He declared himself to be "highly enthusiastic about Voltaire"[125] and possessed the skills to seduce high society. He could be found at the houses of the comtesse de Boufflers, the comtesse d'Egmont, the comtesse de Brionne, the maréchale de Luxembourg, Madame de Mesmes, Madame Geoffrin, and the comtesse de La Marck. After his return to Sweden, Gustav III began an exchange of letters with the comtesse de La Marck and with the comtesse de Boufflers that was to continue for fifteen and twenty years, respectively.[126] To what extent were these correspondences motivated by friendship, by the pleasure that the king took in writing in French, having news of Paris life, and consulting his correspondents on the various events in his private life, or by his understandable interest as king? In the context of unstable domestic politics, an alliance with France was imperative for Gustav III, and it was crucially important for him to have contacts at the French court and in the high society of Paris. Creutz, who looked after the king's interests, guided his epistolary choices, relying on his own familiarity with the political geography of the salons. Several months after the king's departure, Creutz congratulated himself on seeing "with what vivacity everyone here takes an interest in [the king's] glory: Mme d'Egmont, Mme de Brionne, Mme de Luxembourg, Mme de La Marck, etc., all breathe only for Your Majesty."[127] As a consequence, Creutz encouraged the king to pursue those correspondences. At first, the comtesse d'Egmont seemed to be a highly valuable correspondent. Thanks to family connections, she was close to the duc d'Aiguillon, her cousin, while her ties to the comtesse de Brionne and her liberal opinions attached her to the Choiseul clan.[128] In contrast, when the duc d'Aiguillon was named minister of foreign affairs and quarreled with the comtesse d'Egmont, she became a hindrance to the negotiations that Creutz was carrying on, and he asked the king to write less often to the countess so as to avoid offending the duc d'Aiguillon.[129] Three years later the political terrain had again shifted: the duc d'Aiguillon was no longer in power and the Choiseul party had revived. At that point Creutz encouraged Gustav III to correspond actively with the comtesse de Brionne: "I beg of Your Majesty, if a sure occasion presents itself, to continue your correspondence with Mme de Brionne; that might be useful, or even necessary."[130]

These communications were all the more useful to the diplomacy of Gustav III when, in August 1772, only a few months before his accession to the throne, he carried out a coup d'état that allowed him to reinforce the royal power by promulgating a new constitution. He received the support of France, and the duc d'Aiguillon took it upon himself to have the new constitution printed. In Paris salons, even those who had no words harsh enough to stigmatize Maupeou's absolutism rejoiced at this reinforcement of Swedish absolutism. Morellet commented ironically, "You would laugh to see the enthusiasm here, the tenderness for the king of Sweden shown by some great ladies of the court who have had him for supper in Paris and who believe they share in his elevation."[131] Gustav III's female correspondents also enabled him to keep abreast of all the goings on in Paris and at

Versailles. For twenty years the comtesse de Boufflers sent him letters on the political situation, quite detailed and well informed.

Madame Geoffrin was not indifferent to the diplomatic aspects of worldly sociability. The correspondence that she kept up with Catherine II was for her a source of pride and importance. From the sovereign's point of view, it was Madame Geoffrin's ability to circulate the letters, by reading them in her own salon or by showing them to her friends, that made this correspondence valuable. Still, when Stanisław August Poniatowski became king of Poland, Madame Geoffrin was especially able to serve as an intermediary and put her knowledge of the world to political use. For Stanisław August, the friendship of Madame Geoffrin was a precious aid, given that one of the early priorities of his reign was to be recognized by France. His early letters justify his election and his behavior and attempt to reestablish the facts, which he feared had been distorted in France. At that point, Madame Geoffrin reinvented herself as an unofficial ambassador, and her salon became the place where one talked about Polish affairs.[132] She made the acquaintance of Monsieur de Sainte-Foix, the *premier commis* in the Affaires Étrangères and the favorite of the minister, because she thought that it was a relationship that might be useful for Stanisław August. Since the king had not been officially recognized by France, when the minister wanted to get word to him of something, Sainte-Foix informed Madame Geoffrin, who transmitted the communication. She even attempted to negotiate directly with Choiseul, to whom she sent a letter from Stanisław August in which he spoke of his hope for an alliance with France. Diplomacy requires apprenticeship, and Madame Geoffrin discovered, on receiving Choiseul's response, that "politics has its own particular ways":[133] the king of Poland's letter had not been redacted in diplomatic terms since it was addressed to Madame Geoffrin, and it had displeased Choiseul. Diplomatic correspondence, she learned, had different rules from worldly correspondence. Madame Geoffrin was not discouraged, however. She justified herself to Choiseul, and she decided to send him no more letters, but rather to keep them to be read, judged, and heard in her own home. Thus an intermediary had to be found, and she decided to use Baron Gleichen, a friend of Choiseul and a former diplomat, in this role, showing him all the letters so that he could give an account of them to the minister.[134]

The role of intermediary that sealed her reputation and made her the direct interlocutor of a king and a minister meant much to Madame Geoffrin. When she discovered that an envoy of the king of Poland had made the trip to Paris to give a code to the French cabinet without her being informed of the voyage, she was angry. Her disappointment was all the greater because Sainte-Foix had asked her for information regarding this envoy, and she had been obliged to admit that she knew nothing of his visit.[135] When Madame Geoffrin left for Poland, many people thought that she had been charged with a diplomatic mission. She herself thought that she might be able to play the role of adviser to the new king. She underestimated the complexity of the Polish courts, however, and her hopes were dashed. On her return to Paris and after a few months of chilly relations, Madame Geoffrin once more became something of an agent for Stanisław August Poniatowski, with whom she continued to keep up a thick correspondence. She received all the Poles whom he recommended to her and who declared their loyalty to the king. Madame de La Marck told Gustav III of Sweden, "She supports his party in Paris and refuses her doorway to those who are in that of the confederates."[136]

Madame Geoffrin also found her political relations useful when her own reputation was challenged. In 1767, taking advantage of the rumors that had accompanied her trip to Poland, abbé Guasco published some previously unpublished letters of Montesquieu saying extremely negative things about her, to which he added acidic commentaries of his own. The affair was already an embarrassment for Madame Geoffrin when the *Gazette d'Utrecht* published an article that mentioned the book and repeated the criticisms aimed at her. The article stated that in Paris she was called "the fishwife of the fashionable world" and "the *dame de charité* of literature."[137] At that point, Madame Geoffrin turned to Choiseul, who ordered the king's agent at The Hague to intervene with the gazette and have a denial printed, which Choiseul himself redacted and in which Madame Geoffrin—who had become Madame de Geoffrin—obtained a complete retraction.[138] Choiseul transmitted the response to Madame Geoffrin and, for good measure, also had an article inserted in the *Gazette de France*, which took care not to cite Madame Geoffrin by name but denounced Montesquieu's letters as false.[139] This means that while attempting to play the role of diplomatic intermediary between Poniatowski and Choiseul, Madame Geoffrin also used her ties with the minister to have diplomacy intervene in the service of her reputation.

POLICE, POLITICIZATION, REVOLUTION
Police Surveillance

Far from being literary gatherings cut off from all connection with political life, the salons were an important interface between royal power and high society and between Versailles, the epicenter of struggles of influence, and the Parisian circulation of news. Thus it is not surprising that the police did their utmost to keep an eye on worldly life. In addition to the oversight of diplomats by the Contrôle des étrangers, the police attempted to provide more general surveillance of the principal salons of the capital. To be sure, they were more difficult to observe than public spaces where the police were on the look-out for *mauvais discours* (bad talk) and could arrest suspects.[140] Yet the police had spies and informants within the salons. Quite often these were servants, but at times the Paris police used spies better integrated into society life, like one "young and poor author" who turned in regular reports to the lieutenant of police.[141] There was even one salon hostess, whose name Lenoir (lieutenant of police) unfortunately does not mention, who served as a police spy. After a past of gallantry, this sixty-year-old woman had access to the "best houses of Paris." Several times a week she received "courtiers, socialites, men of letters, and the idle." In his memoirs Lenoir stated that he was often better informed by her reports than by the police reports.[142]

The salon habitués were not dupes. The young author who wrote reports for Lenoir was soon suspected and told that he was no longer welcome.[143] Everyone took precautions, and meals with many participants were not considered suitable for overly heterodox discussions. Invited to dinner in the company of Mably, whose writings he admired, Bombelles waited to have a private conversation with him before launching a philosophical discussion. During dinner he was happy to keep to less interesting matters: "One does not speak out before people when one has a modicum of prudence; all the more so because in Paris one is almost always sure to have a police spy among their number."[144]

As a domestic space, the salon was not directly subjected to police surveillance, unlike the public spaces of the capital. At the same time, the presence of many guests and of domestics allowed the police to be informed of what was said and done. Just as much as it was a surveillance of seditious discourse, this was a surveillance of behavior, and the police lieutenant was perfectly up to date on people's reputations, to the point that on occasion he was consulted in family and matrimonial affairs. In the eyes of the police, surveillance of the salons was not so much aimed at controlling seditious spaces as it was at obtaining information. The Doublet salon, for example, which has long been presented as an oppositional salon that gave rise to manuscript journals such as the *Memoires secrets*, was in reality tolerated, but kept under surveillance and perhaps even in part controlled by the Paris police. Far from being an institution of the Parisian public sphere, the salon of Madame Doublet was instead an interface between the police and high society that permitted the government to take an active role in the circulation of news.[145]

It is obvious that certain assumptions about the history of information under the ancien régime need to be revisited. It is easy to imagine a face-to-face opposition between, one the one hand, monarchical propaganda carried out according to monarchical rituals and by governmental gazettes and, on the other, a welter of discourses, rumors, and critical commentaries. In reality, the circulation of information was much more complex and lent itself to more ambiguous strategies. The same sites or the same circuits could transmit news that had opposite effects. Those effects depended on the context in which the news circulated, the credit that was lent to a news item, and the persons to whom it was addressed. At times, the surveillance of news jointly engaged the police, members of the social world, and men of letters.

An odd game developed between the police and the diplomats. For the police, it was important to keep high society under surveillance. The diplomats were well aware of this surveillance and knew how to get around it by making use of the police informants for their own purposes. In 1785, for example, the Venetian ambassador wanted to keep a trip to England secret, so he paid his kitchen boy to give false information to the police inspector who habitually interrogated him.[146] In this manner, he managed to turn police surveillance to his own advantage by having false information about his presence in Paris travel up through the police structure as far as Vergennes, while he himself was in London. It also might happen that the police and the diplomats had converging interests and cooperated to establish surveillance over certain foreigners. When a Russian named Bobrinski, instead of frequenting the "good houses and distinguished societies," became known for his escapades, visiting gambling dens and fighting at the Palais-Royal, he attracted the attention of both the police and Grimm, who feared a scandal that would reflect badly on Catherine II. Inspector Bossenet informed Lenoir that he had reached an agreement with Grimm to keep a close watch on Bobrinski by paying one of his servants to inform him about the man's words and deeds.[147] Finally, the police were one actor in the worldly game of information, which they attempted to use and control. It is striking, reading the police reports, to see the inspectors evaluating the reliability of rumors, doubting the news that was circulating in the salons, and at times exercising a critical sense that was more vigilant than that of the *gens du monde*.

The Politicization of the Salons?

Were the salons the prime victims of the political turmoil of the final years of the ancien régime? Two fairly widespread hypotheses merit examination. The first asserts that the salons declined to the advantage of new forms of male and political sociability of which clubs were the archetype. The proliferation of clubs and societies did in fact attract a number of salon habitués. Thus the reports of the Contrôle des étrangers indicated that, beginning in early winter 1789, the diplomats spent many evenings "at the ambassadors' club," which was very probably the Club des Étrangers. Later witnesses insisted on the role of the clubs in the political effervescence of the years from 1787 to 1789.[148] Certain clubs were even regarded by the police as "baleful for good order" because of the "seditious statements" that could be heard there, which led to their prohibition in 1786 by the baron de Breteuil.[149] Still, their political dimension before the Revolution should not be overestimated. Most of those clubs were primarily places of sociability and amusement. A chess club called the "Sallon [sic] des Échecs," for example, located at the Palais-Royal, was a very exclusive aristocratic group to which new members were admitted only with the unanimous agreement of the existing members.[150] When they were not simply gambling dens reserved for a worldly clientele, the clubs were places for reading the newspapers and, possibly, having a conversation. Bombelles commented, after his first visit to the Salon des Échecs: "Today for the first time I made my entry into the *Salon* in which I had been received on April 28. This establishment is decent and comfortable. For the price of 5 louis per year, one finds several well-heated rooms, all the journals, writing materials equal to those at home, and refreshments such as tea, lemonade, or syrup drinks."[151]

Far from having replaced or supplanted the salons, the clubs added a different form of sociability, one that owed much to the English model but that fit in well with the continued existence of the salons. The latter had not disappeared, and on the eve of the Revolution Madame de La Ferté-Imbault, Madame de La Vallière, the Neckers, abbé Morellet, the comtesse de Boufflers, Madame de Beauharnais, Madame de Flahaut, Madame de Brionne, Madame de Sabran, Madame de Beauvau, Madame de La Reynière, and many others continued to receive guests on a weekly basis. During the meeting of the Estates General, the minister plenipotentiary of the United States, Gouverneur Morris, frequented a number of the salons of the capital, and he remarked that people talked politics there. At the home of the comtesse de Flahaut, a populous society was "in the midst of Politics" but also busy gaming.[152] At the home of Madame de Chastellux, where he took tea, he noted that "two ladies come in and talk politics."[153]

People and information circulated rapidly between the clubs and the salons. On July 9, 1789, while he was discussing Louis XVI's response to the Third Estate at the Club de Valois, Morris received a note from Madame de Flahaut asking him to come sup with her to "tell her the News."[154]

The second hypothesis focuses on political activity in the salons on the eve of the Revolution and insists on their sudden politicization. But, given that worldly conversation had long included current diplomatic and political events, it is hardly surprising that the salons were touched by political fever. Beginning with the Assembly of Notables and even more clearly with the meeting of the Estates General, political questions became the most important topic of salon conversation. This was not a radical transformation of the salons, but rather a sensitivity of high society to the political climate of pre-Revolutionary France.

After 1787 the tense international situation and the Assembly of Notables were increasingly the main topic of conversation within Parisian high society. When Madame de Sabran went to visit the comtesse Diane de Polignac at Montreuil, she spent the evening "chatting, laughing, and politicking."[155] Madame de Créqui found this enthusiasm for political discussions amusing: "There is no neighborhood gossip who does not propose plans, give lessons, and have a remedy for everything."[156] This is hardly astonishing, given that several members of every salon sat on the Assembly of Notables and, at a later date, were candidates for election to the Estates General. Moreover, the monarchy's financial and political difficulties, the flood of pamphlets and polemics, and an acute awareness of being in the midst of a political crisis led to neglect of other topics of conversation. "I have no literary news," stated Madame Necker, who added, "That conversation is no longer fashionable; the crisis is too serious: one does not propose a game of chess on the edge of a precipice; our attention is entirely brought to other objects."[157]

As these political discussions became more numerous, more exclusive, and more virulent, the salons tended to polarize around the principal ministers or those who aspired to become ministers.[158] Thus Madame de Montesson supported Loménie de Brienne, while Calonne found support in the salons of Versailles, in particular that of Madame de Polignac, and Sénac de Meilhan became the favorite of the hôtel de Noailles. The Beauvaus' salon backed both Necker and Loménie de Brienne. The baron de Breteuil, finally, "was the second in many houses, the first nowhere."[159] The model remained the Neckers' salon, which was more active than ever, especially after Necker's return to power. During the Estates General, all the partisans of the minister gathered there, their enthusiasm fanned by Madame de Staël.

The Estates General corresponded to a decisive stage in this polarization of high society around such questions as the doubling of the Third Estate, the position of the nobility, and the reactions of the king. Political positions became sharper, and they brought on a redistribution of worldly topography. Certain salons seemed liberal strongholds, as was that of the comtesse de Tessé, whose husband was a deputy to the Estates General and was enthusiastic about the reforms. La Fayette was received there and fêted, as were most of the deputies of the nobility who took a stand within the minority of the Second Estate.[160] Similarly, the house of the duchesse d'Enville became the rallying place for friends of her son, the duc de La Rochefoucauld.[161] Other salons, in contrast, had divided loyalties. During the Assembly of the Notables, the salon of the comtesse de Brionne had been the "rallying point of all the malcontents"—that is, one of the leading worldly centers of the aristocratic *fronde* of 1787–88. Bombelles found the salon to be in a state of total confusion.[162]

Despite this growing politicization of the salons, the salons continued to grant an important place to the various forms of worldly entertainment. As perfect representatives of the liberal nobility and men used to worldly success, the comte de Narbonne and the vicomte de Ségur devoted time to both politics and theatrical entertainments. "In the midst of everyone's occupation with the Assembly of Notables," Madame de Sabran wrote, "the vicomte de Ségur finds a way to get people talking about him. He has just given a short play in his usual fashion, which he had performed at the house of Mademoiselle Contat, at Auteuil, which is called *Le Parti le plus gai*. It seems to me that it is always what he chooses to do, and especially in this moment, for he himself acted before more than a hundred people of good company."[163] Certain salons kept their more literary tone, however. This was the case of the salon of Fanny de Beauharnais in particular, where Cubières arranged for Mercier to be invited, who then introduced Rétif de La Bretonne in 1787. Morris dined there in March 1789: the company talked about the works of one guest or another and of the theatrical successes of the moment.[164]

Political affairs continued to be discussed alongside traditional forms of society entertainment. Political news gave rise to witticisms that were repeated in all the societies: after the royal session of the Estates General, for example, people repeated from salon to salon that "the king has just presented his *carnet* too; all that is left to do is to verify his powers."[165] Political and worldly concerns often intermingled, as shown by the case of the comte de Narbonne and Madame de Staël. Narbonne was the archetype of the fashionable man during the 1780s. At the time of the Assembly of the Notables and again during the Estates General, he had ambitions for playing a political role, and at the beginning of the Revolution he appeared as one of the representatives of the liberal aristocracy. At the same time, he was still exchanging jokes and songs with Madame de La Ferté-Imbault.[166]

As for Madame de Staël, she had become an important figure in Necker's political and worldly apparatus. Her marriage in January 1786 had enabled her to receive, even while she continued to animate the salon of her mother, Madame Necker, just as her father regained a favorable position.[167] In April 1787, when Necker had been exiled for four months, the nerve center of his partisans' political and worldly activities shifted to the home of Monsieur and Madame de Staël, where "all the partisans of M. Necker, who are in great number among those of high degree, gather," along with "all who are most remarkable at the Court and in the City by birth, talent, and reputation."[168] Germaine de Staël did not limit herself to the simple role of hostess that her mother had faithfully filled with great constancy. She asserted herself as a woman of letters as much as a woman of the world, for which she became the target of satires within proper society. This was perceived as a political threat to Necker. His partisans mobilized, and it was once again Madame de La Ferté-Imbault who was charged with intervening to "reform" Madame de Staël, whose ridiculous moments were exaggerated and exploited by her father's political enemies.[169] The elderly marquise de La Ferté-Imbault, who viewed the young woman quite favorably, set up an entire series of schemes, at times fairly subtle ones, to persuade her not to show herself "on the stage of the *grand monde* as a ridiculous *précieuse* or a *femme savante*."[170] More simply, drawing on her long experience with the world and with the court, she also gave the younger woman some advice about good worldly politics, recommending, for example, that when she went to the home of the maréchal de Biron and that she should behave amiably toward the comtesse de Gontaut, who favored her and whose friendship she should cultivate.[171]

All that was missing in this mixture of sociability and politics was amorous intrigue. In a long dispatch dated April 23, 1789, Count Salmour, minister plenipotentiary of Saxony, tells how Madame de Staël succeeded in stealing the comte de Narbonne, "famous for his trickery and his conquests," from Mademoiselle Contat, an actress. He relates that in order to seduce him, Madame de Staël "did all that she could to draw him into her society, found in him qualities that were attributed to him, and managed to have him take a liking to her manners."[172] Whatever the reasons for this liaison, the couple, with the knowledge and to the detriment of the baron de Staël, later played an important role in the worldly and political life of the early years of the Revolution. It is interesting that Salmour, in a dispatch sent in April 1789, took the trouble to inform his minister at length about these happenings. He seems to have considered that this bit of news, which he reported with a light tone and in worldly language, had political interest, and that it was within his duties to report on it. Was this worldly gossip or a political event? The register on which the news item was placed and the intermingling of interests clouded distinctions, even as, in that month of April, deputies to the Estates General were flowing into the capital.

The Revolution in the Salon

In many ways, the Revolution opened a new period in salon history. Michelet portrayed the first years of the Revolution as the apogee of society life.[173] Since his day, however, studies of sociability have quite properly focused on the major phenomenon of the revolutionary years, and the emergence of new forms of sociability in the political societies that developed rapidly beginning in the autumn of 1789.[174] The salons did not disappear along with the ancien régime, however.

The reports of the Contrôle des étrangers, which continued until 1791, became more and more laconic and incomplete as the police seem first to have been overwhelmed by the events of the summer of 1789, then preoccupied by other tasks.[175] Despite these limits, the reports show that high society survived the fall of the Bastille and that some salons continued to open their doors, including those of Madame de La Reynière, the princesse de Beauvau, the comtesse de Sabran, and the duchesse de La Vallière. Journals and correspondence confirm that during the early years of the Revolution the practices of sociability founded on hospitality were maintained. The young Victorine de Chastenay made her entry into le monde in 1790–91. She was bored in the company of "respectable prudes" whose habits seemed untouched by the political turmoil.[176]

After the summer of 1789, a number of salons continued to receive and to animate a worldly life with an undeniable political role, if only because they permitted encounters and discussions among people who played an active role in the Revolution. These salons included those of Madame de Flahaut, Madame de Condorcet, Madame de Staël, Madame Roland, and Madame de Chastellux, most of whom had begun to receive visitors before the Revolution. The comtesse de Flahaut, for example, received guests in her Louvre apartment beginning in 1787.[177] During the Estates General and in the early years of the Revolution, her salon was one of the rallying points for the liberal aristocracy. Talleyrand, who fathered one of the countess's children, was one of the important men who frequented her salon.

One might also meet there the counts of Narbonne, Montmorin, Ségur, and Guibert, but also Condorcet, Madame de Staël, and the Lavoisiers.[178]

The diary that Gouverneur Morris kept from his arrival in Paris in January 1789 until the summer of 1792 bears witness to the vitality of that sociability. Sent as a representative of the Congress of the United States, then as minister, Morris was charged with several diplomatic missions that led him to take a close interest in the ups and down of politics during the Revolution. An accomplished man of the world, he went from one salon to another, where he discovered Parisian high society within the revolutionary context. His *Diary* gives a clear-sighted view of the intermingling of worldly amusements and political intrigues at the heart of a society that strove to live the Revolution according to the political models of the ancien régime. It notes alternating analyses of the political situation, accounts of conversations with La Fayette or Talleyrand, and relations of gallant intrigues that Morris strove to decode. But if he discovered a host of implications behind every anodyne word, he found the political conversations of the salons lacking in subtlety, and he showed little admiration for such discussions, in which he found much enthusiasm, but little political good sense. His diary highlights the gap between this man of experience, already familiar with revolutionary political struggles, and the worldly folk who were discovering new forms of the political game. He demonstrates some condescension, especially when he expresses his surprise at their lack of seriousness in their approach to political questions.

Although politics occupied an important place in Morris's *Diary*, political questions sit alongside remarks on attempted seductions and on the worldly regards and strategies deployed by those whom he met. Morris complacently reported the gallant phrases with which he gratified one mistress of the house or another and the witticisms that he delivered.[179] When he went to see Necker, who was minister at the time, to negotiate sizable orders for wheat, he began by dining at his home. He sat next to Madame de Staël, and he engaged her in a long conversation about her affair with Narbonne and about her other suitors, a conversation that they carried on in English so that her husband would not understand it. Later, after having signed a treaty in Necker's *cabinet*, he moved on to the home of Madame de Chastellux, to "make Tea for the Dutchess [d'Orléans] and introduce the eating of a Rye Bread Toast which is found to be excellent."[180] As Morris moved in worldly circles, politics and worldliness were permanently intermingled: a game of trictrac interrupts a political conversation; the quality of a meal is as important as the political opinions of the master of the house; ministerial appointments are negotiated in the corner of a room while the guests are writing verse. The very style of conversations, when politics were the topic, conformed to the model of salon conversations in which the most important things are left unsaid. Morris reported that at Madame de Staël's gatherings the reigning mode was the triumph of "the sententious Style. To arrive at Perfection in it, one must be very attentive and either wait till one's Opinion be asked or else communicate it in a whisper. It must be clear, pointed, and perspicuous and then it will be remembered, repeated, and respected."[181]

In the midst of political turmoil, Paris high society maintained its habits, including seasonal departures for the countryside. During the autumn of 1789, Morris reported that, as pleasure was everyone's greatest preoccupation, all had gone to their country houses and came to the city for business only every three or four days. Literary entertainments continued to enliven worldly life, however, and Morris attended several readings. At the home of Madame de Chastellux he heard Delille recite verse and the vicomte de Ségur read a play. Madame de Staël read her tragedy *Montmorency* at her own gatherings.[182]

Thus worldly practices continued, but the break caused by the Revolution accentuated the polarization of the worldly space that had begun as early as 1788. Social ties did not always resist the violence of political engagements, and each person had to choose his camp, which led to ruptures. The example of Morellet clearly displays the partisan breakdown of sociability. At the eve of the Revolution, he was at the center of a dense network of worldly and political relations. He retained certain of these during the first months of the Revolution, continuing to go to the Neckers, where on several occasions he encountered Montmorin, the minister of foreign affairs. On the other hand, his opinions obliged him to break with other houses that had welcomed him. Favoring the doubling of the Third Estate, he published a memoir during the second Assembly of Notables. The comtesse de Boufflers, whose positions were aristocratic, reacted violently and shut her door to him.[183] Morellet soon found himself less favorable to the Revolution, and he quarreled with Cabanis and abbé La Roche, who lived in the house of Madame Helvétius. Their opinions, which diverged more and more, gave rise to arguments that were all the more intense because Madame Helvétius, rather than remaining neutral, took the side of the more democratic opinions. In 1790, Morellet, at the demand of the deputies from Tulle, wrote a defense of proprietors against the critics of the Jacobins, which led to a definitive break with his friends. This rupture took place in Madame Helvétius's salon and was carried out by a simple refusal to follow the rites of politeness: "Two days after the publication, I go to Auteuil, as was my custom. It was evening. Those gentlemen entered the salon: they did not return my salute, did not give any answer when I addressed them, and, leaving soon, left me alone with Madame Helvétius."[184] After this humiliating scene, Morellet never returned there.

The society of Madame Helvétius may represent the limit of political radicalism in this context. Her political engagement, expressed in the mode of enthusiasm, lent itself poorly to a respect of the practices of sociability, as shown by the treatment inflicted on Morellet. She cut herself off from the worldly sociability of the capital and lived at Auteuil. At Auteuil she welcomed the radical partisans of the Revolution according to a model that much resembled political society. When Gouverneur Morris paid a visit to her in August 1791—perhaps because of her friendship with Franklin—he was struck by the difference in tone from the Paris salons that he attended and by the political enthusiasm that reigned there. "Call on Mr. Franklin and we go out to Auteuil where we dine with Madame Helvétius. A raving mad democracy forms this society," he noted laconically.[185] Other societies, to the contrary, were hostile to the Revolution. Madame de Marchais, who became Madame d'Angiviller, had made her salon a center for the support of the king and for hostility to the Assembly. Still, she maintained social ties with some moderate partisans of the Revolution such as Madame de Staël, whom she received at her home. Madame de La Ferté-Imbault, on the other hand, found it inconceivable that some of the habitués of her salon were favorable to the Revolution, as was Le Pelletier de Saint-Fargeau. She reproached him for his democratic ideas before some fifteen people in her home, calling him mad and a renegade.[186] The great figures of Parisian high society who were hostile to the revolutionary developments also included the Beauvaus, with whom Morellet continued to sup quite regularly, both in Paris and at their property of Le Val. Still, as the Revolution advanced, such houses became increasingly suspect and were no longer popular.[187]

The summer of 1792 marked a decisive turning point for the high society of Paris. The fall of the monarchy, the disappearance of what remained of the court, the proclamation of the Republic and the entry into a new cycle of urban violence overturned the foundations of worldly life. Emigration accelerated, and those who remained in France, as did the Beauvaus, sought to avoid attention. Political conflict became too intense to be treated according to the forms of salon conversation. Fanny de Beauharnais, who had left Paris for Italy in October 1789 and later settled in Lyon, tried to reopen her salon in Paris in 1792, but the political quarrels were too much for her. She did not really begin to receive guests again until 1795.[188] Eventually a new era of political surveillance, which culminated in the Terror, made it difficult to maintain the practices of sociability. Diplomats left Paris. Morris even stopped keeping his diary for fear of compromising the people he mentioned in it. Madame Broutin, a friend of several men of letters, had continued to receive in her house at Cernay during the early years of the Revolution. Her guests were on the whole favorable to the Revolution, as were Lacretelle, Destutt de Tracy, and André Chénier, or else more moderate, as was Morellet. In 1792, Madame Broutin thought that Cernay was not sufficiently safe and took refuge in Normandy, putting an end to the hospitality that she had offered for many years.[189] By the autumn of 1792, the Parisians salons had been greatly reduced, leaving only a few Girondin societies such as those of Madame Roland or Madame de Condorcet. For the rest, the political sociability of the clubs had carried the day, in Paris as in the provinces.

The disappearance of worldly sociability in Paris from 1792 to 1795 thus has fairly clearly identifiable causes, but has sparked debate nonetheless over the place of women in the Revolution. Did the disappearance of the salons correspond to the exclusion of women from the political sphere, as asserted, for example, by Joan Landes and others after her?[190] Actually, it was the very space of society as a form of sociability founded on a regular dispensation of hospitality that was discredited by Jacobin political thought. That thought insisted on the distinction between a public and civic space, which was the domain of men, and a domestic space, where women reigned. That domestic space was not removed from the political. Because it was the place for the education of the future citizen, it must be subjected to the regard of the city. The demands of political virtue that reigned in the public sphere must also govern domestic virtue, according to an ideal of the transparency of private behaviors.

The trial of Madame Roland, which put an end to the last salon of the Revolution, bears witness to the incompatibility between a form of sociability inherited from the ancien régime and the new sociopolitical order. In 1789, at the beginning of the Revolution, Manon Phlipon already had a certain experience of intellectual life. The daughter of a master engraver, she had been brought up hearing of the authors of the century and had adhered to enlightened ideas at an early age, as shown by her correspondence. In 1780, she married Jean-Marie Roland, an inspector of manufactories, who took her to Amiens, then to Lyon, but who also permitted her to frequent certain Parisian circles, notably Mesmerist milieux. In Lyon, she enthusiastically welcomed the beginnings of the Revolution and participated in her husband's engagements, while taking care not to promote herself, refusing, for example, to sign the articles that she wrote for Brissot. "I do not think," she wrote, "that our mores permit women to show themselves yet."[191] The couple settled in Paris in February 1791 and began to receive guests on rue Guénégaud. Her salon was frequented by the deputies the farthest to the left of the Constituent Assembly, especially by Brissot and his friends. During the two ministries of her husband (March to June 1792, and August 1792 to January 1793), she played a political role, received at dinners on Mondays and Fridays,[192] and appeared to many to be one of the instigators of Girondin policies. This meant that her salon followed in the tradition of the salons of the ancien régime, mixing sociability, political action, intellectual conversation, and even amorous intrigue. Arrested along with her husband, Madame Roland was not included in the act of accusation of October 24, 1793, against the Girondins, but she was interrogated beginning on October 31 and tried on November 8. Condemned to death, she was executed the same day. Her detention and her death have become famous thanks to her prison memoirs that were published under the title *Appel à l'impartiale postérité*, and thanks to her bravery as she stood before the guillotine. The phrase she is alleged to have uttered on the scaffold, "Liberty, how many crimes are committed in your name!" is part of the revolutionary legend. There has been less interest in the actual conditions of the trial.

The principal accusation against which Madame Roland had to defend herself concerned the people she had received in her house. In the new political culture there was no longer any room for the worldly sociability that had been women's domain of action. The revolutionary dynamic operated in two ways: first, the new public and political space, henceforth reserved to men and dominated by the demand for public action and civic virtue, contrasted with a domestic and familial space to which women were relegated; second, the Jacobin view imagined a transparent domestic sphere subject to public requirements. Any form of intermediate action could be understood only as a plot, a conspiracy, a secret association, or the deleterious influence of women over politics. Madame Roland cleverly adapted her self-justification to the denunciations of her judges. She tried desperately to counter the accusation against her "ordinary societies," her "circle," and the "lectures" that she had held at her house. She contrasted her own "ties of amity" and her "special affections" to the "very public conversations" carried on by her husband's friends and in which she claimed to have had no part.[193] This defense was nonetheless in vain, as her manner and her language betrayed the worldly ethos that was no longer acceptable and the refinement of her responses became evidence against her. Even after she had been condemned the judges found it difficult to force her into silence, humiliate her, and reproach her for speaking "spiritedly." Carla Hesse rightly insists on the revolutionaries' mistrust of the female speech typical of the ancien régime and now become illegitimate.[194] And the old commonplace of the *femme savante* still permitted the disqualification of any woman who departed from her natural female role: after the execution of Madame Roland, *Le Moniteur* asserted that "the desire to be *savante* led her to forgetting the virtues of her sex, and that forgetfulness, always dangerous, ended up having her perish on the scaffold."[195] But the threat that Madame Roland represented in the eyes of her judges corresponded, above all, to a form of sociability that no longer had a place of its own between civic duties and the domestic retreat. In the new political culture, the space that it had occupied held nothing but the fantasy of a control of opinions, a surveillance of the public spirit, and its flip side, an ongoing fear of plots. The old satirical tradition of the *bureau d'esprit* shifted to become political accusation by confusion with the *bureau d'esprit public* created by the Girondins and which the revolutionary tribunal accused Madame Roland of having upheld.[196]

The politics of the ancien régime and worldliness appear to have been closely connected. The salons were not public spaces. They did not form an enlightened, liberal, or critical opinion separate from the traditional mechanisms of politics in the ancien régime. The political specificity of worldliness was based on the circulation of news, which furnished fodder for conversation and constituted a powerful force for sociability. The dynamics inherent in high society and the inscription of the salons within the urban topography of Paris made the salons strategic places at the juncture of information networks and political solidarities. It was precisely their hybrid nature, between the court society and urban sociabilities, that allowed them to occupy that place within the political system of the ancien régime, but that sort of worldly politics was not well adapted, in the years 1792–94, to the new political and ideological clashes. Still, the disappearance of the salons during those years should not conceal either the persistence of worldly practices during the early years of the Revolution nor the resurgence, after Thermidor, of a patent worldliness that was one of the prime features of sociability under the Directory.[197]

Conclusion

M adame Geoffrin once wrote on the back of a playing card, "The great lords are often familiar with one another out of pleasure, but out of dignity they do not want others to be familiar with them."[1] This solitary king of spades is a curious object, preserved in the archives along with bundles of correspondence and household bills. It stands as a symbol for the complexity of worldly sociability: Madame Geoffrin, whose society is often taken as an archetype of the Enlightenment salon, makes use of a playing card to note her remarks on the snobbery of the nobility and the ambiguities of politeness. This card bears witness to the intermingling of the supposed "literary salons" with groups that met for gaming or stressed social distinction, realms that have often been studied separately. This book has aimed to approach the salons as places that cannot be assigned to any single social group or cultural function. It has then focused on worldliness, conceived a set of social practices and cultural representations, which played a central role in the dynamics of high society during the Enlightenment.

It should be clear by now that the distinction between literary salons and aristocratic salons is artificial. Certain salons welcomed more writers; others devoted more time to theatricals, music, or games; but the societies of Madame Geoffrin and the duchesse de La Vallière, of Madame Necker and the duchesse de Luxembourg, were all part of the same sociability, based on the regular hospitality offered by the hosts or hostesses. This sociability defined a social sphere that was called *le monde* or *la société*. It had a center in the leading salons of Paris and quite fluid borders at the court, among the Paris bourgeoisie, or among the provincial elites. This worldly sphere was organized by the circulation of news, which might contain a mixture of political information, word about literary happenings, and social gossip. Such news nourished social connivance, fashioned individual and collective reputations, distinguished and stigmatized. Mastery of the distribution of news was thus important socially and politically: it established a hierarchy within the worldly sphere by constructing positions of authority, and it offered possibilities for action, both in the literary field and in the political sphere. Worldly sociability appeared as a place for transactions among social spaces whose borders were not as tightly closed as has often been thought. By that token, it was also a mechanism of power, thanks to the formation and circulation of reputations.

Certain prominent figures in this world of the salons have been discussed throughout this book. The duchesse de Luxembourg, who was the incarnation of the importance of the court nobility in Paris sociability, is one of these. Wealthy, bearing an illustrious name, and very well placed at court, she achieved a privileged position within Parisian high society. She received and protected such writers as Rousseau, Hume, and La Harpe, but she took care not to be dragged into literary quarrels. At the same time, her intransigence concerning worldly codes made her a recognized authority whose verdicts were feared. Moreover, coming to her salon was an obligatory rite of passage; reputations were made or unmade there, which gave it an eminently political dimension. That central position is manifest in the duchess's worldly relations, since she frequented both the salons of the court nobility and those of Madame Necker and Madame Geoffrin.

Socially, Madame Geoffrin enjoyed a much lower status than the duchesse de Luxembourg. One can see in her success the effects of an increased flexibility in worldly hierarchies in the melting-pot of Enlightenment Paris. Undeniably, her career proves that being a commoner was not an insurmountable handicap to occupying a choice place in high society. But Madame Geoffrin's wealth and the hospitality that she offered friends and artists for forty years do not tell the whole story. The success of her salon owed just as much to her constant effort to conform to the customs of *le monde*. The reputation of the writers and artists whom she protected made her salon attractive because she was skilled at proving the traditional aristocratic forms of sociability, at managing her reputation as a hostess who cared little for *le bel esprit*, and at making clear all the signs of a hyper-vigilance to polite manners. In return, her insertion into the aristocratic networks gave her the means for arranging effective protection for the writers whom she received. Throughout her career, however, her reputation remained fragile and was subject to satire. Comparison with other careers, such as those of the La Reynières or Madame Du Boccage, confirms, on the contrary, that neither wealth nor receiving writers guaranteed membership of *la bonne société*.

The dynamics of worldly society were both gendered and social. Recent historiography has amply insisted on the first of these, at times to the point of identifying the salon with feminism. Even though certain salons were led by men, it is undeniable, they were places of mixed-sex sociability, whose unique qualities were largely due to the role of women and their conversation, whether those women were praised for that or denounced for their softening effect. Worldly sociability, centered on female conversation and its civilizing role, has been thought to be an element of the sociopolitical system of a French monarchy founded on honor, gallantry, and civility. That sociability permitted women of Parisian high society to play a cultural role that was at times significant, but the mechanisms of worldly reputation assured a conservative control of the norms of female *honnêteté* and were clearly incompatible with a claim to intellectual or literary ambitions. It was the Revolution, even though it denounced the effects of worldliness and in fact destroyed the social foundations of the *beau monde*, that offered women broader opportunities in the field of editorial endeavors.[2] Thus the role of women in the salons should not be approached exclusively in terms of intellectual history, but also on the basis of the social mechanisms of worldliness. "The person who said that Paris was ruled by women," Dutens notes, "had judged it fairly well, provided that this opinion be restricted to the Court and among the Nobility; for it is in that class above all that their influence on minds is most marked."[3]

The salons allowed the court nobility to reconfigure its social and symbolic domination, thanks to its mastery of social codes and customs. All too often, debates about social hierarchies during the final years of the ancien régime oppose heterogeneous criteria of classification, such as birth, money, and talent. The novelty of the eighteenth century in fact resides in the rivalry among those criteria of social standing and in the risks of confusion that they imply. In that context, worldliness played an important role of social control, in which the court nobility reinterpreted honor as reputation and integrated into the bosom of high society those who best acquired its norms of behavior and recognized its preeminence. The sources of social distinction (birth, wealth, proximity to the court, talent) passed through the prism of worldly practices to produce a hierarchy in which the *homme du monde* dethroned the courtier. That evolution would continue unabated in the first half of the nineteenth century, after the abolition of privileges under the Revolution, when an elegant lifestyle was all that was left to slake the social elites' thirst for distinction. "The moment that two books of parchment no longer stand for everything," Balzac wrote, "differences have vanished in our society; all that remains are nuances, good breeding, elegant manners, the *je ne sais quoi*, the fruits of a complete education—these form the only barrier separating the man of leisure from the busy man."[4]

For that reason the history of worldliness is also a history of amusement. Mercier writes, "Among the people of the salons, the first pursuit, that of every day, is to amuse themselves."[5] Here the formula should be taken literally. At a time when the beginnings of a consumer society entailed a rising commercialization of culture, society amusements, on the contrary, allowed for distinguishing a leisured elite defined by a relationship to time that differed from that of professionalization, and by an education in which theater, music, and gaming played an important part. On the other hand, those amusements cannot be reduced to a social pageant. The very operation of worldly sociability moves beyond artificial oppositions between amusement and culture or between the pleasures of an idle elite and the artistic or intellectual manifestations of the Enlightenment. Music and society theater were the amusements of great lords, and at times they led to remarkable performances, mobilizing the energies and passion of the participants. Literature furnishes a similar example. Readings were worldly events that could make the reputation of a salon and the career of an author and in which the *esprit de société* elicited more decorous applause than it prompted a critical spirit. Still, readings bear witness to the importance of belles-lettres in the taste of the elites. Literature and learned conversations appeared in the salons as entertainment, but they nonetheless gave Parisian worldliness its particular flavor.

Worldly sociability sheds new light on the social history of Enlightenment writers. One of the most salient results is the participation of writers in the sociability networks of Parisian high society. Writers and philosophes contributed to making the reputation of the salons; they obtained from them material advantages and protections. The model for their participation in aristocratic amusements was the figure of the *homme du monde*, which provided a social horizon that men of letters could aspire to. It did not, however, efface social distinctions and did not make the salons egalitarian and peaceful places, but it did establish shared values among the urban aristocracy and some men of letters. Even though the relations of the writers with the worldly elites were indeed asymmetrical, they were able to represent such a relationship through the paradigm of sociability. The adherence of many men of letters to the practices and representations of high society does not imply any abdication of criticism, as shown by the case of the baron d'Holbach. The writers' intellectual autonomy was not necessarily asserted by a formal break with the elites, but could also take place, within certain limits, through a commitment to some of their cultural values.

The ideal of the man of letters as an *homme du monde* was extremely strong during the second half of the eighteenth century, but it was the target of lively polemics. The book has stressed the importance of the rupture associated with Rousseau, a rupture that arose from a harsh criticism of worldly alienation, but that was also due to the elaboration of a new public figure, that of the writer who had broken with the worldly forms of social domination. Rousseau left the regime of worldliness, defined by enclosure and connivance, and inaugurated the regime of celebrity. He suffered the pain of the contradictions inherent in that celebrity and the impossibility of reconciling his feelings about himself and the public personage that his readership had constructed. For writers of the 1770s and the 1780s, however, the figure of Jean-Jacques, the persecuted writer, and the great Rousseauist themes went hand in hand with a new patriotic discourse that elevated the nation against despotism, the public against the privileged, and the virtuous transparency of sentiments against the falseness of politeness and wit. That convergence is critically important to understanding the cultural and political dynamics of the end of the ancien régime. It sheds light on the emergence of a new topic, that of the writer-patriot, which was taken over by the new generation of writers to replace the worldly figure of the man of letters.

Since the salons were institutions of the worldly sphere, they were not considered to be public spaces that had public effects, and the sociability they fostered did not correspond to Habermas's model of the public sphere. Although many recent historians, following Habermas himself, perceive a continuity between salon sociability and the affirmation of a rational public as an enlightened instance of judgment, the study of salons rejects the validity of such a schema. The principal authors of the Enlightenment drew a vigorous distinction between the public effects of printing and the social effects of worldliness, between public and society. *Société* was an important word in eighteenth-century political thought. It did not only denote the general form of collective life. It had other meanings which designate voluntary associations and social collectives founded on worldly sociability and polite manners. *La société* was a synonym for *le monde*.

Consequently, the valorization of the "public" as the privileged audience for works, but also as a political figure that justifies the act of writing, was not a linear process. For men of letters between 1750 and 1770, the relationship with the public remained extremely ambiguous, whereas monarchical institutions and the spaces of sociability seemed natural. This can be seen in the legacy of social and cultural divisions inaugurated in the preceding century under the auspices of the absolute monarchy, when the exercise of philosophical criticism was connected to a disqualification of popular beliefs and knowledge. In the eighteenth century, the cultural connivance among the social elites was challenged by positive representations of the "public" as a legitimate judge of works, as a tribunal of mores, and as a political body.

In the domain of letters, the semantic field of "publication" shifted. Whereas the term had previously referred to the various forms of the divulgation of news, the circulation of texts, or the making of reputations, its meaning in the eighteenth century was gradually reduced to the field of print, bringing together the political sense of the publication of laws and that of the publication of books within a broader horizon of a destination that potentially extended to include the whole society. For writers who were familiar with the practices of high society, the worldly forms of the circulation of texts, and the social consecration of reputations, a tension developed that was not resolved until the Revolution. The very nature of literary works was at stake, as shown by society poetry, which was torn between its worldly value and its gradual public devaluation. This evolution continued into the nineteenth century with the triumph of a literature emancipated from the forms of conversation, most visibly in the novel. The literary work was no longer the spoken word communicated within a practice of sociability rather, it was a public book and a text to be read.[6] That rupture with worldly forms of literature nourished an intense discourse of loss about the salons of the eighteenth century.

The Parisian salons of the latter half of the eighteenth century corresponded to a peak in the history of high society and they gave rise to serious reflection on sociability. Still, worldliness in France stretches back at least to the late sixteenth century and continued on through the Belle Époque, to say nothing of the heritage of medieval and Renaissance courtesy or the mores of the contemporary jet set. Its peak, from the mid-seventeenth century to the mid-nineteenth century, coincides with a long period of a reconfiguration of aristocratic grandeur, in which the military heroism of a hereditary nobility slowly gave way to the social prestige of an aristocracy of manners. Contrary to appearances, the Revolution did not bring a definitive rupture. The salons reappeared with Thermidor and even more strongly with the Restoration. By then they were thought of as a legacy from a moribund tradition. The worldly sphere, which had become established under the ancien régime through a subtle interplay of proximity to and distance from the royal court and distrust of the public, was increasingly subjected to criticism and exposure. The definitive disappearance of a court society, along with the commercialization of leisure and the advance of a mass culture, finally led to the exhaustion of the salon model at the turn of the nineteenth into the twentieth centuries.

On a European scale, the mobility of the elites encouraged the circulation of worldly practices. In the eighteenth century, a pan-European worldly sociability imitated French practices. Still, elsewhere, men of letters participated in this broader movement much less than in France, and mixing of the sexes was at times less evident. In England, worldliness flourished in particular in male circles of sociability such as coffee houses and clubs, while female sociability was animated by female authors working to create a place for women in the intellectual sphere.[7] In Germany in the late eighteenth century, the emergence within the Jewish society of Berlin of such salons as those of Henriette Hertz and Rahel Levin Varnaghen was a localized and ephemeral phenomenon (1780–1810) connected with a particular historical situation.[8] In Italy, the Grand Tour permitted the introduction of French practices that were grafted onto local forms of sociability. In Florence, *conversazioni* developed during the 1730s. In Turin in the late eighteenth century, the house of the contessa Caterina Vignati di Saint-Gilles was a center of worldly life that was assiduously frequented by foreigners. Even in Rome, where the Curia maintained a male model of cultural and political sociability, some women began to receive during the latter half of the eighteenth century.[9] On the whole, the French model was not easily transplanted, as the opposition between the world of the court elites and intellectual circles often remained a strong structural factor.

Travel accounts highlight the place of worldly sociability in the constitution of national stereotypes. Whether that sociability was the object of praise or condemnation, the importance accorded to worldly practices and their aestheticization (in politeness, the art of conversation, wit) seems to have been an outstanding trait in representations of the French character, seen through the prism of Paris. It would be a mistake, however, to be content with an inventory of those representations, as the geography of wit often has a social origin. In the eighteenth century, German aristocrats continued to use Paris as a European model in which the prestige of Versailles was gradually replaced by that of the salons, while bourgeois travelers or intellectuals made criticism of French frivolity an essential element of their representation of Germany as a *Kulturnation*.[10]

The durable prestige of French sociability owed less to the inherent merits of Parisian conversation than it did to the intense work done to publicize it by men of letters. Carried on by historiography and by literary criticism, a similar effort continues to provide fodder for representations of a French specificity. Still, it would be reductive to see the connections between the social world and literature as nothing more than a process of legitimation. If worldliness exerted such a great influence on French writers, it is also because it was based, as Roland Barthes remarked, on a social imaginary of enclosure: "Before literature raised the problem of political realism, worldliness was a precious means for the writer to observe social reality yet remain a writer; worldliness is indeed an ambiguous form of reality: committed and uncommitted; referring to the disparity of the human condition but remaining in spite of everything a pure form; enclosure guarantees access to the psychological and the social without passing through the political; this is why, perhaps, we have had a great literature of worldliness in France, from Molière to Proust."[11]

Worldliness is indeed an essential part of Proust's work. *À la Recherche du temps perdu* offers general lessons on the evolution of social groups, on their languages, their practices, and their positions, illustrated by the crossed destinies of Madame Verdurin and the duchesse de Guermantes. The novel also displays the microcosm of worldliness and its laws. The amiability of the duchesse de Parme, the encrypted language of Norpois, Bloch's efforts to show a distant irony toward the customs to which he conforms, the virtuous denials of the duc de Guermantes, who claims to attach no importance to honors but is nonetheless obsessed with them, the humiliating reception of Charlus at the Verdurins—these are all signs that the narrator learns to interpret and that make the novels a formidable reservoir of sociological analysis. Proust invites readers to be suspicious of any overly rapid identification between practices and their representations. The prestige of literature enables the Goncourt brothers' *Journal* to give a misleading image of salon conversations: the *Mémoires* of Madame de Villeparisis give a picture of worldly ease, even though her salon is far from prestigious and she herself lacks a light touch; Oriane de Guermantes, finally, claims to scorn the world, an attitude that is the height of worldliness: "She again assumed her society-woman attitude, that is to say, contemptuous of fashionable doings."[12] The account of worldliness given in Proust's novel is particularly ambivalent, with the result that the reader is divided between an admiration of the author's virtuosity in deciphering worldly signs and the revelation of the insignificance of those signs, to the profit of art and literature. Even when literature loudly proclaims its autonomy, it finds it difficult to renounce worldliness.

The salons of eighteenth-century Paris are the most visible and most significant episode in the history of elective affinities between literature and worldliness. Beginning in the mid-seventeenth century, the development of worldliness corresponded to closer contact between writers and certain segments of the urban nobility. This shift of courtly practices into Parisian homes was followed by reciprocal forms of legitimation among the cultural, social, and political elites. An important segment of French literature is thus tied, from the start, to a worldly sphere that durably contributed to nourishing the social and cultural imaginary of France. The importance of literature in French social and political life and the persistence of an elitist model of the writer are the most notable legacies of this history.

Diplomats: Participation in Paris Salons (1774–89)

	1774	1775	1776	1777	1778	1779	1780	1781	1782	1783	1784	1785	1786	1787	1788	1789	Total
Adhémar (Cᵉˢᵉ d')	2																2
Aiguillon (Dˢˢᵉ)	2	4															6
Albaret (Cᵗᵉ d')			1			1	2	3	8	8	17	14	7	7			68
Bacelli (Mᵉˡˡᵉ)												5					5
Beauvau (Pᶜᵉˢˢᵉ)	4	1		2	1	3	4			12	3	31	28	28	31	25	173
Bentheim (Cˢˢᵉ)													1				1
Beringhem (Mˢᵉ de)		3	2														5
Biron (duc de)				4	5	38	43	48	50	31	43	14	1				277
Boufflers (Cˢˢᵉ de)	5	3	5	2		6	9	10	24	5	22	20	24	32	20	13	200
Boulainvilliers, Mˢ					1		1	3	9								14
Boutin (M)	1	1															2
Brancas (marquis de)		5	3	1	3	15	20	20	5	11							83
Breteuil (baron de)		2	2								1	2	1				8
Broglie (duc de)		2															2
Caraman (Cᵉˢᵉ de)	1	4		1				1	1	7	4	4					23
Castries (marquis)		2															2
Choiseul (Dˢˢᵉ de)	2	2				1	5										10
Civrac (Dˢˢᵉ de)	2	3	1														6
Coigny (Mˢᵉ de)										1		9	14	16	8	14	62

(Continued)

(CONTINUED)

	1774	1775	1776	1777	1778	1779	1780	1781	1782	1783	1784	1785	1786	1787	1788	1789	Total
Coislin (Csse de)								15	5								20
Cossé (Dsse de)	1	1	1														3
Du Deffand (Mise)	18	48	45	17	4	34	40										206
Du Dreneux (Mise)							3										3
Dupin (Mme)	1			4			1		2		4						12
Enville (Dsse d')	1	3	1				3	8	22		13	17	7				75
Epinay (Mme d')				13	1				6	1							21
Estrées (Dsse d')											18	20	3				41
Ferté-Imbault (Mise de La)	7	17	15		6	4	27	21	28	20	25	17	10	5	7		209
Forcalquier (Csse de)				3													3
Galitzine (Prince)											1	3	27	14	7	12	64
Geoffrin (Mme)	22	40	41	1													104
Gramont (Dsse de)					7	17	32	5									61
Havré (Dsse d')									1		3						5
Helvétius (Mme)										3	1						4
Holbach (Bon d')	2						2		5	6	6	9	13	30	15	3	91
Infantado (Dsse de l')									2					5	1	40	48
La Borde (M. de)						1			2						1		4
La Marck (Csse de)	3	6	11					4	1	4							29
La Reynière (Mme de)		6	31	1	16	12	65	62	39	14	2	1		17	61	31	358
La Rochefoucauld, duc															1	4	5
La Vallière (Dsse de)		1	6	4		12	25	43	66	64	87	89	80	81	37	15	610
La Vaupalière (Mise)				1		1		1	6	1	15	3	12	12	11	2	65
Lespinasse (Mlle de)	5	16															21
Luxembourg (Dsse)	2	8	26	1	4	7	9	3	22	5	15	7	10				119

Marchais (Bone de)		3	11								1					15
Magon de Balue (Mme)															2	2
Mirepoix (Dsse de)	1	3	3								1					8
Modène (Csse de)					9	5	1									15
Montalembert (Mis)		2														2
Montbarrey (Pce de)							3									3
Mouchy (Dsse de)											1	2	4	10	2	19
Necker (M/Mme)	21	39	33	51	42	83	139	69	41	13	21	25	17	31	15	640
Neukirken (Bone de)			3													3
Nivernais (duc de)		1	1	6	7	2			3		1			1		22
Polignac (Dsse de)		1										2				3
Praslin (Dsse de)	14	13	70	80	45	29										251
Rasoumofsky (Csse)											10				21	31
Richelieu (duc de)	1	11		41		20			1	1	21	11		1		108
Rieben (Bone de)	14	28														42
Rochefort (Csse de)	2	2	1	24	12											41
Rohan-chabot (duc)	2	17	9													28
Rondé (Mme)	1	7	3													11
Sabran (Csse de)															4	4
Schuwalof (Csse)	4	19	37	6												66
Soubise (Pce de)	1	1	15	47	11	70										145
Stroganov (Cte)	14	4	3	1	5											27
Sulkowski (Pce)			8	10												18
Tourton (M)	6	20	17	11	9	36	41	19	16	1						187
Tremoille (Dsse)	1	1	2	7	1											12
Trudaine (M)	4	4	1													9

Source: Archives des Affaires étrangères, *Contrôle des étrangers*, vols. 2–82.

NOTES

INTRODUCTION

1. John Lough, "À propos d'un tableau de Lemonnier: *Une soirée chez Mme Geoffrin en 1755*," *Recherches sur Diderot et sur l'Encyclopédie*, 12 (April 1992): 4–18. The original painting is in the Musée de Malmaison; a signed copy is in the Musée de Rouen.

2. Pierre Larousse, *Grand Dictionnaire universel du XIXe siècle* (Paris: Larousse, 1866–75), vol. 14 (1875), s.v. "Salon."

3. During a television show in 2003, Robert Ménard, the founder of "Reporters sans frontières," reproached Arno Klarsfeld with frequenting "the salons." Klarsfeld, beside himself, repeated the word: "les salons, les salons, quels salons?" then threw a glass of water at Ménard. As one journalist noted, the word "salon" was what "set off" the incident (*Tout le monde en parle*, France 2, January 18, 2003; *Télérama*, no. 2768, January 20, 2003, 66).

4. Roger Picard, *Les Salons littéraires et la société française (1610–1789)* (New York: Brentano's, 1943); Marguerite Glotz and Madeleine Maire, *Salons du XVIIIe siècle* (Paris: Hachette, 1944).

5. Alan Charles Kors, *D'Holbach's Coterie: An Enlightenment in Paris* (Princeton: Princeton University Press, 1977); Daniel Roche, "Lumières et engagement politique: La coterie d'Holbach dévoilée," *Annales E.S.C.* 4 (1978): 720–28, reprinted in Roche, *Les Républicains des lettres: Gens de culture et Lumières au XVIIIe siècle* (Paris: Fayard, 1988), 243–54.

6. Marc Fumaroli, "La conversation," in *Les Lieux de Mémoire*, ed. Pierre Nora, 3 vols. (Paris: Gallimard, 1984–92), vol. 3, *Les France*, part 2, 679–743.

7. Jacqueline Hellegouarc'h, *L'Esprit de société: Cercles et "salons" parisiens au XVIIIe siècle* (Paris: Garnier, 2000); Benedetta Craveri, *The Age of Conversation* (New York: New York Published Books, 2005); Marc Fumaroli, *When the World Spoke French* (New York: New York Published Books, 2011).

8. Alain Viala, *Naissance de l'écrivain: Sociologie de la littérature à l'âge classique* (Paris: Éditions de Minuit, 1985); Pierre Bourdieu, *The Rules of Art: Genesis and Structure of the Literary Field*, trans. Susan Emanuel (Stanford: Stanford University Press, 1996).

9. Robert Darnton, "The High Enlightenment and the Low-Life of Literature in Pre-Revolutionary France," *Past and Present* 51 (1971), 81–115, reprinted in Darnton, *The Literary Underground of the Old Regime* (Cambridge, MA: Harvard University Press, 1982); translated into French by Eric De Grolier as "Dans la France Prérévolutionnaire: Des philosophes des Lumières aux 'Rousseau des ruisseaux,'" reprinted in Darnton, *Bohême littéraire et révolution: Le monde des*

livres au XVIIIe siècle (Paris: Seuil, 1983), 17–41. See also Darnton, *Gens de lettres, gens du livre*, trans. Marie-Alyx Revellat (Paris: Odile Jacob, 1992), which develops and revisits his earlier analyses.

10. Dena Goodman, *The Republic of Letters: A Cultural History of the French Enlightenment* (Ithaca: Cornell University Press, 1994).

11. Carolyn C. Lougee, *Le Paradis des femmes: Women, Salons, and Social Stratification in Seventeenth-Century France* (Princeton: Princeton University Press, 1976). The idea of the salon as a fundamentally female sphere has been common in historical writing since Jules and Edmond de Goncourt, *La femme au XVIIIe siècle* (Paris: Firmin Didot, 1862; Flammarion, 1982), trans. Jacques Le Clercq and Ralph Roeder as *The Woman of the Eighteenth Century* (New York: Minton, Balch, 1927). Among many more recent titles, see Joan Dejean, *Tender Geographies: Women and the Origins of the Novel in France* (New York: Columbia University Press, 1991); Erica Harth, *Cartesian Women: Versions and Subversions of Rational Discourse in the Old Regime* (Ithaca: Cornell University Press, 1991); Myriam Maître, *Les Précieuses: Naissance des femmes de lettres en France au XVIIe siècle* (Paris: Honoré Champion, 1999); Carla Hesse, *The Other Enlightenment: How French Women Became Modern* (Princeton: Princeton University Press, 2001); Faith Evelyn Beasley, *Salons, History, and the Creation of Seventeenth Century France: Mastering Memory* (Aldershot: Ashgate, 2006).

12. Jürgen Habermas, *The Structural Transformation of the Public Sphere*. Trans Thomas Burger and Frederick Lawrence (Cambridge, MA: MIT Press, 1989).

13. Jolanta T. Pekacz, *Conservative Tradition in Pre-Revolutionary France: Parisian Salon Women* (New York: Peter Lang, 1999). Steven D. Kale, "Women, the Public Sphere and the Persistence of Salons," *French Historical Studies* 25, no. 1 (Winter 2002): 115–48; Kale, *French Salons, High Society and Political Sociability from the Old Regime to the Revolution of 1848* (Baltimore: Johns Hopkins University Press, 1994, 2004). For a recent and comparative discussion, see Brian Cowan, "English Coffeehouses and French Salons: Rethinking Habermas, Gender and Sociability in Early Modern French and British Historiography," in *Making Space Public in Early Modern Europe: Performance, Geography, Privacy*, Angela Vanhaelen and Joseph P. Ward, eds. (London: Routledge, 2013), 41–53.

14. Maurice Agulhon, *Pénitents et Francs-Maçons de l'ancienne Provence: Essai sur la sociabilité méridionale* (Paris: Fayard, 1968); Agulhon, *Le Cercle dans la France bourgeoise (1810–1848): Étude d'une mutation de sociabilité* (Paris: Armand Colin, 1977); Daniel Roche, *Le Siècle des Lumières en Province: Académies et académiciens provinciaux, 1680–1789*, 2 vols. (Paris and The Hague: Mouton, 1978). For a sociological approach, see Georg Simmel, *Sociologie et épistémologie*, trans. L. Gasparini (Paris: Presses Universitaires de France, 1991).

15. Daniel Gordon, *Citizens without Sovereignty: Equality and Sociability in French Thought, 1670–1789* (Princeton: Princeton University Press, 1994), 115.

16. Daniel Roche, "République des Lettres ou royaume des mœurs: La sociabilité vue d'ailleurs," *Revue d'histoire moderne et contemporaine* 43, no. 2 (April–June 1996): 293–306.

17. The Littré dictionary immediately associates the salon with the eighteenth century, adding: "The salons of Mme Geoffrin, the marquise Du Deffand, were famous in the eighteenth century": Émile Littré, *Dictionnaire de la langue française*, 4 vols. (Paris: Hachette, 1863–69), s.v. "Salon."

18. Sébastien-Roch-Nicolas Chamfort, *Produits de la civilisation perfectionnée: Maximes et pensées; Caractères et anecdotes*, ed. Jean Dagen (Paris: Garnier-Flammarion,

1968), 74, 108. Originally published as *Maximes, pensées, caractères et anecdotes in Œuvres IV* (Paris: an III [1795]); quoted from *Products of the Perfected Civilization: Selected Writings of Chamfort*, trans. W. S. Merwin (New York: Macmillan, 1969), 153. Dictionaries usually date the term to Madame de Staël's *Corinne*, published in 1807, its first occurrence in the current meaning.

19. Roger Chartier, *The Cultural Origins of the French Revolution*, trans. Lydia G. Cochrane (Durham, NC: Duke University Press, 1991).

20. Norbert Elias, *The Court Society*, trans. Edmund Jephcott (New York: Pantheon, 1983), 267.

21. For a striking example concerning the salon of the marquise de Rambouillet, see Christian Jouhaud, *Les Pouvoirs de la littérature: Histoire d'un paradoxe* (Paris: Gallimard, 2000), 131.

22. Antoine Lilti, *Le Monde des salons: Sociabilité et mondanité à Paris au XVIIIe siècle* (Paris: Fayard, 2005).

CHAPTER 1

1. Jean-François Marmontel, *Mémoires*, ed. Jean-Pierre Guicciardi and Gilles Thierrat (Paris: Mercure de France, 1999), 106; translated as *Memoirs of Marmontel*, 2 vols. (New York: Merill & Baker, 1903); Archives des Affaires étrangères (AAE), *Contrôle des étrangers*, vol. 7, report of December 1, 1775.

2. Marie-Thérèse Geoffrin, letter of December 6, 1867: *Correspondance inédite du roi Stanislas-August Poniatowski et de Madame Geoffrin (1764–1777)*, ed. Charles de Mouÿ (Paris: Plon, 1875), 317.

3. Marmontel, *Mémoires*, 206.

4. AAE, *Contrôle des étrangers*, vol. 8, report of December 1, 1775.

5. Madame de la Ferté-Imbaut, "Anecdotes sur Helvétius, sur Turgot, sur d'Alembert et sur l'archevêque de Paris": Archives nationales, 508 AP 38; Letter of Madame Geoffrin to Véri of May 24, 1768, published in Maurice Tourneux, "Madame Geoffrin et les éditions expurgées des lettres familières de Montesquieu," *Revue d'histoire littéraire de la France* 1 (1894): 52–64.

6. Horace Walpole, "Paris Journal," in *The Yale Edition of Horace Walpole's Correspondence*, ed. W. S. Lewis, 48 vols. in 47 pts. (New Haven: Yale University Press; London: Oxford University Press, 1937–83), 7, 5:257–417. During his stay in Paris from September 1765 to April 1766, Walpole went thirty-one times to Madame Geoffrin's house. He dined there five times, supped six times, for the rest contenting himself with paying a simple visit.

7. Jean-Baptiste Morvan de Bellegarde, *Réflexions sur ce qui peut plaire ou déplaire dans le commerce du monde* (Paris: A. Seneuze, 1688), 258.

8. Lady Crewe, "A Journal Kept at Paris from December 24th 1785 to March 10th 1786," British Library, Add. MSS 37 926, fol. 31.

9. Lady Crewe, "Journal," fol. 40.

10. Eustache Le Noble, *L'École du monde, ou Instruction d'un père à son fils*, 2 vols. (Amsterdam, 1715), bk. 2, p. 30.

11. AAE, *Contrôle des étrangers*, vol. 7, report of September 29, 1775.

12. Henriette-Louise, baronne d'Oberkirch, *Mémoires de la baronne Oberkirch sur la cour de Louis XVI et la société française avant 1789* (1853) (Paris: Mercure de France, 1989), 164; translated as *Memoirs of the Baroness d'Oberkirch, Countess de Montbrison*, ed. Count de Montbrison, 3 vols. (London: Colburn, 1852).

13. Marie-Thérèse Geoffrin, MS notebook, "Différentes choses dont je veux garder le souvenir," private archives of the comte de Bruce.

14. AAE, *Contrôle des étrangers*, vol. 3, reports of December 2 and December 16, 1774.

15. AAE, *Contrôle des étrangers*, vol. 3, reports of December 2 and December 16, 1774.

16. Georges-Louis Leclerc de Buffon, *Correspondance générale* (Paris: Levasseur, 1885), reprint, 2 vols. (Geneva: Slatkine, 1971). See, for example, his letters to Madame Necker of September 12, 1776 (1:322), or December 15, 1777 (1:367).

17. AAE, *Contrôle des étrangers*, vol. 43, report of April 19, 1782, and vol. 56, report of May 6, 1785.

18. This was true to the point that Tourton, a banker who received at dinner on Wednesdays, thought himself obliged, on one occasion when the dinner could not be held, to send notes to his usual guests to warn them: AAE, *Contrôle des étrangers*, vol. 9, report of March 22, 1776.

19. Louis-Sébastien Mercier, *Tableau de Paris* (Amsterdam, 1787–88); ed. Jean-Claude Bonnet, 2 vols. (Paris: Mercure de France, 1994), 1:150.

20. Madame Du Deffand, letter to Horace Walpole, January 8, 1779: Walpole, *Correspondence*, 7, 5:102.

21. Marquise de La Tour du Pin, *Journal d'une femme de cinquante ans (1778–1815)* (Paris: Mercure de France, 1979), 8; quoted from *Memoirs: Laughing and Dancing Our Way to the Precipice*, trans. Felice Harcourt (London: Harvill, 1999), 17. From a more critical viewpoint, Rousseau made this distinction an essential element of Parisian sociability: Jean-Jacques Rousseau, *Julie, ou La Nouvelle Héloïse (1761)*; ed. René Pomeau (Paris: Garner, 1960), 223–24.

22. AAE, *Contrôle des étrangers*, vol. 18, report of November 7, 1777.

23. AAE, *Contrôle des étrangers*, vol. 6, report of July 28, 1775. Similarly, the duchesse de Praslin received on a specific day (Monday, in the autumn of 1781) and also gave *soupers priés* on other evenings: AAE, *Contrôle des étrangers*, vol. 40, reports of September 14 and October 19, 1781.

24. Pierre de Ségur, *Le Royaume de la Rue Saint-Honoré: Madame Geoffrin et sa fille* (Paris: Calmann-Lévy, 1897), 28.

25. Charles Hénault, *Mémoires du président Hénault*, ed. François Rousseau (Paris: Hachette, 1911), 120.

26. Madame de Lambert to the duchesse du Maine: "Here, madame is the respectable Tuesday, which comes to render homage to Your Highness": letter of August 23, reproduced in Hellegouarc'h, *L'Esprit de société*, 53.

27. Goodman, *Republic of Letters*.

28. André Morellet, *Mémoires inédits de l'abbé Morellet de l'Académie française sur le dix-huitième siècle et sur la Révolution*, 2 vols. (Paris: Ladvocat, 1821), ed. Jean-Pierre Guicciardi (Paris: Mercure de France, 1988), 211–12.

29. Morellet, *Mémoires*. See also Amélie Suard, *Essais de mémoires sur M. Suard* (Paris: Didot, 1820), 97.

30. Morellet, *Mémoires*, 187. Letter from Morellet to Suard of July 2, 1772, in *Lettres d'André Morellet*, ed. Dorothy Medlin, Jean-Claude David, and Paul LeClerc, 3 vols. (Oxford: Voltaire Foundation, 1991–96), 1:169–70.

31. Biron's wife is never mentioned in the various collections of correspondence or in the reports of the Contrôle des étrangers, even though they mention all the maréchal de Biron's weekly dinners.

32. "The best society attended his suppers and his parties": Marmontel, *Mémoires*, 134. In 1739, the duc de Biron acquired the house in which these receptions were held, for 105,000 livres. Jacques Hillairet, *La Rue de Richelieu* (Paris: Minuit, 1966), 53.

33. Georges Cucuël, *La Poupelinière et la musique de chambre au XVIIIe siècle, Thèse de lettres, 1913* (Paris: Fischbacher, 1913).

34. In her correspondence with Walpole, Madame Du Deffand often speaks of her evenings with "the Neckers": for example, she states, "I supped yesterday evening in Saint-Ouen at the Neckers" (Madame Du Deffand, letter to Horace Walpole, August 5, 1775: Walpole, *Correspondence*, 6, 4:210); "The Neckers' day is changed; it is Monday instead of Saturday" (letter, November 26, 1775; Walpole, *Correspondence*, 6, 4:239–41); "I sup. . . on Mondays at the Neckers, Tuesdays at the Carrousel or at the Caramans" (letter, February 16, 1776; Walpole, *Correspondence*, 6, 4:268); "I sup once a week with the Neckers" (letter, June 7, 1778; Walpole, *Correspondence*, 6, 5:48). In her journal for 1779–80, she notes every Tuesday, "Supper at the home of M. Necker" ("Journal de Madame Du Deffand"; Walpole, *Correspondence*, 7:5).

35. Or, to be exact, the two baronesses. D'Holbach, who was born in 1725, arrived in Paris as a young man in 1748 after studying in Leiden. His first wife, Suzanne d'Aine, well liked by both Diderot and Rousseau, died in 1754. Two years later, d'Holbach married her sister Charlotte, who, despite lingering bad health, survived him. She is the baroness d'Holbach in question here, and I shall return to her.

36. Diderot, letter to Sophie Volland, September 24, 1767: Denis Diderot, *Correspondance*, ed. Georges Roth, 16 vols. (Paris: Éditions de Minuit, 1955–70), 6:140.

37. Diderot, letter to Sophie Volland, December 1, 1760: Diderot, *Correspondance*, 3:281.

38. I might note, however, that after the death of the baron in January 1789, the reports of the Contrôle des étrangers tell us that Grimm continued to go to the d'Holbach home.

39. Gregory S. Brown, *Literary Sociability in the Old Régime: Beaumarchais, the Société des auteurs dramatiques and the Comédie-Française* (Farnham, UK: Ashgate, forthcoming).

40. Maurice Agulhon, "La sociabilité est-elle objet d'histoire?" in *Sociabilité et société bourgeoise en France, en Allemagne et en Suisse (1750–1850)*, ed. Étienne François, 13–22 (Paris: Éditions recherche sur les civilisations, 1986), 16.

41. Pierre-Yves Beaurepaire, *L'Espace des franc-maçons: Une sociabilité européenne au XVIIIe siècle* (Rennes: Presses Universitaires de Rennes, 2003).

42. AAE, *Contrôle des étrangers*, vol. 53, report of August 27, 1784. Similarly, during his first stay in Paris in 1765, Horace Walpole was presented by Madame Du Deffand at the salon of the maréchale de Luxembourg. The following day he joined those ladies in the box of the prince de Conti at a performance of *Le Philosophe sans le savoir*: Horace Walpole, "Paris Journals," December 12, 1765, in Walpole, *Correspondence*, 7, 5:284.

43. Adèle d'Osmond, comtesse de Boigne, *Mémoires de la comtesse de Boigne, née d'Osmond, de Louis XVI à 1820*, 2 vols. (Paris: Mercure de France, 1971), 57.

44. AAE, *Contrôle des étrangers*, vol. 66, report of November 9, 1787.

45. Katia Béguin, *Les Prince de Condé: Rebelles, courtisans et mécènes dans la France du Grand Siècle* (Seyssel: Champ Vallon, 1999), 329–86.

46. Hénault, *Mémoires*, 29.

47. The duchess went on Wednesdays to Madame de Lambert's, who in turn visited Sceaux and Saint-Aulaire, thus assuring a regular connection between the two salons. On the salon of Madame de Lambert and the *seconde préciosité*, see Roger Marchal, *Madame de Lambert et son milieu* (originally his Thèse de lettres,

1988), *Studies on Voltaire and the Eighteenth Century* 289 (Oxford: Voltaire Foundation, 1991); and, more recently, Katharine Hamerton "A Feminist Voice in the Enlightenment Salon: Madame de Lambert on Taste, Sensibility and the Feminine Mind," *Modern Intellectual History* 7, no. 2 (August 2010): 209–38.

48. René Pomeau, *Voltaire en son temps* (Paris: Fayard; Oxford: Voltaire Foundation, 1995), 1:524–31.

49. According to the duc the Luynes, quoted in Pomeau, *Voltaire en son temps*, I:256.

50. Madame Geoffrin, letter to Gabriel Cramer, August 18, 1748: Bibliothèque publique universitaire de Genève, DO Geoffrin.

51. Jean-Jacques Rousseau, *Émile, ou, de l'Éducation* (1762), ed. Charles Wirz (Paris: Gallimard, 1995), 296, 772; see also *Emile: Or, On Education*, trans. Allan Bloom (New York: Basic Books, 1979).

52. Nicolas Boileau Despréaux, "Satire X," in *Œuvres complètes*, 4 vols. (Paris: Garnier, 1870–73), 2:83.

53. Jean-Jacques Rutlidge, *Le Bureau d'esprit* (Liège, 1776). Féraud was the author of the first dictionary to mention the expression, which, he states, was connected with a "waggish and critical style": Abbé Jean-François Féraud, *Dictionnaire critique de la langue française*, 3 vols. (Marseille: Jean Mossy, 1787–88), s.v. "Bureau."

54. Charles Collé, *Journal et mémoires de Charles Collé sur les hommes de lettres, les ouvrages dramatiques et les événements les plus mémorables du règne de Louis XV*, 3 vols. (Paris: Didot, 1868), reprint, 3 vols. (Geneva: Slatkine, 1967), 3:11, 170, 344.

55. Stéphanie Félicité du Crest, comtesse de Genlis, *Dictionnaire critique et raisonné des étiquettes de la cour*, 2 vols. (Paris: Mongie aîné, 1818).

56. Oberkirch, *Mémoires*, 405. This particular evening was Friday, August 29, 1777: AAE, *Contrôle des étrangers*, vol. 17, report of September 5, 1777.

57. *Dictionnaire de l'Académie françoise* (Paris, 1694), s.v. "Cercle."

58. *Encyclopédie, ou, Dictionnaire raisonné des arts, des sciences et des métiers par une société de gens de lettres*, 31 vols. (Paris: Briasson, 1751–80).

59. Friedrich Melchior, von Grimm, letter of February 1756, in *Correspondance littéraire, philosophique et critique par Grimm, Diderot, Raynal, Meister*, ed. Maurice Tourneux, 16 vols. (Paris: Garnier, 1877–82), 2:164.

60. Mme de La Ferté-Imbault, "Cahier de Mme de La Ferté-Imbault sur les gens qui jouent un rôle à Paris en 1774," Archives nationales, 508 AP 38.

61. *Dictionnaire de l'Académie françoise*, s.v. "Maison."

62. AAE, *Contrôle des étrangers*, vol. 62, report of December 8, 1786, fol. 135.

63. Antoine Furetière, *Dictionnaire universel* (The Hague, 1690), s.v. "Compagnie."

64. AAE, *Contrôle des étrangers*, vol. 12, report of September 6, 1776; vol. 11, report of July 19, 1776; vol. 19, report of January 21, 1778. Other mentions are of the *société* of Madame Du Deffand (AAE, *Contrôle des étrangers*, vol. 1, report of July 22, 1774); Madame Bacelli (vol. 56, report of May 21, 1785); of the duchesse d'Enville (vol. 55, report of January 21, 1785), and more. For the ambassadors, see AAE, *Contrôle des étrangers*, vol. 18, report of November 14, 1777.

65. Jean le Rond d'Alembert, "Éloge de Saint-Aulaire," in *Œuvres d'Alembert*, 5 vols. (Paris: A. Belin, 1821–22), 3:295–96.

66. Florimond-Claude-Charles, comte de Mercy-Argenteau, *Correspondance secrète du comte de Mercy Argenteau avec l'empereur Joseph II et le prince de Kaunitz, publiée par M. le chevalier Alfred d'Arneth et M. Jules Flammermont*, 2 vols. (Paris: Imprimerie Nationale, 1889–91), 2:323.

67. Gordon, *Citizens without Sovereignty*, 51–54.

68. *Dictionnaire de l'Académie* (1694), s.v. "Société."

69. *Dictionnaire de l'Académie* (1798), s.v. "Société."

70. Duchesse de Rohan, letter to the marquise de La Ferté-Imbault, May 24, 1775: Mme de la Ferté-Imbault, correspondence, Archives nationales, 508 AP 37.

71. *Dictionnaire universel français et latin vulgairement appelé Dictionnaire de Trévoux* 3 vols. (1704), 8 vols. (Paris: Compagnie des libraires associés, 1771), s.v. "Société."

72. Marquise de Pons, letter to her husband, July 24, 1773: Archives des Affaires étrangères, *Mémoires et documents*, France 319, fol. 242.

73. Genlis, *Dictionnaire critique et raisonné des étiquettes*.

74. Jean-Jacques Rousseau, *Les Confessions*, vol. 1 of Rousseau, *Œuvres complètes*, ed. Bernard Gagnebin and Marcel Raymond, 5 vols. (Paris: Gallimard, La Pléïade, 1959–95), 1:116, quoted from Rousseau, *Confessions*, trans. Angela Scholar (Oxford: Oxford University Press, 2000), 114.

75. Letter to the comtesse Mniszech, quoted in Marek Bratún, "Paris aux yeux des jeunes Sarmates éclairés en 1766–1767, d'après une correspondance inédite de Joseph et Michel-Georges Mniszech," *Studies on Voltaire and the Eighteenth Century* 371 (1999): 257–74, esp. p. 264.

76. Mirabeau, letter to Madame de Rochefort, October 11, 1759: Musée Arbaud, Aix-en-Provence, Archives Mirabeau, Correspondence, marquis de Mirabeau and the comtesse de Rochefort, vol. 34, fol. 348.

77. Manon Phlipon, letter to Sophie Canet, March 20, 1772: Marie-Jeanne Roland, *Lettres de Madame Roland*, ed. Claude Perroud, 4 vols. (Paris: Imprimerie Nationale, 1900–15), vol. 2 (1913), pt. 1, p. 92.

78. AAE, *Contrôle des étrangers*, vol. 10, report of May 17, 1776.

79. Sonia Branca-Rosoff and Jacques Guilhaumou, "De 'société' à 'socialisme': L'invention néologique et son contexte discursif: Essai de colinguisme appliqué," *Langage et société* 83–84 (March–June 1988): 39–77.

80. Jacques-François Blondel describes this building under the name of the *hôtel du Maine* in his *Cours d'architecture, ou, Traité de la décoration, distribution, & construction des bâtiments*, 6 vols (Paris: Desaint, 1771–77).

81. Louis Hautecoeur, *Histoire de l'architecture classique en France*, 7 vols. (Paris: Picard, 1948–67), 4:483–84. See also Yves Durand, *Les Fermiers généraux au XVIIIe siècle (1971)* (Paris: Maisonneuve et Larose, 1991), 513; Ned Rival, *Grimod de La Reynière, le gourmand gentilhomme* (Paris: Le Pré aux clercs, 1983), 37–38.

82. Archives nationales, T 163–32, no. 174. See also Durand, *Les Fermiers généraux*, 112.

83. Oberkirch, *Mémoires*, 112.

84. La Reynière fils, quoted by Misette Godard in her preface to Alexandre-Balthasar-Laurent Grimod de La Reynière, *Manuel des Amphitryons (1808)* (Paris: Métailié, 1983), xii.

85. Edward Gibbon, letter to his stepmother, February 12, 1763, quoted from *The Letters of Edward Gibbon*, ed. J. E. Norton, 3 vols. (London: Cassel; New York: Macmillan, 1956), 1:33.

86. Claude Pris, "La Manufacture royale des glaces de Saint-Gobain, une grande entreprise sous l'Ancien Régime," 2 vols. (Lille: Service de reproduction des thèses de l'Université, 1975). See also Maurice Hamon, *Mme Geoffrin* (Paris: Fayard, 2010).

87. Marmontel, *Mémoires*, 196, quoted from *Memoirs of Marmontel*, 2 vols. (Paris: Société des Bibliophiles; New York: Merrill & Baker, 1903), 1:250.

88. Family accounts: "État des revenus de madame, 1788," Archives nationales, 508 AP 36.

89. Ségur, *Royaume de la Rue Saint-Honoré*, 111.

90. Geoffrin, MS notebook, "Differents marchands et artisans," private archives of the comte de Bruce. For a list of domestics, see the "inventaire après décès" for Madame Geoffrin, Archives nationales, Minutier central, Étude CXVII, 879, October 15, 1777.

91. Heinrich Carl, baron von Gleichen, *Souvenirs de Charles Henri, Baron de Gleichen*, trans. Paul Grimblot (Paris: Léon Techener fils, 1868), 99.

92. Madame de Staël, letter to her husband, June 1786, in Germaine de Staël, *Correspondance générale*, ed. Béatrice W. Jasinsky, 6 vols. in 11 pts. (Paris: Jean-Jacques Pauvert, 1960–93), 1:75.

93. "Inventaire après décès" dated May 31, 1776: Archives nationales, Minutier central, Étude LXXXIII, 579.

94. Letters of Mme de La Ferté-Imbault to a friend, eighth letter, May 5, 1777: Mme de la Ferté-Imbault, correspondence, Archives nationales, 508 AP 37.

95. Grimm joked: "Sister Lespinasse tells people that her fortune does not permit her to offer either dinner or supper, and that she nonetheless would like to receive at home the brothers who are willing to come there to digest": Grimm, *Correspondance littéraire*, 8:138.

96. Pierre Tyl, "Madame d'Épinay: Son salon, et son oeuvre littéraire," Thèse de doctorat sous la direction de Daniel Roche, Université de Paris I (1993).

97. Madame d'Épinay, letter to Galiani, June 24, 1770, in Ferdinando Galiani and Louise d'Épinay, *Correspondance*, ed. Georges Dulac and Daniel Maggetti, 5 vols. (Paris: Desjonquères, 1992–97), 1:193.

98. Madame Du Deffand, letter to Horace Walpole, March 8, 1770: Walpole, *Correspondence*, 4, 2:386–87.

99. At the death of her husband in 1750, Madame Du Deffand regained control of her *douaire* of 4,000 livres per year, which was added to the yearly income of 15,600 livres she already enjoyed: see the "inventaire après décès" for Madame Du Deffand taken from the archives of the département du Drône, published by W. S. Lewis in Walpole, *Correspondence*, 6:10–47. In 1764, Madame de Lunes bequeathed 6,000 livres to Madame Du Deffand, which she invested and which paid a yearly income of 5,340 livres. In 1770, she estimated her income at 35,190 livres (letter of March 8: Walpole, *Correspondence*, 2:387). When a reform of pensions threatened a reduction, she addressed a memo to the king (taking care to undervalue her revenues to 28,190 livres, in particular by omitting the *rentes* in favor of her servants, the lifetime income from which she enjoyed). On this, see a copy of the *mémoire* to the king in her letter to Walpole of January 29, 1770: Walpole, *Correspondence*, 2:355.

100. Morellet, *Mémoires*, 129. The baron's "inventaire après décès" is not known, but his library contained 2,777 volumes and the sale of his collection of paintings and prints brought in over 40,000 livres.

101. Guy Chaussinand-Nogaret, *La Noblesse en France au XVIIIe siècle: De la féodalité aux Lumières (1978)* (Brussels: Complexe, 1984), 77.

102. Amélie Suard, *Essais de mémoires*, 84.

103. Théodore Tronchin, letter to Jacob Tronchin, 1766: Bibliothèque publique universitaire de Genève, Archives Tronchin, vol. 199, Théodore Tronchin with his parents. See also, for example, the correspondence between Madame de Graffigny and Mademoiselle Quinault, which often mentions the carriage that Mademoiselle Quinault put at Graffigny's disposition: Letters of Mlle Quinaut to Mme de Graffigny, Bibliothèque nationale, Département des MSS, Nouvelles acquisitions françaises, 15579, Graffigny and Devaux.

104. Morellet, *Mémoires*, 96, 136.

105. Denis Diderot, letter to Sophie Volland, August 18, 1765: Diderot, *Correspondance*, 4:94–95.

106. Madame Du Deffand, letter to d'Alembert, March 22, 1753, in Marie de Vichy Chamrond, marquise Du Deffand, *Correspondance complète avec ses amis*, ed. Mathurin de Lescure, 3 vols. (Paris: Plon, 1865), 1:169.

107. Robert S. Tate, Jr., *Petit de Bachaumont: His Circle and the Mémoires secrets, Studies on Voltaire and the Eighteenth Century* 65 (Oxford: Voltaire Foundation (1968)), 102.

108. Mme de la Ferté-Imbault, "Portraits de différentes personnes": Archives nationales, 508 AP 38.

109. AAE, *Contrôle des étrangers*, vol. 10, report of June 7, 1776.

110. Stanislas-Auguste Poniatowski, *Mémoires du roi Stanislas-Auguste Poniatowski*, 2 vols. (St. Petersburg: Imprimerie de l'Académie Impériale des sciences, 1914), 79.

111. Suzanne Necker, letter to Horace Bénédict Saussure, June 21, 1786, published in appendix to Valérie Hannin, "Une ambition de femme au siècle des Lumières: Le cas de Mme Necker," *Cahiers Staëliens* 36 (1985): 5–29.

112. Mme de Necker, letter to Mme Reverdill, April 7, 1770, Bibliothèque publique universitaire de Genève, Archives Horace-Bénédict Saussure, MS suppl. 717.

113. Marie-Thérèse Geoffrin, MS notebook, "Noms et adresses des personnes de ma connaissance," private archives of the comte de Bruce.

114. Geoffrin, "Noms et adresses."

115. Edward Gibbon, "Journal du séjour de Gibbon à Paris du 28 janvier au 9 mai 1763," in *Miscellanea Gibboniana*, ed. Gavin E. De Beer et al., Université de Lausanne, publications de la Faculté des Lettres, 10 (Lausanne: F. Rouge, 1952), 102. Madame Geoffrin notes in her address book, "M. Gibbon, Englishman recommended by milady Hervey. Author of a work, Essai sur la littérature": Geoffrin, "Noms et adresses."

116. Gibbon, letter to Dorothea Gibbon, February 1, 1763: Gibbon, *Letters*, 1:132–34.

117. Gibbon, letter to his father, February 24, 1763: Gibbon, *Letters*, 1:134–38.

118. Edward Gibbon, *Memoirs of My Life*, ed. Betty Radice (London and New York: Penguin, 1984); in French translation as *Mémoires* (Paris: Criterion, 1992), 180.

119. Galiani, letter to Madame d'Épinay, August 7, 1774: Galiani and d'Épinay, *Correspondance*, 4:169.

120. Mme Geoffrin, letter to Grimm, December 17, 1770: Archives nationales, 508 AP 34, Mme Geoffrin.

121. During the same year, Visconti, who served as papal nuncio in Vienna, whom Madame Geoffrin had met in Warsaw four years earlier but who had never written to her, broke "years of epistolary silence" to recommend to her his nephew, the marchese Visconti, who was about to come to Paris and hoped to be received at her home on the rue Saint-Honoré: Letter of papal nuncio Visconti to Madame Geoffrin, November 9, 1770): Archives nationales, 508 AP 34, Mme Geoffrin.

122. Grimm, *Correspondance littéraire*, August, 1767, 7:391. See also Collé, *Journal et mémoires*, III, 170, and the souvenirs of Madame de La Ferté-Imbault, Archives nationales, 508 AP 34, March 15, 1783. Guasco took revenge by adding attacks against Madame Geoffrin to his edition of the familiar letters of Montesquieu: Tourneux, "Madame Geoffrin et les éditions expurgées."

123. Grimm, *Correspondance littéraire*, May 1770, 9:10.

124. Gleichen, *Souvenirs*, 100.

125. Madame Helvétius, letter to Malesherbes, August 24, 1759: Claude Helvétius, *Correspondance générale d'Helvétius*, ed. Peter Allan et al., 3 vols. (Oxford: Voltaire Foundation, 1981–2004), 2:267.

126. AAE, *Contrôle des étrangers*, vol. 21, report of Friday, January 30, 1778.

127. AAE, *Contrôle des étrangers*, vol. 29, report of Friday, April 30, 1779.

128. Alexandre-Balthasar-Laurent Grimod de La Reynière, *Lorgnette philosophique: Trouvée par un R.P. capucin sous les Arcades du Palais Royal et présentéee au public par un célibataire*, 2 vols. in 1 (London and Paris: Chez l'auteur, 1785), 61–62.

129. Marie de Vichy Chamrond, marquise Du Deffand, *Cher Voltaire: La correspondance de Madame Du Deffand avec Voltaire*, ed. Isabelle Vissière et al. (Paris: Des Femmes, 1987), 98.

130. Madame Du Deffand, letter to the duchesse de Choiseul, October 7, 1771, Marie de Vichy Chamrond, marquise Du Deffand, *Correspondance complète avec la duchesse de Choiseul, l'abbé Barthélemy et M. Craufurt, publiée avec une introduction par M. le Marquis de Sainte-Aulaire*, 3 vols. (Paris: Michel Lévy frères, 1877), 2:62.

131. Henry Swinburne, *The Courts of Europe at the Close of the Last Century*, 2 vols. (London, 1841), 2:44. Swinburne was presented to the duchesse de La Vallière on January 19, 1787.

132. "I remember; I have seen all of Europe, Circling her armchair with a triple circle, Watching out for a word, spying a glance": Jacques Delille, *La Conversation, poème* (Paris: Michaud, 1812), 161.

133. Madame Du Deffand, letter to Horace Walpole, April 30, 1775: Walpole, *Correspondence*, 6, 4:183.

134. Madame Geoffrin, letter to the abbé de Véri, May 24, 1768: Tourneux, "Madame Geoffrin et les éditions," 61–63.

135. Morellet, *Mémoires*, 97.

136. The word *salonnier* did exist, but it designated the journalist who wrote about the salons. The adjective *salonnier/salonnière* was rare, but in the late nineteenth century it was used to designate activities connected with the salon. Finally, rarer still, the *Trésor de la langue française* mentions a few exceptional occurrences of *salonnière* as a noun (or a noun used as an adjective) in the nineteenth century to designate a person, but it applied to a woman who frequented a salon, not to a woman who received guests.

137. Morellet, for example, describing the society of Helvétius and his wife, speaks of Madame Helvétius as the "mistress of the house," and he adds that Helvétius himself often went out, even if there were visitors in his own house, "leaving his wife to do the honors of the house for the rest of the day": Morellet, *Mémoires*, 135, 136.

138. Jean-Baptiste de La Lande, marquis du Deffand, died in 1750; François Geoffrin in 1749; the duc d'Enville in 1746. Madame Du Deffand had already separated from her husband. As for Madame Geoffrin, she had to overcome the resistance of her husband when she began to receive at home.

139. Frederick King Turgeon, "Fanny de Beauharnais," PhD diss., Harvard University, 1929.

140. Madame Du Deffand was staying in the provinces with her brother, the comte de Vichy, when she met Julie, illegitimate daughter of the count and sister of the countess. The count and countess, startled by the perspective of one day seeing the young woman demand her portion of an inheritance that had been denied her, for two years opposed Madame Du Deffand's desire to make Julie her *demoiselle de compagnie*. See Marie de Vichy Chamrond, marquise Du Deffand, *Lettres à Julie de Lespinasse*, ed. Warren H. Smith; *Letters to and from Madame du Deffand and Julie de Lespinasse*, trans. Warren H. Smith (New Haven: Yale University Press, 1938).

141. Genlis, *Dictionnaire critique et raisonné des étiquettes*, s.v. "Maîtresse de maison," 1:352.

142. Marie Angélique de Neufville de Villeroi (1707–87) first married the duc de Boufflers, who died in 1747. In 1750, she married the duc de Luxembourg. She is not to be confused with the comtesse de Boufflers (Marie Charlotte Hippolyte de Campet de Saujon) or the marquise de Boufflers (Marie Françoise Catherine de Beauvau), both of whom played important roles in Paris social life.

143. Oberkirch, *Mémoires*, 209.

144. Swinburne, *Courts of Europe*, 2:44. The phrase *comme les autres* is in French in the text.

145. Inspector d'Hémery, "Du Boccage": Bibliothèque nationale, Département des MSS, Nouvelles acquisitions françaises, 19783.

146. David Hume, "Of the Rise and Progress of the Arts and Sciences," in Hume, *Essays: Moral, Political and Literary* (1742), revised edn., ed. Eugene F. Miller, 2 vols. (Indianapolis: Liberty Classics, 1987), 1:111–37, esp. p. 131. In French translation as "De la naissance et du progrès des arts et des sciences" (1742), in *Essais moraux, politiques et littéraires et autres essays*, ed. Gilles Robel, trans. Jean Pierre Cléro (Paris: Presses Universitaires de France, 2001), 268–97, esp pp. 284, 288–89.

147. Mercier, *Tableau de Paris*, 1:626.

148. Jean-François de La Harpe, *Letters to the Shuvalovs*, ed. Christopher Todd, *Studies on Voltaire and the Eighteenth Century* 108 (1973), 74.

149. *Correspondence littéraire*, May 1776, 11:264.

150. Jean Le Rond d'Alembert, "Portrait de Julie de Lespinasse," in Julie de Lespinasse, *Lettres de Julie de Lespinasse suivies de ses autres œuvres et de lettres de Mme Du Deffand, de Turgot, de Bernardin de Saint-Pierre*, ed. Eugène Asse (Paris: Charpentier, 1876), 346, reprint (Geneva: Slatkine, 1971).

151. Marmontel, *Mémoires*, 260.

152. Madame Geoffrin, letter to Martin Folkes, May 17, 1743: Archives of the Royal Society (London), MS 250, vol. III, fol. 83.

153. Morellet, *Mémoires*, 8.

154. Madame Geoffrin, letter to Martin Folkes, January 16, 1743: Archives of the Royal Society, MS 250, vol. III, fol. 13.

155. Geoffrin, "Note autobiographique de Mme Geoffrin sur son éducation," Archives nationales, 508 AP 34.

156. André Morellet, "Portrait de Mme Geoffrin" (1777), in André Morellet, Jean le Rond d'Alembert, and Antoine Léonard Thomas, *Éloges de Mme Geoffrin, contemporaine de Madame Du Deffand, suivis de lettres et d'un Essai sur la conversation par l'abbé Morellet* (Paris: Nicolle, 1812), 14.

157. Grimm, letter to Catherine II, quoted in Ségur, *Royaume de la Rue Saint-Honoré*, 108.

158. The only books in Madame Geoffrin's library written by authors who attended her salon were the novels of Duclos (*La Comtesse de Luz, Les Confessions du comte de ****, and *Les Mœurs du siècle*): Madame Geoffrin, "Notes sur les bibliothèques de mon cabinet de compagnie," in her notebook headed, "Différentes choses dont je veux garder le souvenir," private archives of the comte de Bruce.

159. Geoffrin, "Noms et adresses."

160. Madame Geoffrin, letter to the baron de Gleichen, Archives nationales, 508 AP 34.

161. Rutlidge, *Bureau d'esprit*. See also the critical edition: Rutlidge, *Les comédiens, ou, Le foyer; Le Bureau d'esprit; Le Train de Paris, ou, Les Bourgeois du temps*, ed. Pierre Peyronnet (Paris: Honoré Champion, 1999, 2002).

162. Charles Palissot de Montenoy, *Les Philosophes* (Paris, 1760), ed. Thomas James Barling (Exeter: University of Exeter, 1975). English Showalter has put forward the thesis that the model for Cydalise was not Madame Geoffrin but Madame de Graffigny: English Showalter, "'Madame a fait un livre,' Madame de Graffigny, Palissot et les Philosophes," *Recherches sur Diderot et l'Encyclopédie* 23 (October 1997): 109–25.

163. Dejean, *Tender Geographies*; Maître, *Les Précieuses*.

164. Madame d'Épinay, letter to Galiani, January 4, 1771: Galiani and d'Épinay, *Correspondance*, 2:26.

165. Marchal, *Madame de Lambert*.

166. The duchesse d'Aiguillon, who was her friend, tells of the poor reception that Madame Du Châtelet received at Fontainebleau after the publication of one of her books: "You know that wit and knowledge are not the best ways to succeed." Even while praising the book, the duchess writes: "When I have just read it and I find that head loaded with pompons and I think of what has come of it, I do not know where I am": letter of the duchesse d'Aiguillon to Maupertuis, Bibliothèque nationale, Département des manuscrits, Nouvelles acquisitions françaises, 10398, Maupertuis, fol. 30.

167. Archives nationales, Minutier central, Étude LXXXIII. 579, testament dated December 11, 1776.

168. Necker justifies this attitude in his preface to his wife's manuscripts, which he published after her death: Suzanne Necker, *Mélanges extraits des manuscrits de Mme Necker*, ed. Jacques Necker, 3 vols. (Paris, 1798), and *Nouveaux mélanges*, ed. Jacques Necker, 2 vols. (Paris, 1801). She had written a poem on the *avantages de l'esprit*, which she sent to her friend George Louis Lesage. He described the effects of that initiative to Mademoiselle Reverdill: "It is distressing that an amiable *demoiselle* of merit should have thus bothered her mind with nonsense (*fariboles*) that cover her with an ineffaceable ridicule": Lesage, letter to Mlle Reverdill, September 27, 1759: Bibliothèque publique universitaire de Genève, Papiers Georges-Louis Lesage, MS 2041.

169. Mme Necker, letter to Suard, July 4, 1791: Institut et Musée Voltaire (Geneva), Archives Suard, vol. 6, fol. 34.

170. "I have the misfortune to pass for a *bel esprit*, and that impertinent and unfortunate reputation makes me open to all displays and all the emulation of those who have pretensions in that direction. I often break a lance with them, and that is the occasion on which I stand apart from your precepts of prudence": Mme Du Deffand, letter to Horace Walpole, January 18, 1767: Walpole, *Correspondence*, 3, 1:1, 215.

171. Mme de Boufflers, letter to Bentinck, September 10, 1764: British Library (London), Bentinck correspondence, Egerton 1749, vol. 5, fol. 305.

172. See, for example, the remarks in Bombelles, *Journal*, July 23, 1786, 2:154.

173. For a bibliography and a study of the literary works of Madame Du Boccage, see Grace A. Gill-Mark, *Une femme de lettres au XVIIIe siècle: Anne-Marie Du Boccage, Thèse de lettres* (Paris: Honoré Champion, 1927; Geneva: Slatkine, 1976).

174. Collé, *Journal et mémoires*, 1:85.

175. Collé, *Journal et mémoires*, 1:96.

176. *Correspondance littéraire*, November 1764, 6:111–12.

177. *Correspondance littéraire*, November 1764, 6:113.

178. *Correspondance littéraire*, November 1764, 6:114. For Madame Du Boccage's point of view, see her letter to her sister, Madame Le Hayer du Perron, published by Madame Du Boccage in *Receuil des œuvres de madame Du Boccage*, 3 vols. (Lyon, 1764), 3:403.

179. Collé, *Journal et mémoires*, 85. Inspector d'Hémery noted these suspicions and asserted that Linant was "the author of all the verse that has passed under her name": Inspecteur d'Hémery, "Du Boccage," Bibliothèque nationale, Département des MSS, Nouvelles acquisitions françaises, 10783.

180. Alexandre de Tilly, *Mémoires du Comte Alexandre de Tilly pour servir à l'histoire des mœurs de la fin du XVIIIe siècle*, ed. Christian Melchior-Bonnet, 2 vols. (Paris: Mercure de France, 1965), 1:296.

CHAPTER 2

1. Marie de Vichy Chamrond, marquise Du Deffand, letter to Walpole April 12, 1767: Walpole, *Correspondence*, 3, 1:283.

2. AAE, *Contrôle des étrangers*, vol. 11, report of August 2, 1776.

3. Madame Du Deffand, letter to Walpole, February 20, 1767: Walpole, *Correspondence*, 3, 1:244.

4. AAE, *Contrôle des étrangers*, vol. 47, report of December 27, 1782.

5. Madame Du Deffand, letter to Horace Walpole, July 9, 1775: Walpole, *Correspondence*, 3:351.

6. AAE, *Contrôle des étrangers*, vol. 3, report of November 1, 1774.

7. AAE, *Contrôle des étrangers*, vol. 8, report of December 29, 1775: "The house of this lady was formerly much in fashion among the diplomatic corps, but for several years it is much less frequented by the ministers that make it up."

8. Oberkirch, *Mémoires*, 405.

9. AAE, *Contrôle des étrangers*, vol. 62, report of November 17, 1786.

10. Horace Walpole's Paris Journals: Walpole, *Correspondence*, 7, 5.

11. Herbert Lüthy, *La Banque protestante en France de la Révocation de l'édit de Nantes à la Révolution*, 2 vols. (Paris: SEVPEN, 1959), esp. 2:160–79.

12. The comtesse de Coislin is cited twenty times between August 1781 and October 1782 for suppers frequented by the Spanish ambassador, but also by the ambassadors of Sweden, Venice, and Denmark. The duchesse d'Estrées is mentioned thirty-eight times from 1784 to 1785: her Monday suppers, but also her Thursday and Saturday affairs, attracted a number of diplomats. The following year mentions drop to three: the ambassadors seem to have deserted her suppers.

13. Here the year 1774 covers only six months.

14. Madame Du Deffand, letter to Horace Walpole, January 22, 1767: Walpole, *Correspondence*, 3, 1:205.

15. Madame Du Deffand, letter to Horace Walpole, January 16, 1776: Walpole, *Correspondence*, 6, 4:258.

16. Madame Du Deffand, letter to Horace Walpole, January 6, 1779: Walpole, *Correspondence*, 6, 5:101.

17. AAE, *Contrôle des étrangers*, vol. 57, reports of August 5, 1785 and August 11, 1786.

18. Madame Du Deffand, letter to Horace Walpole, February 3, 1767: Walpole, *Correspondence*, 3, 1:229.

19. This episode has been recounted thousands of times and has often been fictionalized on the basis of different and contradictory sources. See, for example, Pierre de Ségur, *Julie de Lespinasse* (Paris: Calmann-Lévy, 1906); English translation as *Julie de Lespinasse* (London: Chatto & Windus, 1907).

20. Julie de Lespinasse, letter to Guibert, October 21, 1774: Lespinasse, *Lettres*, ed. Jacques Dupont (Paris: La Table Ronde, 1997), 168.

21. The duc de Lauzun was the son of the duc de Gontaut and Antoinette du Châtel, the sister of Louise Honorine du Châtel, duchesse de Choiseul.

22. It is difficult to date this connection. As early as 1738, Madame de Tencin wrote to François Tronchin that she was seeing much of "Mme Joffrin" (letter of April 4, 1738: Bibliothèque publique universitaire de Geneva, Tronchin archives, vol. 179). She declared at a later date: "Do you know why Geoffrin comes here? She wishes to see how much she can pick up out of my inventory": Marmontel, *Mémoires*, 196; quoted from *Memoirs of Marmontel*, 2 vols. (New York: Merill & Baker, 1903), 1:250. Madame Geoffrin's daughter wrote: "It is Mme de Tencin who placed at the feet of my mother the Fontenelles, the La Mottes, the Saurins, the Mairans, and the Montesquieus": Archives nationales, 508 AP 38, "Mémoires intéressants de la marquise d'Estampes née de La Ferté-Imbault."

23. AAE, *Contrôle des étrangers*, vol. 10, report of May 24, 1776.

24. Fanny Mouchard de Chaban, comtesse de Beauharnais, *À la mémoire de Madame Du Boccage* (Paris: Imprimerie Richard, 1802).

25. For the comtesse de La Marck, see Creutz, letter to Gustav III of November 31 [*sic*], 1783: *Gustave III par ses lettres*, ed. Gunnar von Proschwitz (Paris: Touzot, 1986), 240.

26. Palissot, letter to Lebrun, n.d.: Ponce Denis Écouchard Lebrun (called Lebrun-Pindare), *Œuvres*, ed. Pierre Louis Ginguené, 4 vols. (Paris, 1812), vol. 4, *Correspondance*, 161.

27. "Do I dare beg you, if the Thursday is not interrupted, to convey all my regrets for being absent there and all of my gratitude for the kindnesses that the persons who make up [that company] have been good enough to show to me": Condorcet, letter to Madame de La Ferté-Imbault, undated: Archives nationales, 508 AP 37.

28. AAE, *Contrôle des étrangers*, vol. 4, report of February 3, 1775.

29. "Anecdotes sur Helvétius, sur Turgot, sur d'Alembert, et sur l'archevêque de Paris": Archives nationales, 508 AP 38.

30. Michel Pinçon and Monique Pinçon-Charlot, *Dans les beaux quartiers* (Paris: Seuil, 1989); Christophe Charle, "Noblesse et élites en France au début du XIXe siècle," *Les Noblesses européenes au XIXe siècle*, 407–33, Collection de l'École française de Rome, 107 (Paris: Boccard, 1988).

31. Daniel Roche, "Recherches sur la noblesse parisienne au milieu du XVIIIe siècle: La noblesse du Marais," *Actes du 86e congrès des sociétés savantes*, Montpellier, 1961, 541–78 (Paris: Imprimerie Nationale, 1962); Natacha Coquery, *L'Hôtel*

aristocratique: Le marché du luxe à Paris au XVIIIe siècle (Paris: Publications de la Sorbonne, 1998); Mathieu Marraud, *La Noblesse de Paris au XVIIIe siècle* (Paris: Seuil, 2000).

32. Marc, marquis de Bombelles, *Journal*, ed. Jean Grassion and Franz Durif, 7 vols. (Geneva: Droz, 1977–82), 2:242.

33. Madame Du Deffand, letter to Horace Walpole, May 10, 1767: Walpole, *Correspondence*, 3, 1:292.

34. Madame d'Épinay, letter to abbé Galiani, July 19, 1771: Galiani and Épinay, *Correspondance*, 2:145.

35. Madame d'Épinay, letter to abbé Galiani, October 13, 1771: Galiani and Épinay, *Correspondance*, 2:210, quoted from *The Memoirs of Madame d'Épinay*, 3 vols. (Paris: Société des Bibliophiles; New York: Merrill & Baker, n.d.), 3:341.

36. Morellet, letter to Beccaria, July 1766: Morellet, *Lettres*, 1:56.

37. AAE, *Contrôle des étrangers*, vol. 3, report of November 11, 1774.

38. Galiani, letter to Madame d'Épinay, December 15, 1771, in Galiani and Épinay, *Correspondance*, 2:246.

39. Because he had been obliged to move between Saint-Ouen, La Chevrette, and Paris, Suard complains that he had become "a wandering Jew": "I went to dine yesterday at Saint-Ouen, from which I was taken to La Chevrette, from where I returned for supper at Saint-Ouen and to bed in Paris. Today I am going again to dine in Saint-Ouen, to spend the night at La Chevrette, and I shall return here Saturday": Suard, letter to his wife, 1773, Institut et Musée Voltaire, archives Suard, vol. 2.

40. Henri Lafon, *Espaces romanesques du XVIIIe siècle, 1670–1820: De Madame de Villedieu à Nodier* (Presses Universitaires de France, 1997), 150.

41. Mme de La Rochefoucauld, letter to Mme Suard, Institut et Musée Voltaire, archives Suard, vol. 4, fol 56, undated.

42. AAE, *Contrôle des étrangers*, vol. 5, report of June 30, 1775.

43. Duchesse d'Enville, letter to Horace Bénédict de Saussure, August 1, 1782: Bibliothèque publique universitaire de Genève, archives Saussure, vol. 223.

44. Morellet, letter to Jean-Baptiste Suard, August 11, 1772: Morellet, *Lettres*, 1:170.

45. Mercier, *Tableau de Paris*, ed. Bonnet, 1:857.

46. Morellet, letter to Turgot, October 12, 1775: Morellet, *Lettres*, 1:289.

47. Morellet, letter to Voltaire, October 21, 1775: Morellet, *Lettres*, 1:289.

48. Marmontel, *Mémoires*, 284; Morellet, letters to Lord Shelburne, July 17, 1778, and January 27, 1784: Morellet, *Lettres*, 1:385–87; 501–05.

49. Louis-Philippe, comte de Ségur, *Mémoires, ou, Souvenirs et anecdotes*, vols. 1–3 of Ségur, *Œuvres complètes*, 33 vols. in 34 pts. (Paris: A. Eymerie, 1824–26), 1:80; quoted from *Memoirs and Recollections of Count Ségur* (Boston: Wells and Lilly, 1825), 60.

50. Suard, letter to his wife, July 22, 1782: Institut et Musée Voltaire, Geneva, Archives Suard, vol. 2, fol. 59.

51. Karlheinz Stierle, *Mythos von Paris* (Munich and Vienna: Hanser, 1993); French translation by Marianne Rocher-Jacquin as *La Capitale des signes: Paris et son discours* (Paris: Éditions de la Maison des sciences de l'homme, 2001).

52. Mercier, *Tableau de Paris*, 1:857; quoted from *Paris Delineated, from the French of Mercier*, 2 vols. (London: H. D. Symonds, 1802), 1:70–71.

53. Roche, "Recherches sur la noblesse parisienne."

54. Hénaut, letter to Madame Du Deffand, July 13, 1742: Du Deffand, *Correspondance avec ses amis*, 1:48.

55. *Correspondance littéraire*, 9:241.

56. Diderot, letter to Sophie Volland, August 18, 1767: Diderot, *Correspondance*, 4:94–95.

57. Voltaire, letter to Madame Du Deffand, May 18, 1767: Du Deffand, *Cher Voltaire*, 223.

58. Oberkirch, *Mémoires*, 327.

59. Anne Martin-Fugier, *La vie élégante, ou, La formation du Tout-Paris (1815–1848)* (Paris: Fayard, 1990; Seuil, 1993), 100–12.

60. Franco Moretti, *Atlante del romanzo europeo, 800–1900* (1950); French translation, *Atlas du roman européen 1800–1900* (Paris: Seuil 2000), 99–114; English translation, *Atlas of the European Novel, 1800–1900* (London and New York: Verso, 1998).

61. Mercier, *Tableau de Paris*, 2:1211–13.

62. Mercier, *Tableau de Paris*, 2:1213.

63. Tilly, *Mémoires*, 1:102–103.

64. Tilly, *Mémoires*, 1:102–103.

65. Charles Duclos, *Considérations sur les mœurs de ce siècle (1751)*, ed. Carole Dornier (Paris: Honoré Champion, 2000), 71.

66. Duclos, *Considérations*, 71.

67. Mercier, *Tableau de Paris*.

68. Louis Antoine de Caraccioli, *L'Europe française* (Paris: Veuve Duchesne, 1776); Louis Réau, *L'Europe française au siècle des lumières* (Paris: A. Michel, 1938); René Pomeau, *L'Europe des Lumières: Cosmopolitisme et unité européenne au XVIIIe siècle* (Paris: Stock, 1966); Fumaroli, *When the World Spoke French*.

69. Daniel Roche, *Humeurs vagabondes: De la circulation des hommes et de l'utilité des voyages* (Paris: Fayard, 2003); Jean-François Dubost, "Les étrangers à Paris au XVIIIe siècle," in *La ville promise: Mobilité à Paris, fin XVIIe–début XIXe siècle*, ed. Daniel Roche, 221–88 (Paris: Fayard, 2000).

70. John Moore, *Lettres d'un voyageur anglois sur la France, la Suisse, et Allemagne*, 4 vols. (Geneva: Bardin, 1781–82), 1:64.

71. Madame d'Épinay, letter to Galiani, September 17, 1771: Galiani and Épinay, *Correspondance*, 2:198–99.

72. Walpole, letter to Lady Suffolk, September 20, 1765: Walpole, *Correspondence*, 31:48–50. For the impressions of Edward Gibbon, who visited Paris two years earlier, see Gibbon, *Memoirs*.

73. Walpole, letter to Gray, January 25, 1766: Walpole, *Correspondence*, 14, 2:148–57. Four years later Walpole was still known for this letter. Tronchin wrote to his daughter that he had dined with "Mr. Walpole, who wrote the famous letter of the king of Prussia to Jean-Jacques Rousseau": Tronchin, letter to his daughter, 1769, Bibliothèque publique universitaire de Genève, Archives Tronchin, 200, fol. 224. During this first visit, Walpole was received in forty different houses, and in particular in the most prestigious salons: those of Madame Du Deffand, the comtesse de Rochefort, the Choiseuls, Madame Geoffrin, the Maurepas, the duchesse d'Aiguillon, and the prince de Conti: "Paris Journals," in Walpole, *Correspondence*, 7, 5:257–417.

74. Madame Du Deffand, letter to Horace Walpole, November 12, 1777: Walpole, *Correspondence*, 4, 6:492.

75. William Beckford, letter, 1784: John Walter Oliver, *The Life of William Beckford* (London: Oxford University Press, 1932), 162. See also Lady Crewe, "Journal Kept at Paris," fol. 42.

76. AAE, *Contrôle des étrangers*, vol. 41, report of December 28, 1781.

77. Cited by Jadwiga Hoff, "Images des Français dans les mémoires et le manuels de savoir-vivre polonais," in *Mœurs et Images: Études d'imagologie européenne*, Actes du colloque, Paris, October 1995, ed. Alain Montandon, 23–26 (Clermont-Ferrand: Université Blaise Pascal, Centre de recherches sur les littératures modernes et contemporaines, 1997), 23.

78. AAE, *Contrôle des étrangers*, esp. vol. 36, reports of November 24 and December 15, 1780, and vol. 37, report of January 12, 1787.

79. AAE, *Contrôle des étrangers*. Several reports are dedicated to them: vol. 16, July 25, 1777; vol. 30, July 9, 1779; vol. 38, March 31, 1781.

80. AAE, *Contrôle des étrangers*, vol. 36, report of October 13, 1786.

81. AAE, *Contrôle des étrangers*, report of November 11, 1786.

82. On Lady Dunmore's two stays in Paris, see AAE, *Contrôle des étrangers*, vol. 12, fol. 66, report of October 4, 1776; vol. 65, fol. 146, report of September 28, 1787.

83. AAE, *Contrôle des étrangers*, vol. 3, report of November 25, 1774.

84. AAE, *Contrôle des étrangers*, vol. 6, report of July 21, 1775.

85. Many members of the Galitzine family visited Paris. When he arrived there in 1758, Sergei Galitzine noted that there were five Galitzines in Paris! See Wladimir Berelowitch, "La France dans le 'grand tour' des nobles russes de la seconde moitié du XVIIe siècle," *Cahiers du monde russe et soviétiques* 34, nos. 1–2 (January–June 1993): 193–210. The Galitzines mentioned here are Wladimir Galitzine and his wife, Natalia Petrovna, whose arrival is noted in the report for September 17, 1784, and departure in that of March 12, 1790: AAE, *Contrôle des étrangers*, vol. 76, fol. 69.

86. Mercier, *Tableau de Paris*, 1:387.

87. Dubost, "Les étrangers à Paris," 236, 242.

88. AAE, *Contrôle des étrangers*, vol. 23, report of July 31, 1778.

89. J. G. Herder, *Journal meiner Reise im Jahr 1769*, cited in Thomas Grosser, "Les voyageurs allemands en France," in *Deutsche in Frankreich: Franzozen in Deutschland (1715–1789)*, ed. Jean Mondot, Jean-Marie Valentin, and Jürgen Voss, 209–37 (Sigmaringen: Thorbecke, 1992), esp. p. 213.

90. Denis Fonvizin, letter to Piotr Ivanovitch Panin, June 25, 1778: Denis Ivanovitch Fonvizin, *Lettres de France (1777–1778)*, trans. Henri Grosse, ed. Jacques Proust and Piotr Zaborov (Paris: CNRS; Oxford: Voltaire Foundation, 1995), 137.

91. Fonvizin, letter to his sister, April 30, 1778: Fonvizin, *Lettres*, 126.

92. Tilly, *Mémoires*, 189.

93. Madame Necker, letter to Gibbon, September 30, 1776: British Library, Gibbon Papers, ADD. 34 886, fols. 89–90.

94. See, for example, Walpole's letter to Lady Hervey, October 3, 1765: Walpole, *Correspondence*, 31:50–58.

95. François-Antoine Hartig, *Lettres sur la France, l'Angleterre et l'Italie par le Comte François de Hartig, chambellan de sa majesté impériale et royale* (Geneva, 1785), 16.

96. Grosser, "Voyageurs allemands," 216–17.

97. Anonymous, *Interessante emerkungen eine Reisenen durch Frankreich und Italien* (Leipzig, 1793), 81ff.; quoted in Grosser, "Voyageurs allemands."

98. Mme Du Deffand, "Journal": Walpole, *Correspondence*, 6:421–61.

99. Without belonging to the upper echelons of society, the best-known physicians were warmly received there: see Victorine de Chastenay, *Mémoires (1771–1815)*, ed. Guy Chaussinand-Nogaret, 2 vols (Paris: Plon, 1896; Paris: Librairie

académique Perrin, 1987), 38. The marquis de Mirabeau complained that physicians were judged only on their art of bowing: letter to Mme de Rochefort, October 11, 1759: Musée Arbaud, Archives Mirabeau, vol. 34, fol 348.

100. Madame Geoffrin, "Connaissances et visites à faire," in the notebook titled "Adresses de la province et de Paris," *Carnets*, Private archives of the comte de Bruce. Exceptions include Abbé Desfontaines, Foncemagne, the Neckers, and Madame Dupin. Also mentioned are the duc and duchesse de Bouillon, the prince and princesse de Beauvau, the comte and comtesse de Noailles, the princesse de Monaco, the comtesse de La Marck, the marquise de Brézé, the Duke and Duchess Fitz-James, the comtesse de Narbonne, the prince and princesse de Poix, Madame de Courcelles, the marquise de Béthune, the vicomtesse de Durfort, the archbishop of Toulouse (Loménie de Brienne), the marquis de Félino, the marquis and marquise de Sérens, the Rohan-Chabots, the marquise de Flavacourt, the marquise de Castries, the vicomte and vicomtesse de Clermont-Tonnerre, the Marquis and Marchioness Fitz-James, the Duke and Duchess of Berwick, Madame de Blot, and Count Schomberg.

101. "Paris Journals": Walpole, *Correspondence*, 7:5.

102. See Madame Geoffrin, letter to Marmontel, July 29, 1769, in which she speaks of her "friendship for that amiable and respectable lady": Bibliothèque nationale de France, Département des MSS, *Nouvelles acquisitions françaises*, 4748.

103. Madame Geoffrin, letter to Madame de La Ferté-Imbault, June 8, 1766: Bibliothèque nationale de France, Département des MSS, *Nouvelles acquisitions françaises*, 4748.

104. AAE, *Contrôle des étrangers*, vol. 4, report of January 13, 1775; vol. 7, report of December 1, 1775. This report notes that on November 24, 1775 "Mme Geoffrin gave a dinner comprising in part the society of the duc de Rohan, which is made up of the ambassador of Sweden, the comte and comtesse de Benthein, the archbishop of Lyon, the comte de Montazet, his brother, Mmes the marquises and countess de Cossé, the duchesse de Caylus, Mme de La Ferté-Imbault, the marquise de Brezé, the marquise de Pont, the wife of the minister of the King of Prussia, M. and Mme de Blondel, etc."

105. Joseph Marie Vien, "Mémoires," in Thomas W. Gaehtgens and Jacques Lugand, *Joseph-Marie Vien: Peintre du roi (1716–1809)*, 287–320 (Paris: Arthéna, 1988).

106. Jean de Viguerie, "Salons," in Viguerie, *Histoire et Dictionnaire du temps des Lumières* (Paris: Robert Laffont, 1995), 1363–65.

107. Madame Geoffrin, letter to Martin Folkes, January 16, 1743: Archives of the Royal Society (London), MS 250, fol. III, 13.

108. See, in particular, William Doyle, *The Parlement of Bordeaux and the End of the Old Regime, 1771–1790* (New York: St. Martin's, 1974); Robert A. Schneider, *Public Life in Toulouse, 1463–1789: From Municipal Republic to Cosmopolitan City* (Ithaca and London: Cornell University Press, 1989); Olivier Chaline, *Godart de Balbeuf: Le Parlement, le Roi et les Normands* (Luneray: Bertout, 1996); Clarisse Coulomb, "Les Parlementaires de Grenoble au XVIIIe siècle," thèse d'histoire, Université de Besançon, 2001.

109. Charles Pougens, *Mémoirs et souvenirs commencés par lui et terminés par Madame de Saint-Léon* (Paris: H. Fournier, 1834), 51.

110. Notes of inspector d'Hémery : Bibliothèque nationale, Département des manuscrits, *Nouvelles acquisitions françaises*, 10783.

111. Charles Collé, *Journal historique inédit pour les années 1761 et 1762*, ed. Adolphe van Bever and Gabriel Boissy (Paris: Mercure de France, 1911), 1:298–99.

112. The notebook of the "visits of Mme Dupin" published by the comte de Villeneuve-Guibert contains 223 names and addresses that reflect almost all of Paris "society": Gaston, comte de Villeneuve-Guibert, *Le portefeuille de Madame Dupin* (Paris: Calmann-Lévi, 1884). See also Rousseau, *Confessions*, ed. Gagnebin and Raymond, 292. Madame Dupin's salon had an extraordinarily long life, lasting until the Revolution.

113. Durand, *Fermiers généraux*, 551–70.

114. Madame Suard, letter to her husband, 1773: Institut et Musée Voltaire, Archives Suard, vol. 1, fol. 6; Marmontel, *Mémoires*, 168, 228–29, 248–49.

115. François Joseph Pérlisse, duc des Cars, *Mémoires du duc des Cars*, 2 vols. (Paris: Plon, 1890), 2:342.

116. Durand, *Fermiers généraux*, 240.

117. Durand, *Fermiers généraux*, 275ff.

118. This was according to a police informer: see Durand, *Fermiers généraux*, 255, 517.

119. Oberkirch, *Mémoires*, 211.

120. Bombelles, *Journal*, January 11, 1783, 1:189.

121. Louis de Narbonne was also a ladies' man and the lover of Madame de Staël. During the Revolutionary period he was a representative of the liberal aristocracy and, briefly, minister of war in 1792.

122. Necker, *Mélanges*, 1:141.

123. Pascal Briost, Hervé Drévillon, and Pierre Serna, *Croiser le fer: Violence et culture de l'épée dans la France moderne, XVIe–XVIIIe siècle* (Paris: Champ Vallon, 2002).

124. Roger Chartier, "Georges Dandin, ou, Le social en représentation," *Annales, Histoire, Sciences sociales* 2 (March–April 1994): 277–309; reprinted in Chartier, *Culture écrite et société: L'ordre des livres, XIVe–XVIIIe siècle*, 155–204 (Paris: Albin Michel, 1996).

125. Mercier, *Tableau de Paris*, 2:217.

126. Charles Duclos, *Œuvres complètes*, 10 vols. (Paris: Delaunay, 1806), 7:82.

127. Chamfort, *Maximes, pensées, cractères*, 193.

128. Jean le Rond d'Alembert, *Essai sur la société des gens de lettres et des grands, sur la réputation, sur les mécènes, et sur les récompenses littéraires* (1752), in *Œuvres de d'Alembert*, 5 vols. (Paris: A. Belin, 1821–22), 4:337–73.

129. D'Alembert, *Essai sur la société*, 4:357–58.

130. D'Alembert, *Essai sur la société*, 4:357–58.

131. Maréchal de Richelieu, letter to Madame Favart, August 30, 176*, in Charles-Simon Favart, *Mémoires et correspondance littéraires, dramatiques, et anecdotiques*, 3 vols. (Paris: Collin, 1808; Geneva: Slatkine, 1970), 3:91.

132. Diderot, letter to M ***, September 1776: Diderot, *Correspondance*, 14:224.

133. Daniel Gordon resolves this question in a radical manner by asserting the complete autonomy of salon sociability in relation to its social environment: Gordon, *Citizens without Sovereignty*, 94–95.

134. D'Alembert, *Essai sur la société*, 4:337–73.

135. Madame Du Deffand, letter to Horace Walpole, May 18, 1766: Walpole, *Correspondence*, 3, 1:43.

136. Jean-Baptiste Suard, "Des sociétés de Paris," in *Mélanges de littérature*, 5 vols. (Paris: Dentu, 1803–1804), vol. 5, *Fragments de morale*, 120.

137. Suard, "Des sociétés de Paris."

138. Marcel Proust, *Sodome et Gomorrhe, 2, 1*, in *À la recherche du temps perdu*, 4 vols. (Paris: Gallimard, 1989), 3:62.

139. Denis Richet, "Autour des origines idéologiques lointaines de la Révolution: Élite et despotisme," *Annales E.S.C.*, 24, no. 1 (January–February 1969), reprinted in Richet, *De la Réforme à la Révolution: Études sur la France moderne* (Paris: Aubier, 1991), 389–410. See also the critique of Michel Vovelle, "L'Élite, ou le mensonge des mots," *Annales E.S.C.* 29, no. 1 (1974): 49–72. The most determined defender of the thesis of a fusion of the elites is by Guy Chaussinand-Nogaret, in *La noblesse en France and Histoire des élites en France du XVIe au XXe siècle* (Paris: Tallandier, 1991). Mathieu Marraud takes roughly the same position in *Noblesse de Paris*.

140. Jay M. Smith, *The Culture of Merit: Nobility, Royal Service, and the Making of Absolute Monarchy in France, 1600–1789* (Ann Arbor: University of Michigan Press, 1996).

141. Alexis de Tocqueville, *The Old Régime and the Revolution*, trans. Alan S. Kahan, ed. François Furet and Françoise Mélonio, 2 vols. (Chicago: University of Chicago Press, 1998), 1:152.

142. Julie de Lespinasse, letter to Condorcet, June 3, 1769: Lespinasse, *Lettres à Condorcet (1769–1776)*, ed. Jean Noël Pascal (Paris: Desjonquères, 1990), 25.

143. *Dictionnaire de l'Académie françoise*, 1798, s. v. "Monde."

144. Elias, *Court Society*, 103.

145. Marquise de La Tour du Pin, *Mémoires d'une femme de quarante ans*, 76; quoted from *Memoirs: Laughing and Dancing Our Way to the Precipice*, trans. Felice Harcourt (London: Harvill Press, 1999), 52.

146. Stéphanie Félicité du Crest, comtesse de Genlis, *Mémoires inédits sur le XVIIIe siècle et la révolution française depuis 1756 jusqu'à nos jours*, 10 vols. (Paris: Ladvocat, 1825), 2:125; in English translation as *Memoirs of the Countess of Genlis*, 2 vols. (London: Henry Colburn, 1825–26).

147. See *Littératures classiques* 22 (autumn 1994), special issue dedicated to "La notion de monde au XVIIe siècle," in particular, the article by Marc Fumaroli, "Monde, mode, moderne," 7–23.

148. Corneille, *Nicomède*, act III, scene 8, v. 1113.

149. Furetière, *Dictionnaire universel*, s.v. "Monde."

150. Pierre Richelet, *Dictionnaire français, contenant les mots et les choses et plusieurs remarques nouvelles sur la langue française*, Genève, Widerhold, 1680, s v. "Monde."

151. Nicholas Cronk, "The Epicurean Spirit: Champagne and the Defence of Poetry in Voltaire's *Le Mondain*," *Studies on Voltaire and the Eighteenth Century* 371 (1999): 53–80.

152. Charles-Maurice, duc de Talleyrand-Périgord, *Mémoires*, ed. Duc de Broglie, 5 vols. (Paris: Calmann-Lévy, 1891–92), 1:46–48; quoted from *Memoirs of the Prince de Talleyrand*, trans. Raphaël Ledos de Beaufort, 3 vols. (London: Grifffith Farran Okeden and Welsh, 1891; facsimile reprint, Whitefish, MT: Kessinger, 2007), 1:35–36.

153. Mme de La Ferté-Imbault, "Anecdotes du règne de Louis XV": Archives nationales, 508 AP 38.

154. Madame Du Deffand, letter to Horace Walpole, June 1, 1766: Walpole, *Correspondence*, 3, 1:59.

155. "Mémoires intéressants de Mme la marquise de La Ferté-Imbault": Archives nationales, 508 AP 38, Madame de la Ferté-Imbault papers.

156. She was so proud of these portraits, that they figured among the few dates in her life that she thought worthy of inclusion her notebooks: "Différentes choses

dont je veux garder le souvenir plus différentes choses dont je veux me souvenir des prix": Voltaire Foundation (Oxford), private archives of the comte de Bruce.

157. Galiani, letter to Madame d'Épinay, March 23, 1771: Galiani and Épinay, *Correspondance*, 2:76.

158. This episode occupies nearly one-half of the autobiographical notes mentioned in n. 156.

159. Madame Geoffrin, letter to Stanisław August Poniatowski, December 7, 1764: Geoffrin, *Correspondance du roi Stanislas-Auguste Poniatovski*, 130.

160. See below Chapter 6, 219–20.

161. Poniatowski, *Mémoires*, I, 568.

162. Marietta Martin, *Une française à Varsovie en 1766: Madame Geoffrin chez le roi de Pologne, Stanislas-Auguste*, Centre d'études polonaises de Paris, Mémoire no. 1 (Paris: Bibliothèque Polonaise, 1936).

163. Those letters, as well as the gazette articles that were based on them, form the only source on this voyage for Madame Geoffrin's biographers. Ségur, in particular, cites them and paraphrases them at length without casting any doubt on the tale they tell and without even supposing that Madame Geoffrin might have other motives than those of friendship and happiness: Ségur, *Royaume de la Rue Saint-Honoré*, 254, 266.

164. Madame Geoffrin, letter to Madame de La Ferté-Imbault, June 12, 1766: "Autographes de Mme Geoffrin et de Mme de la Ferté-Imbault," Bibliothèque nationale, Département des MSS, 4748.

165. Madame Geoffrin, letter to the younger Boutin, June 12, 1766: "Autographes de Mme Geoffrin et de Mme de la Ferté-Imbault."

166. Madame Geoffrin, letter to Madame de La Ferté-Imbault, June 30, 1766: "Autographes de Mme Geoffrin et de Mme de la Ferté-Imbault."

167. Madame Geoffrin, letter to Gentil-Bernard, undated: "Autographes de Mme Geoffrin et de Mme de la Ferté-Imbault."

168. "Journal de l'année 1766": anonymous manuscript, Bibliothèque historique de la Ville de Paris, Ms 679.

169. *Mémoires secrets*, July 12, 1766, 3:49. For an announcement of her return, see *Mémoires secrets*, November 16, 3:99.

170. Madame Geoffrin, letter to Boutin, June 12, 1766: "Autographes de Mme Geoffrin et de Mme de la Ferté-Imbault."

171. Madame Geoffrin, letter to the marquise de La Ferté-Imbault, June 24, 1766: "Autographes de Mme Geoffrin et de Mme de la Ferté-Imbault."

172. Madame Geoffrin, letter to Marmontel, July 30, 1766: "Autographes de Mme Geoffrin et de Mme de la Ferté-Imbault."

173. Manuscripts left by Julie de Lespinasse, vol. 2, fols. 403–10. Reproduction of the commonplace books of Julie de Lespinasse (Oxford: Voltaire Foundation, Taylor Institution, xxxx)

174. Morellet took care to delete the reference to *tapage* (noise, rumpus), which seemed to him to reflect poorly on Madame Geoffrin's modesty. See Morellet, d'Alembert, and Thomas, *Éloges de Mme Geoffrin*.

175. *Correspondance littéraire*, November 1766, 7:169.

176. Mariette, letter to Paciaudi, November 8, 1766: Anne-Claude, comte de Caylus, *Correspondance inédite du comte de Caylus avec le P. Paciaudi, théatin (1757–1765), suivie de celles de l'abbé Barthélemy et de P. Mariette avec le même*, ed. Charles Nisard, 2 vols. (Paris: Imprimerie nationale, 1877), 2:343.

177. Madame Geoffrin, letter to Madame Necker, summer 1766: Bibliothèque publique universitaire de Genève, Archives Horace-Bénédict Saussure, MS suppl. 717, Mme Necker to Mme Reverdill, fol. 15. See also the letter of July 15.

178. *Correspondance littéraire*, November 1766, 7:168.

179. Collé, *Journal historique*, 1:176.

180. Collé, *Journal historique*, 1:177. The two letters are reproduced on pp. 177–81.

181. Madame Geoffrin, letter to the comtesse de Noailles, 1771: Archives nationales, 508 AP 34: Mme Geoffrin.

182. La Harpe, *Letters to the Shuvalovs*, 58.

CHAPTER 3

1. Gordon, *Citizens without Sovereignty*, 127.

2. Robert Darnton, "A Police Inspector Sorts His Files: The Anatomy of the Republic of Letters," in *The Great Cat Massacre and Other Episodes in French Cultural History* (New York: Basic Books, 1984), 145–90. See also Eric Walter, "Les auteurs et le champ littéraire," in *Histoire de l'édition française*, ed. Henri-Jean Martin and Roger Chartier, 4 vols. (Paris: Promodis, 1982–84), vol. 2: *Le livre triomphant, 1660–1830*, 383–99; Roche, *Républicains des lettres*; Roger Chartier, "The Man of Letters," in *Enlightenment Portraits*, trans. Lydia G. Cochrane (Chicago: University of Chicago Press, 1997), 142–89; Didier Masseau, *L'Invention de l'intellectuel dans l'Europe du XVIIIe siècle* (Paris: Presses Universitaires de France, 1994); Gregory S. Brown, "After the Fall: The *Chute* of a Play, *Droits d'Auteur*, and Literary Property in the Old Regime," *French Historical Studies* 22, no. 4 (1999), 465–91; Geoffrey Turnovsky, *Authorship and Modernity in the Old Regime* (Philadelphia: University of Pennsylvania Press, 2009).

3. Madame d'Épinay, letter to Galiani, June 30, 1770: Galiani and d'Épinay, *Correspondance*, 1:201.

4. Jean-François Georgel, *Mémoires pour servir à l'histoire des événements de la fin du XVIIIe siècle*, 6 vols. (Paris, 1817), I:221.

5. Amélie Suard, *Essais de mémoires*, 68.

6. Morellet, *Mémoires inédites*, 8.

7. Morellet, in Morellet, d'Alembert, and Thomas, *Éloges de Mme Geoffrin*, 26.

8. Catherine Duprat, *Le Temps des philanthropes, vol. 1, La Philanthropie parisienne, des Lumières à la monarchie de Juillet* (Paris: Éditions du CTHS, 1993).

9. *Correspondance littéraire, philosophique et critique par Grimm, Diderot, Raynal, Meister*, ed. Maurice Tourneux, 16 vols. (Paris: Garnier, 1877–82), January 1777, 11:407.

10. Gidéon Tallement des Réaux, *Historiettes*, ed. Antoine Adam (Paris: Gallimard, Pléïade, 1990), 1:444.

11. For a more general presentation of the place of the gift in French society in the early modern era, see Natalie Zemon Davis, *The Gift in Sixteenth-Century France* (Madison: University of Wisconsin Press, 2000), in French translation as *Essai sur le don dans la France du XVIe siècle* (Paris: Seuil, 2002).

12. Amélie Suard, *Essais de mémoires*, 46. The anecdote was also noted by Naigeon in *Le Journal de Paris*, June 12, 1789.

13. Marivaux received 3,000 livres and Saurin 2,000: Masseau, *Invention de l'intellectuel*, 94. On Turpin, who wrote "biting verse," see Inspector d'Hémery, "Turpin," Bibliothèque nationale, Département des manuscrits, *Nouvelles acquisitions françaises*, 10781–83, where d'Hémery notes that "Helvétius protects

him and has given him a pension." See also the document setting up a lifetime income (*rente viagère*) for Saurin: Archives nationales, Minutier central, Étude LVI, vol. 10, July 30, 1751.

14. *Correspondance littéraire*, March 1770, 8:471.

15. Amélie Suard, *Essais de mémoires*, 71. See also Jeanne Carriat, "Meister," in Jean Sgard (dir.), *Dictionnaire des journalistes* (Oxford: Voltaire Foundation, 1999), 2:703.

16. Madame d'Épinay, letter to Galiani, November 30, 1771: Galiani and d'Épinay, *Correspondance*, 2:236.

17. "Family accounts," constitutions of income in favor of Morellet (January 21, 1772), d'Alembert (March 9, 1773), and Thomas (March 24, 1775): Archives nationales, 508 AP 36. The income was arranged through Jean Joseph de Laborde, to whom Madame Geoffrin paid the money (respectively, 15,000 livres, 60,000 livres, and 15,000 livres), and who promised to pay the installments to Madame Geoffrin and the secondary beneficiaries, then to the latter alone after her death. Madame Geoffrin notes on the back of the income contract for d'Alembert: "D'Alembert receives the income. I will come after him." Copies of the *rente* contracts to d'Alembert can also be found in the minutes of the study by maître Diraudeau: Archives nationales, Minutier central, Étude CXVII, 853, April 20, 1771, and 856, January 21, 1772. These income payments were made public after Madame Geoffrin's death by André Morellet in his *Portrait de Madame Geoffrin* (Amsterdam; Paris: Chez Pissot, 1777), where the sums mentioned are slightly different. It was Morellet who noted the 1760 *rente* to d'Alembert: Morellet, d'Alembert, and Thomas, *Éloges de Mme Geoffrin*, 30–35.

18. Morellet, d'Alembert, and Thomas, *Éloges de Mme Geoffrin*, 32.

19. Viala, *Naissance de l'écrivain*, 51–84; Daniel Roche, "Les modèles économiques du mécenat," in *Les Républicains des lettres*, 51–84; Christian Jouhaud and Hélène Merlin, "Mécènes, patrons et clients: Les méditations textuelles comme pratiques clientélaires au XVIIe siècle," *Terrain* 21 (October 1993): 47–62.

20. Barbara Scott, "Mme Geoffrin: A Patron and Friend of Artists," *Apollo* (February 1967): 98–103.

21. Charlotte Guichard, *Les amateurs d'art à Paris au XVIIIe siècle* (Seyssel: Champ Vallon, 2008); see also Nathalie Heinich, *Du peintre à l'artiste: Artisans et académiciens à l'âge classique* (Paris: Éditions de Minuit, 1993).

22. Vien, "Mémoires," esp. pp. 302, 310.

23. Inspector d'Hémery, "Geoffrin": Bibliothèque nationale française, Département des MSS, NAF 10781.

24. Cochin, letter to Madame de La Ferté-Imbault, October 28, 1777: Archives nationales, 508 AP 34.

25. Madame Geoffrin, letter to Stanisław August Poniatowski, March 13, 1766: Geoffrin, *Correspondance du roi Stanislas-Auguste Poniatovski*, 219.

26. Marmontel, *Mémoires*, 135.

27. Amélie Suard, *Essais de mémoires*, 96. See Darnton, "High Enlightenment and the Low-Life of Literature." For a different view of Suard's career, see Gordon, *Citizens without Sovereignty*, chap. 4.

28. Amélie Suard, *Essais de mémoires*, 116.

29. Prince de Beauvau, letter of June 16, 1772: Institut et Musée Voltaire, Geneva, archives Suard, vol. 4, Letters received, Suard, fol. 14.

30. To help in the election of Marmontel to the Académie française, Madame Geoffrin worked to reconcile him with Hénault, with whom his quarrel was superficial: Marmontel, *Mémoires*, 258–59.

31. Bombelles, *Journal*, March 29, 1785, 2:43–44.

32. Montesquieu, letter to Madame Du Deffand, September 13, 1752: Du Deffand, *Correspondance complète*, 1:145.

33. Formont, letter to Madame Du Deffand, December 4, 1754: Du Deffand, *Correspondance avec ses amis*, 1:224.

34. Duchesse de Choiseul, letter to Madame Du Deffand, n.d.: Du Deffand, *Correspondance avec ses amis*, 1:15.

35. Madame Geoffrin, letter to Gabriel Cramer, August 18, 1748, Bibliothèque publique universitaire de Genève, D. O. Geoffrin.

36. Madame Geoffrin, letter to Gabriel Cramer, June 26, 1750: Tourneux, "Madame Geoffrin et les éditions expurgées," 53.

37. Duchesse d'Enville, letter to Georges-Louis Lesage, November 15, 1768: Bibliothèque publique universitaire de Genève, Papiers Georges-Louis Lesage, Ms sup. 512.

38. Bibliothèque publique universitaire de Genève, Ms sup. 512.

39. Archives des Affaires étrangères, *Contrôle des étrangers*, vol. 4, report of March 17, 1775, and Madame Du Deffand, letter to Horace Walpole, March 10, 1775 (addition of Monday, March 13): Walpole, *Correspondence*, 6, 4:169.

40. Amélie Suard, letter to Condorcet, October 1775: Institut et Musée Voltaire (Geneva), Archives Suard, vol. 1, fol. 75. See also Condorcet's letter to Madame Suard (October 1775): *Correspondance inédite de Condorcet et Mme Suard*, ed. Elisabeth Badinter (Paris: Fayard, 1988), 175.

41. Madame de Graffigny had visited Cirey in 1738. She was accused by Madame Du Châtelet of having circulated the manuscript of *La Pucelle*. From that moment on, they became irreconcilable enemies.

42. The dossier of Crébillon's successive refusals and Madame de Graffigny's disillusions can be found in the latter's correspondence for the year 1744: Françoise de Graffigny, *Correspondance*, 7 vols (Oxford: Voltaire Foundation, 1985–2003), vols. 5 and 6. See also Vera L. Grayson, "Trois Lettres inédites de Crébillon fils à Mme de Graffigny," *Dix-huitième siècle* 28 (1996): 223–28.

43. Morellet, *Mémoires*, 136.

44. Jouhaud, *Pouvoirs de la littérature*. See also Nicolas Schapira, *Un professionnel des lettres au XVIIe siècle: Valentin Conrart, une histoire sociale* (Seyssel: Champ Vallon, 2003).

45. Marmontel, who lodged at Versailles for five years (1753–58), continued to frequent the Parisian salons. When he left the court, he went directly to Madame Geoffrin's.

46. Marmontel, *Mémoires*, 172.

47. Marmontel, *Mémoires*, 252–53. See the commentary of Roger Chartier, "Patronage et dédicace," in *Culture écrite et société: L'ordre des livres, XIVe–XVIIIe siècle*, 81–106 (Paris: Albin Michel, 1996), esp. 91–92.

48. Suard, letter to his wife, May 6, 1766: Institut et Musée Voltaire (Geneva), Archives Suard, vol. 2.

49. Amélie Suard, letter to her husband, May 15, 1766: Institut et Musée Voltaire (Geneva), Archives Suard, vol. 1.

50. Boufflers, letter to William Bentinck, Duke of Portland, June 24, 1764: British Library, Bentinck correspondence. Egerton 1749, vol. 5, fol. 286.

51. Bentinck, letter to the comtesse de Boufflers, July 6, 1764: British Library, Bentinck correspondence. Egerton 1749, vol. 5, fol. 296.

52. This is why the discourses in praise of Madame Geoffrin published at her death by Morellet, d'Alembert, and Thomas are exceptional texts, in that their

publication in print broke with worldly practices to rejoin those of a more classic relationship to patronage. This situation can be explained by the context of Madame Geoffrin's death: a veritable battle had ranged around the bed of the old woman when her daughter refused entry to the philosophes. And the memory of Madame Geoffrin and her salon was attacked by Rutlidge in *Le Bureau d'esprit* (1776), a biting satire aimed in particular at men of letters. The authors' praise was thus a public response to a public attack.

53. Théodore Tronchin, letter to his daughter, September 4, 1765: Bibliothèque publique universitaire (Geneva), Archives Tronchin, vol. 200, fol. 156.

54. La Harpe, *Letters to the Shuvalovs*, 58.

55. Marmontel, *Mémoires*, 202.

56. *Mémoires secrets pour servir à l'histoire de la République des lettres en France depuis 1762 jusqu'à nos jours*, 31 vols. (London. 1777–89), January 18, 1773, 6: 260.

57. Madame de La Ferté-Imbault, letter about her mother, March 28, 1777: Archives nationales, 508 AP 37.

58. Denis Diderot, letter to Madame d'Épinay, October 1767: Diderot, *Correspondance*, 7:155–56.

59. Diderot, letter to Sophie Volland, September 19, 1767: Diderot, *Correspondance*, 7:130.

60. Marmontel, letter to the marquise de Créqui, May 1766: Jean-François Marmontel, *Correspondance*, ed. John Renwick, 2 vols. (Clermont-Ferrand: Institut d'Études du Massif Central, 1974), 1:1–119.

61. Laurence Sterne, letter to David Garrick, January 31, 1762: *Letters of Laurence Sterne*, ed. Lewis Perry Curtis (Oxford: Clarendon Press, 1935), 151; quoted in Diderot, *Correspondance*, 4:32.

62. Collé, *Journal et mémoires*, 1:433.

63. Favart, *Mémoires et correspondance*, 2:6.

64. Collé, *Journal et mémoires*, 3:36.

65. Bourdieu, *Le Sens pratique*, Paris: Editions de Minuit, 1980.

66. Jean-Louis Briquet, "Des amitiés paradoxales: Échanges intéressés et morale du désintéressement dans les relations de clientèle," *Politix* 45 (1999): 7–20.

67. Here again, an analysis of this vocabulary as an enticement dictated by strategies that were totally foreign to it prevails at times. It does, for example, in Sharon Kettering, *Patronage in Sixteenth- and Seventeenth-Century France* (Aldershot: Ashgate, 2002), 139–58.

68. Mably, letter to Madame Dupin and a letter to an unknown correspondent: François Moureau, "Condillac et Mably, dix lettres inédites ou retrouvées," *Dix-huitième siècle* 23 (1991): 193–200; the letter to Madame Dupin is cited in a note on p. 200. See also Aldo Maffey, "Intorno agli inediti del Mably," *Studi francesi* 4 (1960), 32.

69. Moureau, "Condillac et Mably," note 22.

70. Duclos, "Sur la reconnaissance et l'ingratitude," in *Considérations*, 226–33.

71. Jacques Delille, "Ode à la bienfaisance," *Œuvres*, ed. Pierre François Tissot, 10 vols. (Paris: Furne, 1832–33), 10:240–45, esp. p. 244. Delille returns to the theme in an epistle entitled "Parallèle de la bienfiasance et de la reconnaissance, écrite pour la comtesse Potocka qui avait offert une paire de bracelets à la belle-soeur du poète": *Œuvres*, 10:327–30.

72. Jouhaud, *Pouvoirs de la littérature*.

73. I am borrowing the notion of "topic" quite freely; it comes from the rhetorical tradition and from the sociology of Luc Boltanski and Laurent Thévenot,

De la justification: les économies de la grandeur (Paris: Gallimard, 1991), trans. Catherine Porter as *On Justification: Economies of Worth* (Princeton: Princeton University Press, 2006); and Luc Boltanski, *Distant Suffering: Morality, Media and Politics* (Cambridge, UK: Cambridge University Press, 1999). What I mean is a group of coherent arguments and values that support moral positions and are utilized for self-justification.

74. See Dinah Ribard, "D'Alembert et la 'société des gens de lettres': Utilité et autonomie des lettres dans la polémique entre Rousseau et d'Alembert," *Littératures classiques* 37 (1999): 229–45.

75. Jean Marie Goulemot and Daniel Oster, *Gens de lettres, écrivains et bohèmes: L'imaginaire littéraire, 1630–1900* (Paris: Minerve, 1992), chap. 4.

76. The notion of *honnêteté* (a term with no immediate English equivalent, and that involved honor, integrity, and civility) has long been minimized by historians of the eighteenth century. Gregory S. Brown has demonstrated its full importance for the identity and the status of men of letters in *A Field of Honor: Writers, Court Culture and Public Theater in French Literary Life from Racine to the Revolution* (New York: Columbia University Press, 2002), electronic edition, http://www.Gutenberg-e.org.

77. Voltaire, "Questions sur l'Encyclopédie" (1770), in *Œuvres complètes de Voltaire*, 52 vols. (Paris: Garnier, 1877–85), 1:496–501. See also Roger Chartier, "Trajectoires et tensions culturelles de l'Ancien Régime," in *Histoire de la France, choix culturels et mémoires*, ed. André Bourguière and Jacques Revel, 29–142 (Paris: Seuil, 2000), esp. pp. 123–24.

78. *Encylopédie*, s.v. "Gens de lettres," 7:599–600, quoted from "Men of Letters" (Voltaire), in Denis Diderot, *The Encyclopedia: Selections*, ed. and trans. Stephen J. Gendzier (New York: Harper & Row, 1967), 166–68, esp. p. 168.

79. *Encyclopédie*, s.v. "Gens de lettres"; Diderot, *Encyclopedia: Selections*, 168.

80. Voltaire, letters to Helvétius, January 2, 1761, in Voltaire, *Correspondence*, ed. Theodore Besterman, 50 vols. (Oxford: Voltaire Foundation, 1968–77), XXII:435–36.

81. Voltaire, letter to Helvétius, October 27, 1760, in Voltaire, *Correspondence*. XXII:248–49.

82. Voltaire, letter to Madame Du Deffand, July 14, 1760, in Voltaire, *Correspondence*, XXI:465–66.

83. *Correspondance littéraire*, February 1756, 3:164.

84. *Correspondance littéraire*, 4:159. In this manner, Grimm saw in d'Alembert's *Essai sur la société des gens de lettres et des Grands* nothing but "the impudent boasting of a schoolboy," and he reproached him for contrasting the "Greats" and men of letters: "That quarrel that one claims subsists between people of the court and men of letters should never be an object of meditation for a philosopher": *Correspondance littéraire*, February 1759, 4:159.

85. *Correspondance littéraire*, February 1767, 7:215–18; October 1770, 9:129.

86. *Correspondance littéraire*, 9:122–30.

87. Darnton, *Bohême littéraire et révolution*, 9.

88. Eric Francalanza, *Jean-Baptiste-Antoine Suard, journaliste des Lumières* (Paris: Honoré Champion, 2002), 215–317.

89. Jean-Baptiste Suard, *Réponse au discours prononcé dans l'Académie française le mardi XV juin, MDCCLXXXIV à la réception de Monsieur le Marquis de Montesquiou* (Paris: Demonville, 1784), 29.

90. *Encyclopédie*, s.v. "Dictionnaire de langues."

91. Stéphanie Félicité du Crest, comtesse de Genlis, *Adèle et Théodore, ou, Lettres sur l'éducation*, 3 vols. (Paris: Lambert, 1782), 127, quoted from *Adelaide and Theodore, or, Letters on Education*, trans. P. Wogan, 3 vols. (1796), 2:86; ed. Gillian Dow, 2 vols. (London and Brookfield, VT: Pickering & Chatto, 2007).

92. That convergence was already in operation at the end of the seventeenth century: see Ann Goldgar, *Impolite Learning: Conduct and Community in the Republic of Letters, 1680–1730* (New Haven: Yale University Press, 1995), 237ff.

93. Collé, *Journal et mémoires*, 1:271–72, note added in 1780.

94. Bernard Joseph Saurin, *Œuvres choisies* (Paris: Firmin Didot, 1812), 264.

95. Collé, *Journal et mémoires*, 3:127.

96. *Correspondance littéraire*, 9:111.

97. The same opposition between the sociability of the cafés and that of the world is at work in Madame de Graffigny's judgment of Declos, whom she saw at Mademoiselle Quinault's receptions in 1743. In the year during which he had been "in that good company," she writes, he had "begun to leave off the tone of the café." She adds: "I hope that very soon he will speak like a man of the world": letter to Devaux, June 6, 1743: Graffigny, *Correspondance*, 4:313.

98. On the posterity of Cléon as a figure for a schemer, see Michel Delon, *L'Idée d'énergie au tournant des Lumières (1770–1820)* (Paris: Presses Universitaires de France, 1984, 1988), chap. 7, "Le méchant," pp. 462–91.

99. Boltanski and Thévenot, *De la justification*, 270–74.

100. Charles Palissot de Montenoy, *La Dunciade, ou, la Guerre des sots* (Chelsea [Paris], 1764); Palissot de Montenoy, *L'Homme dangereux* (Amsterdam: 1770).

101. Antoine Poinsinet, *Le Cercle, ou, la Soirée à la mode* (Paris: Duchesne, 1764), in *Répertoire général du théâtre français*, 46: 289–346 (Paris: Ménard et Raymond, 1813), esp. scene 12, p 334.

102. Diderot, d'Alembert, Marmontel, and La Harpe figure in Rutlidge's play as Version, Rectiligne, Faribole, and Duluthe.

103. Rutlidge, *Bureau d'esprit*, act 1, scene 11, pp. 40–41.

104. Claude-Joseph Dorat, "Épître aux grands hommes des coteries," *Merlin bel-esprit* (Paris, 1780). The same epistle opens the second volume of Dorat, *Coup d'oeil sur la littérature, ou, Collection de différents ouvrages*, 2 vols. (Amsterdam, 1780).

105. Diderot, *Le Neveu de Rameau*, in *Œuvres*, ed. André Billy, 395–474 (Paris: Gallimard, 1951), esp. p. 435; trans. Jacques Barzun and Ralph H. Bowes as *Rameau's Nephew and Other Works* (Indianapolis: Bobbs Merrill, 1964), 48, 49, 50.

106. On this point, see the analysis of Stéphane Pujol, "L'espace public du neveu de Rameau," *Revue d'histoire littéraire de la France* 5 (1993): 669–84.

107. Jean-Jacques Rousseau, *Julie, ou, la Nouvelle Héloïse (1761)*, ed. René Pomeau (Paris: Garnier, 1960), 209.

108. A note in fact specifies that the judgments expressed are those of a young man of twenty-four who is discovering the world and that the author, who "has learned to know it only too well, does not share." The note does not figure in the manuscript that Rousseau offered to Madame de Luxembourg: Rousseau, *Julie*, 207.

109. Rousseau, *Julie*, 212.

110. Rousseau, *Julie*, 227.

111. Rousseau, *Julie*, 281.

112. Rousseau, *Julie*, 214.

113. Rousseau, *Julie*, 219.

114. Rousseau, *Julie*, 229.

115. Rousseau, *Julie*, 229.

116. Rousseau, *Julie*, 221.

117. Rousseau, *Julie*, 233.

118. The parallel between the author's personal experience and the Parisian career of his personage is indicated, in particular, by the episode just cited, which was inspired by a similar misadventure of Rousseau's. He states, "I remembered my own story in writing his": Rousseau, *Confessions*, 1:355; trans. Scholar, 345.

119. Rousseau, *Julie*, 281–82.

120. Jean Starobinski, *Jean-Jacques Rousseau: La Transparence et l'obstacle: suivi de sept essais sur Rouseau (1951)* (Paris: Gallimard, 1971); trans. Arthur Goldhammer as *Jean-Jacques Rousseau, Transparency and Obstruction* (Chicago: University of Chicago Press, 1988); Bronislaw Baczko, *Rousseau, solitude et communauté*, trans. Claire Brendhel-Lamhout (Paris and The Hague: Mouton, 1974); Barbara Carnevali, *Romanticismo e riconoscimento: Figure della coscienza in Rousseau* (Bologna: Il Mulino, 2004).

121. Rousseau, *Julie*, 210.

122. Benoît Mély, *Jean-Jacques Rousseau: Un intellectuel en rupture* (Paris: Minerve, 1985).

123. Rousseau, *Confessions*, 367; trans. Scholar, 358.

124. Rousseau, *Confessions*, 367; trans. Scholar, 358.

125. Rousseau, *Confessions*, 543; trans. Scholar.

126. Jean Fabre, "Rousseau et le prince de Conti," *Annales Jean-Jacques Rousseau* 36 (1963–65): 4–48.

127. Claude Labrosse, *"La Nouvelle Héloïse" et ses lecteurs* (Lyon: Presses Universitaires de Lyon, 1985); Daniel Roche, "Les primitifs du rousseauisme, une analyse sociologique et quantitative de la correspondance de Jean-Jacques Rousseau," *Annales E.S.C.* 26 (January–February 1971): 151–72; Robert Darnton, "Readers Respond to Rousseau: The Fabrication of Romantic Sensitivity," in *The Great Cat Massacre*, 215–56.

128. On Rousseau's relations with printed publication, which is not just a question of financial autonomy, but also involved the construction of the figure of a writer, see Geoffrey Turnovsky, "The Enlightenment Literary Market: Rousseau, Authorship, and the Book Trade," *Eighteenth-Century Studies* 36, no. 3 (2003): 387–410; Raymond Birn, *Forging Rousseau: Print, Commerce and Cultural Manipulation in the Late Enlightenment* (Oxford: Voltaire Foundation, 2001); Yannick Seïté, *Du livre au lire: "La Nouvelle Héloïse," roman des Lumières* (Paris: Honoré Champion, 2002); Christopher Kelly, *Rousseau as Author: Consecrating One's Life to the Truth* (Chicago: University of Chicago Press, 2003).

129. Jean-Jacques Rousseau, *Lettre à d'Alembert sur les spectacles (1758)*, ed. Michel Launay (Paris: Garnier-Flammarion, 1967), 100.

130. Sarah C. Maza, *Private Lives and Public Affairs: The causes célèbres of Prerevolutionary France* (Berkeley: University of California Press, 1993).

131. David A. Bell, *The Cult of the Nation in France: Inventing Nationalism, 1680–1800* (Cambridge, MA: Harvard University Press, 2001), 68–77.

132. Bell, *Cult of the Nation*, 74–75, 159–68.

133. Brown, *Field of Honor*, chap. 3: *"Politesse perdue*: The Patriot Playwright between Court and Public."

134. Grimod de La Reynière, *Lorgnette philosophique*, 125.

135. On the connection between personal identity, moral values, and the narration of a life, see Charles Taylor, *Sources of the Self: The Making of the Modern Identity* (Cambridge, MA: Harvard University Press, 1989).

136. Louis-Sébastien Mercier, *Du théâtre* (Amsterdam: Van Harrevelt, 1773), 78.

137. Mercier, *Tableau de Paris*, 2:1170–71.

138. Jean-Jacques Rousseau, letter to Madame d'Épinay, March 16, 1757: *Correspondance complète de Jean-Jacques Rousseau*, ed. R. A. Leigh, 52 vols. (Geneva and Oxford: Voltaire Foundation, 1965–98), 4:183.

139. Diderot, letter to Sophie Volland, November 15, 1768: Diderot, *Correspondance*, 8:223.

140. Diderot, *Correspondance*, 14:227.

141. Denis Diderot, *Essai sur les règnes de Claude et de Néron* (1782), in *Œuvres*, ed. Laurent Versini, vol. 1, *Philosophie* (Paris: Robert Laffont, 1994), 1029–36, esp. p. 1036.

142. Diderot, *Essai sur les règnes*, 1103.

143. Alexis-Jean Le Bret, *Nouvelle école du monde, nécessaire à tous les états et principalement à ceux qui veulent s'avancer dans le monde* (Lille: J.-B. Henry, 1764).

144. Voltaire was both admiring and jealous of this "man who speaks to the queen" and who "had his entries with the king": letters to Madame Du Deffand, March 21, 1764, and to Richelieu, August 31, 1751, and March 3, 1754, quoted in Geneviève Haroche-Bouzinac, introduction to Moncrif, *Essai sur la nécessité et sur les moyens de plaire* (Paris, 1738) (Saint-Étienne: Publications de l'Université de Saint-Étienne, 1998), 12–13.

145. Moncrif, *Essai sur la nécessité et sur les moyens de plaire*, 32–34.

146. Pons-Augustin Alletz, *Manuel de l'homme du monde, ou, Connaissance générale des principaux états de la société et de toutes les manières qui sont le sujet des conversations ordinaires* (Paris, 1761).

147. Erasmus, *De civilitate morum puerilium* (1530); *La Civilité puérile*, trans. Alcide Bonneau (1537) (Paris: Ramsay, 1977), in a modern edition with a preface by Philippe Ariès. See also the commentary of Roger Chartier in "Distinction et divulgation," in *Lectures et lecteurs dans la France d'Ancien Régime* (Paris: Éditions du Seuil, 1989), 50–54.

148. Antoine de Courtin, *Nouveau traité de la civilité qui se pratiquee en France parmi les honnêtes gens (1671)*, ed. Marie-Claire Grassi (Saint-Étienne: Publications de l'Université de Saint-Étienne, 1996); Jean-Baptiste de La Salle, *Règles de la bienséance et de la civilité chrétienne à l'usage des écoles chrétiennes (1782)*. (Paris: Ligel, 1956). Jean Pungier demonstrates Courtin's influence in *La Civilité de Jean-Baptiste de La Salle: Ses sources, son message*, 3 vols. (Rome: Maison Jean-Baptiste de La Salle, 1996–2000), esp. 135–95.

149. Chartier, "Distinction et divulgation," 64–68. See also Robert Granderoute, *Le Roman pédagogique de Fénelon à Rousseau* (Geneva: Slatkine, 1985).

150. *L'Honnête homme chrétien* (Paris, 1715). This was also more or less the argument of Louis Antoine Caraccioli in *La Religion de l'honnête homme* (Paris: Nyon, 1766).

151. Morvan de Bellegarde's oeuvre is abundant. His principle treatises on civility are: *Réflexions sur ce qui peut plaire ou déplaire dans le commerce du monde* (Paris: A. Seneuze, 1688); *Réflexions sur le ridicule et les moyens de l'éviter* (Paris, 1696); *Réflexions sur la politesse des mœurs* (1698); *Modèles de conversations pour les personnes polies* (1697). These works were reprinted several times, and the latter three were grouped together in Morvan de Bellegarde, *Œuvres diverses*, 4 vols. (Paris: C. Robustel, 1723).

152. François Marin, *L'homme aimable, dédié à M. le Marquis de Rosen, avec des Réflexions et des Pensées sur divers sujets* (Paris: Prault, 1751), pp. 5, 14–17.

153. Marin, *L'homme aimable*, 50–54.

154. François Vincent Toussaint, *Les Mœurs* (1748), esp. pp. 356–70.

155. Isvan Hont, "The Language of Sociability and Commerce: Samuel Pufendorf and the Theoretical Foundations of the Four Stages," in *The Languages of Political Theory in Early Modern Europe,* ed. Anthony Pagden, 233–76 (Cambridge, UK, and New York: Cambridge University Press, 1987); Catherine Larrère, *L'Invention de l'économie au XVIIIe siècle: Du droit natural à la physiocratie* (Paris: Presses Universitaires de France, 1992), chap. 1: "Sociabilité."

156. Larrère, *L'Invention de l'économie,* 74.

157. Jean-Claude Perrot, "Le Dieu caché et la main invisible," in *Une histoire intellectuelle de l'économie politique, XVIIe–XVIIIe siècle,* 333–54 (Paris: EHESS, 1992).

158. On the distinction between "sympathy" and egotism in Hume's *A Treatise on Human Nature,* see Gilles Deleuze, *Empirisme et subjectivité* (Paris: Presses Universitaires de France, 1953).

159. Denis Diderot, *Principes de la philosophie morale, ou, Essai de M. S*** sur le mérite et la vertu* (Paris, 1745).

160. *Encyclopédie,* s.v. "Sociabilité."

161. Albert Hirschman, *The Passions and the Interests: Political Arguments for Capitalism before its Triumph* (Princeton: Princeton University Press, 1977; translated into French by Pierre Andler as *Les Passions et les intérêts* (Paris: Presses Universitaires de France, 1980); Larrère, *L'Invention de l'économie,* chap. 5.

162. Hirschman notes that the emergence of the phrase *doux commerce* in the late seventeenth century owed much to the polysemy of the word and to its connections with civility: Hirschman, *Les Passions et les intérêts,* 58–60.

163. Diderot, *Essai sur les règnes de Claude et de Néron,* 65.

164. J. G. A. Pocock, *The Machiavellian Moment: Florentine Political Thought and the Atlantic Republican Tradition* (Princeton: Princeton University Press, 1975, 2003); and Pocock, "Virtues, Rights, and Manners: A Model for Historians of Political Thought," in *Virtue, Commerce and History: Essays on Political Thought and History, Chiefly in the Eighteenth Century* (Cambridge, UK: Cambridge University Press, 1985).

165. Quoted in Peter France, *Politeness and its Discontents: Problems in French Classical Culture* (Cambridge, UK, and New York: Cambridge University Press, 1992), 76.

166. Dinah Ribard, *Raconter, vivre, penser: Histoires de philosophes (1650–1766)* (Paris: Vrin, 2003).

167. Stéphane Pujol, "Le Dialogue d'idées au XVIIIe siècle," thèse de Lettres, Université de Paris X, 1994.

168. Michel Delon, "La marquise et le philosophe," *Revue des sciences humaines* 182 (1994): 65–78.

169. Anthony Ashley Cooper, Lord Shaftesbury, *Sensus communis: An Essay on the Freedom of Wit and Humour* (London, 1709), reprinted in *Characteristics of Men, Manners, Opinions, Times,* vol. 1 (London, 1711). See Laurence Klein, *Shaftesbury and the Culture of Politeness: Moral Discourse and Cultural Politics in Early Eighteenth-Century England* (Cambridge, UK: Cambridge University Press, 1994); and Laurent Jaffro, *Éthique de la communication et Art d'écrire: Shaftesbury et les Lumières anglaises* (Paris: Presses Universitaires de France, 1998).

170. Céline Spector, *Montesquieu. Pouvoirs, richesse et société* (Paris, Presses Universitaires de France, 2004). According to Spector, Montesquieu distinguishes between two models for the formation of civil society through a convergence of interests. The first, identified with England, is a "paradigm of commerce." The second, identified with France, is a "paradigm of manners."

Montesquieu thus holds himself at a distance from both the contractualist theories of the voluntarist edification of political and social order and the liberal theories of the "invisible hand."

171. See the famous passage in *De l'esprit des lois*, where Montesquieu asserts: "Should there happen to be a country whose inhabitants were of a social temper," there would be no need to change its spirit by laws. Immediately following this, he associates this "social temper" with an "open-hearted, cheerful" manner, men's "taste and a facility in communicating their thoughts," and a reliance on "a certain notion of honor": Charles Louis, baron de Montesquieu, *De l'esprit des lois* (Amsterdam: F. Grasset, 1761), ed. Victor Goldschmidt, 2 vols. (Paris: Garnier-Flammarion, 1979), 1–461, quoted from *The Spirit of the Laws*, trans. Thomas Nugent, 2 vols. in 1 (New York: Fahner, 1966), 1:294. On the place of Montesquieu in the genealogy of the debates on the national character and the spirit of nations, see Bell, *Cult of the Nation*, 143–54.

172. Spector, *Montesquieu*.

173. Jacques Domenech, *L'Éthique des Lumières: Les fondements de la morale dans la philosophie française du XVIIIe siècle* (Paris: Vrin, 1989).

174. Voltaire, "Vertu," *Dictionnaire philosophique*, 374, quoted from *A Philosophical Dictionary*, 10 vols. (Paris: E. R. Du Mont, 1901), 10:163–64.

175. Franck Salaün, *L'Ordre des mœurs: Essai sur la place du matérialisme dans la société française du XVIIIe siècle (1743–1784)* (Paris: Kimé, 1996).

176. "These sentiments are natural, that is, they derive from the essence of the nature of a being who seeks to preserve himself, who loves himself, who wants to render his existence happy, and who ardently seizes the means to do so. Everything proves to man that social life / life in society is advantageous to him; he gets used to it, and he is unhappy when he is deprived of the presence of his like. That is the true principle of sociability": Paul-Henri Thiry, baron d'Holbach, *La Politique naturelle; ou, Discours sur les vrais principes du gouvernement*, 2 vols. (London, 1773); 2 vols. (Paris: Fayard, 1998), discourse 1, "De la société," I. La sociabilité, 12–13.

177. Paul-Henri Thiry, baron d'Holbach, *Système social, ou, Principes naturels de la morale et de la politique* (London, 1773), 1:119, cited by Robert Mauzi, *L'Idée du bonheur dans la littérature et la pensée française au XVIIIe siècle (1964)* (Paris: Armand Colin, 1994), 580.

178. Paul-Henri Thiry, baron d'Holbach, *La Morale universelle, ou, Les devoirs de l'homme fondés sur la nature*, 3 vols. (Tours: Letourny, 19782). See Jacques Domenech, "D'Holbach et l'obsession de la morale," *Corpus* 22–23 (1992): 103–15; Gordon, *Citizens without Sovereignty*, 69.

179. D'Holbach, *Morale universelle*, 1:224.

180. D'Holbach, *Morale universelle*, 1:227; 3:252.

181. D'Holbach, *Morale universelle*, 2:337.

182. "The sciences suppose reflection and reflection makes us polite because it renders us sociable by teaching us the considerations/respect that are owed to beings brought together in society": D'Holbach, *Morale universelle*, 3:321.

183. D'Holbach, *Morale universelle*, 3:337.

184. On this point my reading differs from Daniel Gordon's, according to whom d'Holbach's sociability autonomizes a "sphere of practices" founded on egalitarian premises (politeness) in an inegalitarian political order: see Gordon, *Citizens without Sovereignty*, 69.

185. The term *civilisation* appears for the first time in 1766 in Mirabeau's *L'Ami des hommes* (1756), but an increasingly frequent use of the terms *civiliser* and *civilisé*

had already established the idea. The bibliography on the notion is considerable: Lucien Febvre, "Civilisation: Évolution d'un mot et d'un groupe d'idées," in
Civilisation: Le mot et l'idée (Paris: La renaissance du livre, 1930), 1–55; Norbert
Elias, *The Civilizing Process*, trans. Edmund Jephcott, 3 vols. (New York: Pantheon,
1982; Oxford and Cambridge, MA: Blackwell, 1994); Jean Starobinski, *Le Remède
dans le mal: Critique et légitimation de l'artifice à l'âge des Lumières* (Paris: Gallimard,
1989), trans. Arthur Goldhammer as *Blessings in Disguise, or, The Morality of Evil*
(Cambridge, MA: Harvard University Press, 1993), chap. 1.

186. Adam Ferguson, *An Essay on the History of Civil Society* (Edinburgh, 1766).
187. Hont, "Language of Sociability and Commerce."
188. Georges Benrekassa, *Le Langage des Lumières: Concepts et savoirs de la langue*
(Paris: Presses Universitaires de France, 1995), 59–60.
189. In chapter 5 ("Sur les gens à la mode") in his *Considérations sur les mœurs*, Duclos
contrasts "l'homme aimable," who seeks only to please and who likes no one,
and "l'homme sociable," who has all the "qualities appropriate for society," such
as "politeness without falsity," and who is thus "the citizen par excellence."
190. D'Holbach, *Morale universelle*, 3:340.
191. Gordon, *Citizens without Sovereignty*, 65.
192. André Morellet, "De la conversation," in Morellet, Thomas, and d'Alembert,
Éloges de Madame Geoffrin; Morellet, "Essai sur la conversation, traduit de
l'anglais du Dr Swift," *Mercure de France* 5 (November 1778), 5–22. Swift's
text, *Hints toward an Essay on Conversation* (1708), can be found, along with
his *Introduction to Polite Conversation* in *The Prose Works of Jonathan Swift*, ed.
Temple Scott, 12 vols. (London: George Bell, 1897–1908), vol. 11.
193. Morellet, "De la conversation," 156.
194. Necker, *Mélanges*, 2:63.
195. Morellet, "De la conversation," 166.
196. Morellet, "De la conversation," 191.
197. Morellet, "De la conversation," 180.
198. Morellet, "De la conversation," 188.
199. Antoine Gombault, chevalier de Méré, "De la conversation" (1668), in *Œuvres
complètes du chevalier de Méré*, ed. Charles H. Boudhors, 3 vols. (Paris: Fernand
Roches, 1930), 2:17.
200. Morellet, "De la conversation," 195. Nicolas Trublet, "De la conversation," in
Essais sur divers sujets de littérature et de morale, 2 vols. (Paris: Briasson, 1735),
section 8.
201. Morellet, "De la conversation," 157.
202. Morellet, "De la conversation," 161.
203. Morellet, "De la conversation," 166.
204. Morellet, "De la conversation," 170.
205. Morellet, "De la conversation," 170.

CHAPTER 4

1. On these amusements of the salons, from the table to gambling and from theater to society music, see the chapter "Les plaisirs du salon," in the French edition of Antoine Lilti, *Le monde des salons: Sociabilité et mondanité à Paris au XVIIIe
siècle* (Paris: Fayard, 2005), 225–72 (not included in the present translation).
2. Jacques Rancière, *La Parole muette: Essai sur les contradictions de la littérature*
(Paris: Hachette, 1998), 28.

3. Staël, *Correspondance générale*, vol. 1, *Lettres de jeunesse*, pt. 1, 65.

4. Amélie Suard, *Essais de mémoires*, 39–40.

5. Notebooks of Madame Geoffrin, private archives of the comte de Bruce.

6. The comtesse de Boufflers also quotes Madame de Sévigné's *bons mots*. See, for example, her letter to Gustav III of August 24, 1785: Marie-Charlotte-Hyppolite, comtesse Boufflers, *Lettres de Gustave III à la comtesse de Boufflers et de la comtesse au roi, de 1771 à 1791*, ed. Aurélien Vivie (Bordeaux, 1900), 358.

7. Talleyrand-Périgord, *Mémoires*; quoted from *Memoirs of the Prince de Talleyrand*, 5 vols. (New York: G. P. Putnam's Sons, 1891–92; facsimile reprint, Whitefish, MT: Kessinger, 2007), 1:34.

8. Charles Augustin Sainte-Beuve, "La femme au XVIIIe siècle," December 1, 1862, *Nouveaux lundis*, 13 vols. (Paris: Michel Lévy frères, 1863–70), 4:25.

9. When Madame Du Deffand repeated to the duchesse de Choiseul a *bon mot* of Richelieu's, the duchess answered her that she did not see anything amusing about it. Madame Du Deffand shot back that the duchess was "a bit rusty": Madame Du Deffand, letter to the duchesse de Choiseul, July 2, 1769: Du Deffand, *Correspondance complète de Mme du Deffand avec la duchesse de Choiseul, l'abbé Barthelemy, et M. Craufurt, publiée avec une introduction par M. le Marquis de Sainte-Aulaire*, 3 vols. (Paris: Michel Lévy frères, 1877), 1:229.

10. Crébillon's friends decided one day to mystify him and persuade him that he was no longer witty by pretending not to laugh at his sallies for an entire evening: Mercier, *Tableau de Paris*, 1:385–88.

11. François de Callières, *Des bons mots et des bon contes: De leur usage, de la raillerie des anciens, de la raillerie et des railleurs de notre temps* (Paris: Barbin, 1692).

12. François-Georges Maréchal, marquis de Bièvre, "Dissertation sur les jeux de mots," in *Calembours et autres jeux sur les mots d'esprit*, ed. Antoine de Baecque, 47–57 (Paris: Payot, 2000). This text was first published in his *Bievrana* in 1799.

13. Pierre-Marc-Gaston, duc de Lévis, *Souvenirs-portraits du Duc de Lévis, suivis de Lettres intimes de Monsieur, Comte de Provence au Duc de Lévis (1787–1792)* (Paris: Mercure, 1993), 187–90.

14. "Shepherdess, let us detach ourselves / from Newton, from Descartes: / Those two fools / have never seen the underside / of the cards, of the cards, of the cards": Hénault, *Mémoires*, 136.

15. Antoine De Baecque, *Les éclats du rire: La culture des rieurs au XVIIIe siècle* (Paris: Calmann-Lévy, 2000); 57–106; Dominique Quéro, *Momus philosophe: Recherches sur une figure littéraire du XVIIIe siècle* (Paris: Honoré Champion, 1995).

16. Pierre Zoberman, "Entendre raillerie," in *Thèmes et genres littéraires aux XVIIe et XVIIIe siècles: Mélanges en l'honneur de Jacques Truchet*, ed. Nicole Ferrier-Caverière, 179–184 (Paris: Presses Universitaires de France, 1992); Jacques Cheyronnaud, "La raillerie, forme élémentaire de la critique," in *Critique et affaires de blasphème à l'époque des Lumières*, ed. Jacques Cheyronnaud, Elisabeth Claverie, Denis Laborde, and Philippe Roussin, 73–128 (Paris: Honoré Champion, 1998).

17. Nicolas Faret, *L'Honneste homme, ou, L'art de plaire à la cour*, ed. Maurice Magendie (Paris: Presses Universitaires de Franc, 1925), 81–82; Madeleine de Scudéry, *"De l'air galant" et autres conversations (1653–1684): Pour une étude de l'archive galante*, ed. Delphine Denis (Paris: Honoré Champion, 1998); Dominique Bertrand, "Le bon usage du rire et de la raillerie selon le discours de la civilité au XVIIe siècle en France," in *Savoir Vivre 1*, ed. Alain Montandon, 63–84 (Lyon: Meyzieu Césura, 1991).

18. D'Holbach, *Morale universelle*, section 3, chap. 12, 290, 163; Charles-François-Nicolas Le Maître de Claville, *Traité du vrai mérite de l'homme* (Paris: Saugrain, 1736), 171.

19. Chamfort, *Produits*, 93.

20. Élisabeth Bourguinat, "Le Persiflage dans la littérature française du dix-huitième siècle (1735–1810): Modernité d'un néologisme," thèse de doctorat, Littérature Française, Paris 4, 1995; published as *Le Siècle du persiflage, 1734–1789* (Paris: Presses Universitaires de France, 2000).

21. Mercier, *Tableau de Paris*, 1:384.

22. Gleichen, *Souvenirs*, 201.

23. Marmontel, *Mémoires*, 202; quoted from *Memoirs*, 1:260.

24. Marmontel, *Mémoires*, 202; *Memoirs*, 1:260.

25. Diderot, letter to Sophie Volland, September 30, 1760; Diderot, *Correspondance*, 3:104.

26. Diderot, *Correspondance*, 3:104. On another occasion, when Galiani was relating *contes*, Diderot wrote: "All this is not too good; but timeliness and gaiety give it a volatile salt that dissipates and is nowhere to be found when the moment passes": Letter to Sophie Volland, September 26, 1762; Diderot, *Correspondance*, 4:170–71.

27. Diderot, letter to Sophie Volland, October 20, 1760 Diderot, *Correspondance*, 3:164–70.

28. Marmontel, *Mémoires*, 131–32; *Memoirs*, 1:261, 260.

29. Morellet, *Mémoires*, 202.

30. Morellet, *Mémoires*, 202. Diderot had similar things to say about the actor's talents that made Galiani so amusing: Letter to Sophie Volland, October 20, 1760; Diderot, *Correspondance*, 3:169–70.

31. Marmontel, *Mémoires*, 198; *Memoirs*, 1:254.

32. Julie de Lespinasse, letter, October 21, 1774; Lespinasse, *Lettres*, 168.

33. Bombelles, *Journal*, May 13, 1786, 2:138.

34. Madame Du Deffand, letter to Walpole, May 31, 1767; Walpole, *Correspondence*, 3, 1:21–25. Madame de La Ferté-Imbault also speaks of d'Alembert's "very comical talent, which was to copy all the actors of the Opéra and the Comédie to make you die laughing": Lettre sur d'Alembert, March 28, 1777; Archives nationales, 508 AP 37.

35. Oberkirch, *Mémoires*, 315, quoted from *Memoirs of the Baroness d'Oberkirch, Countess de Montbrison*, ed. Count de Montbrison, 3 vols. (London: Colburn, 1852), 2:243. See also Genlis, *Mémoires inédits*, 1:360.

36. Madame Du Deffand, letter to Walpole, April 30, 1766; Walpole, *Correspondence*, 3, 1:302.

37. Madame Du Deffand, letter to Walpole, May 3, 1766; Walpole, *Correspondence*, 1, 3:27.

38. *Correspondance littéraire*, March 1771, 9:262. It is possible that this was the same Touzet that Madame Du Deffand saw at the home of Trudaine de Montigny three years earlier: "We were given the spectacle of a man who places himself behind a screen and who plays, all alone, the matins of a convent or a village morning; you think you are listening to twenty different people; among other things there is a high mass with [music from] the serpent and the organ, a sermon, a quarrel at the church door, and dogs barking": Madame Du Deffand, letter to Walpole, March 14, 1769; Walpole, *Correspondence*, 4, 2:210–11.

39. Suzanne Necker, *Mélanges*, 2:66–67.

40. Suzanne Necker, *Mélanges*, 2:66–67.

41. *Le Petit Tableau de Paris*, 1783, 35–36.

42. Jean Starobinski, "Sur la flatterie," in *Remède*; quoted from *Blessings*, 36.

43. Starobinski, *Remède*, 62; *Blessings*, 37.

44. Charles-Joseph, prince de Ligne, *Mémoires, lettres et pensées*, preface by C. Thomas (Paris: F. Bourin, 1990), 698.

45. Suzanne Necker, *Mémoires*, 1:234.

46. Ligne, *Mémoires*, 168.

47. Alain Viala, "L'esprit galant," *Biblio 17 Papers on French Seventeenth-Century Literature* 101 (1997): 53–74; Alain Viala, *La France galante* (Paris: Presses Universitaires de France, 2009).

48. Philip Stewart, *Le Masque et la parole: Le langage de l'amour au XVIIIe siècle* (Paris: José Conti, 1973), chap. 2, "Une société en conversation," 59–89.

49. Madame Du Deffand, letter to Horace Walpole, October 23, 1775; Walpole, *Correspondence*, 6, 4:224.

50. Poniatowski, *Mémoires*, 1:84.

51. Poniatowski, *Mémoires*, 86.

52. Gleichen, *Souvenirs*, 95.

53. Bibliothèque Nationale, Département des MSS, *Nouvelles acquisitions françaises* 10235: Hénault.

54. Julie de Lespinasse, letter to Guibert, September 22, 1774: Lespinasse, *Lettres*, 133.

55. Galiani, letter, February 16, 1771: Galiani and Épinay, *Correspondance*, 2:51.

56. Galiani, letter, May 11, 1771: Galiani and Épinay, *Correspondance*, 2:112.

57. The archetype of private correspondence is that between lovers. While reading a letter from the duc de Chartres, Madame de Genlis was surprised by the arrival of the chevalier de Durfort, whom she feared had recognized the duke's handwriting: Madame de Genlis, letter to the duc de Chartres, July 23, 1772: Archives des Affaires étrangères, *Mémoires et documents*, France 319, fol. 60.

58. Galiani, letter, October 30, 1772: Galiani and Épinay, *Correspondance*, 3:134.

59. When Madame d'Épinay complained of not having seen a letter full of mocking banter that Galiani had sent to Morellet, with whom she had chilly relations, Galiani responded that all she had to do was to ask Morellet for the letter, thus implying that he could not refuse to show it to her: Galiani, letter, May 19, 1770: Galiani and Épinay, *Correspondance*, 1:169.

60. Madame d'Épinay, letter, February 5, 1772: Galiani and Épinay, *Correspondance*, 2:272.

61. Madame d'Épinay, letter, June 30, 1770: Galiani and Épinay, *Correspondance*, 1:200.

62. Madame d'Épinay, letter, July 2, 1770: Galiani and Épinay, *Correspondance*, 1:217.

63. Madame d'Épinay, letter, August 9, 1770: Galiani and Épinay, *Correspondance*, 1:226–27.

64. Madame d'Épinay, letter, August 9, 1771: Galiani and Épinay, *Correspondance*, 2:158.

65. Scholars usually ignore or minimize these aspects. At best, such considerations are presented as constraints that only marginally fetter "the astonishing encounter of two thoughts that reply to one another": Jürge Siess, "La marquise et le philosophe: La rencontre épistolaire entre Mme Du Deffand et Voltaire," in *Penser par lettre*, ed. Benoît Mélançon, 311–25 (Quebec: Fidès, 1998).

66. Du Deffand, *Cher Voltaire*, 103.

67. Madame Du Deffand, letter of March 22, 1768: Du Deffand, *Cher Voltaire*, 236.

68. Voltaire, letter of August 18, 1761: Du Deffand, *Cher Voltaire*, 106.

69. Madame Du Deffand, letter of July 17, 1764: Du Deffand, *Cher Voltaire*, 153.

70. Voltaire, letter of July 1, 1764: Du Deffand, *Cher Voltaire*, 161.

71. Voltaire, letter of July 26, 1764: Du Deffand, *Cher Voltaire*, 164.

72. Walpole, letter to Thomas Gray, January 25, 1766: Walpole, *Correspondence*, 14:148–57.

73. *Mémoires secrets*, January 11, 1774.

74. Madame Du Deffand, letters of March 7, 1764, and April 15, 1769: Du Deffand, *Cher Voltaire*, 131, 298.

75. Madame Du Deffand, letter of December 20, 1769: Du Deffand, *Cher Voltaire*, 326.

76. Voltaire, letter of March 15, 1769: Du Deffand, *Cher Voltaire*, 287.

77. Duchesse de Choiseul, letter to Madame Du Deffand, March 20, 1769: Du Deffand, *Cher Voltaire*, 289.

78. Madame Du Deffand, letter of April 15, 1769: Du Deffand, *Cher Voltaire*, 298.

79. Madame Du Deffand, letter of April 10, 1768: Du Deffand, *Cher Voltaire*, 239–40.

80. Duchesse de Choiseul, letter to Madame Du Deffand, July 16, 1769: Du Deffand, *Cher Voltaire*, 305. She thanks Madame Du Deffand for having "saved her from falling into a most awkward trap."

81. Voltaire, letter of September 6, 1769: Du Deffand, *Cher Voltaire*, 315.

82. Voltaire, letter of September 6, 1765: Du Deffand, *Cher Voltaire*, 188.

83. Voltaire, letter of January 1, 1766: Du Deffand, *Cher Voltaire*, 195.

84. Voltaire, letter of March 14, 1764: Du Deffand, *Cher Voltaire*, 135.

85. Voltaire, letter of March 14, 1764: Du Deffand, *Cher Voltaire*, 135.

86. Jacqueline Hellegouarc'h, "Mélinade ou la duchesse du Maine: Deux contes de jeunesse de Voltaire: *Le Crocheteur borgne* et *Cosi-Sancta*," *Revue d'histoire littéraire de la France* (September–October 1978), 722–35.

87. Frank A. Kafker, "L'Encyclopédie et le cercle du baron d'Holbach," *Recherches sur Diderot et sur l'Encyclopédie* (1987): 118–24, esp. p. 118.

88. This society has at times been presented as a philosophical and literary cenacle frequented by Diderot, Rousseau, and d'Alembert, and a place where very free discussions were held on religious topics. The publication of the abundant correspondence of Madame de Graffigny and the works of Judith Curtis have done away with these historiographical legends and have shown that the society of Mademoiselle Quinault was above all inspired by a quest for worldly amusement. See in particular Judith Curtis, "Mademoiselle Quinault and the Bout-du-Banc: A Reappraisal," *Studies on Voltaire and the Eighteenth Century* 8 (2000): 35–56.

89. Madame de Graffigny, letter to Devaux, January 31, 1743: Graffigny, *Correspondance*, 4:117. She warns Devaux to keep the project a secret: "Do not speak of this trifle with any living soul. It is the secret of the society."

90. Madame de Graffigny, letter to Devaux, August 17, 1744: Graffigny, *Correspondance*, 5:411–12. On the genesis of this collection, see Jacqueline Hellegouarc'h, "Un atelier littéraire au XVIIIe siècle: La société du bout-du-banc," *Revue d'histoire littéraire de la France* 1 (2004): 59–70, and the remarks of Aurelio Principato in the critical edition of Crébillon's *Dialogues des morts*, in Claude Prosper Jolyot de Crébillon, *Œuvres complètes*, ed. Jean Sgard, 4 vols. (Paris: Garnier, 1999–2000), 2:465–84.

91. *La Journée de l'amour, ou, Heures de Cythère* ([Paris]: Gnide, 1776).

92. Curtis, "Mademoiselle Quinault"; David Warner Smith, "La composition et la publication des contes de Mme de Graffigny," *French Studies* 3 (July 1996), 275–84.

93. Madeleine de Scudéry, Paul Pellisson, and others, *Chroniques du Samedi, suivies de pièces diverses*, ed. Alain Niderst, Delphine Denis, and Myriam Maître (Paris: Honoré Champion, 2002); Myriam Maître, "Les escortes mondaines de la publication," in *De la publication entre renaissance et lumières*, ed. Christian Jouhaud and Alain Viala, 249–65, Groupe de recherches interdisciplinaires sur l'histoire du littéraire (Paris: Fayard, 2002).

94. *Les Étrennes de la Saint Jean* (Paris, 1739). The *Recueil de ces messieurs* includes two "Spanish novels," an Oriental tale, a fairy tale, and a "moral story."

95. Suard, letter to his wife, Institut et Musée Voltaire (Geneva), Archives Suard, vol. 2, fol. 14.

96. Madame Du Deffand, letter to the duchesse de Choiseul, June 30, 1773: Du Deffand, *Correspondance avec la duchesse de Choiseul*, 2:445.

97. *Graffigny Papers*, LV, 235; cited in Helvétius, *Correspondance*, 1:65.

98. Roger Chartier, "Du lire au croire: Les pratiques citadines de l'imprimé, 1660–1780," in Chartier, *Lectures et lecteurs*, 207–208; "Urban Reading Practices, 1660–1780," in Chartier, *The Cultural Uses of Print in Early Modern France*, trans. Lydia G. Cochrane, 183–239 (Princeton: Princeton University Press, 1987). See also Chartier, "Loisir et sociabilité: Lire à haute voix dans l'Europe moderne," *Littératures classiques* 12 (January 1990): 127–47.

99. Bombelles, *Journal*, April 29, 1783, 1:216.

100. Chastellux, letter to Guibert, August 29, 1774: François-Jean de Chastellux, *Lettres inédites de Chastellux à Wilkes*, ed. Gabriel Dominique Bonno, University of California Publications in Modern Philology, vol. 15, no. 2 (Berkeley: University of California Press, 1932), 121.

101. Madame Du Deffand, letter to Craufurt, January 17, 1773; Madame Du Deffand, letter to Barthélemy, January 28, 1773: Du Deffand, *Correspondance avec la duchesse de Choiseul*, 2:328, 337.

102. Alexis Piron, *La Métromanie*, in *Théâtre du XVIIIe siècle*, ed. Jacques Truchet, 2 vols. (Paris: Gallimard, Pléïade, 1972–74).

103. Nicole Masson, *La Poésie fugitive au XVIIIe siècle* (Paris: Honoré Champion, 2002).

104. Masson, *Poésie fugitive*. See also Walter Moser, "De la signification d'une poésie insignifiante: Examen de la poésie fugitive au XVIIIe siècle et de ses rapports avec la pensée sensualiste en France," *Studies on Voltaire and the Eighteenth Century* 94 (1972): 277–415.

105. On occasion, women of high society versified in social gatherings as well. The duchesse d'Aiguillon, for example, added some satirical verse on the Académie to a letter to Maupertuis: Duchesse d'Aiguillon, undated letter (ca. 1746–49), Bibliothèque nationale, Département des MSS, *Nouvelles acquisitions françaises*, 10398, fol. 29.

106. Nicole Vaget-Grangeat, *Le Chevalier de Boufflers et son temps, étude d'un échec* (Paris: Nizet, 1976). His poems and occasional pieces were published in Stanislas-Jean, chevalier de Boufflers, *Poésies diverses du chevalier de Boufflers*, ed. Octave Uzanne (Paris: A. Quantin, 1886). For his tales, see Stanislas-Jean, chevalier de Boufflers, *Contes*, ed. Alex Sokalski (Paris: Société des textes français modernes, 1995).

107. *Correspondance littéraire*, August 1772, 10:31–32. See also the article "Parfilage" in Genlis, *Dictionnaire critique et raisonné des étiquettes*, 1:38, in which Madame de Genlis denounces the activity as an "extravagant and most ignoble fashion" and gives herself credit for making it fall out of use by criticizing it in *Adèle et Théodore*.

108. Madame Du Deffand, letter to Walpole, November 15, 1772: Walpole, *Correspondence*, 3, 5:281–86.

109. Archives nationales, 508 AP 38: Madame de La Ferté-Imbault, papers: "Poems that were made for me in my youth and in my mature age, beginning at age 25 until age 55. These poems were made in various societies and families that I followed until the death of the heads of those societies and families."

110. In the four volumes of manuscripts that she bequeathed to d'Alembert, there are hardly any texts of Julie de Lespinasse herself (one exception is the continuation of the *Voyage sentimental*). Rather, they include extracts from printed works, copies of correspondence (from Voltaire in particular), and a large number of society pieces (portraits, verse, etc.) that at times date to the first half of the century and from the Sceaux court, along with epistles from Voltaire and songs of Piron. This handwritten transmission allowed a long memoir about daily life to be put together Voltaire Foundation (Oxford), Manuscripts bequeathed by Julie de Lespinasse, 4 vols.

111. Masson, *Poésie fugitive*, 105.

112. Masson, *Poésie fugitive*, 110, citing Thomas Bouhier, *Correspondance littéraire du président Bouhier*, ed. Henri Duranton, 5 vols. (Saint-Étienne: Publications de l'Université de Saint-Étienne, 1976–82).

113. Masson, *Poésie fugitive*, 110.

114. The poems of Voltaire were avidly sought after and were the object of competition among hostesses. Knowing that Voltaire had written verse for Madame Du Deffand, Madame Necker ask Moultou to obtain from Voltaire a poem explicitly dedicated to her: Madame Necker, letters of October 29, 1772, and January 4, 1774, cited by Edouard de Callataÿ, *Madame de Vermenoux: Une enchanteresse au XVIIIe siècle* (Geneva: La Palatine, 1956), 70.

115. Claude-Henri-Fuzée, abbé de Voisenon, *Œuvres mêlées*, 4 vols. (Paris, 1881), 3:372, 380, 425.

116. Patrick Wald Lasowski, *L'Ardeur et la galanterie* (Paris: Gallimard, 1986). See, in particular, "Deux ou trois papillons," 63–100.

117. Roger Fayolle, "La dépindarisation de Ponce Denis Écouchard Lebrun, dit Le Brun-Pindare," *Œuvres et Critiques* 7, no. 1 (1982): 87–100.

118. "À madame la comtesse de Brancas, qui venait de me faire éveiller à six heures du matin," Ponce Denis Écouchard Lebrun, *Œuvres*, ed. Pierre Louis Ginguené, 4 vols. (Paris: Crapelet, 1811), 3:404.

119. Lebrun, *Œuvres*, 4:76.

120. Madame de Staal, letter to Madame Du Deffand, August 15, 1747: Du Deffand, *Correspondance avec ses amis*, 1:90–92.

121. Madame de Staal, letter to Madame Du Deffand, August 20, 1747: Du Deffand, *Correspondance avec ses amis*, 1:94.

122. Bibliothèque publique universitaire de Genève, MS fr. 322: *Bouts rimés* of Mme Necker to Mme de Vermenoux, fols. 133, 134.

123. Abbé Pierre-Joseph-André Roubaud, *Nouveaux synonymes français*, 4 vols. (Paris: Moutard, 1785–86).

124. See Renée Caroline de Froulay, marquise de Créquy, *Lettres inédites de la marquise de Créquy à Sénac de Meilhan (1782–1789)*, ed. Edouard Fournier, preface

by Charles Augustin Sainte-Beuve (Paris: L. Potier, 1856). In a letter dated February 1786, she warmly recommends to Sénac abbé Roubaud's book, which had just been published: Créquy, *Lettres*, 59.

125. Voltaire Foundation (Oxford), Manuscripts bequeathed by Julie de Lespinasse, vol. 2, fols. 33–113.

126. *Correspondance littéraire*, April 1786, 14:351, 353.

127. *Correspondance littéraire*, May 1786, p. 365.

128. His synonym began thus: "Expression[s] that the common run of men use indifferently to speak of the female of the ass. The nuances between these two denominations are quite distinct, however, and easily strike the subtle and profound spirits who weigh the value of terms and want to speak or write with elegance": *Correspondance littéraire*, May 1786, p. 365.

129. Maître, *Précieuses*, 652.

130. See Michel Butor's responses to Jean Roudaut in "La poésie du XVIIIe siècle lue au XXe siècle depuis 1950: Réponses à un questionnaire," *Œuvres et Critiques* 7, no. 1 (1982): 139–50, esp. pp. 142–44.

131. Émile Pierrot, *Étude sur Saint-Lambert* (Nancy: Berger-Levrault, 1875), 36.

CHAPTER 5

1. Genlis, *Dictionnaire critique et raisonné*, s.v. "Auteur," 1:62.

2. Duchesse d'Aiguillon, letter to Maupertuis, August 22, 1746: Bibliothèque nationale, Département des MSS, *Nouvelles acquisitions françaises*, 10398.

3. Denis Fonvizin, letter to Piotr Ivanovitch Panine, March 31, 1778: Fonvizin, *Lettres de France*.

4. Mercier, *Tableau de Paris*, 1:42–43.

5. Horace Walpole, letter to Mary Coke, January 4, 1766: Walpole, *Correspondence*, 31:93.

6. Madame Du Deffand, letter to Walpole, January 2, 1770: Walpole, *Correspondence*, 4, 2:370.

7. Armand, comte d'Allonville, *Mémoires secrets de 1770 à 1830*, 6 vols. (Paris: Werdet, 1838–45), 1: 394.

8. *Correspondance littéraire*, March 1789, 15:418.

9. *Correspondance littéraire*, March 1789, 15:418.

10. When he was brought to d'Holbach's salon, George Louis Schmid noted: "By telling fables, recounting the news of the day, and saying something amusing about others and rarely saying anything true is how one pays one's share here" (extracts from Schmid's journal published in Hans-Ulrich Seifert, "Banquets de philosophes: Georges Louis Schmid chez Diderot, d'Holbach, Helvétius et Mably," *Dix-huitième siècle* 19 (1987), 223–26).

11. Norbert Elias, "Neighbourhood Relations in the Making," in *The Established and the Outsiders: A Sociological Enquiry into Community Problems*, ed. Norbert Elias and John L. Scotson, 13–23 (London: Frank Cass, 1965). See also chapter 7 of the same work, "Observations on Gossip" (167–84). The term "established" refers to both the length of time that a group has existed in a given place (here, an English suburb) and its dominant position in terms of power and prestige.

12. Madame Du Deffand, letter to Walpole, June 3, 1766: Walpole, *Correspondence*, 3, 1:61.

13. Mercier, *Tableau de Paris*, 2:217.

14. Fonvizin, *Lettres de France*, 135.

15. Duclos, *Considérations*, 170.

16. "The maréchale, as I have already said, was the oracle of *bon ton*. Her decisions on the manner of being in the greater world were without appeal": Genlis, *Mémoires inédits*, 1:383.

17. Genlis, *Mémoires inédits*, 1:196.

18. Genlis, *Mémoires inédits*, 1:196.

19. Daniel Roche, *The Culture of Clothing: Dress and Fashion in the "Ancien Régime,"* trans. Jean Birrel (Cambridge, UK: Cambridge University Press, 1994), 515.

20. Gabriel Tarde, *Les Lois de l'imitation* (1893) (Paris: Kimé, 1993), trans. Elsie Clews Parson as *The Laws of Imitation* (New York: Holt, 1903; reprint Charleston: Bibliolife, 2010), 341.

21. Genlis, *Dictionnaire critique et raisonné*, 2:211.

22. "You measure friendship, probity, wit, in fact everything, on the greater or lesser number of homages rendered to you. That is what determines your approbations and your judgments, which vary from one choice to another. Get rid of—or at least pretend to get rid of—that personal measurement (*toise personnelle*); and believe that one can have a good heart without always being in your study": Walpole, letter to Madame Du Deffand, March 16, 1770: Walpole, *Correspondence*, 4, 4:387.

23. Bombelles, *Journal*, December 27, 1783, 1:296.

24. Baczko, *Rousseau, solitude et communauté*, 13–56.

25. Genlis, *Dictionnaire critique et raisonné*, 1:311.

26. La Harpe, *Letters to the Shuvalovs*, 47.

27. Genlis, *Mémoires inédits*, 2:19–20.

28. Madame Du Deffand, letter to Walpole, August 23, 1777: Walpole, *Correspondence*, 6, 4:469.

29. Antoine Lilti, "Public ou sociabilité? Les théâtres de société au XVIIIe siècle," in *De la publication, entre Renaissance et Lumières*, ed. Christian Jouhaud and Alain Viala, (Paris: Fayard, 2002), 281–300.

30. Jeffrey S. Ravel, *The Contested Parterre: Public Theater and French Political Culture, 1680–1791* (Ithaca: Cornell University Press, 1999).

31. Jean-François de La Harpe, *Lycée ou cours de littérature ancienne et moderne*, 17 vols. (Paris: H. Agasse, 1799–1805), 8:448–56. Jean Antoine Roucher was born in Montpellier in 1745. Sources dating from the 1770s testify to his brilliant but short-lived success in the salons of the capital; he was a "shining meteor" for whom "all Paris felt enthusiasm": *Correspondance littéraire* 11:168. When the work was published, disappointment was general. See Georges Buisson, "Roucher après *Les Mois*: Une 'réputation étouffée," *Cahiers Roucher-Chénier*: part 1, "L'année 1780" (1985); part 2, "D'une chute à l'autre" (1987).

32. Hélène Merlin, *Public et littérature en France au XVIIe siècle* (Paris: Les Belles-Lettres, 1994); Merlin, "Figures du public au XVIIIe siècle: Le travail du passé," *Dix-Huitième siècle* 23 (1991): 345–56; Ravel, *Contested Parterre*.

33. Ravel, *Contested Parterre*, chapter 1; Jeffrey S. Ravel, "Le théâtre et ses publics, pratiques et représentations du parterre à Paris au XVIIIe siècle," *Revue d'histoire moderne et contemporaine* 49, no. 3 (July–September 2002): 89–118.

34. On this theme, see Tarde, *Les Lois de l'imitation*, 201–15.

35. For the ways in which the mechanisms (including material mechanisms) of interaction engaged the forms of ordinary judgments and the principles of justice and coordination to which those judgments referred, see Laurent Thévenot, "Jugements ordinaires et jugements de droit," *Annales E.S.C.*, no. 5 (September–October 1992).

36. Immanuel Kant, *What is Enlightenment?* In *Foundations of the Metaphysics of Morals and What is Enlightenment?* trans. Lewis White Beck, 2nd rev. ed. (New York: Macmillan, 1990), 87. See also the analyses of Chartier, *Cultural Origins of the French Revolution*, 23–27; Daniel Roche and Vicenzo Ferrone, "Historiographie des Lumières," in *Le Monde des Lumières*, ed. Roche and Ferrone (Paris: Fayard, 1999), 501–503.

37. On the point fact that the "public" in Kant is not defined on the basis of forms of intellectual sociability, see Chartier, *Cultural Origins*, 27.

38. Alletz, *Manuel de l'homme du monde*, 12–13.

39. Necker, *Mélanges*, 3:257.

40. Madame Du Deffand, letter to Walpole, December 27, 1768: Walpole, *Correspondence* 4, 2:174.

41. Genlis, *Mémoires*, 1:396.

42. Madame Necker, letter to Lesage, September 25, 1768: Bibliothèque publique universitaire de Genève, MSS suppl. 514, fol. 68.

43. Julie de Lespinasse, letter to Guibert, August 16, 1773: Lespinasse, *Lettres*, 64.

44. Madame Necker, letter to Gibbon, September 30, 1776: British Library (London), Add. 34 886, fols. 89–90.

45. Madame Necker, letter to Gibbon, September 30, 1776: British Library (London), Add. 34 886, fols. 89–90.

46. *Correspondance littéraire*, February 1770, 8:459.

47. *Correspondance littéraire*, March 1770, 8:475.

48. Joseph de La Porte, *Anecdotes dramatiques*, 3 vols. (Paris: La Veuve Duchesne, 1775); 3 vols. (Geneva: Slatkine, 1971), 1:81.

49. Claude Helvétius, *De l'esprit, or, Essays on the Mind (1759)* (Bristol, UK: Thoemmes Press, 2000), in Essay 2, "Of the Mind Relative to Society," 72–76.

50. Collé, *Journal et mémoires*, 2:333–34.

51. Hume's "succinct exposé" (1766) has been republished: David Hume, *Exposé succinct de la contestation qui s'est élevée entre M. Hume et M. Rousseau, avec les pièces justificatives et la lettre de M. de Voltaire à ce sujet*, ed. Jean-Pierre Jackson (Paris: Éditions Alive, 1998). The texts relating to the quarrel and the correspondence exchanged have been published in Rousseau, *Correspondance complète*, ed. Leigh, vols. 27–35 (in the following notes, *CC*). Leigh's editorial presentation is among the most nuanced. One might also consult Margaret Hill Peoples, "La querelle Rousseau-Hume," *Annales Jean-Jacques*, 18 (1927–28): 1–331; Henri Guillemin, *"Cette affaire infernale": L'affaire J.-J. Rousseau–Hume–1766* (Paris: Plon, 1942); Dena Goodman, "The Hume-Rousseau Affair: From Private Querelle to Public Process," *Eighteenth-Century Studies* 25 no. 2 (Winter 1991–92): 171–201.

52. Hume, letter to the comtesse de Boufflers, August 12, 1766: Rousseau, *Correspondance complète*, 30:233.

53. D'Alembert, letter to Hume, July 6, 1766: Rousseau, *CC*, 30:19.

54. "Let me beg of you not to think of publishing anything": Smith, letter to Hume, July 6, 1766; Rousseau, *CC*, 30:16.

55. "Stand this ridicule, expose his brutal letter, but without giving it out of your own hand, so that it may never be printed": Rousseau, *CC*, 30 :16.

56. D'Holbach, letter to Hume, July 7, 1766: Rousseau, *CC*, 30:20–21.

57. D'Alembert, letter to Hume, July 6, 1766: Rousseau, *CC*, 30:19.

58. D'Holbach, letter to Hume, July 7, 1766: Rousseau, *CC*, 30:20–21.

59. D'Alembert, letter to Hume, July 6, 1766: Rousseau, *CC*, 30:21.

60. Turgot, letter to Hume, July 27, 1766: Rousseau, *CC*, 30:178.

61. Duchesse d'Enville, letter to Moultou, July 21, 1766: Rousseau, *CC*, 30:134.

62. François Coindet, letter to Rousseau, July 21, 1766: Rousseau, *CC*, 30:182.

63. Since d'Holbach later destroyed Hume's letters, we know of them only by citations (in particular, the designation of Rousseau as "the blackest and most atrocious villain that ever disgraced human nature") through quotations in several correspondence collections: see Rousseau, *CC*, vol. 39, appendix A 439: 306–307.

64. Coindet, letter to Rousseau, July 21, 1766: Rousseau, *CC*, 30:182.

65. See the letters of the comtesse de Boufflers to Julie de Lespinasse of July 21, 1766 (Rousseau, *CC*, 30:129) and to Hume of July 22, 1766 (Rousseau, *CC*, 30:139).

66. Madame Du Deffand, letter to Walpole, July 9, 1766: Rousseau, *CC*, 30:27.

67. Turgot expressed his regret about the *bruit* and the *éclat* of Hume's letter to baron d'Holbach: Turgot, letter, September 7: Rousseau, *CC*, 30:335. He went so far as to assert that Hume's letter had been "as public as it could have been": Turgot, letter, July 23: Rousseau, *CC*, 30:147.

68. The *Courrier d'Avignon*, which had spoken of Rousseau's difficulties in England in an issue of July 1, spoke of the affair of July 12 (in the edition of July 22), and again on three other occasions during the month of August: Rousseau, *CC*, appendix A 450–454, 30:401–404. A number of articles appeared in England in the *Saint James's Chronicle*: Rousseau, *CC*, appendix A 461, 31:336–46.

69. Turgot used the term *publicité* in his letter to Hume of July 27: Rousseau, *CC*, 30:175–80.

70. "We also think that as the public is currently very occupied by this affair, you should lose no time before printing": D'Alembert, letter to Hume, July 21 1776: Rousseau, *CC*, 30:131.

71. Rousseau, letter to Guy, August 2, 1766: Rousseau, *CC*, 30:198.

72. Raymond Trousson, *Jean-Jacques Rousseau jugé par ses contemporains: Du Discours sur les sciences et les arts aux Confessions* (Paris: Champion, 2000), 415–16.

73. See Rousseau, *CC*, 30: appendix A 436–437.

74. Antoine Lilti, "The Writing of Paranoia: Jean-Jacques Rousseau and the Paradoxes of Celebrity," *Representations* 103 (Summer 2008), 53–83. Antoine Lilti, *Figures publiques. L'invention de la célébrité (1750–1850)* (Paris: Fayard, 2014).

75. *Remarques d'un anonyme* (Yverdun, 1766), 196; reprinted in Rousseau, *CC*, 33: appendix 539.

76. "Eh! What can one say to you, Monsieur, after a letter so little worthy of your pen that it is impossible for you to justify it, no matter how offended you might believe yourself to be": Madame de Boufflers, letter to Jean-Jacques Rousseau, July 27, 1766: Rousseau, *CC*, 30:174.

77. Turgot, letter to Hume, July 23, 1766: Rousseau, *CC*, 30:147. Turgot later returned to the topic: "The printing and the publication of this story can only have the object of justifying you in the imputations of villainy, blackness, and atrocity that you made against Rousseau and of which it is impossible that he not be aware": Rousseau, *CC*, 149.

78. "You are his benefactor; that title imposes duties on him in your regard," wrote Madame des Meinières: Rousseau, *CC*, 30:22.

79. Julie de Lespinasse, letter to Hume, July 6, 1766: Rousseau, *CC*, 30:18.

80. Duchesse de Choiseul, letter to Madame Du Deffand, July 17, 1766: Rousseau, *CC*, 30:109.

81. Madame Geoffrin, letter to Marmontel, July 30, 1766, Bibliothèque nationale française, Département des MSS, *Nouvelles acquisitions françaises* 4748.

82. Dominique Joseph, comte Garat, *Mémoires historiques sur la vie de M. Suard, sur ses écrits, et sur le XVIIIe siècle*, 2 vols. (Paris: A. Belin, 1820), 2:175.

83. Starobinski, *Jean-Jacques Rousseau: Transparence*, 162–63.

84. Turgot, letter to Hume, July 23, 1776: Rousseau, *CC*, 30:149.

85. Madame de Boufflers, letter to Jean-Jacques Rousseau, July 27, 1766: Rousseau, *CC*, 30:174.

86. Hume, letter to Pierre Guy, August 2, 1766: Rousseau, *CC*, 30: 197.

87. François Coindet, letter to Rousseau, July 21, 1766: Rousseau, *CC*, 30:128.

88. Comtesse de Boufflers, letter to Rousseau, July 27, 1766: Rousseau, *CC*, 30:175.

89. Rousseau, letter to the comtesse de Boufflers, August 30, 1766: Rousseau, *CC*, 30:292.

90. D'Holbach, letter to Hume, September 1, 1766: Rousseau, *CC*, 30:300. Hume followed that recommendation to the letter. His succinct exposé presents the items in the correspondence in an irreproachable transcription.

91. Rousseau, letter to Hume, July 10, 1766: Rousseau, *CC*, 30:29.

92. See, for example, Rousseau's letter to Madame Verdelin: "M. Hume has promised to publish all the pieces relating to this affair. If he keeps his word, you will see in the letter that I wrote to him on July 10 the details that you ask for, [or] at least enough to make the rest superfluous": Rousseau, letter, August 30, 1766: Rousseau, *CC*, 30:298. This was precisely where the greatest gap was created between Rousseau and his defenders, who were attempting to recall him to a regime of proof: "If you do not have quite clear and clearly stated facts to oppose, it is impossible for you to justify what you have done," Coindet wrote: Coindet, letter to Rousseau, July 28: Rousseau, *CC*, 30:181.

93. Rousseau, letter to Madame de Boufflers, August 30, 1877: Rousseau, *CC*, 30:292.

94. Rousseau, letter to Hume, July 10, 1766: Rousseau, *CC*, 30:29.

95. Rousseau, letter to the marquise de Verdelin, ca. August 30, 1766: Rousseau, *CC*, 30: 300.

96. Marquise de Verdelin, letter to François Coindet, July 24, 1766: Rousseau, *CC*, 30:134; letter to Rousseau, October 9, 1766: Rousseau, *CC*, 31:21–22.

97. D'Holbach, letter to Hume, September 1, 1766: Rousseau, *CC*, 30:309.

98. D'Alembert, letter to Hume, July 21, 1766: Rousseau, *CC*, 30:130.

99. Hume, letter to Adam Smith, September 9, 1766: Rousseau, *CC*, 30:343.

100. See, for example, the letters exchanged by d'Alembert and Suard in early October 1766: Rousseau, *CC*, 31:2–10. D'Alembert wrote to Hume: "M. Suard has already translated your papers, we have made, together with the baron, the called-for changes in conformity with your wishes, we will add to it a brief notice": D'Alembert, letter to Hume, October 6, 1766: Rousseau, *CC*, 31: 16.

101. D'Alembert, letter to Hume, October 6, 1766: Rousseau, *CC*, 31:16.

102. George Keith, letter to Rousseau, November 22, 1766: Rousseau, *CC*, 31:196.

103. See, for example, Madame Verdelin's letter to Rousseau of July 24, 1766: Rousseau, *CC*, 30:152.

104. Madame de Verdelin, letter to François Coindet, ca. July 24, 1766: Rousseau, *CC*, 30:154.

105. Rousseau, *CC*, 30:154.

106. See d'Alembert, letter to Suard, October 5, 1766: Rousseau, *CC*, 31:15.

107. On receiving a letter from Hume, she wrote to Julie de Lespinasse, "I do not claim to hide that this seemed to me much too late and that I thought I was to be

informed before anyone else of this occurrence": Comtesse de Boufflers, letter, July 21, 1766: Rousseau, *CC*, 30:129.

108. Théodore Tronchin, letter to Jacob Tronchin, August 17, 1766: Rousseau, *CC*, 30:211.

109. Madame de Boufflers, letter to Hume, July 22, 1766: Rousseau, *CC*, 30:142.

110. Rousseau, *CC*, 143.

111. Madame Du Deffand, letter to Walpole, July 16, 1766: Rousseau, *CC*, 30:103.

112. Madame Du Deffand, letter to Walpole, August 6, 1766: Rousseau, *CC*, 30: 217.

113. Madame Du Deffand, letter to Walpole, September 11, 1766: Rousseau, *CC*, 30:367.

114. Madame Du Deffand, letter to Walpole, July 16, 1766: Rousseau, *CC*, 30:103.

115. *Correspondance littéraire*, October 1766, 7:129–46.

CHAPTER 6

1. Marie de Rabutin-Chantal, marquise de Sévigné, *Lettres*, rev. ed., ed. Louis Jean Nicolas Monmerqué, 14 vols. (Paris: Hachette, 1862–66), 8:502. The term *politiquer* reappears in the great literary classics of the eighteenth century (*Jacques le Fataliste* and *La Nouvelle Héloïse*) and in correspondence.

2. Madame Du Deffand, letter to abbé Barthélemy, March 13, 1772: Du Deffand, *Correspondance avec la duchesse de Choiseul*, 2:148.

3. Madame Du Deffand, letter to abbé Barthélemy, February 24, 1773: Du Deffand, *Correspondance avec la duchesse de Choiseul*, 2:367.

4. Maurepas was one of the major song collectors. Bernis had certain of these songs sent to him in Rome, such as "Apologie de la nouvelle administration des finances" (about Turgot) and "Vers à Mme la comtesse Du Barry au sujet de la disgrâce de M. le duc de Choiseul": Bibliothèque de l'Arsenal, MS 15041, Bernis.

5. Chamfort, *Maximes, pensées, caractères*, 227.

6. Archives nationales, 508 AP 38.

7. Robert Darnton, "Poetry and the Police in Eighteenth-Century Paris," *Studies on Voltaire and the Eighteenth Century* 371 (1999): 1–22.

8. Horace Walpole, letter to Thomas Gray, Paris, November 19, 1765: Walpole, *Correspondence*, 22:142–45.

9. Blbliothèque publique universitaire de Genève, Archives Tronchin, vol. 200. See also Madame Du Deffand's correspondence with Walpole.

10. Lespinasse, *Lettres*, 130; quoted from *Letters of Mlle de Lespinasse*, trans. Katherine Prescott Normeley (Boston: Hardy, Pratt, 1902), 135.

11. When Turgot became Secretary of the Navy, Boufflers wrote that he was among her "friends," and enjoyed a "general esteem," and she praised his intelligence (*lumières*), his "abilities," and his "probity": Letter, July 20, 1774; Boufflers, *Lettres de Gustave III*, 89. Immediately after Conti's death, she stated that the last service that he had rendered to his country had been to stand opposed "to the dangerous and unjust systems of M. Turgot": Letter, January 24, 1777; Boufflers, *Lettres de Gustave III*, 105.

12. Boufflers, letter, January 24, 1777: Boufflers, *Lettres de Gustave III*, 104.

13. Madame de Forcalquier was an old friend of Madame Du Deffand's but their relations had always been complicated. Madame de Forcalquier's alliances connected her with the Brancas and the Maurepas. She was quite close to the duchesse d'Aiguillon, which, in the confrontation between d'Aiguillon and Choiseul, put her in a position directly opposed to that of Madame Du Deffand.

14. Madame Du Deffand, letter to Walpole, March 7, 1770: Walpole, *Correspondence*, 4, 2:382.

15. Madame Du Deffand, letter to Walpole, March 28, 1770: Walpole, *Correspondence*, 4, 2:390–91.

16. Madame Du Deffand, letter to the duchesse de Choiseul, January 7, 1771: Walpole, *Correspondence*, 5, 3:308.

17. François-Vincent Toussaint, *Anecdotes curieuses de la cour de France sous le règne de Louis XV*, ed. Paul Fould (1905) (Paris: Plon, 1908), 236–37.

18. See Jean Sareil, *Les Tencin: Histoire d'une famille au dix-huitième siècle, d'après de nombreux documents inédits* (Geneva: Droz, 1969).

19. Allonville, *Mémoires secrets*, 1:170.

20. *Correspondance littéraire*, August 1772, 10:39.

21. Madame Suard, letter to Condorcet, autumn 1772: Condorcet, *Correspondance inédite*, 99.

22. Madame de La Ferté-Imbault, "Histoire de l'amititié dont le prince de Condé m'honore depuis 1762": Archives nationales, 508 AP 38.

23. See the letter of Mary Wilkes to John Wilkes, August 5, 1772, which states that Pezay was "extremely intimate with the baron d'Holbach, and knows well all of his *société* [in French in the original]": Diderot, *Correspondance*, 12:100. On the ambiguous relations between Pezay and the Encyclopedists, see Frank A. Kafker and Serena L. Kafker, *The Encyclopedists as Individuals: A Biographical Dictionary of the Authors of the Encyclopédie*, Studies on Voltaire and the Eighteenth Century 257 (Oxford: Voltaire Foundation at the Taylor Institution, 1988), 310–12.

24. His real name was Jacques Masson, and not everybody appreciated this social transformation: "This little Masson de Pezay who wears red heels and gets his lackey and even his printer to call him 'Monsieur le marquis' right in front of our faces—we who have known Madame Masson his mother and who used to take the liberty of calling monsieur le marquis *le petit Massonet*": *Correspondance littéraire*, 9:455–56.

25. Madame de Rochfort, letter to Mirabeau, January 29, 1761: Musée Arbaud, Aix-en-Provence, Archives Mirabeau, vol. 34, fols. 424–25.

26. Marquis de Mirabeau, letter to Madame de Rochefort, August 9, 1767: Musée Arbaud, Archives Mirabeau, vol. 35, fol. 375.

27. Bombelles, *Journal*, August 15, 1786, 2:159.

28. Madame de La Ferté-Imbault, letter about Bernis, August 10, 1776: Archives nationales, 508 AP 37. Madame de La Ferté-Imbault was a close friend of Bernis and had closely followed his rising career.

29. Madame de La Ferté-Imbault, letter about Bernis, August 10, 1776: Archives nationales, 508 AP 37.

30. François Joachim de Pierres, cardinal de Bernis, *Mémoires*, ed. Philippe Bonnet (Paris: Mercure de France, 1980, 2000), August 15, 1786, 2:159, quoted from *Memoirs and Letters of Cardinal de Bernis*, trans. Katharine Prescott Wormeley, 2 vols. (London: Heinemann, 1902), 2:138.

31. Bernis, *Mémoires*, 2:159; *Memoirs and Letters*, 2:140.

32. Madame de La Ferté-Imbault, letter about Bernis, August 10, 1776: Archives nationales, 508 AP 37.

33. Madame de La Ferté-Imbault, letter about Bernis, August 10, 1776: Archives nationales, 508 AP 37. See also "Anecdotes du règne de Louis XV": Archives nationales, 508 AP 38, fol. 65; and Hénault, *Mémoires*, 214–15.

34. "Histoire de l'amitié dont le prince de Condé m'honore depuis 1762": Archives nationales, 508 AP 38.

35. Madame de La Ferté-Imbault, letter to the comte d'Albaret, December 21, 1778: British Library (London), Morisson Collection, Add. MS 39673, fol. 186.

36. See, for example, Bombelles on the sociability of the baron de Breteuil: Bombelles, *Journal*, 1:250; 2:242, 250.

37. Rohand d'Olier Butler's weighty *Choiseul* (Oxford: Clarendon Press, 1980), vol. 1, *Father and Son, 1719–1754* stops in 1754. The many biographies of Choiseul repeat the information given in the two works of Henri Maugras on Choiseul: *Le duc et la duchesse de Choiseul, leur vie intime, leurs amis et leur temps* (Paris: Plon, 1902), and *La Disgrâce du duc et de la duchesse de Choiseul, la vie à Chanteloup, le retour à Paris, la mort* (Paris: Plon, 1903, 1976).

38. Madame Du Deffand, letter to Abbé Barthélemy, May 5, 1773: Du Deffand, *Correspondance avec la duchesse de Choiseul*, 2:401.

39. Madame Du Deffand, letter to Walpole, January 6, 1772: Walpole, *Correspondence*, 5, 3:169.

40. Abbé Barthélemy, letter to Madame Du Deffand, September 23, 1771: Du Deffand, *Correspondance avec la duchesse de Choiseul*, 2:49.

41. Madame Du Deffand, letter to the duchesse de Choiseul, January 7, 1771: Du Deffand, *Correspondance avec la duchesse de Choiseul*, 1:309.

42. Madame Du Deffand, letter to Walpole, January 19, 1771: Walpole, *Correspondence*, 5, 3:13.

43. Madame de Choiseul, letter to Madame Du Deffand, July 18, 1771: Du Deffand, *Correspondance avec la duchesse de Choiseul*, 2:13–14.

44. Du Deffand, *Correspondance avec la duchesse de Choiseul*, 2:13–14.

45. Bathélémy, Letter, July 17, 1771: Du Deffand, *Correspondance avec la duchesse de Choiseul*, 2:15.

46. Madame Du Deffand, letter to Walpole, February 21, 1775: Walpole, *Correspondence*, 6, 4:161; letter of January 19, 1775, Walpole, *Correspondence*, 6, 4:142.

47. "M. de Sénac is the oracle of some circles and belongs within the society of M. de Choiseul by his connections with the prince and princesse de Beauvau. That society is no longer predominant, but it has not lost all direct or mediated means for serving its partisans": Bombelles, *Journal*, May 6, 1783, 1:218.

48. See John Hardman, *French Politics, 1774–1789, from the Accession of Louis XVI to the Fall of the Bastille* (London and New York: Longman, 1995), 52–53; Jean Égret, *Necker, ministre de Louis XVI, 1776–1790* (Paris: Honoré Champion, 1975), 27–29.

49. Condorcet, letter to Madame Suard, June 1775: Condorcet, *Correspondance inédite*, 167.

50. Condorcet, letter to Madame Suard, 1778: Condorcet, *Correspondance inédite*, 194–95. When Madame Suard jokingly proposed to Condorcet that he be named Minister of War, he responded, "It is a good idea to name me Minister of War; it is like M. Necker [as] contrôleur général. Happily, I do not have any great suppers": Condorcet, *Correspondance inédite*, 184.

51. "It was neither for us nor for herself that she took all these pains; it was for her husband. To bring us acquainted with him, to make him be viewed with favor and talked of with praise in *le monde*, and thus to lay the foundations of his renown, was her powerful motive in founding her literary society": Marmontel, *Mémoires*, 331; quoted from *Memoirs of Marmontel*, 2:98.

52. Madame Necker, letter to Gibbon, July 29, 1781: British Library, Add. 34 886, Gibbon Papers, fols. 121–22.

53. AAE, *Contrôle des étrangers*, vol. 3, report of December 16, 1744.

54. André Morellet, *Mémoire sur la situation actuelle de la Compagnie des Indes* (Paris: Dessaint, 1765); Morellet, *Examen de la réponse de M. N. au mémoire de M. l'abbé Morellet, sur la Compagnie des Indes, par l'auteur du Mémoire* (Paris: Dessaint, 1769).

55. See, for example, *Correspondance littéraire*, 9:16; or Diderot's letter to Sophie Volland of August 23, 1769: Diderot, *Correspondance*, 9:120.

56. André Morellet, *Analyse de l'ouvrage intitulé "De la législation et du commerce des grains,"* (1775). See also his letter to Shelburne, April 12, 1776: Morellet, *Lettres*, 1:336–41.

57. Morellet, letter to Shelburne, September 2, 1780: Morellet, *Lettres*, 1:429.

58. Marmontel, *Correspondance*, 2:207.

59. Morellet, letter to Shelburne, September 2, 1780: Morellet, *Lettres*, 1:429.

60. Necker's career as a banker in the early years of the salon is well known thanks to Lüthy, *Banque protestante*, 369–420.

61. This was according to Alexandre-Marie-Léonor de Saint-Mauris, prince de Montbarey, *Mémoires autographes*, 3 vols. (Paris: A. Eymerie, 1826–27), 2:244–45, 3:123–24; cited in Égret, *Necker*, 41. The duchesse d'Enville, who was fairly close to Maurepas, had already played a role two years earlier in favor of Tugot: Madame de La Ferté-Imbault, "Anecdotes relatives à M. le comte de Maurepas, 16 mai 177," Archives nationales, 508 AP 38. On Turgot's rise to power and on the satires inspired by his connections with the women of high society (Madame de Marchais, Madame d'Enville, Julie de Lespinasse, Madame Blondel), see Edgar Faure, *La Disgrâce de Turgot* (Paris: Gallimard, 1961), 464.

62. See, in particular, the letters of the duchesse de Choiseul of April 26, 1776, and July 6, 1776: Du Deffand, *Correspondance avec la duchesse de Choiseul*, 3:213, 226.

63. Madame Du Deffand, letter to the duchesse de Choiseul, October 23, 1776: Du Deffand, *Correspondance avec la duchesse de Choiseul*, 3:250.

64. The Choiseuls failed to appreciate her efforts, and reproached her with not furnishing news rapidly enough. She was thus obliged to justify herself: Letter of October 26, 1776; Du Deffand, *Correspondance avec la duchesse de Choiseul*, 251.

65. "Anecdotes sur Necker," June 10, 1781: Archives nationales, 508 AP 38.

66. Madame de La Ferté-Imbault, letter to d'Albaret, n.d.: British Library (London), Add. MS 39673, fol. 186.

67. In her personal papers Madame de La Ferté-Imbault changed her tone toward the former minister. Her "Anecdotes sur M. et Mme Necker" of June 10, 1780 strongly praise both Necker and his wife: Archives nationales, 508 AP 38. In the "Lettre sur la démission de M. Necker" (June 5, 1781), she is very critical and blames Necker's errors on "his wife" and "his society." Two weeks after Necker's resignation, she paid a visit to them at Saint-Ouen on the condition that they had no other visitors.

68. According to Turgot, "He brought together the most opposed sorts of support, as Madame Du Deffand spoke of him just as did Mademoiselle de Lespinasse": Letter, September 2, 1773; Anne Robert Jacques Turgot, *Lettres de Turgot à la duchesse d'Enville, 1764–74 et 1777–1780*, ed. Joseph Ruwet (Louvain: Bibliothèque de l'université, 1976), 87.

69. *Correspondance littéraire*, April 1770, 9:16.

70. Madame de Créqui, letter, September 6, 1788: Créquy, *Lettres*, 168.

71. Dena Goodman, "Pigalle's *Voltaire nu*: The Republic of Letters Represents Itself to the World," *Representations* 16 (1986): 86–109; Goodman, *Republic of Letters*, 180, 226–28.

72. Voltaire, "Stances à Mme Necker," in *Œuvres de Voltaire*, ed. A. J. Q. Beuchot, 72 vols. (Paris: Firmin Didot, 1829–40), 12:549.

73. Voltaire, "Épître à Mme Necker," *Œuvres*, 13:332–33. Even Necker's enemies tried to procure a copy of it. Turgot, who was at La Roche-Guyon at the home of the duchesse d'Enville, had copies made for Condorcet and for Madame Blondel: Turgot, letter to Condorcet, November 21, 1776: Anne Robert Jacques Turgot, in Jean-Antoine-Nicolas Caritat, marquis de Condorcet, *Correspondance inédite de Condorcet et de Turgot 1770–1779*, ed. Charles Henry (Paris: Charavay frères, 1882; Geneva: Slatkine reprints, 1970), 286.

74. Joseph Alphonse, abbé de Véri, *Journal*, 2 vols. (Paris: Tallandier, 1928–1930), 1:126.

75. Keith Michael Baker, *Inventing the French Revolution: Essays on French Political Culture in the Eighteenth Century* (Cambridge, UK, and New York: Cambridge University Press, 1990), 167–99.

76. Baker, *Inventing the French Revolution*, 190–97.

77. Necker, *De l'administration des finances de la France*, Paris, 1784, lviii; quoted from *A Treatise on the Administration of the Finances of France*, trans. Thomas Mortimer, 3 vols. (London: Logographic, 1785), 1:lv.

78. *De l'administration*, lxx; *Treatise*, 1:lxvii.

79. *De l'administration*, lxii; *Treatise*, 1:lix.

80. Necker, letter to Maurepas, October 1776; Égret, *Necker*, 29.

81. Letters of Suard and his wife, January 2, 1783, and response of Madame Necker, January 17, 1783: Institut et Musée Voltaire (Geneva), Archives Suard, vol. 1, fol. 94, and vol. 6, fol. 27.

82. Madame de La Ferté-Imbault, letter to Madame Necker, March 22, 1788 and undated response: Archives nationales, 508 AP 37.

83. See, for example, Jean Pierre, marquis de Luchet, *Les Amusements des gens du monde* (s.l., 1785), 12–17, which publishes a false letter of Necker's to Madame de Beauvau.

84. Lucien Bély, *Espions et ambassadeurs au temps de Louis XIV* (Paris: Fayard, 1990), 391.

85. See, for example, Géraud Poumarède, "La querelle du sofa: Étude sur les rapports entre gloire et diplomatie," *Histoire, économie et société* 2 (2001): 185–97.

86. François de Callières, *De la manière de négocier avec les souverains. . .* (Paris, 1716); quoted in Bély, *Espions et ambassadeurs*, 392.

87. AAE, *Contrôle des étrangers*, vol. 6, report of June 2, 1775. Habitual guests of this "Monday society" included the ministers of Sweden, Russia, and Prussia, as well as Prince Baratinski and Count Stroganov.

88. AAE, *Contrôle des étrangers*, vol. 6, report of July 21, 1775.

89. AAE, *Contrôle des étrangers*, vol. 2, report of January 2, 1778.

90. AAE, *Contrôle des étrangers*, vol. 3, report of November 11, 1774.

91. AAE, *Contrôle des étrangers*, vol. 3, report of November 18, 1774.

92. AAE, *Contrôle des étrangers*, vol. 21, report on the English ambassador, March 20, 1779.

93. AAE, *Contrôle des étrangers*, vol. 7, report of October 13, 1775.

94. AAE, *Contrôle des étrangers*, vol. 7, report of October 27, 1775.

95. Jules Flammermont, *Les Correspondances des agents diplomatiques étrangers en France avant la Révolution, conservées dans les archives de Berlin, Dresde, Genève, Turin, Gênes, Florence, Naples, Simancas, Lisbonne, Londres, La Haye, Vienne* (Paris: Imprimerie Nationale, 1896), 86–95.

96. AAE, *Contrôle des étrangers*, vol. 60, report of May 5, 1786.

97. AAE, *Contrôle des étrangers*, vol. 21, report of April 3, 1778.

98. AAE, *Contrôle des étrangers*, vol. 21, report of April 3, 1778.

99. AAE, *Contrôle des étrangers*, vol. 15, report of May 30, 1777.

100. AAE, *Contrôle des étrangers*, vol. 14, report of March 28, 1777; vol. 15, report of April 4, 1777.

101. AAE, *Contrôle des étrangers*, vol. 21, report of March 13, 1778.

102. AAE, *Contrôle des étrangers*, vol. 18, report of October 24, 1777.

103. AAE, *Contrôle des étrangers*, vol. 19, report of December 12, 1777. The news referred to the battle of Saratoga.

104. "On the public rumors about a treaty between France and America": AAE, *Contrôle des étrangers*, vol. 20, report of January 9, 1778. The duchesse de Deux-Ponts, who was also known as the comtesse de Forbach, received Franklin on Saturdays. She enthusiastically supported the American struggle, and her son Christian, who was delighted to speak English with Franklin at his mother's house, later served in Rochambeau's expeditionary corps. See, for example, the letter of the duchess to Franklin, Tuesday March 10, 1778: Benjamin Franklin, *Papers*, 39 vols. (New Haven: Yale University Press, 1959–2008), March 1–June 30, 26:86–87.

105. Duc de La Rochefoucauld, letter to Franklin, February 18, 1778, and Franklin's response: Franklin, *Papers*, 25:686–87.

106. Ambassador Stormont and his wife received 152 visits during the four final days of his stay in Paris, March 17–20: a list is annexed to AAE, *Contrôle des étrangers*, report of March 20, 1778, vol. 21.

107. AAE, *Contrôle des étrangers*, vol. 21, report of March 27, 1778.

108. Duc de La Rochefoucauld, letter to Franklin: Franklin, *Papers*, 26:180.

109. AAE, *Contrôle des étrangers*, vol. 17, report of August 1, 1777.

110. AAE, *Contrôle des étrangers*, vol. 40, report of September 28, 1781.

111. AAE, *Contrôle des étrangers*, vol. 6, report of August 13, 1784, dossier "Boden"; copy of the report of December 27, 1771.

112. AAE, *Contrôle des étrangers*, vol. 6, report of August 13, 1784; copy, December 27, 1771.

113. AAE, *Contrôle des étrangers*, vol. 33, report of February 18, 1780.

114. Bibliothèque de l'Arsenal, MSS 11981, fol. 29, report of the search of her premises, January 27, 1757.

115. Bibliothèque de l'Arsenal, MSS 11981, fol. 29, report of January 23, 1756. See also the report of February 19, 1758, fol. 312.

116. Bibliothèque de l'Arsenal, MSS 11981, fol. 29, fol. 310, report of Duval.

117. Unfortunately, the dossier kept in the archives of the Bastille for the most part concerns the 1757 episode alone. For later events there are only a few fragmentary reports, for example Duval, letter to Vergennes, July 1774: Bibliothèque de l'Arsenal, MSS 11981, fol. 403.

118. Abraham de Wicquefort, *L'Ambassadeur et ses fonctions* (Amsterdam, 1730), quoted in Hugues Marquis, "L'espionnage britannique et la fin de l'Ancien Régime," *Histoire, économie et sociétés* 2 (1998): 261–76.

119. Bombelles, *Journal*, August 12, 1783, 1:250.

120. Lucien Bély, *La Société des princes, XVIe–XVIIIe siècle* (Paris: Fayard, 1999), chap. 25: "Le temps des despotes éclairés."

121. Madame Du Deffand, letter to Walpole, May 18, 1777: Walpole, *Correspondence*, 6, 4:442–43. Madame Blondel, the daughter of a receveur général des Finances and the wife of a diplomat, was one of Turgot's closest friends.

122. Madame Du Deffand, letter to Walpole, May 18, 1777: Walpole, *Correspondence*, 6, 4:442–43.

123. Cars, *Mémoires*, 2:31. AAE, *Contrôle des étrangers*, vol. 53, reports of August 27 and September 3, 1784.

124. See the dispatches of the Saxon chargé d'affaires, Rivière, in October 1784, cited in Flammermont, *Correspondances des agents diplomatiques*, 200–01.

125. Madame d'Épinay, letter to Galiani, March 1, 1771: Galiani and Épinay, *Correspondance*, 2:62–63.

126. Lucien Maury, "Les comtesses de la Marck et de Boufflers et Gustave III, d'après les corespondances conservées à Upsala," *Revue Historique* 1 (1905): 302–309; 2 (1905): 92–110; Marie-Charlotte-Hyppolite, comtesse Boufflers, *Lettres de Gustave III à a comtesse de Boufflers et de la comtesse de Boufflers au roi, de 1771 à 1791*, ed. Aurélien Vivie (Bordeaux, 1900).

127. Creutz, letter to Gustav III, August 30, 1771: Maury, "Les comtesses de La Marck et de Boufflers," 307.

128. Gustav III asked the comtesse d'Egmont to act as an intermediary for him with the comtesse de Brionne, who exerted a great influence over Choiseul. Madame d'Egmont wrote to Gustav III about transmitting to her friend the request of the king of Sweden to have her portrait. The gallant exchange is political here. This letter is published in Marie de Ségur, comtesse d'Armaillé, *La Comtesse d'Egmont, fille du Maréchal de Richelieu, 1740–1773, d'après ses littres inédites à Gustave III* (Paris: Perrin, 1890), 181.

129. Creutz, letter to Gustav III, January 16, 1772: Maury, "Les comtesses de La Marck et de Boufflers," 307.

130. Creutz, letter to Gustav III, June 25, 1775: Maury, "Les comtesses de La Marck et de Boufflers," 307.

131. Morellet, letter to Shelburne, November 3, 1772: Morellet, *Lettres*, 1:180.

132. Madame Geoffrin, letter to Stanisłas August Poniatowski, August 7, 1765: Geoffrin, *Correspondance du roi Stanislas-Auguste Poniatowski*, 164.

133. Madame Geoffrin, letter to Choiseul: Archives nationales, 508 AP 34, 1765.

134. Madame Geoffrin, letter to Choiseul: Archives nationales, 508 AP 34, 1765.

135. Madame Geoffrin, letter to Stanisław August Poniatowski, December 21, 1765: Geoffrin, *Correspondance du roi Stanislaw-Auguste Poniatowski*, 183–89.

136. Comtesse de La Marck, letter to Gustav III, Paris, February 20, 1772: AAE, *Mémoires et documents*, France 319.

137. Copy of the article of November 3, 1767 of the *Gazette de La Haye*: Archives nationales, 508 AP 34.

138. Choiseul, letter to Madame Geoffrin, December 4, 1767: Archives nationales, 508 AP 34.

139. Choiseul, letter to Desrivaux, November 24, 1767, and Desrivaux's response to Choiseul, November 29, 1767: Archives nationales, 508 AP 34.

140. Lenoir, letter to Vergennes, January 1781: AAE, *Contrôle des étrangers*, vol. 37.

141. Bibliothèque municipale d'Orléans, Lenoir papers, MS 1399, fol. 120.

142. Bibliothèque municipale d'Orléans, Lenoir papers, MS 1400, fol. 28.

143. "He was suspected: he himself warned me that he was suspect there and that someone had said to him that it was odd to see, under a tolerant minister, the inconvenient eye of the police": Bibliothèque municipale d'Orléans, Lenoir papers, MS 1399, fol. 120.

144. Bombelles, *Journal*, July 17, 1782, 1:134.

145. Jeremy D. Popkin and Bernadette Fort, eds., *The Mémoires secrets and the Culture of Publicity in Eighteenth-Century France* (Oxford: Voltaire Foundation, 1998), 15. The traditional presentation of the salon of Madame Doublet can be found in Tate, *Petit de Bachaumont*.

146. Lenoir, letter to Vergennes, July 23, 1785, AAE, *Contrôle des étrangers*, vol. 61, fols. 36–37.

147. AAE, *Contrôle des étrangers*, vol. 60, report of June 2, 1786, "Bobrinsky."

148. Morellet, *Mémoires inédits*, 279.

149. Bibliothèque municipale d'Orléans, Lenoir papers, MS 1401, fol. 235.

150. Luc Vincent Thiery, *Guide des amateurs et des étrangers voyageurs à Paris*, 3 vols. (Paris: Hardouin et Gattey, 1787), 279–80.

151. Bombelles, *Journal*, December 12, 1785, 2:92.

152. Gouverneur Morris, *A Diary of the French Revolution*, ed. Beatrix Cary Davenport, 2 vols. (Boston: Houghton Mifflin, 1939), 1:55.

153. Morris, *Diary*, 1:40.

154. Morris, *Diary*, 1:142. Similarly, several days before, after a political discussion with Jefferson, Morris circulated among the cafés and in the clubs and salons in search of information: *Diary*, 1:104, 105.

155. Madame de Sabran, letter to the chevalier de Boufflers, July 11, 1787: Sabran, *Correspondance inédite de la comtesse de Sabran et du chevalier de Boufflers (1778–1788)*, ed. E. De Magnieu and Henri Prat (Paris: Plon, 1875), 273.

156. Madame de Créqui, letter to Sénac, July 11, 1788: Créquy, *Lettres*, 143.

157. Madame Necker, letter to M. De L.***: Necker, *Mélanges*, 1:153.

158. Talleyrand-Périgord, *Mémoires*, 1:59–60.

159. Talleyrand-Périgord, *Mémoires*, 1:59–60.

160. Morris, *Diary*, 1:6.

161. Morris, *Diary*, 1:6.

162. Bombelles, *Journal*, November 19, 1788, 2:260.

163. Madame de Sabran, letter to the chevalier de Boufflers, January 8, 1787: Sabran, *Correspondance inédite*, 201–202.

164. Morris, *Diary*, 1:3–4.

165. Suard, letter to his wife, June 1789: Institut et Musée Voltaire, Geneva, Suard archives, vol. 2, fol. 79.

166. Madame de La Ferté-Imbault, letter to Narbonne, October 17, 1788, and his response of November 10, 1788: Archives nationales, 508 AP 37.

167. The success of Necker's *Traité sur l'administration des finances de la France*, published in 1784, the presence of the royal family at the marriage of his daughter, the protection of the queen, and the financial difficulties of the monarchy led his partisans to hope for his return to power.

168. Dispatch of Salmour, the minister plenipotentiary of Saxony, April 21, 1787: Flammermont, *Correspondances des agents diplomatiques*, 217.

169. Marquise de La Ferté-Imbault, letter to the comte d'Albaret, undated (early 1786): British Library, Morisson Collection, Add. MS 39673, fol. 203.

170. Madame de La Ferté-Imbault, several letters of January and February 1786: British Library, Morisson Collection, Add. MS 39673, fols. 205–17.

171. Madame de Staël, letter to Madame de La Ferté-Imbault, 1786: Archives nationales, 508 AP 37.

172. Dispatch of Salmour, April 23, 1780: Flammermont, *Correspondances des agents diplomatiques*, 228.

173. Jules Michelet, *Histoire de la Révolution française*, 2 vols. (Paris: Robert Laffont, 1988), 1:517.

174. Jean Boutier and Philippe Boutry, "Les sociétés politiques en France de 1789 à l'an II: Une machine?" *Revue d'histoire moderne et contemporaine* 36 (1989): 29–67. See also *Atlas de la Révolution française*, ed. Serge Bonin and Claude Langlois, 8 vols. (Paris: Éditions de l'EHESS, 1987–), vol. 6, *Les Sociétés Politiques*, ed. Jean Boutier and Philippe Boutry (1992).

175. AAE, *Contrôle des étrangers*, vol. 74, report of July 30, 1789.

176. Chastenay, *Mémoires*, 113.

177. The comtesse de Flahaut was Adélaïde Filleul, the wife of Charles François Flahaut de La Billarderie, who was the brother of the comte d'Angiviller. She is better known for her novels, written during the Restoration under the name of Madame de Souza.

178. Marie-José Fassiotto, "La comtesse de Flahaut et son cercle: Un exemple de salon politique sous la Révolution," Transactions of the Eighth International Congress on the Enlightenment, Bristol, July 21–27, 1991, Studies on Voltaire and the Eighteenth Century, 303 (1992): 344–48.

179. Morris, Diary, 2:147.

180. Morris, Diary, 1:293.

181. Morris, Diary, 1:286.

182. Morris, Diary, December 14, 1789, November 30, 1790, and April 13, 1791: 1:332, 2:75, 2:161.

183. Shelburne, letters to Morellet, December 13, 1789 and February 1790: Morellet, Lettres, 2:154. See also Morellet's account in his Mémoires, 275.

184. Morellet, Mémoires, 307. On this rupture, see David Warner Smith, "Revolution and Personal Relationships: The Rupture between Cabanis and the Abbé Morellet," in Rousseau and the Eighteenth Century: Essays in Memory of R. A. Leigh, ed. Marian Hobson et al., 335–48 (Oxford: Voltaire Foundation, 1992).

185. Morris, Diary, 2:235.

186. Correspondence between Madame de La Ferté-Imbault and Le Pelletier de Saint-Fargeau: Archives nationales, 508 AP 37.

187. It is hard to distinguish, in the counterrevolutionary networks, what was a salon and what was a secret society. The "salon français," a club created in 1782, became a counterrevolutionary group during the Revolution. It stopped meeting in 1790, then was reconstituted in March 1790 on the rue Royale-Saint-Roch, but it inspired protests that led to its closing on May 15 by decision of the police: Jugement rendu qui fait défense à la société connue sous le nom de sallon français de s'assembler à l'avenir dans la maison de la rue Royale no. 29, May 15, 1790 (Paris: Imprimerie de Loltin l'aîné). The members of this group continued to meet clandestinely and drew up plans for the king's escape or for an insurrection in the southeast: See Jacqueline Chaumié, Le Réseau d'Antraigues et la contre-Révolution (Paris: Plon, 1965), 46–47.

188. Colette Piau-Gillot, "Rétif, ou le salon de Mme de Beauharnais," in Vivre la Révolution: Rétif de la Bretonne, Actes du colloque de Tours, June 22–23, 1989; Études Rétiviennes 11 (1989): 109–28, esp. p. 123.

189. Morellet, Mémoires, 309. Madame Broutin was quite closely connected with the Suards, who attended her Wednesday dinners: Institut et Musée Voltaire, Geneva, Suard archives.

190. Kale, "Women, the Public Sphere and the Persistence of Salons."

191. Madame Roland, letter to Bancal, April 5, 1791: Roland, Lettres, 2:258.

192. Madame Roland, letter to Boc, April 15, 1792: Roland, Lettres, 2:418.

193. Records of the interrogations of Madame Roland in Actes du tribunal révolutionnaire, gathered and commented by Gérard Walter (Paris: Mercure de France, 1986), 264, 268, 274. See also Marie-Jeanne Roland, Mémoires de Madame Roland (Paris: Mercure de France, 1986).

194. Hesse, Other Enlightenment.

195. Quoted in Mona Ozouf, Les Mots des femmes: Essai sur la singularité française (Paris: Fayard, 1995; Gallimard, 1999), 87; trans. Jane Marie Todd as Women's Words: Essay on French Singularity (Chicago: University of Chicago Press, 1997).

196. Interrogation of 12 Brumaire (November 1, 1792), in *Actes du tribunal révolu-tionnaire*, 270. The "bureau d'esprit public" signified a Girondin office created to diffuse the revolutionary press in the provinces that was put into place in the summer of 1792. Charles Walton, *Policing Public Opinion in the French Revolution. The Culture of Calumny and the Problem of Free Speech* (New York: Oxford University Press, 2009).

197. Kale, *French Salons*, chap. 2; Bernard Gainot, "Héritages et mutations de la sociabilité politique dans la France du Directoire," in *Élites et Sociabilité au XIXe siècle: Héritages, identités*, Acts du colloque de Douai, 1999, ed. Hervé Leuwers (Villeneuve-d'Asq: Université Charles-de-Gaulle Lille 3, 2001).

CONCLUSION

1. Archives nationales, 508 AP 34.

2. Hesse, *Other Enlightenment*.

3. Louis Dutens, *Mémoires d'un voyageur qui se repose, ou, Dutensiana*, 3 vols. (Paris: Bossange, Masson et Besson, 1806), 3:11; English translation as *Memoirs of a Traveller, now in Retirement* (London, 1806).

4. Honoré de Balzac, *Treatise on Elegant Living*, trans. Napoleon Jeffries (Cambridge, MA: Wakefield Press, 2010), 23.

5. Louis-Sébastien Mercier, *Le Nouveau Paris* (Paris: Mercure de France, 1994), 506.

6. Alain Vaillant and Éric Térouane, "Le roman au XIXe siècle ou la littérature livre," *Revue d'histoire du XIXe siècle* 19 (1999): 15–34, esp. p. 16.

7. Sylvia Harcstark Myers, *The Bluestocking Circle: Women, Friendship, and the Life of the Mind in Eighteenth-Century England* (Oxford: Clarendon Press; New York: Oxford University Press, 1990); Deborah Heller, "Bluestocking Salons and the Public Sphere," *Eighteenth-Century Life* 22 (May 1998).

8. Deborah Hertz, *Jewish High Society in Old Regime Berlin* (New Haven: Yale University Press, 1988).

9. Maria Luisa Betri and Elena Brambilla, eds., *Salotti e ruolo femminile in Italia tra fine Seicento e primo Novecento* (Venice: Marsilio, 2004). On Rome, see also Mirabelle Madigner, "Sociabilité informelle et pratiques sociales en Italie: Les salons romains et florentins au XVIIIe siècle," thesis in History, European University, Florence, 1999, and Maria Pia Donato, *Accademie romane: Una storia sociale, 1671–1824* (Naples: Edizioni scientifiche italiane, 2000).

10. Bernhard Struck, "De l'affinité sociale à la différence culturelle: La France vue par les voyageurs allemands au XVIIIe siècle," *Francia* 28, no. 2 (2001): 17–34; Michel Espagne and Michael Werner, eds., *Transferts: Les relations interculturel-les dans l'espace franco-allemand (XVIIIe et XIXe siècles)* (Paris: Éditions Recherche sur les Civilisations, 1988).

11. Roland Barthes, "La Bruyère," *Critical Essays*, trans. Richard Howard (Evanston, IL: Northwestern University Press, 1972), 227. See also Barthes, "Une idée de recherche," in *Le Bruissement de la langue: Essais critiques*, 4 vols. (Paris: Seuil, 1984, 1993), 4:327–32: "Proust's work is much more sociological than is acknowledged: it describes with great exactitude the grammar of promotion, of class mobility" (330), quoted from *The Rustle of Language*, trans. Richard Howard (New York: Hill and Wang, 1986), 274.

12. Marcel Proust, *Le Temps retrouvé*, in *À la recherche du temps perdu*, 4:601; quoted from *Remembrance of Things Past*, 2 vols. (New York: Random House, 1927, 1932), "The Past Recaptured," trans. Frederick A. Blossom, 1106.

SELECTED BIBLIOGRAPHY

MANUSCRIPT SOURCES

Archives des Affaires étrangères (AAE). *Contrôle des étrangers*, vols. 2–82 (July 1774 to December 1791). (Surveillance notes on prominent foreigners in Paris and weekly reports on foreign ministers.)

Archives des Affaires étrangères (AAE). *Correspondance politique*, Sweden, vol. 276. (Report on the voyage to France of Gustav III.)

Archives des Affaires étrangères (AAE). *Mémoires et documents*, France 319. (Letters seized by the *cabinet noir*.)

Archives nationales. Series AP (Archives privées). 4 AP 184 and 185: Brienne Archives. 29 AP: Roederer papers (correspondence and lecture notes); 29 AP 10, 11, 12: letters; 29 AP 106–108: materials for the history of polite society. 273 AP: Rohan-Bouillon Archives; 273 AP 7: papers of Louis de Rohan; 273 AP 8: papers of the princesse de Guéumenée; 273 AP 26: papers of the comtesse de Marsan; 273 AP 47–49: journal of the prince de Soubise, 1777–81; 273 AP 206: correspondence of the duc de Bouillon. 508 AP: Fonds Geoffrin-Valençay; 508 AP 34: papers of Mme Geoffrin; 508 AP 35: various papers of Mme de La Ferté-Imbault; 508 AP 36: family accounts and papers; 508 AP 37: correspondence of Mme de La Ferté-Imbault; 508 AP 38: personal papers of Mme de La Ferté-Imbault.

Archives nationales. Series T (Saisie des émigrés). T 208: papers of Marguerite de Beauvau-Craon, maréchale et duchesse de Mirepoix; T 477: papers of Amélie de Boufflers; duchesse de Lauzun, and the maréchale de Luxembourg; T 161, 1, 15, 16: papers of M. des Franches de Bossey, correspondence with Mme Geoffrin and Mme de La Ferté-Imbault.

Archives nationales. Minutier central. Étude CXVII, 8335, 836, 838, 939, 839, 840, 841, 842, 843, 844, 849, 850, 853, 857, 861, 862, 863, 864, 869, 871, 873, 874, 877, 879, 880, 886, 890, 896: documents concerning Mme Geoffrin; Étude VII, 439, 445: wills and after-death inventory, Mme Du Deffand; Étude LXXXIII, 579: documents of Julie de Lespinasse: will (May 22, 1776), inventory after death (May 31–June 7, 1776); XXIII, 649: after-death inventory of La Poupelinière (February 4, 1763).

Bibliothèque de l'Arsenal. MS 10028: papers of Inspector Buhot; MS 10248: surveillance of private citizens; MS 11981: dossier of the arrest of Mme de Rieben; MS 14701: Julie de Lespinasse, "Le seigneur du château, suite du voyage sentimental"; MS 15041: poetic works by Bernis.

Bibliothèque municipale d'Orléans. MS 1399–1401: papers of lieutenant de police Lenoir.

Bibliothèque municipale de Valenciennes. MS 756–758: Duc de Croÿ, "Histoire de l'Hermitage."

Bibliothèque nationale. Département des manuscrits. *Fonds français.* 15230: letters received by d'Alembert.

Bibliothèque nationale. Département des manuscrits. *Nouvelles acquisitions françaises.* 1184: letters received by Mme d'Épinay; 2763–2767: collection of autograph letters; 4748: autograph letters of Mme Geoffrin, Mme de la Ferté-Imbaut; 10235: correspondence of Hénault; 19398: correspondence of Maupertuis; 10781–10783: police notes of Inspector d'Hémery; 10844: correspondence of Suard and Dussert; 14898: autograph letters of Mme Du Deffand and Mme Geoffrin; 15579–15592: papers of Graffigny and Devaux; 16598: correspondence of the marquis de Saint-Lambert and the comtesse d'Houdetot; 23639: letters and papers of Condorcet; 23640: letters of Julie de Lespinasse to the Suards, letters from the comtesse de Boufflers and Mme Du Deffand; 24893: letters of Falconet to Mme Geoffrin.

Bibliothèque publique universitaire de Genève. Papiers Georges-Louis Lesage. MS supp. 512, 514, 516, 518: correspondence, duchesse d'Enville, Mme Necker; MS fr. 2041: documents about Mme Necker.

Bibliothèque publique universitaire de Genève. Archives Tronchin. Vols. 179, 181, 183: correspondence of François and Jacob Tronchin with Mme de Tencin, Grimm, etc; Vol. 196: François Tronchin, trip to Paris; Vol. 199: Théodore Tronchin with his parents; Vol. 200: Théodore Tronchin with his children; Vol. 219, correspondence, François and Jacob Tronchin with the Neckers.

Bibliothèque publique universitaire de Genève. Archives Horace-Bénédict Saussure. Vols. 8, 223: duc de Richelieu and the duchesse d'Enville; MS supp. 717: Mme Necker to Mme Reverdill.

Bibliothèque publique universitaire de Genève DO Necker: autograph letters of Mme Necker.

Bibliothèque publique universitaire de Genève DO Geoffrin: letter of Mme Geoffrin to Gabriel Cramer;

MS fr. 322: Bouts rimés of Mme Necker to Mme de Vermenoux.

British Library (London). Gibbon Papers. Add. 34 886: letters of Mme Necker.

British Library (London). Morisson Collection. Add. MS 39673: correspondence of Mme de la Ferté-Imbault with the Franches de Bossey and with comte Albaret (fols. 156–220).

British Library (London). Bentinck correspondence. Egerton 1749, vol. 5: letters of the comtesse de Boufflers (fols. 286–359).

Bibliothèque publique universitaire de Genève. Add MSS 37 926: Lady Crewe, "A Journal Kept at Paris from December 24th 1785 to March 10th 1786."

Institut et Musée Voltaire (Geneva). Archives Suard. Vol. 1: letters of Amélie Suard to her husband (1–67) and to other correspondents (68–105); Vol. 2: letters of Jean-Baptiste-Antoine Suard to his wife; Vol. 3: letters of Suard to other correspondents; Vols. 4–6: letters received, Suard and Mme Suard; Vol. 8: "Relation faite par Mme Suard de sa liaison avec M. Suard"; Vols. 12–14: literary miscellany.

Musée Arbaud, Aix-en-Provence. Archives Mirabeau. Vol. 17: letters of the marquis de Mirabeau to the comtesse de Rochefort and the marquise du Saillant (1752–67); Vol. 34: correspondence, marquis de Mirabeau and the comtesse de Rochefort (1757–62); Vol. 35: correspondence between the bailli de Mirabeau, the marquis de Mirabeau, Mme de Rochefort, the duc de Nivernais, and Mme de Pailly (1763–74); vol. 36: correspondence with the comtesse de Rochefort (1757).

Royal Society (London). Archives. MS 250, fol. I, 61; fol. II, 70; fol. III, 13, 23, 39, 93: letters of Mme Geoffrin to Martin Folkes, president of the Royal Society.

Voltaire Foundation (Oxford). Manuscripts bequeathed by Julie de Lespinasse, 4 vols., microfiches. (A copy of the microfiches made by the Voltaire Foundation is available at the Bibliothèque de la Sorbonne under the title, "Manuscrits légués par Mlle de Lespinasse: A reproduction of the commonplace books of Jeanne-Julie-Eléonore de Lespinasse at the Voltaire Foundation." Taylor Institution, Oxford, Voltaire Foundation, 1986. 4 vols, 18 microfiches.)

Private Archives of the comte de Bruce. Carnets of Mme Geoffrin. "Différentes choses…"; "Noms de mes connaissances"; "Noms et adresses des personnes"; "Adresses de la province et de Paris"; "Différents marchands et ouvriers" (1767–68); "Marchands d'étoffe" (1767–68) ; an untitled notebook containing the names and addresses of foreigners.

PRINT SOURCES

Actes du tribunal révolutionnaire. Edited by Gérard Walter. Paris: Mercure de France, 1986.

Annales politiques, civiles et littéraires du dix-huitime siècle: Ouvrage périodique. 14 vols. London and Brussels, 1774–88.

Bibliothèque de société, contenant des mélanges intéressants de littérature & de morale; une élite de bons mots, d'anecdotes, de traits d'humanité;. . . enfin des divertissements de société. 4 vols. Paris: Delalain, 1771.

Correspondance littéraire, philosophique et critique par Grimm, Diderot, Raynal, Meister. Edited by Maurice Tourneux. 16 vols. Paris: Garnier, 1877–82.

Correspondance secrète sur Louis XVI, Marie-Antoinette, la cour et la ville de 1777 à 1792. 2 vols. Paris: Plon, 1866.

Dictionnaire de l'Académie françoise. Paris: J. J. Smits, 1694, 1718, 1740, 1762, an VI–VII [1799–1800], 1835.

Dictionnaire universel français et latin vulgairement appelé Dictionnaire de Trévoux. 3 vols. (1704); 8 vols. Paris: Compagnie des libraires associés, 1771.

Discours prononcés dans l'Académie française le jeudi 16 février 1785 à la réception de M. De Lamoignon de Malesherbes. Paris: Demonville, 1775.

Encyclopédie ou dictionnaire raisonné des arts, des sciences et des métiers par une société de gens de lettres. 31 vols. Paris: Briasson, 1751–80.

Histoire et recueil des Lazzis. Edited by Judith Curtis and David Trott. *Studies on Voltaire and the Eighteenth Century* 338 (1996). Oxford: Voltaire Foundation.

Journal des gens du monde. Nos. 1–84. Frankfurt, 1782–85.

Jugement rendu qui fait défense à la société connue sous le nom de sallon français de s'assembler à l'avenir dans la maison de la rue Royale no. 29. Paris: Imprimerie de Lottin l'aîné, May 15, 1790.

Mémoires secrets pour servir à l'histoire de la République des lettres en France depuis 1762 jusqu'à nos jours. 31 vols. London, 1777–89.

Recueil de ces messieurs. Amsterdam: Weinstein, 1745.

d'Alembert, Jean le Rond. *Essai sur la société des gens de lettres et des grands, sur la réputation, sur les mécènes, et sur les récompenses littéraires. Vol. 4 of Œuvres de d'Alembert,* 337–73. Paris: A. Belin, 1821–22.

Alletz, Pons-Augustin. *Manuel de l'homme du monde, ou, Connaissance générale des principaux états de la société et de toutes les manières qui sont le sujet des conversations ordinaires.* Paris, 1761.

Allonville, Armand-François, comte d'. *Mémoires secrets de 1770 à 1830*. 6 vols. Paris: Werdet, 1838–45.

Angivillier, comte d'. *Notes sur les mémoires de Marmontel*. Edited by Louis Babé. Copenhagen, [1933].

Argenson, Jean-Baptiste de Boyer, marquis d'. *Journal et Mémoires*. Edited by E. J. B. Rathery. 9 vols. Paris: Veuve Renouart, 1859–67.

Beauharnais, Fanny Mouchard de Chaban, comtesse de. *À la mémoire de Madame du Boccage*. Paris: Imprimerie Richard, 1802.

Bernis, François Joachim de Pierres, cardinal de. *Mémoires*. Edited by Philippe Bonnet. Paris: Mercure de France, 1980, 2000.

Besenval, Pierre-Victor, baron de. *Mémoires*. Paris: Mercure de France, 1987.

Boigne, Adèle d'Osmond, comtesse de. *Mémoires de la comtesse de Boigne, née d'Osmond, de Louis XVI à 1820*. 2 vols. Paris: Mercure de France, 1971.

Bombelles, Marc, marquis de. *Journal*. Edited by Jean Grassion and Franz Durif. 7 vols. Geneva: Droz, 1977–82.

Boufflers, Marie-Charlotte-Hyppolite, comtesse. *Lettres de Gustave III à la comtesse de Boufflers et de la comtesse au roi, de 1771 à 1791*. Edited by Aurélien Vivie. Bordeaux, 1900.

Boufflers, Stanislas-Jean, chevalier de. *Poésies diverses du chevalier de Boufflers*. Edited by Octave Uzanne. Paris: A. Quantin, 1886.

Buffon, Georges-Louis Leclerc de. *Corespondance générale*. Paris: Levasseur, 1885. Reprint, 2 vols. Geneva: Slatkine, 1971.

Callières, François de. *Des mots, de la mode et des nouvelles façons de parler, avec des observations sur diverses manières d'agir et de s'exprimer*. Paris: Claude Barbin, 1692.

Campan, Jeanne-Louise-Henriette. *Mémoires de Madame Campan, première femme de chambre de Marie-Antoinette*. Paris: Mercure de France, 1988.

Caraccioli, Louis-Antoine de. *L'Europe française*. Paris: Veuve Duchesne, 1776.

Caraccioli, Louis-Antoine de. *La Religion de l'honnête homme*. Paris: Nyon, 1766.

Carmontelle, Louis Carrogis. *Amusements de société ou Proverbes dramatiques*. 2 vols. Paris: Jorry, 1769.

Caylus, Anne-Claude, comte de. *Correspondance inédite du comte de Caylus avec le P. Paciaudi, théatin (1757–1765), suivie de celles de l'abbé Barthélemy et de P. Mariette avec le même*. Edited by Charles Nisard. 2 vols. Paris: Imprimerie nationale, 1877.

Chamfort, Sébastien-Roch-Nicolas. *Produits de la civilisation perfectionnée: Maximes et pensées; Caractères et anecdotes*. Edited by Jean Dagen. Paris: Garnier-Flammarion, 1968. Originally published as *Maximes, pensées, caractères*. Paris: an III [1795]. Translated by W. S. Merwin as *Products of the Perfected Civilization: Selected Writings of Chamfort*. New York: Macmillan, 1969.

Chamfort, Sébastien-Roch-Nicolas. *Œuvres*. Edited by Pierre-Louis Gingyené. 4 vols. Paris: Imprimerie des Sciences et Arts, an III [1795].

Chastellux, François-Jean de. *Lettres inédites de Chastellux à Wilkes*. Edited by Gabriel Dominique Bonno. University of California Publications in Modern Philology, vol. 15, no. 2. Berkeley: University of California Press, 1932.

Chastenay, Victorine de. *Mémoires (1771–1815)*. Edited by Guy Chaussinand-Nogaret. 2 vols. Paris: Plon, 1896; Paris: Librairie académique Perrin, 1987.

Cole, William. *A Journal of my Journey to Paris in the Year 1765*. Edited by Francis Griffin Stoke. London: Constable, 1931.

Collé, Charles. *Journal et mémoires de Charles Collé sur les hommes de lettres, les ouvrages dramatiques et les événements les plus mémorables du règne de Louis XV*. 3 vols. Paris: Didot, 1868. Reprint, 3 vols. Geneva: Slatkine, 1967.

Collé, Charles. *Journal historique inédit pour les années 1761 et 1762*. Edited by Adolphe van Bever and Gabriel Boissy. Paris: Mercure de France, 1911.

Collé, Charles. *Théâtre de société*. 3 vols. Paris and The Hague: F. Gueffier, 1777.

Condorcet, Jean-Antoine-Nicolas Caritat, marquis de. *Correspondance inédite de Condorcet et de Turgot 1770–1779*. Edited by Charles Henry. Paris: Charavay, 1883; Geneva: Slatkine, 1970.

Condorcet, Jean-Antoine-Nicolas Caritat, marquis de. *Correspondance inédite de Condorcet et Mme Suard*. Edited by Elisabeth Badinter. Paris: Fayard, 1988.

Courtin, Antoine de. *Nouveau traité de la civilité qui se pratique en France parmi les honnêtes gens (1671)*. Edited by Marie-Claire Grassi. Saint-Étienne: Publications de l'Université de Saint-Étienne, 1996.

Creutz, Gustav Philip. *Un ambassadeur à la Cour de France: Le Comte de Creutz; Lettres inédites à Gustave III, 1779–1770*. Edited by Georges Mary and Marianne Molander. Acta Universitatis Gothoburgensis. Paris: Jean Touzot, 1987.

Croy, Emmanuel, duc de. *Journal*. Edited by Emmanuel Henri Grouchy and Paul Cottin. 4 vols. Paris: Flammarion, 1906; Clermont-Ferrand: Paleo, 2004–.

Delille, Jacques. *La Conversation, poème*. Paris: Michaud, 1812.

Devaux, François-Antoine. *Poésies diverses*. Edited by Angela Consiglio. Bari: Adriatica-Nizet, 1977.

Diderot, Denis. *Correspondance*. Edited by Georges Roth. 16 vols. Paris: Éditions de Minuit, 1955–70.

Diderot, Denis. *Œuvres*. Edited by Laurent Versini. 5 vols. Paris: Robert Laffont, 1994–.

Du Deffand, Marie de Vichy Chamrond, marquise. *Cher Voltaire: La correspondance de Madame Du Deffand avec Voltaire*. Edited by Isabelle Vissière et al. Paris: Des Femmes, 1987.

Du Deffand, Marie de Vichy Chamrond, marquise. *Correspondance complète avec la duchesse de Choiseul, l'abbé Barthélemy et M. Craufurt, publiée avec une introduction par M. le Marquis de Sainte-Aulaire*. 3 vols. Paris: Michel Lévy frères, 1866.

Du Deffand, Marie de Vichy Chamrond, marquise. *Correspondance complète avec ses amis*. Edited by Mathurin de Lescure. 3 vols. Paris: Plon, 1865.

Du Deffand, Marie de Vichy Chamrond, marquise. *Journal (1er juin 1779–10 septembre 1780)*. In *The Yale Edition of Horace Walpole's Correspondence*. Edited by W. S. Lewis. 48 vols. New Haven: Yale University Press, 1937–68), vol. 6, pp. 421–61.

Du Deffand, Marie de Vichy Chamrond, marquise. *Letters to and from Madame du Deffand and Julie de Lespinasse*. Edited by Warren H. Smith, New Haven: Yale University Press, 1938.

Du Préaux, abbé. *Le Chrétien parfait honnête homme ou l'art d'allier la piété avec la politesse et les autres devoirs de la vie civile*. 2 vols. Paris, 1749.

Duclos, Charles. *Considérations sur les mœurs de ce siècle*. 1751. Edited by Carole Dornier. Paris: Honoré Champion, 2000.

Dufort de Cheverny, Nicolas. *Mémoires sur les règnes de Louis XV et Louis XVI et sur la Révolution*. 2 vols. Paris: Plon, Nourrit, 1886.

Dutens, Louis. *Mémoires d'un voyageur qui se repose, ou, Dutensiana*. 3 vols. Paris: Bossange, Masson et Besson, 1806. In English translation as *Memoirs of a Traveller, now in Retirement*. London, 1806.

Épinay, Louise d'. *Histoire de Madame de Montbrillant*. Paris: Mercure de France, 1989.

Faret, Nicolas. *L'Honneste homme, ou, L'art de plaire à la cour (1630)*. Edited by Maurice Magendie. Paris: Presses Universitaires de France, 1925.

Féraud, abbé Jean-François. *Dictionnaire critique de la langue française*. 3 vols. Marseille: Jean Mossy, 1787–88.

Fonvizin, Denis Ivanovitch. *Lettres de France (1777–1778)*. Translated by Henri Grosse, edited by Jacques Proust and Piotr Zaborov. Paris: CNRS; Oxford: Voltaire Foundation, 1995.

Frénilly, baron de. *Souvenirs*. Paris: Plon, 1908.

Galiani, Ferdinando, andLouise d'Épinay. *Correspondance*. Edited by Georges Dulac and Daniel Maggetti. 5 vols. Paris: Desjonquères, 1992–97.

Garat, Dominique-Joseph, comte. *Mémoires historiques sur la vie de M. Suard, sur ses écrits, et sur le XVIIIe siècle.* 2 vols. Paris: A. Belin, 1820.

Genlis, Stéphanie Félicité du Crest, comtesse de. *Dictionnaire critique et raisonné des étiquettes de la cour, des usages du monde, des amusements, des modes, des mœurs, etc., des français de la mort de Louis XIII jusqu'à nos jours; contenant le Tableau de la Cour, de la Société et de la Littérature du dix-huitième siècle, ou, L'Esprit des étiquettes et des usages anciens comparés aux modernes.* 2 vols. Paris: Mongie aîné, 1818.

Genlis, Stéphanie Félicité du Crest, comtesse de. *Mémoires inédits sur le XVIIIe siècle et la révolution française depuis 1756 jusqu'à nos jours.* 10 vols. Paris: Ladvocat, 1825. In English translation as *Memoirs of the Countess of Genlis.* 2 vols. London: Henry Colburn, 1825–26.

Geoffrin, Marie-Thérèse. "Correspondance de Mme Geoffrin et de Wenzel Anton Kaunitz." Edited by Milena Lenderova. *Dix-huitième siècle* 30 (1998): 310–16.

Geoffrin, Marie-Thérèse. *Correspondance inédite du roi Stanislas-Auguste Poniatowski et de Madame Geoffrin (1764–1777).* Edited by Charles de Mouÿ. Paris: Plon, 1875.

Gibbon, Edward. "Journal du séjour de Gibbon à Paris du 28 janvier au 9 mai 1763." In *Miscellanea Gibboniana.* Edited by Gavin E. De Beer et al., 85–107. Université de Lausanne, publications de la Faculté des Lettres, 10. Lausanne: F. Rouge, 1952.

Gibbon, Edward. *The Letters of Edward Gibbon.* Edited by J. E. Norton. 3 vols. London: Cassel; New York: Macmillan, 1956.

Gibbon, Edward. *Memoirs of My Life.* Edited, with an introduction, by Betty Radice. London and New York: Penguin, 1984. Translated by Guillaume Villeneuve as *Mémoires.* Paris: Criterion, 1992.

Gleichen, Heinrich Carl, baron von. *Souvenirs de Charles Henri, Baron de Gleichen.* Translated by Paul Grimblot. Paris: Léon Techener fils, 1868.

Graffigny, Françoise de. *Correspondance.* 7 vols. Oxford: Voltaire Foundation, 1985–2003.

Gresset, Jean-Baptiste. *Le Méchant.* In *Répertoire général du théâtre français,* vol. 46, 11–130. Paris: Ménard et Raymond, 1813.

Grimm, Friedrich Melchior, Freiherr von. *Correspondance inédite de Frédéric Melchior Grimm.* Edited by Joachim Schlobach. Munich: Fink, 1972.

Grimod de La Reynière, Alexandre-Balthasar-Laurent. *Manuel des Amphitryons.* Paris: Capelle et Renaud, 1808; Paris: Métaillé, 1983.

Helvétius, Claude. *Correspondance générale d'Helvétius.* Edited by Peter Allan et al. 3 vols. Oxford: Voltaire Foundation, 1981–2004.

Helvétius, Claude. *De l'Esprit.* Paris: Durant, 1758; Paris: Fayard, 1971. English translation as *De l'esprit, or, Essays on the Mind.* Bristol, UK: Thoemmes Press, 2000.

Hénault, Charles. *Mémoires du président Hénault.* Edited by François Rousseau. Paris: Hachette, 1911.

d' Holbach, Paul-Henri Thiry, baron. *Ethocratie, ou, Le gouvernement fondé sur la morale.* Amsterdam: Marc-Michel Rey, 1776.

Holbach, Paul-Henri Thiry, baron d'. *La Morale universelle, ou, Les devoirs de l'homme fondés sur la nature.* 3 vols. Tours: Letourny, 1792.

Holbach, Paul-Henri Thiry, baron d'. *La Politique naturelle; ou, Discours sur les vrais principes du gouvernement.* 2 vols. London, 1773; 2 vols. Paris: Fayard, 1998.

Hume, David. *A Concise and Genuine Account of the Dispute between Mr. Hume and Mr. Rousseau*. London: T. Becket and P. A. De Hondt, 1766. In French translation by Charles Bordes, edited by J. B. A. Suard, as *Exposé succinct de la contestation qui s'est élevée entre M. Hume et M. Rousseau* (1766). Paris: Alive, 1998.

Hume, David. *Essays: Moral, Political and Literary*. Revised edition, edited by Eugene F. Miller. 2 vols. Indianapolis: Liberty Classics, 1987. In French translation by Jean Pierre Cléro, edited by Gilles Robel, as *Essais moraux, politiques et littéraires et autres essais*. Paris: Presses Universitaires de France, 2001.

Kant, Immanuel. *What is Enlightenment? In Foundations of the Metaphysics of Morals; or, What is Enlightenment?* Translated by Lewis Beck White. 2nd ed. rev. New York: Macmillan, 1990. Edited by Françoise Proust as *Vers la paix perpétuelle? Que signifie s'orienter dans la pensée? Qu'est-ce que les Lumières? et autres textes*. Paris: Garnier-Flammarion, 1991.

Karamzine, Nicolas. *Voyages en France, 1789–1790*. Paris: Hachette, 1885. In English translation as *Letters of a Russian Traveler, 1789–1790*. New York: Columbia University Press, 1957.

La Harpe, Jean-François de. *Letters to the Shuvalovs*. Edited by Christopher Todd. *Studies on Voltaire and the Eighteenth Century* 108 (1973). Oxford: Voltaire Foundation.

La Harpe, Jean-François de. *Lycée ou cours de littérature ancienne et moderne*. 17 vols. Paris: H. Agasse, 1799–1805.

La Porte, Joseph de. *Anecdotes dramatiques*. 3 vols. Paris: La Veuve Duchesne, 1775. 3 vols. Geneva: Slatkine, 1971.

La Tour du Pin, marquise de. *Journal d'une femme de cinquante ans (1778–1815)*. Paris: Mercure de France, 1979. Translated by Felice Harcourt as *Memoirs: Laughing and Dancing Our Way to the Precipice*. London: Harvill, 1999.

Le Maître de Claville, Charles-François-Nicolas. *Traité du vrai mérite de l'homme*. Paris: Saugrain, 1736.

Lespinasse, Julie de. *Lettres*. Edited by Jacques Dupont. Paris: La Table Ronde, 1997.

Lespinasse, Julie de. *Lettres à Condorcet (1769–1776)*. Edited by Jean Noël Pascal. Paris: Desjonquères, 1990.

Lespinasse, Julie de. *Lettres de Julie de Lespinasse suivies de ses autres œuvres et de lettres de Mme Du Deffand, de Turgot, de Bernardin de Saint-Pierre*. Edited by Eugène Asse. Paris: Charpentier, 1876. Reprint. Geneva: Slatkine, 1971.

Lespinasse, Julie de. *Lettres inédites de Lespinasse à Condorcet, à d'Alembert*. Edited by Charles Henry. Paris: E. Dentu, 1887.

Lévis, Pierre-Marc-Gaston, duc de. *Souvenirs-portraits du Duc de Lévis, suivis de Lettres intimes de Monsieur, Comte de Provence au Duc de Lévis (1787–1792)*. Paris: Mercure, 1993.

Ligne, Charles-Joseph, prince de. *Lettres et pensées, d'après l'édition de Mme de Staël*. Edited by Raymond Trousson. Paris: Tallandier, 1989.

Marin, François. *L'homme aimable, dédié à M. le Marquis de Rosen, avec des Réflexions et des Pensées sur divers sujets*. Paris: Prault, 1751.

Marmontel, Jean-François. *Correspondance*. Edited by John Rewick. 2 vols. Clermont-Ferrand: Institut d'Études du Massif Central, 1974.

Marmontel, Jean-François. *Mémoires*. Edited by Jean-Pierre Guicciardi and Gilles Thierrat. Paris: Mercure de France, 1999. Translated as *Memoirs of Marmontel*. 2 vols. New York: Merill & Baker, 1903.

Mercier, Louis-Sébastien. *Tableau de Paris*. Amsterdam, 1787–88. Edited by Jean-Claude Bonnet. 2 vols. Paris: Mercure de France, 1994.

Moncrif, François-Augustin Paradis de. *Essai sur la nécessité et sur les moyens de plaire.* Paris: Prault, 1738; Saint-Étienne: Publications de l'Université de Saint-Étienne, 1998.

Montesquieu, Charles Louis, baron de. *De l'esprit des lois.* Amsterdam: F. Grasset, 1761. Edited by Victor Goldschmidt. 2 vols. Paris: Garnier-Flammarion, 1979. Translated by Thomas Nugent as *The Spirit of the Laws.* 2 vols. in 1. New York: Fahner, 1966.

Montesquieu, Charles Louis, baron de. *Lettres persanes* (1721). In Montesquieu, *Œuvres complètes.* Edited by Roger Caillois. 2 vols. Paris: Gallimard, Pléïade, 1945–1951. Translated and edited by C. J. Betts as *Persian Letters.* London: Penguin, 1873, 1993.

Morellet, André. *Lettres d'André Morellet.* Edited by Dorothy Medlin, Jean-Claude David, and Paul Leclerc. 3 vols. Oxford: Voltaire Foundation, 1991–96.

Morellet, André. *Mémoires inédits de l'abbé Morellet de l'Académie française sur le dix-huitième siècle et sur la Révolution.* 2 vols. Paris: Ladvocat, 1821. Edited by Jean-Pierre Guicciardi. Paris: Mercure de France, 1988.

Morellet, André. *Portrait de Madame Geoffrin.* Amsterdam; Paris: Chez Pissot, 1777.

Morellet, André, Jean le Rond d'Alembert, and Antoine Léonard Thomas. *Éloges de Madame Geoffrin, contemporaine de Madame Du Deffand, suivis de lettres et d'un Essai sur la conversation par l'abbé Morellet.* Paris: Nicolle, 1812.

Morris, Gouverneur. *A Diary of the French Revolution.* Edited by Beatrix Cary Davenport. 2 vols. Boston: Houghton Mifflin, 1939.

Morvan de Bellegarde, Jean-Baptiste. *Le Chrétien honnête homme; ou, L'alliance des devoirs de la vie chrétienne avec les devoirs de la vie civile.* The Hague: A. Van Doll, 1736.

Morvan de Bellegarde, Jean-Baptiste. *Réflexions sur ce qui peut plaire ou déplaire dans le commerce du monde.* Paris: A. Seneuze, 1688.

Necker, Suzanne. *Mélanges extraits des manuscrits de Mme Necker.* Edited by Jacques Necker. 3 vols. Paris: Pougens, 1798.

Necker, Suzanne. *Nouveaux mélanges.* Edited by Jacques Necker. 2 vols. Paris: Pougens, 1801.

Nivernois, Mancini-Mazarin, duc de. *Œuvres.* 8 vols. Paris: Didot le jeune, 1796.

Oberkirch, Henriette-Louise, baronne d'. *Mémoires de la baronne Oberkirch sur la cour de Louis XVI et la société française avant 1789* (1853). Paris: Mercure de France, 1989. Translated as *Memoirs of the Baroness d'Oberkirch, Countess de Montbrison,* ed. Count de Montbrison. 3 vols. London: Colburn, 1852.

Palissot de Montenoy, Charles. *Œuvres complètes.* 6 vols. Paris: L. Collin, 1809.

Pluquet, François-André-Adrien, abbé. *De la sociabilité.* 2 vols. Paris: Barrois, 1767.

Poinsinet, Antoine. *Le Cercle, ou La soirée à la mode.* Paris: Duchesne, 1764. In *Répertoire général du théâtre français,* vol. 46, 289–346. Paris: Ménard et Raymond, 1813.

Poniatowski, Stanislaus-Auguste. *Mémoires du roi Stanislas-Auguste Poniatowski.* 2 vols. St. Petersburg: Imprimerie de l'Académie Impériale des sciences, 1914.

Pougens, Charles. *Mémoires et souvenirs commencés par lui et terminés par Madame de Saint-Léon.* Paris: H. Fournier, 1834.

Proust, Marcel. *À la Recherche du temps perdu.* 4 vols. Paris: Gallimard, 1989. Translated by C. K. Scott Moncrieff and Frederick A. Blossom as *Remembrance of Things Past.* 2 vols. New York: Random House, 1927, 1932.

Richard, abbé Jérôme. *Réflexions critiques sur le livre intitulé Les Mœurs.* Aux Indes, 1748.

Roland, Marie-Jeanne. *Lettres de Madame Roland.* Edited by Claude Perroud. 4 vols. Paris: Imprimerie Nationale, 1900–15.

Roland, Marie-Jeanne. *Mémoires de Madame Roland.* Paris: Mercure de France, 1986.

Roubaud, abbé Pierre-Joseph-André. *Nouveau synonymes français.* 4 vols. Paris: Moutard, 1785–86.

Rousseau, Jean-Jacques. *Correspondance complète de Jean-Jacques Rousseau.* Edited by R. A. Leigh. 52 vols. Geneva and Oxford: Voltaire Foundation, 1965–98.

Rousseau, Jean-Jacques. *Discours sur les arts et les lettres; Lettre à d'Alembert sur les spectacles.* Paris: Gallimard, 1987.

Rousseau, Jean-Jacques. *Julie, ou, La Nouvelle Héloïse (1761).* Edited by René Pomeau. Paris: Garnier, 1960.

Rousseau, Jean-Jacques. *Lettre à d'Alembert sur les spectacles (1758).* Edited by Michel Launay. Paris: Garnier-Flammarion, 1967.

Rutlidge, Jean-Jacques. *Le Bureau d'esprit.* Liège, 1776.

Sabran, comtesse de. *Correspondance inédite de la comtesse de Sabran et du chevalier de Boufflers (1778–1788).* Edited by E. de Magnieu and Henri Prat. Paris: Plon, 1875.

Ségur, Louis-Philippe, comte de. *Mémoires, ou, Souvenirs et anecdotes.* Vols. 1–3 of *Œuvres complètes.* 33 vols. in 34 pts. Paris: A. Eymerie, 1824–26. Translated as *Memoirs and Recollections of Count Ségur.* Boston: Wells and Lilly, 1825.

Sénac de Meilhan, Gabriel. *Considérations sur l'esprit et les mœurs.* London and Paris, 1787.

Sénac de Meilhan, Gabriel. *Des principes et des causes de la Révolution en France.* 1790. Edited by Michel Delon. Paris: Desjonquères, 1987.

Smith, Adam. *The Correspondence of Adam Smith.* Edited by Ernest Campbell Mossner and Ian Simpson Ross. Oxford: Clarendon Press, 1987.

Staël, Germaine de. *Considérations sur la Révolution française (1813).* Paris: Tallandier, 1983. In English translation as *Considerations on the Principal Events of the French Revolution (1818).* Edited by Aurelian Cr_iutu. Indianapolis: Liberty Fund, 2008.

Staël, Germaine de. *Lettres de jeunesse.* Vol. 1, pts. 1 and 2, of *Correspondance générale,.* Edited by Béatrice W. Jasinsky. 6 vols. in 11 pts. Paris: Jean-Jacques Pauvert, 1960–93.

Suard, Amélie. *Essais de mémoires sur M. Suard.* Paris: Didot, 1820.

Suard, Jean-Baptiste. *Correspondance littéraire avec la Margrave de Bayreuth.* Edited by Gabriel Bonno. Berkeley: University of California Press, 1934.

Suard, Jean-Baptiste. *Madame de Staël et J.-B.-A. Suard: Correspondance inédite (1786–1817).* Geneva: Droz, 1970.

Suard, Jean-Baptiste. *Réponse au discours prononcé dans l'Académie française le mardi XV juin, MDCCLXXXIV à la réception de Monsieur le Marquis de Montesquiou.* Paris: Demonville, 1784.

Talleyrand-Périgord, Charles-Maurice, duc de. *Mémoires.* Edited by Duc de Broglie. 5 vols. Paris: Calmann-Lévy, 1891–92. Translated by Raphaël Ledos de Beaufort as *Memoirs of the Prince de Talleyrand.* 3 vols. London: Grifffith Farran Okeden and Welsh, 1891. Facsimile reprint: Whitefish, MT: Kessinger, 2007.

Thiery, Luc Vincent. *Guide des amateurs et des étrangers voyageurs à Paris.* 3 vols. Paris: Hardouin et Gattey, 1787.

Thomas, Antoine Léonard. *À la mémoire de Madame Geoffrin.* Paris: Moutard, 1777.

Thomas, Antoine Léonard. *Correspondance.* Vol. 6 of *Œuvres complètes.* 6 vols. Paris: Verdière, 1825.

Thomas, Antoine Léonard, Mme d' Épinay, and Denis Diderot. *Qu'est-ce qu'une femme?: Un débat.* Edited by Elisabeth Badinter. Paris: P.O.L., 1989.

Tilly, Alexandre de. *Mémoires du Comte Alexandre de Tilly pour servir à l'histoire des mœurs de la fin du XVIIIe siècle.* Edited by Christian Melchior-Bonnet. 2 vols. Paris: Mercure de France, 1965.

Toussaint, François-Vincent. *Les Mœurs*. 1748. In English translation as *Manners* (London, 1749).

Trublet, Nicolas. "Pensées sur l'esprit de société." *Mercure de France* (February 1759): 45–61; (March 1759): 60–72; (May 1759): 58–70; (June 1759): 62–68.

Turgot, Anne Robert Jacques. *Lettres de Turgot à la duchesse d'Enville, 1764–74 et 1777–1780*. Edited by Joseph Ruwet. Louvain: Bibliothèque de l'université, 1976.

Turgot, Anne Robert Jacques. *Œuvres de Turgot*. Edited by Gustav Schelle. 5 vols. Paris: Alcan, 1913–1923.

Véri, Joseph Alphonse, abbé de. *Journal*. 2 vols. Paris: Tallandier, 1928–30.

Verri, Pietro. *Viaggio a Parigi e Londra (1766–1767); Carteggio di Pietro e Alessandro Verri*. Edited by Gianmarco Gaspari. Milan: Adelphi, 1980.

Vien, Joseph-Marie. "Mémoires." In Thomas W. Gaehtgens and Jacques Lugand. *Joseph-Marie Vien: Peintre du roi, 1716–1809*, 287–320. Paris: Arthéna, 1988.

Vigée-Lebrun, Elisabeth. *Souvenirs*. Edited by Claudine Herrmann. 2 vols. Paris: Des Femmes, 1984. Translated by Lionel Strachey as *Memoirs of Madame Vigée Lebrun*. New York: Doubleday, Page, 1903; Braziller, 1989.

Villeneuve-Guibert, Gaston, comte de. *Le portefeuille de Madame Dupin*. Paris: Calmann-Lévi, 1884.

Voltaire. *Dictionnaire philosophique*. (1764). Paris: Garnier-Flammarion, 1964. Translated and edited by Theodore Besterman as *Philosophical Dictionary* . London and New York: Penguin, 1972, 2004.

Voltaire. *Voltaire's Correspondence*. Edited by Theodore Besterman. 107 vols. Geneva: Institut et Musée Voltaire, 1953–1966.

Walpole, Horace. *The Yale Edition of Horace Walpole's Correspondence*. Edited by W. S. Lewis. 48 vols. in 47 pts. New Haven: Yale University Press; London: Oxford University Press, 1937–83.

SECONDARY SOURCES

Agulhon, Maurice. *Pénitents et Francs-Maçons de l'ancienne Provence: Essai sur la sociabilité méridionale*. Paris: Fayard, 1968.

Arditi, Jorge. *A Genealogy of Manners: Transformations of Social Relations in France and England from the Fourteenth to the Eighteenth Century*. Chicago: University of Chicago Press, 1998.

Auerbach, Erich. "La cour et la ville." In *Le culte des passions, essais sur le XVIIe siècle français*, 115–79. Paris: Macula, 1998.

Baczko, Bronislaw. *Rousseau, solitude et communauté*. Translated from the Polish by Claire Brendhel-Lamhout. Paris and The Hague: Mouton, 1974.

Baker, Keith Michael. *Inventing the French Revolution: Essays on French Political Culture in the Eighteenth Century*. Cambridge, UK, and New York: Cambridge University Press, 1990.

Barthes, Roland. "La Bruyère." In *Critical Essays*, 221–37. Translated by Richard Howard. Evanston, IL: Northwestern University Press, 1972.

Beasley, Faith Evelyn. *Salons, History, and the Creation of Seventeenth Century France: Mastering Memory*. Aldershot: Ashgate, 2006.

Beaurepaire, Pierre-Yves. *L'Espace des franc-maçons: Une sociabilité européenne au XVIIIe siècle*. Rennes: Presses Universitaires de Rennes, 2003.

Bell, David A. *The Cult of the Nation in France: Inventing Nationalism, 1680–1800*. Cambridge, MA: Harvard University Press, 2001.

Bély, Lucien. *Espions et ambassadeurs au temps de Louis XIV*. Paris: Fayard, 1990.

Bénichou, Paul. *Le Sacre de l'écrivain, 1750–1830: Essai sur l'avènement d'un pouvoir spirituel laïque dans la France moderne*. Paris: José Corti, 1973; Gallimard, 1996.

Bonnet, Jean-Claude, ed. *La Carmagnole des muses: L'homme de lettres et l'artiste dans la Révolution*. Paris: Armand Colin, 1988.

Bourdieu, Pierre. *Distinction: A Social Critique of the Judgement of Taste*. Cambridge, MA: Harvard University Press, 2000.

Bourguinat, Élisabeth. *Le Siècle du persiflage, 1734–1789*. Paris: Presses Universitaires de France, 1998.

Bravard, Alice. *Le grand monde parisien 1900–1939*. La persistance du modèle aristocratique. Rennes: Presses Universitaires de Rennes, 2013.

Brown, Gregory S. *A Field of Honor: Writers, Court Culture and Public Theater in French Literary Life from Racine to the Revolution*. New York: Columbia University Press, 2002.

Burke, Peter. *The Art of Conversation*. Ithaca: Cornell University Press, 1993.

Callataÿ, Edouard de. *Madame de Vermenoux: Une enchanteresse au XVIIIe siècle*. Geneva: La Palatine, 1956.

Campbell, Peter R. *Power and Politics in Old Regime France, 1720–1745*. London: Routledge, 1996.

Carnevali, Barbara. *Romanticismo e riconoscimento: Figure della coscienza in Rousseau*. Bologna: Il Mulino, 2004.

Chartier, Roger. *The Cultural Origins of the French Revolution*. Translated by Lydia G. Cochrane. Durham, NC: Duke University Press, 1991.

Chartier, Roger. *The Cultural Uses of Print in Early Modern France*. Translated by Lydia G. Cochrane. Princeton: Princeton University Press, 1987.

Chaussinand-Nogaret, Guy, ed., *La Noblesse en France au XVIIIe siècle: De la féodalité aux Lumières*. Paris: Hachette, 1975; Brussels: Complexe, 1984.

Cowan, Brian. *The Social Life of Coffee: The Emergence of the British Coffeehouse*. New Haven: Yale University Press, 2005.

Cowan, Brian. "English Coffeehouses and French Salons: Rethinking Habermas, Gender and Sociability in Early Modern French and British Historiography." In *Making Space Public in Early Modern Europe: Performance, Geography, Privacy*, eds. Angela Vanhaelen and Joseph P. Ward, 41–53. London: Routledge, 2013.

Craveri, Benedetta. *The Age of Conversation*. New York: New York Published Books, 2005.

Craveri, Benedetta. *Madame Du Deffand and her World*. Boston: Godine, 1994.

Crow, Thomas E. *Painters and Public Life in Eighteenth-Century Paris*. New Haven: Yale University Press, 1985.

Curtis, Judith. "Mademoiselle Quinault and the Bout-du-Banc: A Reappraisal." *Studies on Voltaire and the Eighteenth Century* 8 (2000): 35–56.

Darnton, Robert. *The Great Cat Massacre and Other Episodes in French Cultural History*, New York: Basic Books, 1984.

Darnton, Robert. *The Literary Underground of the Old Regime*. Cambridge, MA: Harvard University Press, 1982.

Delon, Michel. *L'invention du boudoir*. Cadeilhan: Zulma, 1999.

Desnoiresterres, Gustave. *Le Chevalier Dorat et les poètes légers au XVIIIe siècle*. Paris: Perrin, 1887.

Dupront, Alphonse. *Qu'est-ce que les Lumières*. Paris: Gallimard, 1996.

Durand, Yves. *Les Fermiers généraux au XVIIIe siècle*. Paris: Presses Universitaires de France, 1971; Maisonneuve et Larose, 1991.

Elias, Norbert. *The Court Society*. Translated by Edmund Jephcott. New York: Pantheon, 1983.

Elias, Norbert. *The Civilizing Process*. Translated by Edmund Jephcott. 3 vols. New York: Pantheon, 1982; Oxford and Cambridge, MA: Blackwell, 1994.

Farge, Arlette. *Subversive Words: Public Opinion in Eighteenth-Century France*. University Park: Pennsylvania State University Press, 1995.

Francalanza, Eric. *Jean-Baptiste-Antoine Suard, journaliste des Lumières*. Paris: Honoré Champion, 2002.

France, Peter. *Politeness and its Discontents: Problems in French Classical Culture*. Cambridge, UK, and New York: Cambridge University Press, 1992.

François, Étienne, and Rolf Reichardt. "Les formes de sociabilité en France du milieu du XVIIIe siècle au milieu du XIXe siècle." *Revue d'Histoire moderne et contemporaine* 34 (1987): 453–72.

Fumaroli, Marc. "La conversation." In *Les Lieux de Mémoire*, vol. 3, pt. 2 : *Les France*, 679–743. Edited by Pierre Nora. 3 vols. Paris: Gallimard, 1984–92.

Fumaroli, Marc. *When The World Spoke French*. New York: New York Published Books, 2011.

Furet, François. *Interpreting the French Revolution*. Cambridge, UK: Cambridge University Press; Paris: Éditions de la Maison des sciences de l'homme, 1981.

Gaulin, Michel. *Le Concept d'homme de lettres en France à l'époque de l'Encyclopédie*. New York: Garland, 1991.

Glotz, Marguerite, and Madeleine Maire. *Salons du XVIIIe siècle*. Paris: Hachette, 1944.

Goldgar, Ann. *Impolite Learning: Conduct and Community in the Republic of Letters, 1680–1730*. New Haven: Yale University Press, 1995.

Goncourt, Edmond de, and Goncourt, Jules de. *La femme au XVIIIe siècle*. Paris: Firmin Didot, 1862; Flammarion, 1982. Translated by Jacques Le Clercq and Ralph Roeder as *The Woman of the Eighteenth Century* . New York: Minton, Balch, 1927.

Goodman, Dena. "Filial Rebellion in the Salon: Madame Geoffrin and her Daughter." *French Historical Studies* 16 (Spring 1989): 27–47.

Goodman, Dena. "The Hume-Rousseau Affair: From Private Querelle to Public Process." *Eighteenth-Century Studies* 25, no. 2 (Winter, 1991–92): 171–201.

Goodman, Dena. *The Republic of Letters: A Cultural History of the French Enlightenment*. Ithaca: Cornell University Press, 1994.

Gordon, Daniel. *Citizens without Sovereignty: Equality and Sociability in French Thought, 1670–1789*. Princeton: Princeton University Press, 1994.

Goulemot, Jean Marie, and Daniel Oster. *Gens de Lettres, écrivains et bohèmes: L'imaginaire littéraire, 1630–1900*. Paris: Minerve, 1992.

Guillois, Antoine. *Les Boufflers à Auteuil*. Lecture, December 22, 1894. Paris, 1895.

Guillois, Antoine. *Le Salon de Mme Helvétius" Cabanis et les idéologues*. Paris: Calmann-Lévy, 1894; New York: B. Franklin, 1971.

Gunn, J. A. W. *Queen of the World: Opinion in the Public Life of France from the Renaissance to the Revolution*. Oxford: Voltaire Foundation, 1995.

Guichard, Charlotte, *Les amateurs d'art à Paris au XVIIIe siècle*. Seyssel: Champ Vallon, 2008.

Habermas, Jürgen. *The Structural Transformation of the Public Sphere*. Translated by Thomas Burger and Frederick Lawrence. Cambridge, MA: MIT Press, 1989.

Hamon, Maurice. *Madame Geoffrin*. Paris: Fayard, 2010.

Harth, Erica. *Cartesian Women: Versions and Subversions of Rational Discourse in the Old Regime*. Ithaca: Cornell University Press, 1992.

Haussonville, Paul Othenin, comte d'. *Le Salon de Mme Necker d'après les documents tirés des archives de Coppet*. 2 vols. Paris: Calmann-Lévy, 1882.

Hellegouarc'h, Jacqueline. *L'Esprit de société: Cercles et "salons" parisiens au XVIIIe siècle.* Paris: Garnier, 2000.

Jouhaud, Christian. *Les Pouvoirs de la littérature: Histoire d'un paradoxe.* Paris: Gallimard, 2000.

Kale, Steven D. *French Salons, High Society and Political Sociability from the Old Regime to the Revolution of 1848.* Baltimore: Johns Hopkins University Press, 1994, 2004.

Kale, Steven D. "Women, the Public Sphere and the Persistence of Salons." *French Historical Studies* 25, no. 1 (Winter 2002): 115–48.

Klein, Lawrence E. *Shaftesbury and the Culture of Politeness: Moral Discourse and Cultural Politics in Early Eighteenth-Century England.* Cambridge, UK: Cambridge University Press, 1994.

Kors, Alan Charles. *D'Holbach's Coterie: An Enlightenment in Paris.* Princeton: Princeton University Press, 1977.

Koselleck, Reinhard. *Le Règne de la critique.* Translated by Hans Hildenbrand. Paris: Éditions de Minuit, 1979.

Lagrave, Jean-Paul, ed. *Madame Helvétius et la Société d'Auteuil. Studies on Voltaire and the Eighteenth Century* 374 (1999). Oxford: Voltaire Foundation.

La Vopa, Anthony. "Conceiving a Public: Ideas and Society in Eighteenth-Century Europe." *Journal of Modern History* 64 (March 1992): 79–116.

Lilti, Antoine. "The kingdom of Politesse: Salons and the Republic of Letters in Eighteenth-Century Paris." *Republics of Letters: A Journal for the Study of Knowledge, Politics, and the Arts* 1, no. 1 (May 2009); http://arcade.stanford.edu/sites/default/files/article_pdfs/roflv01i01_Lilti_071609_0.pdf.

Loménie, Louis de. *La Comtesse de Rochefort et ses amis: Étude sur les mœurs en France au XVIIIe siècle, avec des documents inédits.* Paris: Michel Lévy, 1870; Geneva: Slatkine Reprint, 1972.

Lougee, Carolyn C. *Le Paradis des femmes: Women, Salons, and Social Stratification in Seventeenth-Century France.* Princeton: Princeton University Press, 1976.

Magendie, Maurice. *La politesse mondaine et les théories de l'honnêteté en France au XVIIe siècle de 1600 à 1660.* 2 vols. Paris: F. Alcan, 1925.

Mah, Harold. "Phantasies of the Public Sphere: Rethinking the Habermas of Historians." *Journal of Modern History* 72 (March, 2000): 153–82.

Maître, Myriam. "Les escortes mondaines de la publication." In *De la publication entre renaissance et lumières,* ed. Christian Jouhaud and Alain Viala, 249–65. Groupe de recherches interdisciplinaires sur l'histoire du littéraire. Paris: Fayard, 2002.

Maître, Myriam. *Les Précieuses: Naissance des femmes de lettres en France au XVIIe siècle.* Paris: Honoré Champion, 1999, 2008.

Marchal, Roger, ed. *Vie des salons et activités littéraires: De Marguerite de Valois à Mme de Staël.* Actes du Colloque International de Nancy, October 1989. Nancy: Presses Universitaires de Nancy, 2001.

Martin-Fugier, Anne. *Les Salons de la IIIe République.* Paris: Perrin, 2003.

Maza, Sarah C. *Private Lives and Public Affairs: The causes célèbres of Prerevolutionary France.* Berkeley: University of California Press, 1993.

McMahon, Darrin, *Enemies of the Enlightenment: The French Counter-Enlightenment and the Making of Modernity.* New York: Oxford University Press, 2011.

Melton, James van Horn. *The Rise of the Public in Enlightenment Europe.* New York: Cambridge University Press, 2001.

Mély, Benoît. *Jean-Jacques Rousseau: Un intellectuel en rupture.* Paris: Minerve, 1985.

Merlin, Hélène. "Figures du public au XVIIIe siècle: Le travail du passé." *Dix-Huitième siècle* 23 (1991): 345–56.

Morrissey, Robert. "Sociabilité, la passion de l'échange." *Critique* (January–February, 1997): 78–88.

Myers, Sylvia Harcstark. *The Bluestocking Circle: Women, Friendship, and the Life of the Mind in Eighteenth-Century England*. Oxford: Clarendon Press; New York: Oxford University Press, 1990.

Ozouf, Mona. *Les Mots des femmes: Essai sur la singularité française*. Paris: Fayard, 1995; Gallimard, 1999. Translated by Jane Marie Todd as *Women's Words: Essay on French Singularity* . Chicago: University of Chicago Press, 1997.

Pascal, Jean-Noël. "La muse de l'*Encyclopédie*." In *Femmes savantes et femmes d'esprit: Women Intellectuals of the French Eighteenth Century*. Edited by Roland Bonnel and Catherine Rubinger. New York: Peter Lang, 1994.

Pekacz, Jolanta T. *Conservative Tradition in Pre-Revolutionary France: Parisian Salon Women*. New York: Peter Lang, 1999.

Picard, Roger. *Les Salons littéraires et la société française, 1610–1789*. New York: Brentano's, 1943.

Pinson, Guillaume. *Fiction du monde. De la presse mondaine à Marcel Proust*. Montréal: Presses de l'Université de Montréal, 2008.

Pocock, J. G. A. *Virtue, Commerce and History: Essays on Political Thought and History, Chiefly in the Eighteenth Century*. Cambridge, UK: Cambridge University Press, 1985.

Ravel, Jeffrey S. *The Contested Parterre: Public Theater and French Political Culture, 1680–1791*. Ithaca: Cornell University Press, 1999.

Revel, Jacques. "The Uses of Civility." In *A History of Private Life*, vol. 3: *Passions of the Renaissance*, ed. Roger Chartier, 167–205. Cambridge, MA: Belknap Press of Harvard University Press, 1989.

Roche, Daniel. *Les Républicains des lettres: Gens de culture et Lumières au XVIIIe siècle*. Paris: Fayard, 1988.

Roche, Daniel. "République des Lettres ou royaume des mœurs: La sociabilité vue d'ailleurs." *Revue d'histoire moderne et contemporaine* 43, no. 2 (April–June 1996): 293–306.

Romagnoli, Daniela, ed. *La Ville et la cour: Des bonnes et des mauvaises manières*. Paris: Fayard, 1995.

Russo, Elena. *La Cour et la ville de la littérature classique aux Lumières: L'invention de soi*. Paris: Presses Universitaires de France, 2002.

Russo, Elena. *Styles of Enlightenment, Taste, Politics, and Authorship in Eighteenth-Century France*. Baltimore: Johns Hopkins University Press, 2007.

Sareil, Jean. *Les Tencin: Histoire d'une famille au dix-huitième siècle, d'après de nombreux documents inédits*. Geneva: Droz, 1969.

Scott, Katie. *The Rococo Interior: Decoration and Social Spaces in Early Eighteenth-Century Paris*. New Haven: Yale University Press, 1995.

Ségur, Pierre de. *Julie de Lespinasse*. Paris: Calmann-Lévy, 1906. In English translation as *Julie de Lespinasse*. London: Chatto & Windus, 1907.

Ségur, Pierre de. *Le Royaume de la Rue Saint-Honoré: Madame Geoffrin et sa fille*. Paris: Calmann-Lévy, 1897.

Smith, Jay M. *The Culture of Merit: Nobility, Royal Service, and the Making of Absolute Monarchy in France, 1600–1789*. Ann Arbor: University of Michigan Press, 1996.

Sonenscher, Michel. "Enlightenment and Revolution." *Journal of Modern History* 70 (June 1998): 371–83.

Spector, Céline. *Montesquieu. Pouvoirs, richesse et société*, Paris, Presses Universitaires de France, 2004.

Starobinski, Jean. *Jean-Jacques Rousseau: La transparence et l'obstacle: suivi de sept essais sur Rouseau* (1951). Paris: Gallimard, 1971. Translated by Arthur Goldhammer as *Jean-Jacques Rousseau, Transparency and Obstruction*. Chicago: University of Chicago Press, 1988.

Stewart, Philip. *Le Masque et la parole: Le langage de l'amour au XVIIIe siècle*. Paris: José Conti, 1973.

Tarde, Gabriel. *L'Opinion et la foule*. Paris: Alcan, 1901. Edited by Dominique Reynié. Paris: Alcan, 1913; Presses Universitaires de France, 1989.

Tocqueville, Alexis de. *The Old Regime and the Revolution*. Translated by Alan S. Kahan, edited by François Furet and Françoise Mélonio. 2 vols. Chicago: University of Chicago Press, 1998.

Turnovsky, Geoffrey. *Authorship and Modernity in the Old Regime*. Philadelphia: University of Pennsylvania Press, 2009.

Van Damme, Stéphane. *Paris capitale philosophique: De la Fronde à la Révolution*. Paris: Odile Jacob, 2005.

Veblen, Thorstein. *The Theory of the Leisure Class: An Economic Study of Institutions*. (1899) New York: Modern Library, 1934.

Viala, Alain. *La France galante*, Paris: Presses Universitaires de France, 2004.

Walter, Eric. "Les auteurs et le champ littéraire." In *Histoire de l'édition française*, ed. Henri-Jean Martin and Roger Chartier. 4 vols. (Paris: Promodis, 1982–84), vol 2: *Le livre triomphant, 1660–1830*, 383–99.

Walton, Charles. *Policing Public Opinion in the French Revolution: The Culture of Calumny and the Problem of Free Speech*. New York : Oxford University Press, 2009.

INDEX